HEALING A WOUNDED WORLD

HEALING A WOUNDED WORLD

Economics, Ecology, and Health for a Sustainable Life

*Joseph Wayne Smith,
Graham Lyons,
and Gary Sauer-Thompson*

**Westport, Connecticut
London**

Library of Congress Cataloging-in-Publication Data

Smith, Joseph Wayne.
  Healing a wounded world : economics, ecology, and health for a sustainable life / Joseph Wayne Smith, Graham Lyons, and Gary Sauer-Thompson.
      p.   cm.
  Includes bibliographical references and index.
  ISBN 0–275–95601–6 (alk. paper)
  1. Sustainable development. 2. Environmentalism. I. Lyons, Graham, 1936– . II. Sauer-Thompson, Gary. III. Title.
HC79.E5S536   1997
338.967—dc20   96–44682

British Library Cataloguing in Publication Data is available.

Copyright © 1997 by Joseph Wayne Smith, Graham Lyons, and Gary Sauer-Thompson

All rights reserved. No portion of this book may be reproduced, by any process or technique, without the express written consent of the publisher.

Library of Congress Catalog Card Number: 96-44682
ISBN: 0–275–95601–6

First published in 1997

Praeger Publishers, 88 Post Road West, Westport, CT 06881
An imprint of Greenwood Publishing Group, Inc.

Printed in the United States of America

The paper used in this book complies with the
Permanent Paper Standard issued by the National
Information Standards Organization (Z39.48–1984).

10 9 8 7 6 5 4 3 2 1

Copyright Acknowledgments

The authors and publisher gratefully acknowledge permission to use the following source:

Moore, E. & Smith, J. W. (1995). Climatic Change and Migration from Oceania: Implications for Australia, New Zealand and the USA. *Population and Environment* 17: 105–122.

Contents

Preface		vii
1.	A Wounded World: Can Civilization Be Sustained?	1
2.	Global Meltdown: Population Growth and Environmental Destruction	29
3.	The Unreasonable Silence of the World: Postmodernity and the Crisis of Philosophy, Science and Knowledge	61
4.	Economic Irrationalism: Against Cosmopolitan Economics	101
5.	Endgame: Healing a Wounded World	147
Bibliography		155
Index		199

Preface

> If we are lucky, mankind as it is has about 50 years left. Most of the graphs of human development, population, ecology, technology . . . and the spread of disease are on an explosive curve. The lines shoot off the graph somewhere in the middle of the next century.
> —William Rees Mogg (1992, quoted in Kumar, 1995, 204)

As we approach the end of the twentieth century, and the end of the millennium, there is in most communities throughout the world and especially in the West, an anxious sentiment that the world is spinning toward disaster (Lyons et al., 1995). Millennial cults that foresee the end of the world figure prominently in the news, from "patriotic" bombers, to the Aum Supreme Truth cult's attempt to flood the Tokyo underground system with poison gas, to the mass Winter Solstice suicide of Solar Temple followers in the French Alps (Crawford & Edgar, 1995). A sense of fear, conspiracy, paranoia and angst is also seen in popular culture; in apocalyptic themes in movies (from *Mad Max* and the *Terminator* movies, to *Waterworld*, and the alien-invasion epics, *Independence Day* and *The Arrival*); television (*The X-Files*, *Nowhere Man* and *The Millennium*); popular fiction (a wide range of science fiction, occult and "horror" books) and music (e.g., "rap" music). Twenty-seven percent of Americans believe that America is a police state and increasing infringements of civil liberties will lead to a civil war and social chaos (Wark, 1995, 48). We are not interested here in whether or not all or many of these beliefs are *rationally* held: what is of sociological interest is that such millenarian beliefs are held at all (Cohen, 1970, 1993).[1]

A superficial explanation accounts for these phenomena by saying that they are a response to the approach of a new millennium. A deeper explanation sees these phenomena, as well as massacres by rampaging gunmen (such as Port Arthur, Tasmania, April 1996), as symptoms of the breakdown, alienation and dislocation of modern society, with the collapse of traditional value systems and the loss of faith in political and social institutions. This breakdown has occurred through technological change and the globalization or internationalization of what were once national economies (Lyons et al., 1995). The subjective interpretation that global change is out of control is also held by Zbigniew Brzezinski. In his book *Out of Control: Global Turmoil on the Eve of the 21st Century* (Brzezinski, 1993), he states his belief that the United States faces disintegration, encountering "an increasingly pervasive sense of spiritual emptiness," ailments comprising "the economic, the social and even the metaphysical" (Brzezinski, 1993, 107). Brzezinski believes that we are witnessing a collapse of all established values that once acted as the glue that held society together. Consumerism, "permissive cornucopia" and a cult of self-gratification masquerade as substitutes for moral values. The Western world faces a moral crisis, a crisis of meaning and purpose. We argue in this book, that the West and indeed all of humanity, face another crisis, a crisis of survival.

Brzezinski is not an ecologist and is better known for his support of economic globalization and of a global confederation built around the United Nations (Brzezinski, 1993, 225). However, even he recognizes that there are limits to economic growth, that "much of Western consumption is in fact unattainable by the poor majorities of mankind" (Brzezinski, 1993, 73). Other researchers have advanced the thesis that over the next fifty years the growth in world population and increased economic growth will lead to a shortage of renewable resources such as forests, fisheries, rivers, aquifers and fertile agricultural land. Competition for these scarce resources may lead to violent conflicts, both civil and international (Homer-Dixon et al., 1993; Huntington, 1993a, b; Harries, 1993, 1995; Kaplan, 1994).

In this book and its successor, *Global Meltdown: Immigration, Multiculturalism, and National Breakdown in the New World Disorder*, we explore and defend the idea that the so-called "New World Order" is breaking down and that the world is hurtling toward anarchy and social chaos. We will argue in both books that various "crises of civilization" have not been satisfactorily resolved or healed in the twentieth century and their festering irresolution will lead to the poisoning and ultimately the death of the social and political world which we know. There are two broad crises of civilization; both are dialectically related, positively reinforcing each other and feeding off each other. The first is a crisis of value, meaning and philosophy. It is seen most acutely today in the academy in battles over postmodernism, multiculturalism and relativism. At the community level, this conflict is often manifested in racial and ethnic conflict. We shall discuss this crisis briefly in chapter 3, and shall offer a more detailed consideration in our successor book *Global Meltdown*. The second major crisis of civilization is environmental, ecological and economic. It relates specifically to the question of whether there are limits to growth, both of human numbers and of human economic and industrial activity. Economic growth must be sharply distinguished from economic development. Economic growth involves an increase in the physical dimensions of an economy; more technically, it is a *quantitative* increase in the rate of flow of matter and energy through the economy. By contrast, economic development is "the *qualitative* improvement in the structure, design, and composition of physical stocks and flows, that result from greater knowledge, both of technique *and of purpose*" (Daly, 1987, 323 emphasis added). Consequently, there may be biophysical limits to growth, and either definite limits to development, or no such limits, or no limits to growth and no limits to development. The view that there are no limits to growth but limits to development is a logically consistent position, but is seldom proposed.

In the past century the world's industrial production has increased 100-fold, relative to the century before. Between 1950 and 1985, manufacturing increased by a factor of seven, the number of automobiles also by a factor of seven, the use of electricity by a factor of eight. In the last 150 years human economic and industrial activity has increased the atmospheric concentration of carbon dioxide by 24 percent (Clark, 1989). In the 1990s we face severe environmental problems, such as soil erosion, declining biodiversity, the degradation of ground water resources, the enhanced greenhouse effect and many other problems that will be discussed in this book. Is there a causal connection between the growth of human population numbers and industrial activity on the one hand, and the environmental crisis on the other? Have the exponential rates of industrialization and population growth in the twentieth century precipitated our environmental crisis? If so, for how long can such rates of growth continue before a systems collapse occurs?

The position which we shall call *Limitationism* is a branch of environmentalism that holds that there are limits to human population growth and economic and industrial growth and that humanity is either fast approaching these limits or has already overshot them, living now by "future eating," destroying the ecological capital of future generations (Flannery, 1995). The best-known book arguing for this theme is *The Limits to Growth* sponsored by the Club of Rome (Meadows et al., 1972). That work concentrated primarily on the depletion of nonrenewable resources such as minerals and petroleum. It was soundly criticized in the technical literature and has already been refuted on a number of points simply by the passage of time. However, this early study stimulated interest by environmentalists in the question of limits. While there have been continuing debates about "when will the oil run out," more recent studies have been concerned with *sink constraints* rather than resource limits (Goodland, 1992). The environmental debate in the 1990s is about phenomena such as human biomass appropriation, declining biodiversity, global warming and the rupture of the Earth's ozone shield, rather than about when the world's supply of copper will be exhausted. The focus of the environmental debate has shifted to the end of the production process rather than the beginning (Daly & Cobb, 1989; Goodland et al., 1992; Dauncey, 1988; Douthwaite, 1992; Ekins, 1986; Elgin, 1981; Goldsmith, 1988; Suzuki & Gordon, 1990; Catton, 1982; Meadows et al., 1992). This is recognized by the World Commission on Environment and Development in their report *Our Common Future*:

The scale and complexity of our requirements for natural resources has increased greatly with the rising levels of population and production. Nature is bountiful, but it is also fragile and finely balanced. There are thresholds that cannot be crossed without endangering the basic integrity of the system. Today we are close to many of these thresholds; we must be ever mindful of the risk of endangering the survival of life on Earth. Moreover, the speed with which changes in resource use are taking place give little time in which to anticipate and prevent unexpected effects. (World Commission on Environment and Development, 1988, 32–33)

The World Commission on Environment and Development maintained that absolute poverty in developing countries could only be overcome by an overall growth in national income of 5 percent a year in the developing countries of Asia,

5.5 percent in Latin America and 6 per cent in Africa and West Africa (World Commission on Environment and Development, 1988, 50). This growth must be less material- and energy-intensive. Considerable debate exists about whether or not this is possible, when both the world and those developing countries in question face an environmental crisis where humanity is already close to ecological thresholds, the crossing of which will endanger the basic sustainability of the life-support systems of Earth (Rees, 1990; Hueting, 1990; Ekins, 1991).

Julian Simon is a prolific critic of Limitationism (Simon, 1981, 1990; Simon & Kahn, eds, 1984; Myers & Simon, 1994; Simon, ed., 1995). He has argued that the ecological prophets of doom have proposed since recorded history that their civilizations and societies have been on the verge of collapse and they have all been proved wrong: "the evidence of history is that these positive trends [of increasing utilitarian satisfaction] have indeed gone on forever all throughout our history. And there's no reason that I know of why this cannot continue to go on forever" (Myers & Simon, 1994, 151). For Simon the world in the year 2000 will be less crowded, less polluted, more ecologically stable and life for more people on Earth will be less economically precarious that it is now. These positive trends will continue past the year 2000, past the year 2100, indefinitely into the future. Science and technology will solve all of humanity's threatening problems. There are no limits to growth and economic development and prosperity can continue forever (Simon, ed., 1995).

Simon has argued for this position of technological and economic optimism longer than most other writers in his field. Recently though, he has been joined by a number of other writers who are in general agreement with his position. They are all critical of environmentalism, but are critical of it for different reasons. We now list the most important of these works. Most sympathetic to Simon's cornucopian position is Dennis Avery, *Saving the Planet with Pesticides and Plastic* (1995) and the essays in Ronald Bailey (ed.), *The True State of the Planet* (1995). These books offer a free enterprise and free market internationalist response to environmentalism in general and Limitationism in particular. Other important books include C. T. Rubin, *The Green Crusade: Rethinking the Roots of Environmentalism* (1994); M. W. Lewis, *Green Delusions: An Environmentalist Critique of Radical Environmentalism* (1992); A. Wildavsky, *But Is It True? A Citizen's Guide to Environmental Health and Safety Issues* (1995); G. Easterbrook, *A Moment on the Earth: Why Nature Needs Us* (1995); B. Maley, *Ethics and Ecosystems* (1994); R. Bailey, *Eco-Scam: The False Prophets of Ecological Apocalypse* (1993); D. L. Ray & L. R. Guzzo, *Environmental Overkill: Whatever Happened to Common Sense?* (1993); W. Kaufman, *No Turning Back: Dismantling the Fantasies of Environmental Thinking* (1994); R. D. North, *Life on a Modern Planet: A Manifesto for Progress* (1995b) and W. Beckerman, *Small Is Stupid: Blowing the Whistle on the Greens* (1995). Lewis (1992) is critical of Simon's "cornucopianism," a view he sees as being hostile to nature (Lewis, 1992, 185). He believes that there are limits to the growth of human population but does not believe that there are limits to economic growth—which he defines as economic development, not the increasing consumption of energy and raw materials, but of increasing value-added goods and services (Lewis, 1992, 185). Despite Lewis' differences of opinion with Simon, his position has much in common with him and the other critics of environmentalism. All of these critics are globalists or internationalists; they are critical of the ideal of regional, national or community economic self-reliance or self-sufficiency (*autarky*) and support global free trade, mass immigration and the free movement of people across the world as tourists and workers. North (1995b) adequately summarizes the globalist or internationalist position in the following words:

The 1980s and the 1990s, so far, have developed a consensus that capitalism must be left to operate with as little, and as carefully targeted, political interference as possible . . . the political support for free trade and market economies is now so great that it has marginalized all left-wing thinking, including green-tinged left-wing thought. (North, 1995b, 254)

Common to all the recent critics of environmentalism is an acceptance of the truth and theoretical adequacy of orthodox neoclassical economics, of utilitarianism, of the rational-economic-man model of human behavior and of free trade theory. Rather than call the view held by these critics "cornucopianism," we have decided that "Economism" is a fairer neologism to describe this position. We agree that this neologism is not "pretty," but our concern here is not with beauty, but with truth. All of these critics of environmentalism believe that neoclassical economics is a sound scientific study of the only plausible economic system, globalized capitalism. In this book we will defend environmentalism and Limitationism against these critics by offering a firsthand defense of these positions and a foundational critique of Economism as well as an attack on orthodox economics. We recognize that a minority of economists—the ecological economists—accept Limitationism and acknowledge ecological and biophysical constraints upon human economic activity. By use of the term "Economism" we are not implying that *all* economists are progrowth or cornucopians, although most economists are. However, what we are attacking in this book is a economic version of *scientism*; just as scientism is a reductionist belief that only the natural sciences can deliver genuine knowledge, Economism is the reductionist belief that economics is the most basic science for the understanding of human society. Economism is scientism in the social and human sciences. We have used the term "Economism" to reflect this doctrine's relationship within the reductionist approach to the unity of science, scientism. More will be said about this in chapter 3.

The political and philosophical movement known as environmentalism contains much with which we strongly disagree and we acknowledge here and now the value of many of the criticisms that have been made of environmentalism by Simon, Avery, Rubin, Lewis, Wildavsky, Easterbrook and Kaufman. For example Kaufman (1994) and Lewis (1992) intellectually destroy the idea of the "noble savage" living in balance and harmony with nature. The noble savage presumably was a feminist and an antiracist and embodied all of the politically correct values of liberalism and the left. Kaufman argues strongly for the thesis that "[m]ost primitive people not only put their species first [i.e., over nature], but unashamedly put their own nation or tribe first as well. They are brazenly ethnocentric and racist. Such prejudice should make Romantic anthropologists and liberals blush" (Kaufman, 1994, 60). Primitive populations engaged in tribal warfare and infanticide. Groups such as the Australian Aborigines, looked upon by liberal-left greens as embodying in their traditional societies sensitive new age values, practiced cannibalism (Lumholtz, 1980; Bates, 1938), sexism, patriarchy and other sins of political incorrectness. The native American Indians were not early American liberals as a Hollywood fantasy such as *Dances with Wolves* portrays. These people were highly territorial even though they followed the buffalo in a fixed region. They accepted technological innovations such as Winchester rifles, which they rightly perceived as superior weapons to their bows and arrows. The American Indians' horse was brought to North America from Europe and it became the Indians "traditional" means of travel (Easterbrook, 1995, 93). Even worse for environmentalism, Chief Seattle's famous environmental speech is a fake, having been written by the screen writer Ted Perry for the 1972 film *Home* (Kaiser, 1987; Callicott, 1989). This matter was discussed by the editors of *Environmental Ethics* in 1989 (volume 11, pages 195–196). In stating this we are not criticizing the Australian Aborigine or the American Red Indian; on the contrary it is the fantasies of liberal-left environmentalism which should be rejected. In many cases these activities made perfectly good biological sense in the environment in which these people lived.

Much environmental philosophy is based on the idea of the harmony and balance of nature, seeing the natural world as a highly structured and regulated system in a steadystate (Worster, 1993). This metaphysical paradigm has been challenged by ecologists who have made use of chaos theory (Stewart, 1989; Ruelle, 1991; Gleick, 1988) and complexity theory (Waldrop, 1992; Allen & Hoekstra, 1992). Botkin develops this "new ecology" position in his book *Discordant Harmonies* (1990). He concludes from various studies of animal populations that the numbers of such populations are subject to "chaotic" fluctuations. Variation rather than constancy is the rule of nature, with "harmony" and "balance" existing, if at all, for short time periods (May, 1974). This view fits well with an evolutionary neo-Darwinist view of life, which sees species evolving, struggling for existence, but in the longrun ultimately perishing. The fossil record is, with a few exceptions, a record of the death and extinction of species. We do not accept Botkin's view that the new "chaotic" ecology should therefore be more approving of economic development than the ecology of the 1960s and 1970s. In fact, Botkin demonstrates that we must be even more conscious of human impact on the environment. Orthodox ecology believed that it was possible to determine the normal yield or output for an ecosystem. So, for an animal population such as fish in a certain area, it was thought to be possible to derive the steadystate population in the ecosystem and then determine how many fish could be caught and for how long, without affecting the steady-state population. Botkin argues that this view led to overfishing and the ultimate collapse of the Californian sardine industry in the 1950s. A concern with nonlinear effects, complexity, uncertainty and chaos effects shows, in our opinion, that human economic and industrial activity may have a *greater*, and often more unpredictable, impact than orthodoxy would expect. We argue in defense of this position in chapter 2 of this book (McMichael, 1993, 47).

The same evolutionary biohistorical philosophy of nature is also applicable to human civilizations. Contrary to Simon, the rise and collapse of complex civilizations is an accepted, although neglected, part of economic theory (Olson, 1982). The idea of the collapse of civilization was well known to the ancients. Herodotus said of the Greek city-states of his time:

[T]he cities that were formerly great, have most of them become insignificant; and such as are at present powerful, were weak in olden times. I shall therefore discourse equally of both, convinced that human happiness never continues long in one stay. (Olson, 1982, 1)

Some of the great civilizations that have collapsed include the Western Chou Empire (China, 1122 B.C.); the Harappan civilization of the Indus Valley in northwestern India (2400 B.C.); the Mesopotamian empire (2350–2150 B.C.); Egyptian Old Kingdom (3100 B.C.); the Hittites (1792 B.C.); the Minoan civilization of Crete (2000 B.C.); the Mycenaean civilization of mainland Greece (1650 B.C.); the Western Roman Empire; Olme civilization of Mexico (end of the first millennium B.C.); the Lowland Classic Maya (first millennium B.C.); the Mesoamerican Highlands; the Casas Grandes; the Chacoans; the Hohokam; the Huari and Tiahuanaco Empires (Tainter, 1988, 5–18; Mazzarino, 1966). In more recent times we have seen the collapse of the British empire and the Soviet Union. The rise and fall of civilizations has been dealt with in classic studies by Spengler (1962), Toynbee (1962) and other twentieth-century sociological and anthropological theorists (Kroeber, 1944, 1957; Coulborn, 1954, 1966; Sorokin, 1957; Melko, 1969; Renfrew, 1979; Low, 1985). Tainter (1988) believes that the clear implication which can be drawn from the study of history and archaeology is that "civilizations are fragile, impermanent things" (Tainter, 1988, 1) and civilizations can die because they have died before.

Ecological factors have played a major role in the collapse of past civilizations such as the Roman empire (Simkhovitch, 1916; Hughes, 1975), Easter Island (Diamond, 1991, 296–297) and classic Maya civilization (Sabloff, 1995; Hodell et al., 1995). Consider the case of the collapse of civilization on Easter Island. When the Polynesians arrived on Easter Island, the island was covered with dense forests comprised of the world's largest palm trees. A great civilization arose, one sophisticated enough to erect thirty-tonne stone statues which were probably carved between A.D. 1000 and 1600. However, by the time the statues were erected all of the forests had gone. The Easter Islanders could not build canoes to escape their island. Soil erosion ended agriculture; native terrestrial birds were hunted to extinction. Then the 7000 people on the island turned on each other in cannibalistic warfare (Diamond, 1991, 296–297).

Economists do not believe that modern technoindustrial civilization could suffer ecological collapse. As we will see, they are confident that science and technology will solve whatever problems nature puts in humanity's path. Economists are fond of quoting the spectacularly failed prophecies of doom of ecologists, such as Paul Ehrlich's prediction of the end of animal life in the oceans by 1979, resulting in mass starvation in Asia and genocidal wars (Ehrlich, 1968). We shall also discuss the possibility of global ecological collapse in this book. For the moment, let us note that even a sophisticated technological civilization is not free from the prospects of annihilation. In May 1996 an asteroid discovered by Timothy Spahr and Carl Hergenrother, asteroid 1996JA1, missed the Earth by 450,620 kilometers which is a very small distance in cosmology (Jaroff, 1996). The asteroid was about half a kilometer across and had it hit the Earth the explosion would have been equivalent to a 3,000–12,000-megaton nuclear bomb. Duncan Steel of the Anglo-Australian Observatory in New South Wales, Australia, an asteroid expert, posted this E-mail message at the time: "this object was discovered only days before closest approach, so that if it had been on a collision course with Earth, we would not have had time to do anything much about it." There are over 100 Near Earth Objects (NEOs) from the size of one kilometer to several hundred kilometers across in the asteroid belt between Mars and Jupiter. Two thousand or more are thought to be undetected. Occasionally one gets displaced from its orbit and is hurled in the Earth's direction. A body 10 kilometers in diameter would strike with the force of 10 million thermonuclear bombs and would punch a hole in the Earth's crust more than 60 kilometers in diameter. The intense heat would roast vegetation and animals across the globe and a global nuclear winter would result from dust flung into the sky. Most life would perish (Davies, 1995).[2] The likelihood of death by an asteroid is statistically higher than the likelihood of death from a plane crash, because even though asteroid deaths are very infrequent, when they occur billions could be annihilated. The sudden mass extinctions documented in the fossil record (e.g., 250 million years ago 90 percent of species abruptly vanished) is thought to be explicable by comet or asteroid impacts.[3]

In this book, part of our strategy for refuting Economism will involve demonstrating that modern technoindustrial society is not immune from the dangers of ecological collapse. The argument does not consider exotic cosmological causes further, but goes back to basics, considering questions of water quality and food resources. It is typical in debates between Limitationists and Economists to resort to rather complex arrays of statistics to justify one's position. Both sides of the debate seem to be able to find exactly the statistics which they want to justify their view. As we argue in chapter 2, statistical data are highly fallible and very often theory-relative. Consequently we do not believe that progress can be made by swapping statistics. Instead we have compiled the assessments of the state of various ecological resources by consulting the opinions and practical experience of experts in the field using media reports, electronic communications and recently published material. We have not relied on the work of environmentalists who our Economist opponents would immediately reject.

The first section of chapter 1 ("The Scars of Modernity") presents the case for believing that we are living in a world that is seriously wounded, ecologically speaking. The basic case for Limitationism is stated. We then turn in the following section ("The Environmentalist Backlash") to examine and rebut the broad Economist critique of Limitationism. Then we attempt to refute the technological optimism of Julian Simon, Wilfred Beckerman, Richard North and other critics of Limitationism ("Refuting Technological Optimism"). First we outline some of the social and political problems associated with the information technology revolution and the strong program of artificial intelligence which seeks to build superintelligent machines. Such technological developments threaten to make humanity itself redundant. However, for reasons to be outlined in chapter 3, we doubt whether there is sufficient time left for such technological advances to occur. The chapter concludes with a discussion of emerging diseases and the existence of drug-resistant superbugs. Internationalism and globalization have led to the situation where epidemic diseases that were once locked into a particular area can now be transferred by human vectors or germcarriers, as they jet across the globe. The prospects of coming plagues are examined and both internationalism and Economism are faulted on the ground of promoting pandemics. In globalizing human society, we have also globalized disease.

Chapter 2 furthers our case against Economism by considering the problem of human population expansion. In the first section ("The Population Glacier") we outline some of the shortcomings of official world population projections. It is likely that the world's population in 2050 will be much higher than the projected medium-variant figure of 10 billion people. The United Nations' Population Fund announced on December 28, 1995 that the world's population had increased by 100 million people in the previous 12 months. This figure is much higher than was expected. After rejecting claims made by Julian Simon that people are the "ultimate resource," we examine the devastating effect that human population increase is having on the environment and investigate the question of the human-carrying capacity of the Earth. It is quite likely that humans have already overshot the carrying capacity of the Earth.

Earlier in this preface we mentioned a number of crises of civilization confronting humanity. One of these crises is an intellectual or philosophical crisis concerned with the ultimate meaning of human existence and the grounding and justification of knowledge, science, rationality and understanding. It is manifested in opposition by postmodernists to the Enlightenment doctrines of materialism and naturalism. We are prepared to accept the commonsense realist idea that man is a part of nature. However, we locate in the Enlightenment Project the source of globalism and cosmopolitanism, the belief in the sovereignty of Universal Reason and scientific rationality and the hope of building a universal culture grounded upon science, money and consumerism. This is the culture in which we now live, one which is metaphysically, and morally, materialist. We believe that such a culture is metaphysically, and morally bankrupt and responsible for producing in modern man a sense of cosmic homelessness that Camus called "the unreasonable silence of the world" (Camus, 1955, 29). As Limitationists we recognize the fallibility of all human institutions including science, philosophy, logic and reason itself. Chapter 3 outlines the postmodern debate about the foundations of knowledge and value. We propose that the fallibility of science adequately shows that the doctrine of technological optimism held by Julian Simon and other Economists is false, for the postmodernists have shown that the idea of scientific progress is itself problematic.

Although recognizing the ultimate biological and ecological basis of human life, we reject the metaphysical and social doctrine of materialism. Skepticism and nihilistic despair are not advocated by the authors of this book. Indeed we believe that the postmodern debate is a symptom of a deep philosophical illness permeating Western culture and that illness is universalism, the quest to create a universal global culture. We argue in chapter 4 that insofar as this ideal is manifested and realized in economic activity in the operation of a free trade globalized economy, it is a disaster that will lead to social chaos, increased human misery and further ecological destruction. We attempt to counter the universalism of orthodox economics by attacking it at a foundational level. Surprisingly enough, mathematical economists and econometricians have already unintentionally undermined much of the rational basis for accepting orthodox economics. Our job here is merely to inform the reader of this good news. Economics exercises a vice-like hegemony upon the minds of late-twentieth-century humanity. It is only by realizing that modern economics is largely a mythological system that we can entertain the possibility of an alternative to cosmopolitan economics. As our alternative we propose autarky, national self-reliance and, if possible, national self-sufficiency. Thus the key to creating an ecologically sustainable society lies in abandoning economic globalism. However, we do not naïvely believe that this movement to autarky will occur by force of reason. It will be the cold, bloody forces of biophysical necessity which will ultimately heal the wounds of this wounded world and force what remains of the human race to live within limits.

We are grateful for the assistance of: Professor Virginia Abernethy, Dr. K. Betts, Dr. R. Birrell, Professor H. Caton, Professor Emeritus Max Charlesworth, Professor Paul R. Ehrlich, Dr. Tim Flannery, Dr. Terry Godlove, Karen Gordon, Professor Otis L. Graham, Professor Emeritus Garrett Hardin, Professor Rom Harré, Suzanne Heath, Professor G. Hugo, Dr. David Lamb, Dr. Wayne Lutton, Sue Lyons, Denis McCormack, Professor G. McNicolls, Rose Milton-Head, Evonne Moore, Professor G. Munévar, Roger Porter, Professor David Shearman, Professor R. V. Short, Claire Smith, Professor W. F. Smyth, Professor Roy Sorensen, (the late) Dr. Richard Sylvan, Dr. John Tanton and Professor Ted Wheelwright. These individuals are not responsible for the views and opinions expressed in this work.

Joseph Wayne Smith acknowledges assistance from the Australian Research Council for a Senior Research Fellowship at the University of Adelaide and earlier from the Commonwealth Department for Human Services and Health, for a Human Services and Health Research and Development Grant (RADGAC).

NOTES

1. An interest in apocalypse theory, eschatology (the metaphysics, science and technology of end-times) and doomsday arguments can even be found in American analytic philosophy (e.g., Leslie, 1989, 1992, 1994, 1996; Krieger, 1995).

2. Comets and asteroids *do* strike the Earth. The Earth's surface bears the scars of these impacts, which can be seen in dry areas where slow weathering occurs, as in the Australian deserts. On June 30, 1908, an asteroid exploded above the Siberian forest near Tunguska. On February 1, 1994, a fifteen-meter rock exploded over the Western Pacific with a blast force of many Hiroshima bombs. A 100-meter rock exploding over the Pacific Ocean could produce a tidal wave sufficient to wipe out coastal Pacific Ocean cities such as Los Angeles, Tokyo and Sydney. Collisions of this nature are expected to occur every few thousand years. Rocks less than a mile across can be traced by tracking their speed, but smaller rocks are virtually invisible. Even if it were possible to destroy massive rocks by particle beams or move them off their collision path by a missile, as the discovery of asteroid 1996JA1 shows, Earth may be "shot in the back."

3. There is an even worse possibility than the Earth being hit by an asteroid—it could be hit by a mini-black hole and instantly annihilated. Dr. Mike Hawkins, of the Royal Observatory in Edinburgh, hypothesizes that outer space is populated with mini-black holes that arose a fraction of a second after the big bang. A number of cosmological arguments are advanced in support of this conjecture (e.g., that it accounts for the identity of the so-called "dark matter" (Chown, 1996)). If this hypothesis is correct, the universe may ultimately end by matter being destroyed by "local" black holes.

HEALING A WOUNDED WORLD

1

A Wounded World: Can Civilization Be Sustained?

THE SCARS OF MODERNITY

In 1992 some distinguished scientific bodies issued warnings to humanity about the state of the global environment and the ecological peril which we face:

Human beings and the natural world are on a collision course. . . . The Earth's ability to provide for growing numbers of people is finite; . . . and we are fast approaching many of the Earth's limits. Pressures resulting from unrestrained population growth put demands on the natural world that can overwhelm any efforts to achieve a sustainable future. . . . No more than one or a few decades remain before the chance to avert the threats we now confront will be lost and the prospect for humanity [and Nature] immeasurably diminished. (Union of Concerned Scientists, *World Scientists' Warning to Humanity*, issued 1992)

If current predictions of population growth prove accurate and patterns of human activity on the planet remain unchanged, science and technology may not be able to prevent either irreversible degradation of the environment or continued poverty for much of the world. . . . Some of the environmental changes may produce irreversible damage to the Earth's capacity to sustain life. The overall pace of environmental change has unquestionably been accelerated by the recent expansion of the human population. . . . The future of our planet is in the balance. (US National Academy of Science and [British] Royal Society, *Population Growth, Resource Consumption, and a Sustainable World*, issued 1992 [quoted from Lyons et al., 1995, 1–2])

Japan's environment agency issued a press release on June 5, 1995 predicting that mass production and consumption could lead to the death of civilization. Dr. Seitji Ikkatai, director of the agency's office of public planning and research, noted that the Asia-Pacific region, at present having the world's highest rate of economic and industrial growth, "will suffer the most damage from deforestation and from emissions of carbon dioxide and sulphur dioxide, triggering global warming and acid rain" (AFP news service, June 6, 1995). Projected sulfur dioxide emissions in the Asia-Pacific region will almost quadruple between 1990 and 2025 and carbon dioxide output will double over the same period. The Asia-

Pacific region will consume three times more energy than in 1990 and will become the world's top producer of carbon dioxide. Forty percent of its tropical forests will disappear between the years 1990 and 2100. Japan's environmental agency compared modern civilization to extinct civilizations such as ancient Crete and Mesopotamian civilization, which they believe died because of environmental destruction. Dr. Ikkatai expressed this comparison, unprecedented for Japan's environment agency in these words: "Since humans cannot go to Mars and since the use of coal creates global warming, it seems that the present civilisation is now in the final stage where it is facing its own global limits" (AFP news service, June 6, 1995).

In the preface we mentioned a number of intellectuals and scientists who have warned that human economic activity is approaching or has overshot the absorptive and ecological regenerative capacities of the planet. By way of introduction and lead-in to the general thesis of this book, we will take the reader on a tour of expert scientific *opinion* about the perilous state of our planet. As we have already stated, this is a book about the conflict of ideas and world views between Economists and ecologists, between those who believe that there are limits to growth which we are fast approaching (*Limitationists*) and those who believe that there are no such limits (*Economists*) and who look forward to a new era of economic growth. Consequently, we are concerned in the main with scientific testimony, its truth, justification and rationality. In what follows, the reader should keep an open mind about various assertions made and conclusions inferred from specific data because—as we shall show in chapter 3—there are no concrete, unrevisable, absolutely certain conclusions in science. There are, however, propositions which are reasonable to accept relative to a body of evidence. We believe that the scientific expert testimony to follow puts the burden of disproof on the Economists, those who believe that there are no limits to growth, that the business of capitalism can proceed as usual and that "better management" is all that is required, combined with improved technology.

The Asian region, especially North East Asia, is considered by many to be the principal economic growth region of the twenty-first century (Smith, 1991a). Proponents of this view speak of the "Asian miracle." In the West, we seldom hear of the ecological darkside of this alleged "miracle." This is especially the case in countries such as Australia which are said to be undergoing "Asianization" or integration into the Asian region by both trade arrangements and a large-scale Asian migration program. We do not doubt that many Asian economies have remarkably strong rates of economic growth. But this economic strength is also a source of ecological weakness, as students of Asian philosophies such as Taoism would appreciate.

A conference held in Canberra, Australia on April 16, 1993, "The Food Time-Bomb," brought together some of the Asian region's leading food researchers. They warned that the Asian economic miracle could very well end by a collapse of food supplies and by social chaos brought about by starvation. This grim scenario was not made by Paul Ehrlich but by authorities such as Dr. Klaus Lampe, Director-General of the International Rice Research Institute based in the Philippines. He believes that to survive, Asia must grow 70 percent more rice on less land with less water, labor and less of other inputs. By the early part of the twenty-first century, 85 percent of the Earth's population will be poor and only 15 percent "rich." This situation, according to Lampe, will threaten the stability of social, political and economic systems in Asia (Cribb, 1993a). Dr. George Rothschild, Chief of the Australian Centre for International Agricultural Research, believes that the Asian situation is more serious than even that of Africa. He observes that a major deterioration of the Asian resource base is taking place, especially in the Philippines and Indonesia. Lampe and Rothschild both see Australia facing a future flood of environmental refugees, impelled by starvation. The mass migration of refugees to Australia could number in the tens or hundreds of thousands—depending on the extent of the environmental damage in Asia—and on other events such as war in Asia. At the same conference Dr. Derek Tribe of the Crawford Fund also expressed the opinion that the deterioration of Asia's environment may lead to war in the region. India and Pakistan, for example, could go to war over a water dispute for Pakistan's Punjab region, which is controlled by India (Cribb, 1993a).

Drs. Lampe and Rothschild are well aware of the success that the green revolution has had in Asia but they believe that this very success has resulted in a dangerous complacency, where it is simply assumed that technology will save the day. In Rothschild's opinion "we have used up our stock of great leaps forward. I am not convinced we can reproduce the achievements of the past. Now we have to feed a lot more people on a lot less land" (Cribb, 1993a).

A similar opinion was expressed more recently at the Vision 2020 Conference on Food, Agriculture and the Environment, held in Washington DC in 1995, by the Director-General of the International Food Policy Research Institute, Dr. P. Pinstrup-Anderson (Cribb, 1995a). He believes that severe water shortages could emerge in one in every five countries in the twenty-first century, resulting in a growing hunger that will in turn cause a global refugee crisis with tens of millions of people flooding across international borders. He predicts on the business-as-usual scenario, massive environmental destruction throughout the globe, the collapse of fisheries and social conflict, warfare and violence. At present, he notes, 800 million people suffer malnutrition and 1.1 billion people live in absolute poverty with incomes less than $US 1.00 a day. The number of refugees has increased tenfold in less than twenty years (Cribb, 1995a). Almost one-quarter of the world's forests, pastures and farmlands are degraded; in the past forty-five years more than one-tenth of the world's soils have lost a substantial amount of their natural fertility. In Europe 17 percent of soils have been seriously degraded; in Central America and Mexico the figure is 24 percent and for Africa 14 percent (Cribb, 1995a). Along with the problem of the degradation of soils, the conference was told that existing technology was inadequate to feed a world of eight billion people, expected in the year 2020. Research was needed into new technologies, as had occurred previously with the green revolution, but research budgets were being cut, not increased. Global spending on agricultural research has fallen by almost a third over recent years to the present figure (1995) of $US 12 billion. As there is a twenty-year lag between starting an agricultural research project and seeing the results in farmers' fields, the world is taking a dangerous hold of its breath.

Senator Sartaj Aziz, regarded by some as a future presidential prospect for Pakistan, also doubts whether the green revolution will be repeated in Asia by 2020 and he maintains that the best that can be hoped for is to reduce Asian malnutrition by one half (Cribb, 1995b). This in itself will be a major task as 60 percent of the 1.1 billion poor and malnourished of the world already live in Asia and by 2025 the population of Asia will be as great as the population of the world today (Cribb, 1995b).

The enormity of this task was recognized by Canadian Professor Alex McCalla, Director of Agricultural and Natural Resources for the World Bank, in his 1995 Crawford Oration, which was sponsored by Australia (Cribb, 1995c). In McCalla's opinion the number of the world's hungry could reach 2.3 billion by 2025. To deal with this problem world trade in basic foodstuffs must triple, but a number of factors are coinciding to produce a potential global catastrophe—such as population growth, shortages of land and water, the degradation of soils and a decrease in the rate at which global crop yields are improving. Dr. Gurdev Khush, one of the world's leading rice breeders, also believes that very serious food shortages are possible in the future in the Asian region, as no new rice areas are available for cultivation in many countries and Asian farmers are being increasingly forced into marginal and mountainous areas leading to disastrous environmental consequences (Cribb, 1993b).

The decline of the Earth's biodiversity will also severely impact on the problem of maintaining adequate food stocks (Leakey & Lewin, 1996). The United Nations released at an international conference held in Jakarta on November 15, 1995 a 1140-page *Global Biodiversity Assessment*, which documents the state of the world's biodiversity (Briscoe, 1995). The assessment takes as the minimum number of species threatened with extinction to include 5,400 animals and 4,000 plants. This estimate covers only known species, but the UN report estimates that the total number of species at risk could be as high as 30,000. Economists, the supporters of increased economic growth, are generally highly skeptical of such estimates (Simon & Wildavsky, 1995). Critics of environmentalism have also asked: even if this loss of biodiversity is occurring, does it matter for humans? Without addressing this question it is possible to show that even from a human-centered viewpoint, biodiversity declines may have enormous importance for agriculture. The UN Food and Agricultural Organization (FAO) released in April 1996 an exhaustive survey of the world's phytogenic resources ahead of the First International Conference of Phytogenic Resources, held in Leipzig, Germany, June 17–23, 1996. The report documents that a massive loss of biodiversity has occurred as a result of modern farming methods which have privileged the most profitable varieties. For example, in the United States, 91 percent of maize species have been lost in the past 100 years, and where once 7,098 varieties of apple were grown in the United States in the past century, 86 percent of these have now disappeared. This massive loss of biodiversity has led to a trend toward uniformity in crops, many of which are less resistant to disease and variations in climate. Consequently, vital food resources are left vulnerable to decimation by a single cause. This problem cannot be solved by genetic engineering as genetic engineering requires the genetic raw materials to begin with.

This problem exists not only with plants, but also with animal resources. The Australian marine scientist Dr. Meryl Williams, the Director-General of the International Centre for Living Aquatic Resources, has noted that the global catch of fish is declining and will continue to decline due to overfishing, pollution and marine habitat loss. She believes that it is impossible to increase the total fish harvest from existing stocks. The global catch from natural stocks fell from a peak of eighty-nine million tonnes of sea and fresh water fish in 1989 to eighty-five million tonnes in 1993 and aquaculture production has failed to make up for this shortfall.

Simon and Wildavsky (1995), as we have noted, claim that the rate of known extinctions has been and continues to be low. The ecologist Stuart Pimm accepts Simon's point that assessments of extinction rates are highly contentious—but the reason is because estimates of unnamed species range from several million to a hundred million (Pimm, 1995). Consequently, assessments must operate from incomplete sets of wildlife data and infer general trends from a limited number of case studies of the local extinction patterns. Pimm believes, on the basis of his own research, that over the past few thousand years, species have become extinct at rates of up to 1,000 times greater than the extinction rates likely to have existed in the distant past, exhibited in the fossil record. Norman Myers' argument for the massive contemporary loss of biodiversity (Myers & Simon, 1994, 73–74) is based on the premise that about half of the world's species live in tropical forests and these forests are being destroyed at a rate of not less than 150,000 square kilometers per year, or 2 percent of remaining forests. This is based on Myers' work with the Remote Sensing Center of the European Commission in conjunction with the National Aeronautics and Space Administration. The 2 percent annual rate of forest destruction is translated into an annual species extinction rate by means of the theory of island biogeography (Wilson, ed., 1988). This theory contains the empirically well-tested theoretical deduction that when a habitat loses 90 percent of its original extent, no more than 50 percent of the original species can be supported. This, according to Myers, is a minimum estimate. Myers believes that we will lose 20 percent of all species within thirty years and 50 percent or more after that (Myers & Simon, 1994, 79). Myers is more pessimistic about the contemporary decline of biodiversity than Pimm. He estimates that the "natural" rate of extinction before the human era to be one species every four years, making the present extinction rate 120,000 higher, as in Myers' assessment 30,000 species become extinct each year.

Another one of the main limiting variables in the food equation is water. Rashmi Mayur, Director of the International Institute for a Sustainable Future, Bombay, India, believes that the environmental destruction caused by population growth in Asia, Africa and Latin America will strain the environmental resources of these regions to the breaking point and whole countries may be wiped out as life systems collapse (Kadaba, 1995). Mayur as well is not impressed with high tech fixes, seeing them as mainly for the richer Western world, which can afford them. The problem for the poorer remainder of the world, the vast majority of mankind, is the preservation of basic environmental items such as clean water, which is becoming scarcer each day. The same warning was issued by Professor Hal Mooney of Stanford University at the International Grasslands Conference in February 1993. He noted that the current use of the world's fresh water was more than 3,000 cubic kilometers a year and by the year 2000 will be more than 5,000 cubic kilometers. The total global fresh water available is only 9,000 cubic kilometers. So in Professor Mooney's opinion the world's water usage is unsustainable. The doubling of the world's grain supply which has occurred since the mid-1960s has only been possible because of a ready availability of water and given that it takes 5,000 kilograms of water to grow one kilogram of rice, the availability of water must be considered to be a key limiting variable in food production (Kadaba, 1995; Cribb, 1996).

The shape of global conflict in the twenty-first century may well be based on water, as worldwide demand for water is growing twice as fast as the growth in human population (Cribb, 1996). The per capita availability of water in Asia as a whole has declined by 40 to 60 per cent since 1955 due to the growth of cities, and population and the degradation of water quality due to logging, farming and development in catchment areas. Most Asian countries will experience some shortages by 2025. Dr. P. Pinstrup-Anderson believes that there could be water wars in the twenty-first century. By the year 2000 the water shortfall in the Middle East and Mediterranean basin will be twelve million cubic metres a day. Already there are tensions between Israel, the emerging Palestinian state and Jordan over the River Jordan and its aquifers; tensions between Turkey, the Kurds, Iran and Iraq over the Euphrates and Tigris; Egypt and Ethiopia are in dispute over one of the Nile's sources (Cribb, 1996).

In August 1995 the World Bank also recognized that water would become the most sought after natural resource of the twenty-first century, as well as the most likely cause of war, according to Ismail Serageldin, Vice President for Ecologically Sustainable Development at the World Bank (Connor, 1995). Chronic water shortages are already faced by 40 percent of the world's population and the situation will worsen with population expansion and a resultant increased demand for water. The global demand for water is increasing by 2.3 percent a year and doubling every twenty-one years, leading to a situation where supply cannot keep up with demand. As other authorities have observed, a decline in water resources will also occur because of the contamination of water resources by industrial waste and sewage. Ninety-five percent of the world's sewage is emitted into rivers where it is causing enormous environmental and health damage right across the world. Consequently, almost a billion people in the world do not have access to clean drinking water and almost another billion lack adequate sanitation. In developing countries polluted water is responsible for 80 percent of disease, killing ten million people a year (Harding, 1995). This prediction from the World Bank, of a growing water problem in Asia, is particularly significant as this organization is not usually known for making such predictions. Its orientation is firmly in the direction of economic development and growth. However, the World Bank's present thinking is that unless the water problem can be solved, the Asian miracle will end and economic growth in many countries will be curbed.

China's Yellow River has slowed to a trickle where it passes through the Jiang Gully village and dries up completely 100 kilometers short of where it once emptied into the Bohai Gulf (Hutzler, 1996). Rapid industrialization, extensive irrigation and expanding cities are drying up North China's water resources. Ground water levels are falling, resulting in the sinking of land levels, and near the coast, drinking water is becoming polluted as salt water seeps into it. Wang Guoxin of China's Ministry of Water Resources has been quoted as saying that every day China needs approximately 1.5 billion liters of water more than it can ecologically sustain. Already 300 Chinese cities have water shortages and Beijing and Shanghai are among the top ten of the world's cities with the most severe water problems (Hutzler, 1996).

Africa is, and will continue to be, one of the regions worst hit by water shortages. In the 1960s astronauts rarely observed dust storms over Africa. Today the dust is often so thick that it is difficult for astronauts to make out the African continent at all. Richard Underwood, a former photogrammetric engineer for the

National Aeronautics and Space Administration, tours the world showing photographic evidence of environmental damage. From his space-photographic studies he predicts that Africa could be destroyed by 2020 as a result of environmental degradation and drought causing crop failure and starvation (Ceresa, 1994). British scientists at the University of East Anglia have predicted that Southern Africa (including Zimbabwe, Namibia, Botswana and South Africa) faces a centurylong drought as the result of altered climatic patterns produced by the enhanced greenhouse effect. Some years may be cooler with rainfall, but the long-term trend for the region is to become hotter and drier, with harvests in the region falling by a fifth (Nuttall, 1995).

Australia, looked at as a population haven by much of Asia, is facing a severe water crisis, which is part of a much wider environmental crisis (Boyden et al., 1990; Lines, 1991). Let us consider here only the water problem. Australia has the highest per capita quantity of fresh water of any nation (primarily because of its low population density not because of the richness of its water resources), but this is threatened by the pollution of its waterways by salts, sediments, sewage, agricultural and industrial pollution and algal blooms. The lower Darling River, for example, has already suffered the world's worst toxic algal bloom (Cribb, 1994; Woodford, 1995) and pollution is affecting almost every river in the southern two-thirds of the continent—the main area of human population. This pollution, including the algal blooms, is the outcome of development fueled in large part by Australia's immigration program. Ironically, the degradation of water quality will have a major constraining effect on Australia's population growth. The pollution of waterways through outbreaks of toxic algal blooms has the potential to threaten the future of water supplies in South Australia, for example. In 1991 blooms rendered water in South Australia's two biggest fresh water lakes, Albert and Alexandrina, unfit for human consumption and contact, for more than three months. If the Murray-Darling Basin becomes subject to further algal bloom pollution, not only would fresh water for Adelaide, the capital of South Australia, be threatened, but $AUS 10,000 million worth of agricultural production would also be endangered (Humphries, 1992). Yet in an act of sheer ecological insanity, the present South Australian government is lobbying the federal government for a greater number of migrants to the State. Immigration in Australia, as we shall document in our next book in this series, *Global Meltdown*, well illustrates the power of big business and the ethnic lobby who both press for growth and short-term profits at the expense of the ecological sustainability of Australia.

The Murray-Darling is Australia's biggest and most important river system. This system, like most other Australian river systems, was harnessed for irrigation in the 1880s, and since that time water has been diverted from the Murray-Darling River system to the present point where two thirds of the water that would have originally reached the sea is now diverted. This has had a massive impact on the riverine environment, as recognized by the Murray-Darling Basin Commission's own report *The Impact of River Regulation on the Natural Flows of the Murray-Darling Basin* (October 1992). Reduced flooding has affected the Red Gums that line its banks as well as the breeding cycle of fish and birds. There is much less river flow to dilute the natural inflow to the river of salt and nutrients. Toxic algae feed off nutrients coming from agricultural fertilizers, phosphates, as well as organic materials from urban runoff and human sewage. A sludge of nutrients accumulates at the bottom of rivers, so that given the right flow and right weather, toxic algae blooms can occur for many years. No economic or environmentally satisfactory way of combating algal blooms once they occur exists, according to Dr. Ian Smalls, the principal scientist of the New South Wales Department of Water Resources. For example, to control algal outbreaks in the Nepean-Hawkesbury River—which supplies water to Sydney, Australia's immigration capital—by methods such as flushing would require 10 percent of Sydney's annual water supply with each flush. The flush would then need to be repeated after only 20 days (Higgins, 1992). The Australian Conservation Foundation, one of Australia's leading environmental groups, has described the Murray-Darling River system as little more than a "polluted drain" (Honeysett, 1996). The Murray-Darling Basin Commission itself has recognized that the biodiversity of the river system is "crashing" (Honeysett, 1996). The view that Australia's river systems are facing a major ecological crisis and that there is not enough water to meet environmental and consumption needs is accepted by leading water authorities such as Don Blackmore, Chief Executive of the Murray-Darling Basin Commission, Alan Dodds, water resources manager of Sydney's Water Board, and Klaus Schonfeldt, the executive officer of the Murray-Darling Basin Commission's nutrient management strategy (Higgins, 1992).

In 1995 the Murray-Darling Basin was placed under an immediate damage control moratorium by banning new irrigation leases (Chamberlin, 1995). However conservation and scientific groups believe that water use must be reduced by at least 20 percent if these problems are to be solved. It is difficult to see how this can be achieved as long as Australia's ecologically unsustainable immigration program is in place (Smith, ed., 1991). Professor Peter Cullen, Director of the Co-operative Research Centre for Fresh Water Ecology, Australia, has said about the Hawkesbury-Nepean River, which also serves Sydney's west, an area of concentrated migrant settlement:

Today more than half of the water in the lower Hawkesbury is treated flow from sewage works. The river has suffered enormously from removal of water for city use, from sandmining, from nutrient inflows, catchment erosion and urban runoff. It lies in an area of Australia where population is increasing by almost 400 people a week and extraction of water continues to rise at 5 per cent a year to meet that demand. (Rolls, 1993/94, 36)

The grim state of Australia's environment is confirmed by the publication of Australia's first *State of the Environment Report* released in August 1996 (State of the Environment Advisory Committee, 1996). The Executive Summary released by the Minister of Environment, Senator Robert Hill, says that Australians are destroying their environment through population growth, land clearing and the overuse of water resources. Australia's air pollution can be as bad as New York's; we have cleared 70 percent of the native vegetation of the land since European settlement, have the worst rate of mammal extinctions in the world and lose fourteen billion tonnes of topsoil each year (Bita, 1996).

So far in this chapter we have discussed predictions about the sustainability of key ecological resources, the decline of which will seriously threaten human life. We are certain that as long as human beings exist, they will require uncontaminated drinking water for life to continue. It is true that certain philosophers of artificial intelligence look forward to the day when human consciousness can be downloaded into robot bodies, but as we shall see in chapter

3, even *if* thinking machines could exist, this proposal is untenable. We are primarily biological organisms and as such we cannot escape *entirely* the biophysical limits of our human animal condition. With technology we can extend these limits, but in many cases technology leads us back to an appreciation of our biophysical limits. For example, as Savory (1994) has observed, modern agriculture (involving large-scale monoculture cropping and a heavy reliance on petrochemicals) has enabled millions more people to be fed than if traditional farming methods of, say, the Middle Ages were used. By virtue of this power, modern agriculture is led into a "Catch-22" situation where it directly contributes to the destruction of the ecological base, such as by eroding soils (Poincelot, 1990). Agriculture makes civilizations possible, but destructive agricultural practices have destroyed civilizations.

In this discussion we have emphasized the fragility of basic biological resources (the capital of life) and the limited regenerative capacity of ecological systems (sink constraints). Early work on the limits to growth thesis such as D. H. Meadows (et al.), *The Limits to Growth* (1972), was concerned with source limits such as how long liquid petroleum will last. It is this branch of *Limitationism* which has been criticized by Julian Simon. In this book, sink constraints are considered to be of more relevance to a defense of Limitationism than source limits. However, it is worthwhile to mention, in passing, work that has recently been done on source-Limitationism. If it is correct, it strengthens the central argument of this book.

The Australian Limitationist Ted Trainer believes that since the publication of *The Limits to Growth,* a much stronger case has emerged for Limitationism (Trainer, 1985, 1989, 1991, 1995a, b). He notes that even though the Earth is made of minerals, minerals are not likely to be mined from other than ore deposits, which are usually found close to the surface. To extract minerals from crustal rock would require between ten and 1000 times the amount of energy required for the extraction of minerals from even the poorest grade ores (Skinner & McClaren, eds., 1987). Trainer argues that if eleven billion people (the UN median estimate of the world population in 2065) were to consume minerals at the per capita rate of present U.S. society, most accessible minerals would be exhausted in about three to four decades. This prediction is based on an estimate of all the minerals that exist in the Earth as ore, including low-grade deposits that are not economical to mine at present and deposits that have not yet been found. Seabed deposits, Trainer asserts, would potentially double accessible quantities of only a few items such as copper and manganese (Trainer, 1995b). Following Chapman and Roberts' (1983) estimate that the energy cost of producing minerals is likely to rise at 2 to 3 percent per annum in the next few decades and given that it requires the energy equivalent of 560 liters of oil to provide the minerals consumed by each American annually, Trainer has calculated that by 2035, the amount of energy required to provide one American with minerals will be about 2700 liters of oil (Trainer, 1995b, 24). This is 4 to 5 times the amount of commercial energy, on average, that half of the people in the world now consume. If eleven billion people were to use energy at the per capita rate of Americans, then all nonrenewable energy resources would be exhausted in approximately forty years (2035) (Trainer, 1995b, 27). Trainer also argues that renewable energy resources are not capable of sustaining the energy demands of industrial society because of the large energy loss associated with the storage and transportation of energy in this form (Trainer, 1995c).

David Price of Cornell University (Price, 1995) believes that the exhaustion of fossil fuels will lead to a collapse of the Earth's population and civilization itself. At current rates of consumption, known reserves of petroleum will be exhausted in about thirty-five years, coal in 200 years and natural gas in fifty-two years (Price, 1995, 310; World Resources Institute et al., 1990, 145). Price doubts whether the discovery of new reserves will significantly alter this situation given recent advances in geologic technology. In any case, the demand for energy will grow at an increasing rate—if the demands of increased economic growth are to be met—effectively eliminating the advantages yielded by any such discoveries. Price assesses a number of alternative energy resources, including biomass conversion, hydropower, solar, geothermal and other sources of renewable energy, and concludes that they would not be sufficient to sustain industrial society. Controlled thermonuclear fusion would definitely solve at least the West's energy problems, but the technology is still experimental (Price, 1995, 313). Price concludes that a collapse of the human population will occur because of starvation, war, social chaos (death) and disease, the horsemen of the apocalypse:

[It] may prove impossible for even a few survivors to subsist on the meagre resources left in civilization's wake. The children of the highly technological society into which more and more of the world's peoples are being drawn will not know how to support themselves by hunting and gathering or by simple agriculture. In addition, the wealth of wild animals that once sustained hunting societies will be gone, and topsoil that has been spoiled by tractors will yield poorly to the hoe. A species that has come to depend on complex technologies to mediate its relationship with the environment may not long survive their loss. (Price, 1995, 316)

Lewis Perelman (1980) is much less pessimistic than Price about the sustainability of civilization but he does believe that the transition from societies based on fossil fuels to ones based on renewable sources of energy will lead to the elimination of the liberal-democratic system and its replacement by a new "feudalism" with wealth and power based primarily on land holdings, political decentralization, a steady-state economy and social stratification by class or caste (Perelman, 1980, 395). Renewable sources of energy, such as solar energy, are area-dependent, unlike nonrenewable sources of energy, such as fossil fuels. Perelman means this in the sense that nonrenewable resources offer vast energy resources in relatively small areas of land, but solar collection, for example, by its very nature depends on area. A concentration of economic power in land reserves is a characteristic of feudal society. As well, Perelman argues, after the end of liberal-democratic growth-based society, a theocracy is likely to emerge, where religion provides a social cohesive force once the contemporary religions of consumerism and materialism are abandoned (Perelman, 1980, 396–397).[1]

Perelman's work offers some interesting speculations about the sustainability of human civilization. Economists, the supporters of increased economic growth, could and have contested this Limitationist argument at many points. H. E. Goeller (1995), for example, looks forward to an "age of substitutability" in about two centuries where humanity "should be able to subsist permanently on renewable resources of energy, plus substitutes for some chemical elements, and non-renewable resources of about 36 elements that will be in effectively infinite supply" (Goeller, 1995, 313). This all depends on future science and technology which has not yet been envisioned. Goeller believes that science and technology have the capacity to deliver to us this new age of plenty. Consequently, he does not view as realistic the analysis of current reserve and resource data. Indeed, Goeller takes a large number of minerals and elements to be literally infinite ("∞") in measure (Goeller, 1995, 316–317; Goeller & Zucker, 1984). He admits though that if current resources were to remain constant, many elements such as gold, zinc, lead, copper, tin, mercury and so on might be depleted before 2100. New technology and substitutes will avert a crisis; for example, copper cables in telecommunication have been replaced by fiber optic cables, ultimately made from sand. The recycling of metals is important, in Goeller's opinion, but unless its efficiency is high, it will not make a major difference in the long run (Goeller, 1995, 315).[2]

It is clear that Goeller and many other Economists reject many of the methodological and theoretical assumptions accepted by Limitationists such as Trainer. Therefore, if progress is to be made in the debate about the sustainability of industrial civilization, we must examine the core assumptions of both positions. A convenient way of doing this is to examine, and rebut, the Economist critique of environmentalism and Limitationism. We shall in turn show that the Economist critique fails and that the Economist position is untenable.

THE ENVIRONMENTALIST BACKLASH

The broad critique of environmentalism involves a number of arguments: (1) failed predictions of doom made by many environmentalists; (2) in the case of global warming, the incompleteness of knowledge and the uncertainty of the effects; (3) the costs of reducing environmental damage which are regarded as excessive by industrialists and capitalists; (4) the belief that environmentalism, especially in its *deep ecology* form, involves a rejection of industrial capitalism and the advocation of a new ecological religion—but this is a fantasy of the intellectual elites in the urbanized West (Ray & Guzzo, 1993); (5) the belief that humans in any case no longer need a social relationship with nature and there is no turning back from technological expansion, economic globalization and the unending expansion of liberal capitalism (Easterbrook, 1995; Ferry, 1993; Kaufman, 1994; Lewis, 1992; Maley, 1994; Rogers, 1995; Rubin, 1994; Wildavsky, 1995).

Ronald Bailey's book *Eco-Scam: The False Prophets of Ecological Apocalypse* (1993) follows the above pattern. Although he states that he does not champion "mindless boosterism" or "Panglossian optimism," he does say that "human history shows that our energy and creativity will surmount whatever difficulties we encounter . . . there is nothing out there that we cannot handle" (Bailey, 1993, xii). He comments, as do most recent critics of environmentalism, on Ehrlich's failed predictions of ecocatastrophe (Ehrlich, 1968; Miller, 1991) and Ehrlich's October 1980 bet with Julian Simon about the ten-year price movements of copper, chrome, nickel, tin and tungsten, which exhibited a fall in price. This indicates in Bailey's opinion that "the supply of resources is becoming more abundant, not more scarce" (Bailey, 1993, 54). The same point is made by Richard North in *Life on a Modern Planet: A Manifesto for Progress* (North, 1995b) and by Wilfred Beckerman in *Small Is Stupid: Blowing the Whistle on the Greens* (Beckerman, 1995).

Beckerman's book is more technical than the other books that have been cited here. It contains an interesting discussion of the question of "discounting the future," which we shall address in another book. Beckerman maintains that all environmental problems, including giving a greater proportion of Third World populations access to clean drinking water, can only occur by societies getting richer, and societies only get richer by economic growth (Beckerman, 1995, 41). Further, economic growth can be taken as a rough, imperfect index of welfare. Since growth enables us to consume, and consumption is desirable, then growth is desirable.

Like Bailey, North and Julian Simon, Beckerman denies that resources are finite (Beckerman, 1995, 49). He admits that if resources are finite, "the only way to ensure they last forever is to stop using them" (Beckerman, 1995, 49). This being so, zero growth will fail to save us in the long run. Otherwise, resources are not finite and the limits to growth argument collapses.

Beckerman, like most other Economists, believes that the acceptance of the limits to growth position depends on when the ecocatastrophe is likely to occur (Beckerman, 1995, 50). In our opinion, this argument is irrelevant because Limitationists are pointing to existing problems. Environmental damage is a measure of overshoot *now*. Certainly total global ecological collapse has not occurred, but this in itself does not show that it will not. The situation may well be like that of the alcoholic who systematically damages his liver. Life still goes on even with a damaged liver, but only up to a certain critical point after which systemscollapse occurs and death results. The Limitationist proposes that the environmental crisis is much like this.

Beckerman, like most other Economists, is an economic imperialist. The environment is a subset of the economy. We believe that this position is refuted by mainstream biological and evolutionary theory which does not see mankind as radically distinct from the rest of the animal world. A total neglect of a biophysical approach to the understanding of life, for example, is seen in Beckerman's discussion of global warming. Beckerman in his discussion of global warming in *Small Is Stupid* does not consider the implications of computerized models of the world's climate and economy. This is not because such models are uncertain: computerized models of Western economies are, after all, used by economists to justify a number of their pet obsessions, such as support for mass immigration into countries such as Australia. Beckerman believes that "alarm over the predicted effects of global warming is vastly exaggerated" and this can be demonstrated by consideration of one piece of evidence: the "present dispersion of the world's population over widely different temperature zones" (Beckerman, 1995, 90). Nobody, as far as we are aware, has said that global warming will produce average temperatures that humans cannot adapt to. The problem is the wide-ranging impact on environments of climatic change. But this is not a problem for Beckerman. He says that even if global warming does produce damaging climatic changes, stopping climatic change will cost us more than climatic change itself, so it is better to damage the environment. For example, he proposes that it is in the interest of Bangladesh to make "some kind of deal" whereby they accept that 20 percent of their country is destroyed, but they receive an appropriate proportion of what it would cost the global economy to control greenhouse emissions.

An excellent example of Beckerman's neglect of biological science occurs in his critique of a Limitationist argument based on the human appropriation of the photosynthetic product of the planet (Beckerman, 1995, 51). The argument in question is that humans use, either directly or indirectly, 40 percent of the net primary product of terrestrial photosynthesis, or, if oceans and aquatic ecosystems are included, 25 percent (Vitousek et al., 1986; Goodland, 1992). A doubling of the human population, assuming a constant or increased rate of appropriation (a reasonable assumption), will lead to at least an 80 percent appropriation. A 100 percent appropriation is ecologically impossible, so a human population crash is inevitable (Catton, 1982). Beckerman argues against this, using an argument that was verified by one of his "eminent" Oxford scientific colleagues. (The colleague is so eminent that no name is given or source referencing offered.) Beckerman's argument is given in Box 4.1, "The Photosynthesis Fairy Tale" of his book (Beckerman, 1995, 52):

If there is less vegetation—e.g. because land that had been covered by carbon-absorbing vegetation has been converted for other purposes, such as for building cities or motorways—then there will be less photosynthesis. But this would just have reflected a fall in the "demand" for it from vegetation. Insofar as some, or most, of the vegetation that has been destroyed to make way for other uses of land had not been used for human consumption in one way or another, it must of course be true that the proportion of total photosynthetic product that was "appropriated for our own purposes" will have risen. But this is no cause for concern. It simply means that a lot of the photosynthetic product that had previously been produced was of no use to us. It was, in effect, wasted. Now there is less of it. So what? Would it be better if 99 per cent of the total photosynthetic product had been of no use to the human race, as was the case a few centuries ago?

Beckerman is in effect asserting here that it is of no consequence if humans use the entire photosynthetic product of the planet and if myriad ecosystems collapse. As we have seen from our discussion earlier in this chapter, this assertion is scientific nonsense. Human life would not be able to continue in such a decimated world.

Beckerman's need to show that Limitationism is false arises from his recognition that although the price mechanism is an efficient mechanism for the optimal allocation of resources for competing uses, the price mechanism cannot determine the optimal scale of output (Beckerman, 1995, 142). This would not be important if there were no ecological limits to growth. Hence Beckerman's need to show that Limitationism is false. However, it also follows from this that if Limitationism can be successfully defended, then orthodox economics, assumed by all the critics of environmentalism, is severely defective, for the question of the optimal scale of output is a question that an adequate scientific theory should be able to resolve. We shall demonstrate in chapter 4 that Beckerman's economic framework is theoretically flawed.

The most prolific critic of the limits to growth position and environmentalism is the economist Julian Simon, Professor of Business Administration at the University of Maryland (Simon, 1981, 1990, ed. 1995; Myers & Simon, 1994). Simon advances his critique of environmentalism from the perspective of "absolute liberalism" or "absolute economic rationalism," which sees market mechanisms as perfectly competitive and price the only strict criterion of supply. As Ellul has noted (Ellul, 1990, 20), Simon does not attempt to justify his broad economic framework; in due course we shall demonstrate that it is flawed. Taking price as the only strict criterion of supply, Simon maintains that if something is in short supply, it is costly. Copper fell in price between 1800 and 1980 and more is sold today. Copper, according to Simon, will become even more abundant. Hence copper reserves are unlimited. Likewise with grain, the price of grain has gone down over the last century and this will continue indefinitely. Along with absolute economic rationalism, Simon has an uncritical faith in simple linear extrapolations.

Accompanying his uncritical acceptance of neoclassical economics, Simon also makes four main points in his work. First, scientists cannot give us certain results: indeed, there is no debate about the existence of scientific disagreement! However, economic experts also disagree. He also argues that scientific data relating to pollution and the exhaustion of nonrenewable resources can be dismissed. The only criterion is the market. For some reason, the uncertainty that afflicts the biophysical sciences does not afflict orthodox economic theory and the failed predictions of economists (Ormerod, 1995). Second, there are no limits to growth; Simon denies that any resource is finite. Third, Simon has an absolute belief in technological progress. Technological progress will deal with any difficulty. As we have noted, much is made by Simon's supporters of his successful bet against Ehrlich about the price of a set of five metals. It should be noted that Simon claimed that we could begin mining the moon by 1990 and that satellites for solar energy would supply our energy needs by the year 2000 (Simon, 1981, 89). Finally, the ultimate resource for Simon is people. The faster the population grows, the greater the prosperity of the population increases. The more immigrants taken in, the better off the economy will be. We will now take up these main points.

A major argument in Simon's work is that there are no limits to growth because no resource is finite. Simon rejects the Malthusian assumption that resources are finite because he holds to an open-world vision that resources are increasing in quantity, largely through the expansion of the economy and technological innovation. For example, Simon argues that the number of oil wells that will eventually produce oil is not known at present; hence, it cannot be taken to be meaningfully finite (Simon, 1990, 400). In fact, Simon believes that the supply of natural resources is *infinite* (Simon, 1981, 47):

> the length of a one-inch line is finite in the sense that it is bounded at both ends. But the line within the endpoints contains an infinite number of points; these points cannot be counted, because they have no defined size. Therefore the number of points in that one-inch segment is not finite. Similarly, the quantity of copper that will ever be available to us is not finite, because there is no method (even in principle) of making an appropriate count of it, given the problem of the economic definition of "copper," the possibility of creating copper or its economic equivalent from other materials, and thus the lack of boundaries to the sources from which copper might be drawn.

These arguments are logically defective. It doesn't logically follow from the premise that since the number of oil wells which will eventually produce oil is *unknown*, that the number of oil wells is therefore not meaningly finite in a mathematical sense. The number of hairs on one's head is unknown, but it is finite as male pattern baldness well shows. In Simon's example of the one-inch line, the line is finite in length even though it contains an "uncountable" or nondenumerable infinity of points. The number of points in the line segment is known—it is a nondenumerable infinity, so these points can be "counted" in a mathematical sense. Contrary to Simon, the points do have a definite size—they are of zero dimension or unextended. The example shows exactly the opposite of what Simon wants. The argument that anything which is infinitely divisible is therefore infinite in quantity is fallacious. By way of counterexample, consider our financial assets. These are infinitely divisible, but they are certainly not infinite in quantity.

As Simon is wrong about his basic mathematics, he is wrong in applying this analogy to copper. Garrett Hardin, who debated this issue with Simon in Simon's book *Population Matters* (Simon, 1990, 381–404), accepts that minerals such as copper are finite in quantity—after all, the number of atoms in the universe is thought by physicists to be a mathematically finite number. Hardin, however, agrees with Simon that we are not running out of minerals such as copper. His point is that when copper was first mined in the United States, copper ore was of a 20 percent concentration, but now it is only 0.7 percent. Technology has kept pace with the impoverishment of the ore. But these improvements cannot go on forever because of the principle of diminishing returns, which even orthodox economists recognize. More energy must be used for copper extraction, leading to a price rise. Hardin notes that the copper cost curve from 600 B.C. to 1930 is down, but from 1930 it is up. Simon recognizes this, but says that there are dangers in using trend series because there is no logical way of saying on the basis of a given series what is the appropriate period for forecasting. Hence, he favors the largest run series (Simon, 1990, 386). This, however, is precisely what Hardin has done in presenting his biohistorical view.

In a recent paper, Michael Bronner (1996) argued that the lifespan of liquid petroleum is quite short. Technology will not improve the situation because petroleum is a finite exhaustible resource and without it modern industrial transportation and industry cannot survive. The limitations of this resource are represented by the concept of *Q-infinity*. Q-infinity is "a numerical value denoting the maximum quantity of recoverable liquid petroleum within the geologic composition of our planet" (Bronner, 1996, 374). Important work was done on Q-infinity by M. King Hubbert (1962; Kraushaar & Ristinen, 1993). Hubbert derived Q-infinity estimates by mathematical projections rather than by the analysis of geologic field estimates. He plotted on a logistic curve (an S-shaped curve), the cumulative history of oil discovered in the United States. Another curve was plotted that lags behind the discovery curve by about 10.5 years based on production data for crude oil and the process of actually obtaining it from the ground (Bronner, 1996, 375). The actual time between when oil is discovered and when it is pumped from the ground is on average 10.5 years. Hubbert has mathematically incorporated technological innovations into his analysis. The slope of the discovery curve rises in the early years of oil discovery as easy reserves are pumped from the ground and rapid technological advances are made. If technology improved oil production for a particular year, that would be represented in the total oil output for that year. Hubbert found in plotting the quantitative discoveries and production from 1900 to 1961 that the maximum slope of the curve was reached in 1956 and he hypothesized that from that point the curve would gradually level off, reaching Q-infinity when a tangent to the curve is horizontal (i.e., dy/dx = 0). He predicted that Q-infinity for the United States would be reached by the year 2050. Bronner believes that Hubbert was too conservative in his projection since the slopes of both curves have been decreasing between 1956 and 1970.

Liquid petroleum is, contrary to Julian Simon's opinion, a *finite* resource. Oil was created between ten and 500 million years ago from plants and animals. This organic material was transformed into oil under high temperatures and pressures. There is no technologically possible way of replicating this process on the *same scale*. Oil can be manufactured in the laboratory but not at a price to cheaply power an industrial society. We recognize that there are vast oil fields untapped in the Middle East; we take no position on the question of when the world's oil will run out. However, it is in the very nature of an exponential consumption curve that it soon exceeds all physical bounds. Remove one cell from your body. Nothing happens. Now remove 2 cells, 4 cells, 8 cells, 16 cells ... doubling each time. Very soon you will find yourself bleeding to death as vast chunks of your body are removed: such is the nature of exponential growth (Hardin, 1993).

The uncertainty that afflicts biophysical models is not alleviated by economic models involving historical cost trends (Trainer, 1986). For a start, in almost all of the graphs of historical cost trends of resources used in Simon and Kahn's book *The Resourceful Earth* (Simon & Kahn, 1984), price falls significantly level-out as the present is reached, indicating the operation of the principle of diminishing returns (as extra units of one factor of production are used with the others held constant, the quantity of output produced by each additional unit employed will eventually fall). Trainer (1986, 20) has observed that Simon and Kahn's graph of U.S. mineral prices against the CPI (Simon & Kahn, 1984, 15) rises after 1940, also indicating the operation of the principle of diminishing returns.

The theoretical problem, however, which vitiates much of Simon's work, and much of environmental economics for that matter, is the assumption that there is a coherence relationship between economic theory and ecological or biophysical reality. This is seen in Simon's assertion that economics is a sounder guide to understanding resource scarcity than ecology. Simon commits the fallacy of *misplaced concreteness* (Whitehead, 1925, 200, 1929; Daly & Cobb, 1989; Georgescu-Roegen, 1971, 320)—neglecting the degree of abstraction involved in one's theory and fallaciously drawing inferences about reality. Simon takes the abstract properties of money to be possessed by commodities themselves. Thus, money can grow indefinitely at compound interest and so, therefore, can the economic growth of physical commodities.

Simon's view that economics is a sounder guide to understanding resource scarcity than ecology, geology and other physical sciences puts conceptual weight upon the concept of the cost or price of a given resource. It is a weight that this economic concept cannot bear, and Simon himself supplies the reasons in an afternote to chapter 1 of *The Ultimate Resource* entitled "The 'True' Cost (Price) of Natural Resources" (Simon, 1981, 28–29). Simon admits that there is no true or objective measure of cost or price in economics; rather there are different measures of cost, relative to a certain information base. Simon shows this by outlining the difficulties that exist in measuring the "objective" cost of a commodity—we accept his arguments and refer the interested reader to the primary text. This problem with the relativity of price undermines Simon's basic uncertainty argument against the biophysical account of scarcity. If prices are arbitrarily constructed and relative, then supply-and-demand curves cannot represent anything objectively real. In fact, the price of commodities is seldom a mechanical product of supply and demand. The neoclassical theory which holds that the marginal productivity of factors is the determinant of profit bears little relation to the actual workings of modern global capitalism. Oligopolies set prices, usually using the "cost plus" method, adding a fixed percentage to the estimated "cost." Demand is often created by saturation advertising using sophisticated psychological techniques (which is not to say that advertisements themselves are sophisticated). Neoclassical theory needs to be confronted with real life work situations such as textile and footwear manufacturing in China, often based on the slave labor of prisoners or the sweatshops of Asia where workers receive only a few dollars' pay a day. Their productivity has nothing to do with their minimal wages, beyond the fact that if they do not produce enough they will be punished and replaced by another human robot. We will return to this point again in chapter 4.

REFUTING TECHNOLOGICAL OPTIMISM

There is no doubt that behind the cornucopian optimism of Julian Simon, Wilfred Beckerman, Richard North and the other critics of environmentalism is the view that Limitationists underestimate the power of science and technology. It is one of the key assumptions of modernity and the Enlightenment project that while it may be impossible to know everything, the method by which anything whatsoever can be known is known, and that method is the scientific method (Rosen, 1974, xv; Rodman, 1980; Catton & Dunlap, 1980). It is the belief in the idea that there are no limits to knowledge that is the ultimate justification for the modernist faith in unending technological progress. In chapter 3 we shall directly challenge modernist belief. For the moment let us counter the technological optimism of Julian Simon, without ascending to a high level of sophistication.

A sensible position toward science and technology has been expressed by Professor Richard Levins, Head of the Department of Population Sciences at the Harvard School of Public Health, in a lecture delivered in Edinburgh, April 13, 1996, when he was presented with the annual Edinburgh Medal for his work. He recognized the impressive achievements of science and technology but also its dramatic failures. Science has contributed to the destruction of the environment and new discoveries have been applied without a consideration of the consequences. It has given humanity a "greater capacity to kill and to cause mass death. The promises of understanding and progress have not been kept, and the application of science to human affairs has often done great harm." Levins is not surprised that there has been an antiscience backlash with young people abandoning the subject. Although we are viewed as technological pessimists, we do believe that technology has much to contribute to sustainable living. Biotechnology and artificial intelligence both can make major contributions toward environmental management.

However, all technological progress has a price, carrying with the benefits also costs and unforeseen effects, and in many cases technical progress raises more and greater problems in the *long term* than the short term problems that it solves. Often the harmful effects of technical progress are inseparable from its beneficial effects (Ellul, 1990). There is an extensive literature documenting the "Janus face" of technology for almost all of the technological marvels that impress Julian Simon (Abbott, 1994; Ascher, 1989; Barnaby, 1986; Bellini, 1987; Bequai, 1987; Bessant & Cole, 1985; Blank, 1984; Campbell & Connor, 1986; Cornwell, 1987; Davies, 1992; Forester, ed., 1989; Forester & Morrison, 1990; Fowler & Mooney, 1990; Hayes, 1990; Haynes, ed., 1991; Hill, 1988; Hindmarsh, 1991; Hoffman & Moran, 1986; Keighery, 1995; Kipnis, 1990; Krimsky, 1982; Laudan, 1986; Laura & Ashton, 1991; Lyon, 1990; Lyytinen & Hirschheim, 1987; McDermott, 1987; Michie & Johnston, 1985; Postman, 1985; Reinecke, 1984; Rifkin, 1984, 1985; Schnaars, 1989; Shaker & Wise, 1988; Shallis, 1984; Smith & Best, 1989; Stoll, 1996; Tirman, 1984; Traber, ed., 1986; Webster & Robins, 1986; Wheale & McNally, 1988; Winner, ed., 1992). The technological optimist such as Julian Simon must contend that all of these critics are wrong about all of the substantial issues that they raise, and this is most unlikely.

Let us consider the case of information technology. Simon regards the information technology revolution as a major human achievement, and of course he is, in some respects, right. For example, it has made the writing of a difficult manuscript such as this one much easier than if computers were not available for research. It does not follow, though, that computers have succeeded in improving the human condition in general when a complex costbenefit analysis is conducted. Indeed information technology has its own built-in "Murphy's Law." This is well illustrated by the so-called "productivity paradox" (Attewell, 1996).

In universities and corporations, investments in information technology have not reduced the cost of administration or the concomitant expansion of managerial staff. Investment of massive sums of money has not improved white-collar productivity substantially. Computer technologists and futurologists asserted that information technology would produce major improvements in efficiency enabling a given quantity of administrative work to be done with less workers at less cost. What has happened is that new things are being done by the same workforce: expectations have changed because of the power of computers and word processing software. So documents become more elaborate. Written communications have replaced many spoken communications, and laboratory studies show that written communications tend to be more detailed. Face-to-face and telephone communications are often replaced by electronic mail. Information technology has also increased the number of methods by which a white-collar worker's day can be fragmented, also reducing productivity. Labor costs have been saved by replacing many secretaries and typists, but these savings have often been offset by the need of firms to hire managerial professionals at higher rates of pay. The information technology revolution, rather than reducing information overload, has created "escalating demands for data and [fueled] the growth of a 'management by numbers' culture, which emphasizes quantitative data and spreadsheet modelling as central to good organizational decision making" (Attewell, 1996, 25). Critics see this process as augmenting information overload, not alleviating it (Kipnis, 1990).

The fragility of our modern computer-based society is well illustrated by a simple problem that has enormous ramifications: can computers cope with a change in the millennium? (Reeve et al., 1996). It would appear that a simple change of date presents a problem that could cause a "global millennium meltdown" (Reeve et al., 1996, 53) and would cost at least $US 400 billion to correct. The Julian Simon school of technological optimism is confronted by a problem that human ingenuity should have immediately solved: most computers, upon which modern life in the West depends, can only tell the date in terms of two digits. The year 2000 will be read as "00," so the computer will think it is really the year 1900. This simple fault may prove to be the most costly mistake in human history, for even many powerful mainframe computers have this flaw. The problem arose because in early computers memory space was very expensive, so programmers expressed the year in two digits instead of four. This date format became standardized and manufacturers failed to anticipate the problem. Consequently, at midnight on December 31, 1999 many computers after reaching the year "00" will assume that an error has occurred and will shut down. Others may assume that it really is the year "00" adding 100 years of interest to bank accounts. Many computers will record that they have not been serviced for 100 years and will cease to operate. Other doomsday predictions of the "millennium bomb" include a Pentagon warning that some weapons systems may run out of control and that the United States would not be able to respond to military threats. The problem is not simply solved: it often involves programmers examining every line in a computer's operating instructions, and this can sometimes be more than 100 million lines of code (Reeve et al., 1996). If this problem is not resolved, it could in itself lead to global economic chaos.

There is another reason for rejecting the technological optimism of Julian Simon at least with respect to artificial intelligence. A number of philosophers and theorists in the field of artificial intelligence have already begun discussing the prospects of artificial brains being created that will be equal, or superior, to the brain of humans. This prospect has been discussed by O. B. Hardison in his popular book *Disappearing through the Skylight* (Hardison, 1989) and has become the staple diet of contemporary philosophy of mind. Hugo de Garis (1990) sees a battle emerging in the twenty-first century about who or what will be the dominant species on this planet—man or machine. Dr. William I. McLaughlin of the Jet Propulsion Laboratory, California Institute of Technology, sees humanity losing this battle to machines within 100 years (McLaughlin, 1983). Already advances are being made in a field of science known as *electrically conductive polymer molecules* that may enable artificial muscles to be built. A hypothetical artificial muscle would be able to lift up to 450 times the weight of a human muscle using an electric impulse as low as one volt (Cribb, 1995d). Professor Marwan Jabri of Sydney University's Faculty of Engineering, an expert in neuromorphic engineering, predicts that humanoid machines will appear within the next few years that can sense, react, learn and make decisions (Cribb, 1995d). He recognizes that "humanoids are going to have a far greater impact on our society even than the information revolution," so society must begin to immediately discuss the social and ethical consequences of thinking machines. However, he will in the meantime press ahead with his research and build one.

The technological optimists tell us that these advances in artificial intelligence will benefit humanity. Artificial muscles will help people who have lost a limb. Perhaps they will. But again, this is not the real motivation for the artificial intelligence program. Only a brief glance at the philosophical writings of many of the leading AI theorists tells us that this is not so. Their goal is to create an artificial man, the same goal which Dr. Frankenstein had in the famous novel by Mary Shelley. Their goal is to make humanity—and themselves—ultimately redundant. Some technological optimists deny that superintelligent machines will become our masters and monsters. More honest technological optimists accept the inevitability of this, and look forward to creating the next stage of evolution. They are the true mad scientists of our time and probably the only refutation of their position that is possible is a refutation much along the lines pursued in the movie *Terminator 2: Judgment Day*. But at this point we have established our case against the technological optimist. If the ultimate aim of AI is to make humans redundant, to lead to a situation where robots may annihilate humanity, then we can hardly claim that such a technological advance will improve the *human* condition. Yet these developments are implicit in the AI program. If a superintelligent machine is created with "free will" (a plastic neural system, the capacity to learn, with thoughts and desires of its own), then such a machine could *not* by definition be under our control. It might pursue a lifeplan inconsistent with our interests. The burden of proof is upon the followers of Julian Simon to show that this scenario is not likely to occur. We cannot see how they can do this. We do not believe that the strong AI program will succeed and we offer our reasons for this in chapter 3. Here we are stating a consequence of the strong AI program *if* it succeeds.

Other technological optimists believe that new technologies such as nanotechnology will allow us to escape the limits to growth and our biophysical limits. The idea here is being able to manipulate materials atom by atom. Nanovisionary K. E. Drexler, founder of the Foresight Institute in California, foresees molecular assemblers putting together any structure we want from cheap materials, such as manufacturing meat from vegetable waste (Drexler, 1990). There is no doubt that this will revolutionize technology. Supercomputers the size of a pocket calculator could be created. Indeed, nanotechnology may be required to transcend the technical problems facing the strong AI program in its quest to create the superintelligent machine (Clery, 1992).

However, at present, nanotechnology is a long way from achieving Drexler's vision. Work is being done by IBM with scanning tunneling microscopes, which operate using the quantum mechanical tunneling properties of electron beams, allowing single atoms to be manipulated. This is a very long way from making a pork chop from vegetable waste or reconstructing an extinct species, atom by atom. However, even if it could be done, this would not show that humans have escaped all biophysical limits and that the second law of thermodynamics is inapplicable because the second law of thermodynamics will apply to aggregates of molecules.

Perhaps the greatest achievement of modern technology has been the advent of antibiotics, anesthesia, surgical technology and an array of pharmaceutical innovations. Martin W. Lewis in *Green Delusions: An Environmentalist Critique of Radical Environmentalism* (1992) is right to refute the idea that health standards have been declining in modern times and that premodern times were "healthier." Life was hard and brutal and average life spans were for premodern man sometimes as low as an average of seventeen to eighteen years (Lewis, 1992,

127; Cohn, 1989, 124). (No doubt this low average life span figure was due to high infant and child mortality rates, dragging the "average" life expectancy down, giving us a somewhat artificial statistic.) Michael Haines, in his paper in Julian Simon's *The State of Humanity*, "Disease and Health through the Ages" (Haines, 1995), notes that compared to other animal species "human beings have suffered a disproportionately large share of mortality from infectious and parasitic diseases" (Haines, 1995, 51). Haines goes on to say that it is the reduction and control of these diseases that have led to the rapid growth in the human population which has occurred in modern times. Haines believes that the "Age of Pestilence and Famine" (Omran, 1971), which characterized the premodern era, is over even in developing nations: "We no longer face catastrophic epidemic infections, and even many pervasive endemic microparasitic infections have been banished" (Haines, 1995, 59). If the technological optimists have a strong ground, this area must be it.

It is true that public health measures and antibiotics have made the death rates from infectious disease fall rapidly. But bacteria have been evolving defenses against antibiotics. Indeed, paradoxically, antibiotics themselves breed drug-resistant superbugs. The resistance to antibiotics does not occur by the development of tolerance by individual bacteria, but rather by the process of natural selection. Rare gene mutations occur in the bacteria or new genes are introduced by plasmid "infection" (plasmids are tiny rings of DNA) or genetic transfer between bacteria spreads resistant genes. Natural selection gives a selective advantage to resistant strains (Nesse & Williams, 1995, 55). Mutations have made once harmless bacteria into dangerous ones. This has occurred with the bacterium *Haemophilus aegypticus*, which causes Brazilian purperic fever (Cannon, 1995, xxiv).

Staphylococcal bacteria were all vulnerable to penicillin in 1941. Today 95 percent of these strains show at least some resistance to penicillin (Nesse & Williams, 1995, 53). One-third of all cases of tuberculosis in New York City are antibiotic resistant, and 3 percent of new cases and 7 percent of recurrent cases are resistant to two or more antibiotics (Nesse & Williams, 1995, 54). One of the largest studies of antibiotic resistance in the world was recently completed by the Australian Group on Antimicrobial Resistance. They found that penicillin resistance among the bacteria causing pneumonia and meningitis, *Streptococcus pneumonia*, was six times higher in 1996 than in 1989 (Ferrari, 1996a, b). One of the members of this research team, Dr. Peter Collingnon, head of the infectious diseases unit at Canberra's Woden Valley Hospital, said :

In almost every bacterial species you can think of, resistant rates are going up and the rate of resistance developed to drugs is rising faster than new drugs are being developed. In the 1920s and 1930s it was a disaster—if you had these infections you died from it. We're now getting back to the situation where we're worrying that for some people, we might be back where we were then. (Ferrari, 1996a, 3)

The Monash Medical Centre in Australia found that oral antibiotics are unable to treat multiple-resistant "golden staph" present in most major East Coast teaching hospitals in Australia. Mutant strains of bacteria resistant to all or most antibiotics exist, such as certain strains of enterococci bacteria. According to Dr. Richard Novick of New York, an expert on bacterial drug resistance, these bacteria are likely in time to transfer total drug resistance to Staphylococci and "[t]he result could be a global epidemic, perhaps [the] greatest disaster ever created by modern medical practice" (Cannon, 1995, xxiii; Koshland, 1992). One of Australia's leading microbiologists, Professor Peter McDonald, of the Flinders University of South Australia, has stated that emerging infections by "smart-bugs" and "super-bugs" could lead to the outbreak of "uncontrollable infectious disease." "By the time we humans have worked out ways of coping with germs, environmental changes that favor germs and not us will have gone too far and the dominance of humans will diminish—like the dinosaur" (Hailstone & Starick, 1995, 5).

Diseases once thought to have been conquered by medical technology have reemerged—tuberculosis, cholera, typhoid fever, yellow fever, malaria, dengue fever, diphtheria and whooping cough. Only smallpox seems to have been eliminated. According to the World Health Organization's *World Health Report* (1996), the world is on the brink of an infectious disease crisis. The world death toll from infectious diseases has risen to seventeen million people a year; taken collectively, infectious diseases represent the world's leading cause of premature death: HIV/AIDS > 1 million; measles > 1 million; malaria, 2.1 million; hepatitis B, 1.1 million; tuberculosis, 3.1 million; acute respiratory infections, 4.4 million; diarrheal diseases, 3.1 million; neonatal tetanus, 500,000; whooping cough, 355,000; and roundworm/hookworm, 165,000. From 1994 to 1995, TB deaths rose by 13 percent from 2.7 million to 3.1 million and deaths from malaria rose by 5 percent from 2 million to 2.1 million. The World Health Organization has declared TB a global emergency, predicting that 90 million new cases will be recorded from 1990 to 1999, with 30 million deaths expected in the decade from 1990. TB is the world's major cause of death from a single infectious agent, killing almost 3 million people in 1995, which is a death toll greater than the worst years of the TB epidemic at the turn of the century (2.1 million people died in one year). TB is out of control in developing countries such as sub-Saharan Africa and South East Asia. In the United States alone the number of TB cases reported each year has increased 14 percent from 1985 to 1993, which the American Lung Association sees as an alarming health emergency. The World Health Organization in a press release (March 22, 1996) stated that up to half a billion people could contract TB within the next fifty years, possibly by a TB strain with multiple-drug resistance.

The number of people suffering from AIDS increased by 25 percent in 1995, according to the United Nations. Twenty-one million adults across the world are HIV infected, 42 percent are women and the percentage is rising. More than 90 percent of the world's HIV infected are in developing countries, the worst areas being sub-Saharan Africa and the Caribbean. There has been, fortunately, a decline of HIV cases in the United States. In Australia HIV subtype E, a strain that is 500 times more infectious than the better known HIV subtype B, has already killed a number of Australians. It was spread by Asian prostitutes on visitors' visas (Hailstone, 1995).

Haines and Julian Simon are mistaken in believing that the age of the plague is over, as Laurie Garrett documents in *The Coming Plague: Newly Emerging Disease in a World Out of Balance* (1994) and A. Karlen in *Plague's Progress* (1995). Garrett sees humanity as having been "lulled into a complacency born of proud discoveries and medical triumphs, unprepared for the coming plague" (Garrett, 1994, 12). Perhaps the Ebola virus is one of the most horrific of the newly emerging viruses, liquefying bodies and leaving people to die in a bloody mess. Ebola in 1976 and 1979 killed hundreds of people in Zaire and the Sudan. In 1995 in Zaire it again killed hundreds of people in a horrible fashion. There is no effective treatment for it. In Australia in 1994 a new virus *Equine morbillivirus* killed fourteen horses in Southern Queensland and one person. They died a gasping, wheezing death.

New strains of influenza arise and move through the world's population every ten to forty years. Between 1918 and 1919 a new strain of influenza infected over two billion people and killed between twenty and forty million. The Asian flu of 1957 killed 750,000 people in the United States alone. Could there be another such influenza epidemic? Disease experts met in Bethesda, Maryland in December 1995 to discuss the possibility of a new lethal influenza virus evolving. Dr. Dominick Iacuzio, of the National Institute of Allergy and Infectious Diseases, believes that this is quite possible. Deadly influenzas such as Texas A, Johannesburg A and Beijing B have already killed thousands of people in the Northern hemisphere. Once a bout of the flu put one in bed for about forty-eight hours. Now it is not unusual to be laid out for weeks or months with a lingering, strength-sapping illness and fatigue, with aching joints and agonizing headaches. We all speak from personal experience—and we are relatively strong and fit.

In our own state of South Australia two diseases have caught world headlines. The first was the rabbit calicivirus (RCD), lethal to European rabbits. RCD escaped quarantine on Wardang Island in the Spencer Gulf in October 1995 and spread across Australia. Although the virus was not lethal to humans and most farmers welcomed it, the rabbit meat industry did not. In South Australia ten claims were lodged through the Meat Research Corporation. Overall the industry is claiming millions (Morgan, 1996). RCD's spread showed the easy path that a lethal virus can cut through a vulnerable population.

A second disease that caused public concern in South Australia occurred in 1995 when an otherwise healthy child died because the ameba *Balamuthia mandrillaris* "ate" holes in his brain. How the child contracted the disease remains a mystery. Although the disease has killed fifty-nine people to date, after first being identified in 1990, it is usually associated with immune suppression and has never before been seen in an otherwise healthy person. The disease was the focus of attention of an international conference on amebic disease held at the Adelaide Women's and Children's Hospital on January 8, 1996 (Foster, 1996). Although it was stated that this disease was not a public health concern, it was noted that there is no way to fight it. Because amebae are similar to our own body cells, antibiotics are usually ineffectual. Chemicals that kill amebae are usually toxic to humans. Other deadly amebae include *Acanthamoeba*, causing encephalitis (brain disease) or keratitis (eye disease). It was first identified in Philadelphia in 1968. *Naegleria fowleri*, causing amebic meningoencephalitis, was first identified in South Australia in 1961. *Acanthamoeba* has been a problem for wearers of contact lenses who wash their lenses in unsterilized water. The amebae interact with bacteria and produce chemicals that slowly dissolve the eyeballs. Eventually, if the condition is not rectified, the amebae penetrate the brain and destroy it as well.

Another disease that at the time of this writing is causing social panic in Britain is mad cow disease—*bovine spongiform encephalopathy* (BSE). This disease, like kuru and Creutzfeldt-Jakob disease (CJD, a human form of mad cow disease), is caused by disease entities known as *prions,* which infect the brains and nervous tissue of humans and animals and cause holes in nervous tissue. Prions were discovered by Professor Stanley Prusiner of the California School of Medicine ten years ago. Prions are small proteins, which, through mechanisms not yet fully understood, reproduce themselves without genetic material such as DNA. They are transmitted from animal to animal and between species of animals. In the host organism, prions cause a change in the brain's own proteins. The changes are encoded by the host's genome with the nasty side effect of dissolving small areas of the brain.

Mad cow disease arose in Britain because of the practice adopted in the 1970s by the meat industry of feeding the carcasses of animals, such as sheep, in the ground-up form of a protein supplement to cows. Some of these sheep had died from the prion-caused disease *scrapie*. By the mid-1980s 130,000 cattle had been infected with a disease similar to scrapie, which came to be called mad cow disease. It led to cows going literally mad as the prion destroyed their brains. In 1988 an official report recommended that there should be a ban on the feeding of protein from carcasses. This was not widely enacted or enforced; in any case, it interfered with the economic rationalist policy of the deregulated pursuit by agribusiness of maximum profits through low costs.

A crisis came in the form of a number of human deaths from CJD in 1995/96. CJD usually occurred in older people; now for the first time, it was found in young people. On March 20, 1996 the British government admitted that BSE and CJD are related, but it has not been scientifically proven that eating beef products contaminated by infected tissue might cause CJD. It is, however, probable as other prion diseases have been transmitted through contaminated meat. An example is the disease kuru found in the highlands of Papua New Guinea. The disease was transmitted by cannibalism where people would eat the brains of dead relatives infected by kuru and develop the disease themselves. If this hypothesis is true, it is possible that an explosion of CJD cases may occur in the future, perhaps between 5000 and 500,000 sufferers a year according to some authorities. Professor John Pattison, chair of the British government's scientific advisory body on this matter, believes that CJD has the potential to develop into an epidemic like AIDS in the future. A key question is whether the prion can be transmitted via the blood. The prion causing kuru apparently gets from the stomach to the victim's brain via the blood. At this stage it is impossible to tell what the full extent of the CJD crisis will be.

The socioeconomic effects of the 1996 BSE crisis are immense. At the time of writing in mid-1996, a collapse of public trust in the British beef industry has occurred. British beef has been banned throughout the world. As of May 23, 1996, Prime Minister John Major was engaged in a virtual war with the European Union (EU), threatening to implement policies to paralyze EU business unless the ban on British beef was lifted. If Major did this, it could destroy the EU. But we predict that it will not, that the forces of global money whose members own the media will allow the item to fall from the headlines. But it will not be so easy to do this in the future, if thousands or hundreds of thousands of people have a latent illness. Nevertheless, the BSE crisis does demonstrate the fragility of the economically globalized "new world order" of today. It shows, contrary to economists such as Julian Simon, that biology trumps economics.[3]

Professor Jonathan Mann, former head of the World Health Organization's AIDS program, believes that modern transportation makes the global spread of infectious diseases relatively easy (da Silva, 1995, 64). M. Gladwell, in an article originally published in *The New Republic* (Gladwell, 1995), rejects the view that this situation poses a threat to the globalization of the world. The view of Garrett expressed in *The Coming Plague* (Garrett, 1994), that plagues are a response by nature to ecological imbalance, is also rejected. Gladwell makes the point that nature has been striking back against the "human parasite" for as long as humans have existed. He uses William McNeill's *Plagues and Peoples* (1985) in support of the claim that human attempts to remodel the environment are seldom a source of serious epidemic disease and new microorganisms interact with humans, who build up resistance to the new infections. Consequently, virulent infections such as syphilis become attenuated (as a matter of fact it is *still* virulent). He goes on to say that it was not the conquerors of the new world who were all but wiped out by smallpox, but the native Indians. He does not consider the obvious reply that new emerging diseases are making the whole of humanity like those Indians. In Gladwell's opinion, we should not fear the exposure of microbes from equatorial Africa as we are safer "in a world where new viruses and bacteria are in constant circulation, and where human populations can encounter and build defences against them. Unlocking the viruses of the rain forest is part of the way we tame nature, not the way nature tames us" (Gladwell, 1995, 26).

We agree with Gladwell's basic point that disease organisms seldom result in the extinction of an entire species. Usually, unless the organism "jumps" to another species, this would lead to a balance being reached between parasite and host—otherwise the parasite will die out as well. However, as Haines has recognized (Haines, 1995, 51), humans have, compared to other animal species, a disproportionately large share of mortality from infectious disease. The ecological balance of which Gladwell speaks is likely to be one where the human population is significantly reduced in numbers. We have given reason to believe that medical technology is already losing the battle against newly emerging diseases and old diseases that are reestablishing themselves. The West will face the full impact of these diseases in a globalized open-border world. This constitutes, in our opinion, overwhelming reason for abandoning economic globalization, for closing borders and restricting the mass movement of people across the world—in short, for returning to nationalism, autarky and a more insular world. If this is "isolationism," then long live isolationism.[4]

There are a number of philosophical lessons to be learnt from the reemergence of the age of pestilence. First, for environmentalists, it shows that nature is not, as the idealists think, a warm and fuzzy holistic entity producing "natural balance and harmony" (Bos, 1994). Rather, nature is harsh and is shot through with suffering and disease for individuals of the species or race. The individual is only a passing player in evolutionary terms; what survives is genetic information which is macroscopically expressed in the species or race. For the Economist, the previous considerations refute the naïve technological optimism of Julian Simon and the other critics of environmentalism who have been cited here. They all believe that human ingenuity will save the day for us. Emeritus Professor Frank Fenner, Australia's most distinguished virologist, takes a different view of things, looking from the perspective of biological evolution. Fenner blames the human brain itself for the ecological crisis, especially the population problem, and believes that the evolution of the human frontal lobe may prove to be lethal to us in the long run: "Our brain has enabled us to dominate the planet like it's never been dominated before. But it may be that we've become too clever. All other predictions of the Earth's end flow from the explosion in human population" (Fenner, 1996). Our ability to grow food and fight disease has led to the planetary population problem, which will lead, we will also argue, to environmental destruction and human death and misery.

There is, from an evolutionary perspective, essentially a self-defeating logic embodied in scientific and technological advances. This is not to support what Martin W. Lewis in *Green Delusions* calls "technophobia" (Lewis, 1992, 117–149). It is not technophobic to be critical of aspects of modern technology if one has good reasons and sound arguments. The environmentalist argument that technological advances are responsible in part for the environmental crisis stands on its own merits. Lewis' strategy to refute the environmentalist critique of industrialism, by showing that alternative technoeconomic systems such as the European medieval guild system were socially exploitative, is irrelevant. We have already accepted Lewis' point that "the pre-industrial world was far from the ecological and social paradise imagined by some eco-radicals" (Lewis, 1992, 127). It is no part of our Limitationist position to claim that any golden age has existed for humanity; human life is a biotragedy and a struggle against ecological necessity (Diamond, 1991). In the longrun, we are all dead.

THE STATE OF THE ARGUMENT

In this chapter, we have advanced in broad outline our case against the Economist, the believer in unending economic growth and human progress. In the first section of this chapter we outlined a case for the limits to growth and that humanity is facing a dangerous ecological crisis. We then examined and criticized at first hand Economist attacks on the limits to growth position, especially by Julian Simon. We have also argued that technological optimism—the belief that technological fixes will resolve the environmental crisis—is delusory. Most importantly, through a discussion of disease, we have tried to show that despite human technological and scientific sophistication, we are still a part of nature. The idea of some postmodern sociologists that nature has become a social construction is nonsense.

In the next chapter, we strengthen our critique of the progrowth position by considering human population expansion and its resultant destruction of the environment.

NOTES

1. Professor Ian Angell, London School of Economics, has also predicted that a return to the "new" Dark Ages will occur (Hawkes, 1995). The information age will bring into being a world where corporations take over from nation states as nation states break up, and in the fight to get global business, poorer areas are left to fend for themselves. The elites will defend themselves from the dispossessed masses inside

urban areas protected by electronics, constituting an "electronic castle." This is already happening in Brazil.

2. Bailey in *Eco-Scam: The False Prophets of Ecological Apocalypse* (1993) takes the authors of *The Limits to Growth* to task for predicting that at exponential growth rates the world would run out of gold by 1981, mercury by 1985, tin by 1987, zinc by 1990, petroleum by 1992 and copper, lead and natural gas by 1993 (Meadows et al., 1972, 64–67). Clearly they were mistaken. Bailey goes on to quote U.S. Bureau of Mines estimates that at 1990 rates of production, world gold reserves will last 24 years, mercury 40 years, tin 28 years, zinc 40 years, copper 65 years and lead 35 years, ignoring technological change (Bailey, 1993, 67). Proven reserves of petroleum are expected to last 46 years at 1988 production rates (Bailey, 1993, 67). This does not refute Limitationism; it confirms it. It merely shows that Meadows et al. were wrong about the depletion years, not that they were wrong in theory and principle.

3. In the United States, a high percentage of cows with downer cow syndrome (DCS) are ground up and fed back to other cows. It is possible that such ecologically unnatural practices could lead to another crisis as there are suggestions of a link between DCS and an encephalopathy disease.

4. According to Dr. David McIntosh, of the Preventative Medicine Unit at the Royal Alexander Hospital for Children, New South Wales, Australia, a high proportion of the 900 active TB cases reported in Australia each year occur among persons born overseas, but few migrants and no tourists are fully tested for it (Anon, 1993).

2

Global Meltdown: Population Growth and Environmental Destruction

> The elimination of warfare by military means is tolerable only in a world that has outlawed reproductive warfare. The competitive use of human gonads in a pacifistic world is every bit as vicious and productive of suffering as is the militaristic use of atomic bombs. (Hardin, 1959a, 322)

> Robert Malthus . . . said that food production in 1988 would not be more than seven and a half times what it was in his day, 1800, and . . . that the world's population would not be more than seven and a half times what it was in 1800. . . . [It] was about 900 million in 1800 versus five billion in 1987, an increase of but 5.5 times over 1800. (Luten, 1991, 317)

THE POPULATION GLACIER

During the last decade of the twentieth century as many people will be added to the world population as were alive in the days of the famous Limitationist Robert Malthus. This increase in the world population—the exact extent of which, as we shall see, is a matter of debate—will be reached even if each female presently of reproductive age replaced only herself and partner. Most of the world's population is youthful and has not yet reached reproductive age. The United Nations Population Fund announced on December 28, 1995 that the world's population had increased by 100 million people in the previous twelve months (UN press release, December 28, 1995). This is equivalent to adding another Mexico to the planet. At a press conference held at the UN in New York on that day, the Population Fund president Werner Fornos said that three billion young people will enter their reproductive years in the coming generation and "how well these young people are able to implement the awesome responsibility of parenting will make the difference between our setting a course for an environmental

Armageddon in the 21st century, or a better quality of life" (UN press release, December 28, 1995).

At the present rate of growth, if such a trend continues into the future, the world population could number fourteen billion by 2050. Ninety percent of 1995's growth was in poor countries, most of them torn by brutal poverty and civil strife, Kaplan's "coming anarchy" (Kaplan, 1994). Many of these countries will double their numbers in thirty-two to thirty-six years, while industrialized nations such as Australia would take 430 years to complete a doubling. Thirty countries such as Thailand, Kenya, Zimbabwe, Indonesia, Mexico and Brazil are reporting declining birth rates, but eighty countries' populations are reproducing at a rate that will double their numbers within the next thirty years and forty-three of them are in Africa. In Africa, 45 percent of the population is under the age of fifteen years. Its population will grow 116 percent from 720 million in 1995 to 1.6 billion in 2030. During the same time: Asia's population will increase 47 percent, from 3.4 billion to 5.1 billion; Central and South America by 51 percent, from 475 million to 715 million; Oceania by 36 percent, from 29 million to 39 million; North America by 24 percent, from 295 million to 368 million and Europe by only 1 percent, from 731 million to 742 million. The five most populous countries in 2030 will be China with 1.5 billion; India, 1.4 billion; the United States, 328 million; Indonesia, 275.7 million and Brazil, 231.5 million (UN press release, December 28, 1995).

The United Nations' Population Fund's *The State of World Population* (1995) takes the current world population to be 5.7 billion. Published before the data cited in the paragraphs above, it nevertheless maintains that annual population increments are likely to remain above 86 million until the year 2015. The projections in this document for 2015 range from 7.1 billion to 7.8 billion and for 2050, from 7.9 billion to 11.9 billion. These totals, according to the United Nations Population Fund, are dependent upon whether or not the goals of the Cairo International Conference on Population and Development (ICPD) are achieved or not. Data on low-variant, medium-variant and high-variant projections are published in *World Population Prospects: The 1994 Revision*, by the Department for Economic and Social Information and Policy Analysis, Population Division, of the United Nations (United Nations, 1995, 458-459).

Most demographers accept that ten to twenty years is the limit of reliable population forecasting (Keyfitz, 1981; Poleman, 1995). This raises some difficulty for ecologists and futurologists concerned about the ecological sustainability of human population increases, because an investigation into such a question necessarily requires consideration of long-term population trends. By "long-term" we are not being unrealistic and asking for reliable data that would cover centuries; we would at least like to be able to make judgments on reliable population data extending to 2050 because this period is a crucial one for the survival of the planet. However, as J. Mayone Stycos of Cornell University has documented, population projections have a number of methodological limitations (Stycos, 1995). Population projections are based on data obtained from censuses, vital statistics and surveys, which while being of good quality in the developed world are often poor in the developing world. Cost is but one of many reasons for this. However, poor primary data introduce uncertainty into the final data and population projections can only be as good as the data on which they are based. Stycos maintains that the uncertainty of the projections is seen in the frequency with which they require revision and the simple fact that alternative series of projections are made in the first place (Stycos, 1995, 209). It is very much a "shotgun" approach (Cohen, 1995).

Long-range population projections are based not only on accumulated data, but also on an explicit or implicit theoretical framework (Frejka, 1994). Modern global component projections, first pioneered by the demographer Frank Notestein, have been based on a theoretical framework known as the *demographic transition theory*. This theory has been summarized as follows: "In traditional societies, fertility and mortality are high. In modern societies, fertility and mortality are low. In between there is demographic transition" (Cleland, 1994, 231). In other words, increasing economic growth, affluence, declining infant mortality and modernization will tend to lower the total fertility rate of a society, eventually leading to a stabilization of population numbers (Frejka, 1994, 7). Mortality will decline to a uniformly low rate and fertility will approach the replacement level. This is simply assumed by the UN and World Bank in their predictions, according to demographer Professor Geoffrey McNicoll "from the absence of a more persuasive case for it to be any other value" (McNicoll, 1992, 335).

McNicoll argues that if the fertility assumption is varied, the resulting population growth is dramatic. If the total fertility rate is changed from 2.06 to 2.5, then a long-run projection yields a world population of twenty-eight billion in 2150. Under the "constant fertility" trajectory, based on the 1990 level, a total world population of 694 billion in 2150 results (McNicoll, 1992, 336). Even the UN regards this growth rate as unsustainable: "To many, these data would show very clearly that it is impossible for world fertility levels to remain at current levels for a long time in the future, particularly under assumptions of continuing mortality improvement" (United Nations, 1992, 22).

The demographic transition thesis is subject to considerable criticism but proponents of this view often give an uncritical expression of the position (see, for example, Sen, 1994). Professor Virginia Abernethy, editor of *Population and Environment*, has argued against this thesis in her book *Population Politics* (Abernethy, 1993) and in a number of editorials in the journal *Population and Environment* (Abernethy, 1995). Her basic argument is that the demographic transition theory does not even accurately describe Europe's demographic history. For example, small family sizes were established in France by 1850, but infant mortality did not fall until the twentieth century. The trend to small family size began in other European countries during a period of high infant and child mortality. As well, fertility has risen in many countries during periods of modernization, contrary to the predictions of the demographic transition theory. Abernethy argues at length in support of her theory that the perception of expanding opportunity is followed by rising fertility and experience of worsening conditions is followed by declining fertility. Another demographer, John Cleland, has concluded, after an examination of the demographic transition theory, that this theory "has proved largely inadequate for purposes of description, explanation or prediction. The experience of historical Europe demonstrates that there is no inviolate rule that substantial mortality decline must precede fertility decline" (Cleland, 1994, 234).[1]

It follows from these considerations that long-term population projections are more uncertain than previously thought. It also makes it more reasonable to believe that the world's population is likely to be larger than the optimists think. This is a methodological judgment based on the arguments given above that there is a bias against Limitationism built into orthodox projections of world population. The only scientific alternative to this is to completely suspend judgment on this matter. While this would be correct in a purely theoretical field, it is not correct in a matter affecting our survival. Prudential reasons, then, favor the so-called pessimistic view of human population growth until further evidence is produced. But is this something which should concerned us? It could be argued that even if the demographic transition theory is wrong, there is growing evidence that the availability of contraception is not a minor factor in the family-planning decisions of Third World women, as demographers thought it was in the 1970s. Should we therefore be concerned with the world's population growth? If so, why? Can the world cope with a medium projected number of ten billion people by 2050? It is the aim of this chapter to examine a range of theoretical, philosophical and empirical questions associated with the human population problem and the sustainability of the Earth. In particular it is the explicit aim of this chapter to refute the Economist progrowth position in this field, again best represented by the work of Julian Simon. We turn now to that task.

PEOPLE ARE NOT THE ULTIMATE RESOURCE

Julian Simon, as we have seen already, does not believe that there are limits to growth. He believes that we have the technology and resources to feed an ever-increasing human population for the next seven million years (Myers & Simon, 1994, 174). He argues that in the long run, a higher population size, at least for the West, will lead to a higher standard of living for the West in general: "More people imply more imaginative people to provide new knowledge and new ways of producing things" (Simon, 1990, 393). Simon does not recommend that India increase its birthrate, not because of any logical problem with his economic argument, but because his recommendation involves values (Simon, 1990, 394). He does not explain this further. However, since his recommendation that the West increase its population also involves values, Simon is logically committed to regarding the Third World as underpopulated.

Simon's central argument for increased population growth appears to be this: (1) human population numbers are at an all-time high and rapidly increasing; (2) most of this growth has occurred in this century; (3) rapid technological advance has occurred; (4) population growth is the cause of this because people are the "ultimate resource" as more people lead to more technological developments, therefore, (5) population growth causes economic growth. This argument is never expressed in precise deductive form in Simon's work, but doing so here immediately allows us to see the unsoundness of his reasoning.

Human population numbers have increased in response to technological developments, it has not usually been the other way around. Medical technology, antibiotics and public health measures have lowered mortality, allowing an increase in human numbers to occur. Technological innovations that occur as the result of population increases have usually been in areas where a problem existed that was initially caused by the population increase. We do not deny that there are instances where population growth has led to technological innovations,[2] but it is an absurd overgeneralization to make this into a causal statement and that is what Simon's position entails. In any case, if it was true that population growth and absolute size increased the stock of useful knowledge, then this would make India and sub-Saharan Africa into technological powerhouses and Japan and most of the West, which have relatively smaller populations and growth rates, into technological backwaters. It is not so (Myers & Simon, 1994, 171). More people also means more people to create problems; as Taylor has put it: "More people with more technology spells more pollution, more environmental distortion and less privacy" (Taylor, 1970, 23). Of course, such a pessimistic position would need to be *argued* for if it were to be accepted as generally true, but it is at least as plausible as Simon's unsubstantiated position. The burden of disproof is upon Simon.

Simon also maintains that a large, fast growing population causes or produces an increase in the economic efficiency of industry and business (Simon, 1981, 206). This claim again puts the causal relationship back-to-front. It is more likely that efficient businesses and industries are associated with regions with large populations because these regions have large markets. Often, as we shall see in chapter 4, this association exists because Transnational Corporations capitalize on cheap un-unionized labor.[3]

Julian Simon's work has been influential outside of economics circles. He has endorsed a book by Robert L. Sassone, *Handbook on Population* (1994). Sassone is explicit in his acceptance of no-limits-to-growth. His book is from a Christian perspective and he believes that if the population Limitationists are right, then Christianity is wrong because it teaches, according to Genesis 1:28, "Be fertile and multiply; fill the Earth and subdue it." Now this has certainly been done. But the command was to subdue the Earth, not destroy it. Fundamentalist Christians, be they Catholics or Protestants, may feel that Limitationism is ungodly—how could a good God create a finite world without supplying enough resources for endless growth? By the same token, we may ask these Christians the age-old question: why is there evil in the world if God is all-good and all-powerful? Before we have even finished our sentence, we will be given the traditional freewill defense and a theology of original sin. Well, if freewill and original sin can explain away evil, then it can also explain why there are population-based limits to growth.

Catholics often oppose population Limitationism. However, a statement made by the Pontifical Academy of Sciences at the Population Summit of the World's Scientific Academies, New Delhi, October 24–27, 1993, published in the book, *Population—The Complex Reality* (1994) edited by Sir Francis Graham-Smith, gives us an alternative viewpoint. The Pontifical Academy of Science recognizes that the population problem is only one part of a complex problem encompassing issues such as environmental degradation, idle consumption and wasteful expenditure and "social justice"/compassion issues such as wealth gaps between the rich and poor worlds. But even so, the Pontifical Academy of Sciences accepts that there do exist limits to growth on a finite planet:

In the more distant future, the need for containment of birth rates emerges. This is required to prevent a further surge of irresolvable problems which are bound to occur if we turn our backs on our responsibility toward future generations. (Pontifical Academy of Sciences, 1994, 387)

The Pontifical Academy of Sciences also believes that in Africa, for example, "unlimited fertility" cannot be long maintained. A strict Catholic Limitationist would oppose artificial contraception and abortion and advocate "Natural Family Planning" (NFP) and perhaps abstinence and celibacy. Whether or not these measures are scientifically rational or practical is not for us to decide here. Our point is merely to note that even strict Catholicism is logically consistent with population Limitationism.[4]

Christian defenders of unlimited population such as Sassone (1994) make much of statistics such as that all of the people in the world could stand in an area of about 143 square miles (Sassone, 1994, 44). Let us ignore questions of *ecological* carrying capacity for the moment. Garrett Hardin in *Living within Limits* has pointed out that the Earth's land surface can take 529 trillion human beings in a standing room only situation, but this would take five billion people increasing at 1.7 percent per annum only 686 years to do (Hardin, 1993, 121). Harrison Brown is generally taken to be credited with the observation that a population growth rate of 2 percent per annum, continued for two millennia, would lead to a situation where the Earth would be a mass of human flesh expanding out into the universe at the speed of light (Luten, 1991, 318). This is Julian Simon's vision taken to its logical conclusion.[5]

Why not colonize the planets (Dyson, 1978; Finney & Jones, eds., 1985)? At a 2 percent growth rate, assuming that the Earth is full, it would only take thirty-five years to fill an Earth-sized planet, and thirty-five more years for each Earth-sized planet (Luten, 1991, 319). There is no known planet in our solar system suitable for human life. Only Mars is a remote *theoretical* possibility. Venus has an atmosphere composed primarily of carbon dioxide at temperatures and pressures that would not enable any carbon-based life form to exist. The atmosphere of Mars contains only traces of water and has a pressure of only 1 percent of our atmospheric pressure at sea level. The planet would need to be reconstructed by a type of "Genesis Project," as it was called in one of the *Star Trek* movies. Planet reconstruction is regarded as a technological marvel even in the world of science fiction movies, so there is no need to debate its likelihood with contemporary technology. If it could be done, then it should also be obvious that the same ingenuity should have solved the population and environmental crisis of Earth first. To pin humanity's hopes of survival on planet rehabilitation is an absurd strategy for it is virtually certain that ecological collapse would have destroyed technoindustrial civilization long before the saving technology can be developed.

Thus, if space colonization is to be an answer to the Earth's problem of overpopulation, humanity must search for suitable planets in other solar systems. The nearest star to our own is Alpha Centauri, 4.3 light-years, or 25 quadrillion miles (million million miles), from the Earth. There has been much speculation about how such a journey could be undertaken, but suffice to say by way of summary that all such speculations assume that formidable scientific and technological problems can be overcome. Many scenarios involve placing colonists in suspended animation and it is not known whether it is possible in *theory* to do this with humans, let alone in practice. Consequently, scientific speculators are often forced to resort to exotic suggestions, such as passing a spaceship through a singularity in space-time such as a "worm hole." Who wants to be the first to try this even if such phenomena exist?

Garrett Hardin (1959b, 1993) has given a brilliant *reductio ad absurdum* of interstellar migration as a solution to the Earth's human population problem. He points out that the sorts of people who would be able to leave on the spaceship are precisely those who can control their reproduction (the population of the spaceship must be rigidly controlled over the time of the journey). People who are not willing to control their breeding would not be permitted aboard the interstellar spaceship. But those left behind will continue the problem that initiated interstellar migration in the first place: "the choosing of people as candidates for such migration selects those whose ideals make the extravagant solution unnecessary, while leaving on earth the very ones whose ideals have created the problem in the past and will continue to do so in the future. The 'solution' selects for its own failure" (Hardin, 1993, 13). There is no new frontier.

Julian Simon believes that it has been established "scientifically that population growth is not the bogey that conventional opinion and the press believe it to be" (Myers & Simon, 1994, 23). To refute this we will now consider a range of scientific viewpoints about the population problem starting with the "Science Summit" on World Population held in New Delhi, India, October 24–27, 1993. The Proceedings were published in Sir Francis Graham-Smith (ed.), *Population—The Complex Reality* (1994). The world's scientific academies do express urgent concern about the growth of the world's population and they warn that on a business-as-usual scenario with current predictions of population growth, science and technology may not be able to prevent a major degradation of the life-support system of the planet. Contrary to Simon, the sixty scientific academies recognize that as "human numbers further increase, the potential for irreversible changes of far-reaching magnitude also increase" (World's Scientific Academies, 1994, 379). Indicators of environmental stress ranging from the increasing loss of biodiversity to the enhanced greenhouse effect indicate, again contrary to Simon, that "the earth is finite, and that natural systems are being pushed ever closer to their limits (World's Scientific Academies, 1994, 380). Contrary to the essays published in Simon's edited volume *The State of Humanity*, the academies note that food production from the land and the sea declined over the last decade, relative to the growth in population. Consequently humanity "is approaching a crisis point with respect to the interlocking issues of population, environment, and development" (World's Scientific Academies, 1994, 384). Digby J. McLaren of the Royal Society of Canada believes that "the planet's carrying capacity has long been exceeded and any immediate prospect of sustainability has faded" (McLaren, 1996, 243; see also Abernethy, 1995; Butler, 1994; King & Elliott, 1993; Verkuyl, 1993).

Paul Harrison in *The Third Revolution: Environment, Population and a Sustainable World* (1992) has published a major study examining the historical and ideological basis of the modern debate on population. We will examine this argument here. Present-day followers of Thomas Malthus are the "neo-Malthusians" or "Cassandras" who continue to stress the role of overpopulation in causing poverty and ecological stress. We would no doubt be classified among the "Cassandras." Socialists continue the tradition established by Karl Marx and the anarchist William Godwin in opposing the Malthusian case. Attacking the Cassandras from the left flank, the socialists argue that inequality in all its forms is the problem and that population growth is only a symptom. For the Left, overconsumption in the West is by far the greatest environmental threat and they perceive the neo-Malthusians as engaged in arrogant imperialism in blaming poor Third World people for large families. Then there are the free market conservatives "attacking the Cassandras from the right flank" as they argue that population growth is welcome because it increases human welfare. Harrison presents a lucid and detailed analysis of the main contending arguments. Early in the book he signals his intellectual distance from neo-Malthusianism by supporting the argument of the Danish economist Ester Boserup, who believed that population growth determined changes in agricultural technology. The Boserup thesis is directly counter to that of Malthus, who maintained that it was agriculture which determined population levels. In criticizing Simon it is therefore worthwhile to consider Harrison's work as we can hardly be accused of being selective in our presentation of authorities. While we disagree with him on various points, the general thrust of his book supports our position rather than Julian Simon's.

In a chapter titled "The New Limits to Growth," Harrison points out that the resource shortages which some thought in the 1960s would cause a crisis have not eventuated. There is no obvious global scarcity of minerals, energy, food or fertile land, even though our mineral resources could not support a world of eleven billion consuming like present-day North Americans, as many minerals would quickly run out. Harrison argues that behind the reassuring statistics on global food production, there are nevertheless some worrying trends:

> In terms of food production, the green revolution has worked. Food production per person in China was 94 per cent higher in 1989 than in 1961. In the rest of Asia it was 22 per cent higher. But the sheer size of the Asian countries biased the global averages upwards. Most other regions of the developing world have not done well at all. In Latin America cereal production per person fell by 5 per cent for 1970 to 1989. In the Near East it fell by 18 per cent. Africa fared worst with a 20 per cent decline . . . Between 1978 and 1989 food production lagged behind population growth in no less than 69 out of 102 developing countries . . . (Harrison, 1992, 42–43)

While Western economists generally attribute little importance to national declines in food self-sufficiency, as such declines may provide a spur to international trade, poor countries are invariably in a worse position if they are obliged to pay for imported food out of sparse foreign exchange reserves. Harrison notes that the inability of many poor countries to keep their food production abreast of population growth is an alarming trend. He maintains that while global land reserves are plentiful, they are mostly under rainforest and concentrated in a few equatorial countries. Rainforest soils are usually fragile. He argues that for many individual poor countries, land reserves are less reassuring. While both South America and Africa have plenty of reserves, the Sahel and West Africa are already farming all their suitable land. Harrison believes that while there is much potential for increasing currently low yields in many developing countries through inputs of fertilizer, improved seed strains and irrigation, these cannot be taken for granted. Growth in yields "is a constant battle—of crop-breeding, fertilizer application, expansion in irrigation and fighting pests, diseases and erosion" (Harrison, 1992, 46).

Turning to water resources, he points out that countries in the Middle East and North Africa suffer the most severe shortages. There is rising conflict both within and between countries in these areas over water. Overall Harrison concludes that while many countries face resource shortages that will grow in severity, the world as a whole is not facing such a resource shortage at least for the next decade or two. In our opinion he is mistaken about this. He goes on to suggest that our ecological crisis is not a resource crisis but a "pollution crisis" caused by our consumption and life-style. This pollution includes our solid, liquid and gaseous wastes as well as our wasting of forests and soils. *Homo sapiens*, he argues, are caught in a dilemma because deforestation will accelerate soil erosion, and soil erosion, desertification and salinization will in turn cut food production. Furthermore, if we cut down the rainforest to get at the remaining productive land to grow food for expanding populations, we hasten global warming. Our use of fertilizer to feed growing populations is limited by fears of water pollution from fertilizer runoff. Our use of various nonrenewable fossil fuels, of which we have no shortage, is increasingly limited by our fears of global warming. Renewable resources as well are being destroyed at an increasing rate. Although theoretically renewable, these resources are not being renewed. Forests, soils and biodiversity are most threatened. Harrison devotes several chapters to exploring the threatening processes at work.

Five chapters are devoted to examining environmental problems in developing countries. These issues include loss of biodiversity, deforestation, the process of marginalization both of poor people and of fragile lands and land degradation. In the case of deforestation, to take one example, Harrison points out that this is often attributed to logging and ranching to meet the needs of Western countries for timber products and hamburger meat. But he argues that while logging may cause permanent loss of biodiversity, forests will eventually regrow if allowed to. Permanent deforestation arises from conversion to other uses, such as urbanization (Harrison, 1992, 94). Furthermore, he points out that in the Third World as a whole, from 1973 to 1988, pastureland only expanded by an area equivalent to 7 percent of all forest loss in this period. So, he reasons, ranching is not a major culprit. Indeed, meat is eaten in Latin American homes. Meat for the West's hamburgers is a mere mouthful compared to the massive home consumption. In 1989, for example, Brazil had 137 million head of cattle, but exported only 120,000 tonnes of meat. Harrison goes on to suggest that economically irrational and ecologically disastrous rainforest ranching in Brazil has been largely a result less of demand for meat than of overly generous and misguided government subsidies for ranching (Harrison, 1992, 96).

In the case of timber, he finds that left-wing environmentalists have exaggerated Western consumption, for timber products are in increasing demand in developing countries as well. Most Third World timber is used in the Third World; in 1988, for example, home use of sawnwood exceeded exports by eight to one and industrial roundwood exceeded exports by about eleven to one (Harrison, 1992, 97). Harrison notes that in developing countries, the pillaging of rainforests often serves pork-barrel politics. In much of Latin America, rainforests are sacrificed to the landless instead of governments engaging in the process of land reform. In Asia and Africa ecological sacrifice is an alternative to creating urban jobs or investing in rural areas.

Having allegedly undermined the argument of the left radical school, Harrison goes on to argue that population growth causes deforestation through demand for agricultural and urban land. Of course, if agricultural technologies improve to foster higher crop yields, there may be no need to clear further forests to allow farmland expansion. But the Boserup thesis that growing populations change their technologies to meet the demands of population growth does not apply to all situations. Food production may not keep up with population growth for a range of reasons. Starvation and migration can then become responses to population growth. Harrison observes that Africa has not followed the Boserup path. Much of sub-Saharan Africa, he believes, has fallen into a technology trap over the past twenty-five years aggravated in part by state ownership of land. He points to the often neglected fact that growing populations need more urban land. New towns usually spring up on agricultural land, which then expands into forests, pastures and wetlands. Consequently urban growth results in extensive deforestation. Harrison maintains that the nonagricultural land needs of growing populations will be enormous:

Taking the average figure of 0.06 hectares per person, the non-farm needs of extra populations expected between now and the year 2150 will take up roughly 3.6 million square kilometres of land in developing countries. This will swallow up the equivalent of almost half the total Third World cropland of eight million square kilometres in 1988. To compensate, cropland will have to expand into forest and other marginal areas. (Harrison, 1992, 108)

He believes that population growth, consumption patterns and technology have the main impact on forest loss. While many other factors, such as government policy and staffing and the form of ownership of the forest, also play a part, Harrison concludes that population growth plays the decisive role in forest loss.

After several chapters analyzing crucial ecological issues in developing countries, the author considers the growth of cities, water pollution, air pollution and climate change. Here his focus widens to pay more attention to the environmental problems which are now political issues within developed countries. Regarding pollution within national borders, he points out that consumption levels have played a large role in air pollution. For example, the spread of cars and refrigerators has lifted consumption as well as introducing new technologies. Harrison suggests that when technological change is rapid, the effect of population growth on air pollution is relatively small. While global warming remains our biggest problem, we have not yet begun to grapple with its implications. Cutting carbon dioxide emissions is difficult, as fossil fuels are the basic energy source of techoindustrial society.

Who is most to blame for our ecological ills? Is it the poor scratching out a living on the margins of the Earth or the "rich" driving their gas-guzzling cars and discarding mountains of waste? There is no doubt, Harrison points out, that the rich are the big consumers and polluters. Developed nations are by far the biggest consumers of nonrenewable resources. The affluent 22 percent of the world's population uses 58 percent of fertilizers, 75 percent of oil and 86 percent of natural gas. The typical person in a developed country produces 40 times more industrial waste, 52 times more industrial effluents and 75 times more hazardous waste than does a typical person in a developing country (Harrison, 1992, 256). As a result, Harrison argues, continued population growth in the "North" is a greater environmental threat than population growth in the "South," if the relative consumption and waste output rates remain the same. Nevertheless, he maintains, the picture is changing. Population growth and per capita consumption growth rates are slowing in the richer countries while total consumption is growing in developing countries as the population rapidly grows. Within a few decades, developing countries may be even bigger polluters than today's developed countries (Harrison, 1992, 257).

To what extent are the poor big environmental destroyers? Harrison points out that the poorest families are those headed by women. These are least likely to clear rainforests for farming. He believes that young couples are most likely to clear forest and he finds that the tendency to clear rainforests or marginal land is more a generational matter than one based on a rich-poor divide. Furthermore, he suggests, despite the claim that the poor have more children, it is not the poorest who have the most children. The somewhat better off do. The poor, he concludes, pollute and consume least and tread most lightly on the Earth (Harrison, 1992, 259).

In the light of the Boserup thesis that population growth determines technological change, Harrison maintains that both the agricultural revolution and the industrial revolution were responses to resource crises brought about by population pressures on wild food sources in the first instance and later fuel and wood sources. Each of these revolutions, he believes, was a response to population growth and each in turn fostered further population growth. In the agricultural revolution, humans adjusted technologies and consumption patterns. In the industrial revolution, technologies changed as humans shifted to fossil energy. Harrison goes on to suggest that we are now in the throes of a third major revolution. In this we are trying to adjust our populations and technologies in response to industrialization, urbanization and the environmental crisis. However, he warns, this revolution could stall. While the most promising sign is falling fertility in developed countries and East Asia, we have a near fatal weakness for only taking action when problems are grave.

Harrison concludes that if we are to reach some sort of balance with our environment, we have to tackle population, consumption and technology. In the shorter term, he argues, it is easier to tackle population and technology. While population efforts operate on a slower time frame than technology, if we could achieve the UN low population projection by 2100, this would mean six to seven billion less people than the medium projection. This would make an enormous difference in environmental impact, he says. The agricultural and urban land needs alone of an extra seven billion people would amount to 31 percent of all forest in the world in 1989 and double the area of the world's protected natural areas in 1990. To achieve lower population growth, female education, equality and the right to choose methods of birth control should be supported, the author maintains. He also insists that compulsion has no role to play in family planning as it is inhumane and counterproductive.

We need to improve our technologies, even though technology is no panacea, Harrison argues. Furthermore, as well as tackling the three key causes of environmental decline, we need to work on all the other factors that influence these. Tackling these other, less direct causes of ecological stress involves supporting measures to reduce poverty and to improve equality, improving markets and economic policies and supporting both democratic rights and institutions for controlling the global commons.

Harrison, although not strictly speaking a Limitationist, delivers a telling blow to the cornucopians and Economists. He agrees with them that population growth is a major force producing technological and social change but believes that they err in their complacency. All is not for the best in the best of all possible worlds, as the cornucopians believe, for major adjustments are always forced on us by serious problems. Such problems, Harrison argues, cause suffering or loss on a major scale. Ecological damage can be irreversible. Furthermore, there is no guarantee that successful adjustments will be made. Blockages occur. New technologies do not come without costs as they often have unforeseen negative side effects. Even when sustainable management has been achieved, the author points out, the final outcome may not be an improvement on the original state of affairs (Harrison, 1992, 249).

The present authors disagree with Harrison on a number of points that are not central to our present discussion. Nevertheless his work strongly supports out position against Julian Simon and other Economist critics such as Amartya Sen (1994) who reject the idea that there is a problem of human population numbers and believe that there is only a problem of development. Work done by Partha Dasgupta (1993, 1994, 1995) also counts against the position held by Simon and Sen. In support of our position, we shall also briefly review this work. Dasgupta argues the case for regarding poverty, population growth and the local environment as interconnected. Poverty, population growth and degradation dialectically and synergistically interact: "none of the three elements directly causes the other two; rather each influences, and is in turn influenced by, the other" (Dasgupta, 1995, 27). Dasgupta is critical of population studies for their globalism and internationalism. An almost exclusive concern with the so-called "global population problem" draws attention away from misery that exists at local areas. The poor in many parts of the world do not need to wait for disaster to strike them: they are already experiencing it. Population decisions and associated decisions about food and local resource use are typically made at the household level. Dasgupta believes that if we are to understand the real causes of Third World population growth, we need to understand the microeconomics and psychodynamics of having children.

Third World countries are largely subsistence economies and the cultivation of plants and rearing of animals requires much labor. Children are not merely a future resource for parents in their coming old age, but are also a valuable source of labor in the present. In some Third World countries where forests have been cleared, obtaining adequate firewood is a major task, often taking five to six hours a day. Water too may be in short supply and will have to be searched for. Dasgupta observes that in India children between the ages of ten and fifteen often work as much as one and a half times the number of hours an adult male works (Dasgupta, 1995, 29).

However, the need for many children can have a destructive impact on the local environment and the community. This is especially so when the full cost of bearing children is shared with the community. In sub-Saharan Africa where conjugal bonds are weak, fathers often do not meet the costs of their offspring. It is often necessary for relatives to help raise the children while the father is off inseminating other women. Along with this problem, social norms that for hundreds, if not thousands, of years, have prevented the local commons—the water holes, fields and forests—from overexploitation and consequent degradation are now being broken down by the forces of economic development and increased urbanization (Dasgupta, 1995, 29). The interaction of these factors leads to a situation where the perceived low personal costs and high personal benefits of reproduction lead to too many children being born on a community level—a "tragedy of the commons" situation (Hardin, 1993). As environmental degradation begins, more children are needed for survival, leading to further environmental degradation, so that fertility and environmental degradation positively reinforce each other (Dasgupta, 1995, 30).

Dasgupta's argument forcefully shows the importance of the population component to a locality's environmental quality and he illustrates clearly that population growth questions cannot be considered in isolation from the environmental impact on the population—the technologies of a population and the level of consumption. These concepts are captured in the idea of the *environmental impact equation*, which we shall discuss in the next section. We believe that it is important to explicitly understand this concept before addressing the larger question of the sustainability of the Earth.

In this section we began by criticizing the no-limits-to-growth position of Julian Simon and others. We showed that these positions are inadequate. We ruled out the possibility of space colonization as a realistic solution to the population problem. Thus, since there are no new frontiers, we then examined whether Simon was right in claiming that population growth is not viewed by the experts as a major problem. In the limited space available here we attempted to show that Simon is incorrect in this allegation. We will now show that his views on human population growth are theoretically untenable.

THE ENVIRONMENTAL IMPACT EQUATION AND THE SUSTAINABILITY OF THE EARTH

The environmental impact equation has been used by the Ehrlichs (Ehrlich & Ehrlich, 1990) to explain the relationship between population, consumption and technology. Thus:

(PAT) Environmental impact = Population x affluence x technology.

PAT has the appearance of an equation in mathematical physics, but it is imprecise and as stated is open to some telling criticisms. "Affluence" is difficult to operationalize because it requires a value judgment about what is affluent. How should we measure affluence? Is it GDP? The term "technology" is vague as well and some modern technologies (e.g., solar power) may have less environmental impact than even some subsistence technologies. Further, as Martin W. Lewis points out in *Green Delusions*, on a strict reading of PAT, an advance in pollution control technology would increase the environmental impact (Lewis, 1992, 238). Preston (1994) notes that the environmental impact equation ignores interactions between the components such as the effects of population growth on per capita production, a point also made by Demeny (1991).

Harrison (1992) has attempted to state the environmental impact equation in a more precise form. He suggests replacing the term "affluence" by "consumption per person", which covers every human activity from subsistence consumption to industrial activity. The term "technology" is replaced by "environmental impact per unit of consumption." Harrison's environmental impact equation now reads:

(H1) Environmental Impact = Population numbers x consumption per person x impact per unit of consumption.

Impact covers the use of primary resources, the physical occupation of space and the output of pollutants. The formula shows that for a given level of consumption per person and impact per unit of consumption, a higher population means a higher environmental impact and fewer people means less overall consumption and pollution.

To be able to assess the contribution that population makes to environmental damage, changes over time must be considered. Harrison suggests that population impact be expressed as:

(H2) Population impact = $\dfrac{\text{Annual \% change in population} \times 100}{\text{Annual \% change in use of resource or output of pollutant}}$

By use of this equation, some measure of the relative contribution that the three elements make to environmental impact can be given. It is possible, for example, that one or more of the components of the environmental impact equation may reduce the environmental impact. To deal with this problem Harrison distinguishes between "upward" and "downward" pressures by scoring the upward pressures out of +100 percent and the downward pressures out of -100 percent (Harrison, 1992, 307).

Harrison makes use of the Food and Agriculture Organization *Country Tables 1990* for data in an example he gives to estimate what share of the increase in farmland can be attributed to population growth in the developing world. The population expanded by 2.3 percent a year between 1961 and 1985 in developing countries, while agricultural production rose by 3.3 percent. The production per person, taken by Harrison to be the consumption factor, rose by 0.9 percent. Farmland expanded by 0.6 percent a year. The impact per unit of consumption, in this case the farmland used per unit of agricultural production, declined by 2.6 percent annually, because yields were increasing (Harrison, 1992, 308). Technology exerted a downward pressure on environmental impact, and because it is the only one of the three components of the environmental impact equation exerting a downward pressure on environmental impact, it is given a score of -100 percent. Population growth accounted for +72 percent of the growth of farmland and the increase in consumption per person +28 percent. Yet by Harrison's evaluation, the environmental impact will be negative because of his assignment of a score of -100 percent to the technology component. Not only is this assignment an arbitrary one—he gives no methodology for the scoring of the upward and downward pressures out of 100 percent—but the assignment is counterintuitive. It is quite possible that in an informal sense the environmental impact in Harrison's example was not overall negative but positive. The technology used to produce higher yields may in itself extract an ecological price. The farmland used per unit of agricultural production may have declined by 2.6 percent annually but we cannot say that increasing yields means a decreasing impact per unit of consumption without considering whether these technologies damaged the soil, that is, whether they are in themselves sustainable.

By assigning a score of -100 percent to the technology component, Harrison produces an overall negative environmental impact. In $EI = P \cdot C_{pp} \cdot I_{uc}$, when one variable is negative and the others positive, EI will be negative whatever the size of the negative variable. This is also counterintuitive. Worse, if one component of the environmental impact equation is positive, and the other two components negative, then the environmental impact equation will be positive ($-x \cdot -x = x \cdot x$)

purely because of the multiplicative behavior of the signs, regardless of the magnitudes involved. Clearly, more careful attention needs to be devoted to the algebra of the environmental impact equation. We suggest that the sign of EI be determined in the following way. Let EI = $X.Y.Z$. Then if Z is negative, EI is negative if and only if $|X.Y| > |Z|$ (disregarding the negative sign), where X and Y are positive. If Y and Z are negative, EI can only be positive if $|X| > |Y.Z|$.

In situations where the technology and consumption components of the EI equation are not easily separable—such as in the case of high-technology goods where the product itself creates the consumer need it satisfies—the population component of the environmental impact can be estimated using equation (H2) listed previously. When consumption and technology measures are absent, but thought to be declining, the impact of population growth can be ascertained by:

(H3) Population impact = $\dfrac{\text{Absolute value of the population growth rate} \times 100}{\text{Absolute population growth} + \text{absolute [growth in pollutants - population growth]}}$

But equation (H3) will not give us the population component's share of the change (Harrison, 1992, 313), only the relative strength of the population influence compared to the consumption/technology matrix. Harrison cautions that applying this formula at a global level can lead to "paradoxes." In his example he considers the increases in emissions of carbon dioxide from fossil fuel and cement making, based on United Nations data. In developing countries, between 1960 and 1988 these emissions increased by 5.3 percent a year and population increased by 2.3 percent a year, making the population impact 46 percent. In the same period, the emissions in developed countries increased by 2.41 percent a year and population increased by 0.85 percent, making the population impact 35 percent. However, considering the global level, emissions rose by 3 percent while population rose by 1.9 percent, making the population impact 63 percent. This figure is obviously higher than the average of the two population impact figures, because as Harrison rightly notes, the slower growth in the much higher level of emissions in the developed world when put into the equation gives a lower global figure for emission growth (Harrison, 1992, 314). Consequently the environmental impact equation can only meaningfully be applied to homogeneous regions. When it is applied to the world as a whole, average values will mask deviations from the mean and the resultant variations of the distributions (Harrison, 1992, 314).

We are not entirely satisfied with even this formulation of the environmental impact equation. What are the units of environmental impact? What are the dimensions of the equation and are the dimensions of the components of the equation commensurable? Equation (H1) would seem to require a thermodynamic analysis so that the environmental impact of a specific environment would be a measure of the entropy or disorder of that environment, and ascertaining that is a task of considerable theoretical, methodological and empirical difficulty. Consequently we regard the environmental impact equation as a heuristic device rather than an explicit metric. The formula shows that for a given level of consumption per person and impact per unit of consumption, the higher the population numbers, the higher the consumption of resources, the more pollution produced. All other factors being constant, fewer people mean less total consumption and less pollution. Beyond this though, it is arguable that the components denoted by the variables of the equation interact, we believe in a complex dialectical, nonlinear fashion that cannot be captured by a simple multiplication relationship. Let E_i (P, C_{pp}, I_{uc}) be the environmental impact function for a specified environment for a given time period. Then E_i (P, C_{pp}, I_{uc}) = EI (the environmental impact) but E_i (P, C_{pp}, I_{uc}) is not necessarily equal to E_i (P). E_i (C_{pp}). E_i (I_{uc}). We shall see that the determination of an environmental impact is a highly complex matter that has not yet been adequately resolved by science.

Let us turn now to a consideration of the questions of the optimal human population of a region, or the world, and of the carrying capacity of the world. The carrying capacity of a human environment is often defined by ecologists to be the *maximum* number of people that can be sustained indefinitely by the biological and physical resources of that environment without damaging that environment (Giampietro et al., 1992). However, as Bartlett (1994, 13) has observed, whatever one does as an entropy-producing creature damages the environment, however small. So as far as human carrying capacity is concerned, our interest then is with the largest number of humans that can be sustained indefinitely by an environment. Some nations cannot be sustained at their level of consumption by the local ecology and may in this sense be considered to have overshot the carrying capacity of their environment—they are overpopulated (Pillett, 1993). But because of globalization and international trade, these nations are able to flourish, exchanging value-added goods for basic necessities. However, not all nations can be overpopulated in this sense: someone must produce food. Consequently we must address the question of the carrying capacity of the Earth.

The question of the carrying capacity of the Earth needs to be distinguished from the question of the *optimum* human population size of a region or of the Earth (Singer, ed., 1971). The optimum population is not the same as the maximum sustainable population; rather it is an evaluative choice of a population level that gives some sociopolitically desired life-style that is biophysically sustainable for an indefinite period of time. The optimum population lies somewhere between the biophysical constraints of the minimum viable population size (MVP) for human life to continue at all (Soule, ed., 1987)—which is thought to be 50 to 100 people in several groups totalling 500 people (Daily et al., 1994)—and the biophysical carrying capacity of the planet. G. C. Daily and the Ehrlichs believe that the present population of the Earth has already exceeded sustainable levels (Daily & Ehrlich, 1992; Ehrlich et al., 1993), but based on energy considerations they opt for an optimum human population size for the planet of 1.5 billion people, approximately the number of people who were alive at the turn of the century. This calculation is, they admit, a back-of-an-envelope one.

A study of the question of the optimum population size was conducted by David Pimentel et al. and presented to the American Association for the Advancement of Science in 1994 (Pimentel et al., 1994). They proposed that an optimum population for the United States would be about 200 million people, and one to two billion people for the world. Yet only a cursory consideration of the massive quantity of data and scientific references in this study would lead us to doubt their optimum population size figures. They found that soil erosion is as great as it has ever been in human history. Global food production, even though it has increased in the last few decades will fall by about 20 percent in the next twenty-five years. Fresh water supplies are under increasing strain. The world's irrigation area is decreasing worldwide per capita because of salinization, water logging and population growth (Pimentel et al., 1994, 354). According to Pimentel et al., the world is losing 150 species a day due to human activity. The world supply of oil is projected to last about thirty-five years at current pumping rates (Pimentel et al., 1994, 357). Natural gas and coal reserves will be used up within the next century. If these statistics are correct, it is not reasonable to give the optimum population figures that Pimentel et al. give. We simply have no certain knowledge of the real extent of biophysical damage which man's technoindustrial experiment has done and will do to the planet. Further, as we have already observed, we also lack a precise, scientific way of measuring our environmental impact and indeed even of conceptualizing it. This is perhaps to be expected in a chaotic world (Waldrop, 1992) where we can never do merely one thing (Hardin, 1993).[6]

The problem of the nonlinear and chaotic nature of ecological systems (McMichael, 1993, 47–48) infects the alleged validity of attempts to ascertain the human carrying capacity of the Earth as well. Consider for example a measure based on the Net Primary Production (NPP) of the Earth, the planet's maximum biomass production. The idea here is that food production on Earth is ultimately limited by the energy conversion ratio of photosynthesis and the total solar energy received by the Earth over a specific time period. Estimations of the global human carrying capacity based on the NPP of the Earth ignore all economic, technological and social limitations upon food production. Even so, estimates vary from sixteen billion people to one trillion (Heilig, 1994, 210).[7] However, human biomass appropriation is in itself a threat to ecosystems and a cause of species loss and biodiversity decline. Who knows at the present time what the ultimate ecological and health consequences of this will be (Vitousek et al., 1986)? We agree with Joel E. Cohen's statement in *How Many People Can the Earth Support?* (1995): "The Earth's capacity to support people is determined by processes that the human and natural sciences have yet to understand, and partly by choices that we and our descendants have yet to make" (Cohen, 1995, 11).[8]

This problem can be seen in Smil's recent investigation into how many people the Earth can feed (Smil, 1994). Smil believes that the Earth could support the 1992 UN and 1992 World Bank medium variant prediction of just over eleven billion people by the year 2100. He admits that this supposes that the decline in the life support systems of the planet can be reversed. Smil takes an optimistic view on the question of declining biodiversity and soil and water degradation. This view also supposes that advances in agricultural technology will continue (Smil, 1994, 283). But in Smil's own study of population growth and nitrogen (Smil, 1991), he states that world agriculture will rely increasingly on synthetic nitrogenous fertilizers to maintain yields. Further "there are no immediate prospects for circumventing the applications of synthetic fertilizers by introducing a variety of self-fertilizing crops. Dreams about genetically engineered staple cereals capable of synthesizing their own nitrogen supplies are just that" (Smil, 1991, 592). Consequently the sustainability of the Earth's population will increasingly become dependent on fossil fuel and modern chemical syntheses. Indeed, Smil argues that the survival of peasants is even more dependent than Western urban dwellers on agricultural chemicals (Smil, 1991, 593). There is a growing literature demonstrating that these technologies have an adverse environmental impact with massive social costs (Clunies-Ross & Hildyard, 1992; Fowler & Mooney, 1990; Hobbelink, 1991; Body, 1991). An ecological trap or "Catch-22" situation may arise (Costanza, 1987; Platt, 1973).

Perhaps the best illustration of our thesis is global warming caused by the enhanced greenhouse effect. The Intergovernmental Panel on Climate Change (IPCC) accepted in November 1995 that greenhouse gas concentrations have continued to increase as a result of human activities (Kerr, 1995). Carbon dioxide in the atmosphere has risen 30 percent since the industrial revolution. The observed global warming over the past 100 years is greater than a best estimate of the degree of natural climate variability over at least the last 600 years. Sea levels have risen between ten and twenty-five centimeters over the past 100 years and average temperatures have risen by between 0.3°C and 0.6°C since the late 1800s. The IPCC predicts that by 2100 temperatures will rise another 1° to 3°C; sea levels will rise by an average of fifty centimeters, and this could be as high as ninety-five centimeters by 2100. Up to half of the world's glaciers will melt; deserts will spread and become hotter.[9] Increased desertification will result in increased hunger and famine. This prediction confirms previous research that predicted that global warming will cause a decrease of between 10 and 15 percent of grain yields in Asia, Africa and Latin America, putting the number of people at risk from hunger in the next fifty years at over a billion (Pearce, 1992; Parry & Rosenzweig, 1993). The IPCC believes that even replacing current technology with more efficient technology may not prevent an absolute increase in carbon dioxide emissions in the future because consumer demand for cheap energy is being aroused in China and Indonesia. China, which has vast resources of coal that it intends to use in its program of modernization and industrialization, has refused to accept the objectivity of the IPCC (Pearce, 1995).

Human population numbers have a direct effect on carbon dioxide production regardless of economic activity. People merely being alive and breathing produces an astonishing quantity of carbon dioxide. Banks and Vernon (1990) explain:

Taking the tidal volume as 0.5 litres, the rate of respiration as 12 per min. and the percentage of carbon dioxide in expired air as 4%, then the amount of carbon dioxide produced by each human is 0.5 x 12 x 60 x 24 x 365 x 0.04 = 130,000 litres/year. Remembering that 22.4 litres of carbon dioxide contains 44 g (the molar mass) this means approximately 260,000 g/year. Taking the human population as 6×10^9, this gives a total production of 1.56×10^9 tonnes. This is certainly an underestimate since the values used for the tidal volume and respiration rate are those appropriate for rest. The true figure is certainly greater and may be nearly twice as much. (Banks & Vernon, 1990, 284)

With an increasing human population this quantity of carbon dioxide necessarily increases. Of course, it is human industrial, and more broadly "survival," activities which produce the quantities of carbon dioxide that make human activities a matter of grave concern. Our point is that just being alive makes a contribution to carbon dioxide production and it supports the statement we made earlier that whatever we do, we impact upon the environment.

Global climatic change will have a major impact on human health and hence on population levels (Chivian et al., 1993; Haines et al., 1993; Ewan et al., 1993; WHO, 1990). Dobson (1993) has considered the effects of climate change on biodiversity, concluding that global warming will benefit parasites and other pathogens. Water-borne infections from marine and freshwater sources will also increase (Epstein et al., 1993). Vector-borne diseases are likely to increase in a warmer world (Freier, 1993; Rogers & Packer, 1993; Nicholls, 1993; Almendares et al., 1993). Heat-related mortality is likely to increase (Kalkstein, 1993). Ozone depletion, with a consequent increase in the amount of ultraviolet B from the sun that reaches the Earth's surface, will result in increased sunburn, skin cancers and eye damage (Lloyd, 1993), along with UV-induced immunosuppression (Jeevan & Kripke, 1993). As Haines et al. (1993) note, many of the potential effects of climate change are insidious and will not manifest themselves for some time. The links between ecosystem damage and ill health are often unclear and undefined, and because the underlying climatic processes are global in scale and impact on the Earth's life-support mechanisms themselves, prediction and monitoring of the population health impacts of climate change will prove difficult. Even so, some nations are already recognizing the relationship between a nation's health and the sustainability of the biophysical environment. The Australian Medical Association, at its conference held in Canberra Australia on October 20, 1995, has recognized that Australia faced a risk of diseases spreading under the enhanced greenhouse effect (Cribb, 1995c).

Let us summarize the argument of this section. We began our discussion of the so-called environmental impact equation in an attempt to obtain a more exact understanding of the relationship between technology, economic growth and population growth. We found that understanding this relationship involved surprising complexities that are at present not satisfactorily resolved. We turned then to investigate the question of the carrying capacity of the Earth. Before doing so we examined the idea of the optimum population for a region or the world. We looked at some of the best attempts to explicate this concept and saw that they failed. As well, attempts to ascertain the carrying capacity of the Earth were seen to be problematic because of the chaotic, nonlinear nature of ecosystems. We illustrated this thesis with the case of global warming, showing the dialectical relationships between it, human population growth and human health. Economist critics of Limitationism seldom adopt a systems view of the environmental crisis. They prefer to argue resource by resource, problem by problem so that the small positive probabilities of disaster can be disregarded. However, the small probabilities of disaster do add up. If you get into your car right now and drive for one hour, the odds are against you having a road traffic accident. Drive all day, all week, without sleep and the odds change. With the space limits that we have in this book, we can perhaps best defend this viewpoint by a concrete case study. We have considered, albeit briefly, the ecological ramifications of the enhanced greenhouse effect. We will now round off our discussion by a case study of climatic change and migration from Oceania which illustrates clearly many of the theoretical points we have made in this chapter and the potential for social chaos that arises from ecological disruption.

CASE STUDY: POPULATION, MIGRATION AND CLIMATE CHANGE (with E. Moore)

Predicted warming of the world's climate will have major impacts on human settlements (Schneider, 1989; Kritz, 1990; Houghton et al., 1990; ANZEC,

1990), and the ability of populations to adapt is an issue of concern.[10] Several commentators have offered disturbing scenarios of millions of people forced to flee from areas disrupted by climate change (Gleick, 1989; Jacobson, 1989; Hashimoto & Nishioka, 1991; Tate, 1991; Kennedy, 1993; Kaplan, 1994; Short, 1994; Döös, 1994). The consequences of such population flights could be serious, including racial and ethnic conflict (Kennedy, 1993; Kaplan, 1994; Döös, 1994) and even rising international tensions (Gleick, 1989; Jacobson, 1989). In this section we examine possible population movements from the southwest Pacific region which may be stimulated by climate change over the next thirty years. Even excluding the uncertainties surrounding future climate change, estimating the likelihood of future population flows is a difficult task and such estimates entail a fair degree of uncertainty especially given climate change scenarios. Consequently we aim merely to provide plausible scenarios of migrations that may be spurred by climate change. The focus of this discussion is the area that includes the small island states of the southwest Pacific Ocean. Papua New Guinea is included in the general terminology "island states." Australia, New Zealand and the United States of America are considered in their role as probable destinations for future migrations from the small island states.

The land areas, environments, populations and cultures of the southwest Pacific island states vary. They encompass Polynesian, Melanesian and Micronesian peoples. With a population approaching four million and a territory of 178,000 square miles (World Resources Institute, 1992), Papua New Guinea (PNG) is the largest. Most island states are much smaller. The atoll states in the region are the smallest island states in the world (Roy & Connell, 1989). Despite their differences, the small island states of the southwest Pacific share some characteristics. The average population growth rate in the region is relatively high at 2.2 percent a year (Gannicott, 1993). This growth is due to declining mortality and high fertility. Only a few states, including Samoa and Tonga, have low population growth and this is due to substantial out-migration (Gannicott, 1993). There is some evidence that expectations of emigration opportunities have contributed to high fertility levels with parents hoping for remittances from sons employed overseas (Chambers, 1986; Connell, 1988).

With only 13 percent of the workforce in paid employment, most of the economically active people of the small island states are engaged in subsistence agriculture (Callick, 1993; Gannicott, 1993), primarily agriculture and fishing. A basis of subsistence agriculture with occasional periods of paid labor is a common pattern (Gannicott, 1993). In some Pacific islands, remittances from overseas workers play an important role in domestic economies (Roy & Connell, 1989; Gannicott, 1993). In addition, after political independence was secured by many states, foreign aid made a major contribution to a rise in living standards (Cole, 1993) through improved health and education systems and better infrastructure. However, since the end of the Cold War, strategic interest in the southwest Pacific island region has disappeared. The lucrative Soviet Union "fishing agreements" which island nations once used to attract Western aid are gone. U.S. aid to the region has fallen (Stewart, 1994). Australia and New Zealand are now the main donors of aid to the region (Joint Standing Committee, 1989; NZ Department of Statistics, 1993).

In some of the smaller island states, a limited agriculture base has declined since colonial times (Roy & Connell, 1989). In the atoll states of the Marshall

Islands, Tokelau, Tuvalu and Kiribati, in particular, there has been a decline in *per capita* food production and more food is imported. Many island states have a narrow resource base (Cole, 1993). Some island states rely on exploiting their natural resources to generate income. PNG, the largest state, is fortunate in being rich in minerals, as well as timber and fish. However, the forests and fisheries of many southwest Pacific islands are being exploited in an unsustainable way. Mining of these natural resources is often carried out by Asian companies, with little economic return to the islanders themselves (ABC, 1994). For example, PNG loses as much in illegal logging exports each year as Australia, the main aid donor, gives to PNG in foreign aid (ABC, 1994). In 1993, the Melanesian countries of PNG, the Solomon Islands and Vanuatu lost up to $A350 million in logging revenue due to overlogging and underpayment by foreign companies (Stewart, 1994). Similarly, due to illegal fishing and underreporting of catches, island nations receive only $A74 million of the $A2 billion worth of fish taken from their seas each year (Stewart, 1994). At the 25th South Pacific Forum in Australia in 1994, the then Australian Prime Minister, Paul Keating, criticized Asian companies, primarily those of Japan, South Korea and Malaysia, for overexploiting the natural resources of the southwest Pacific nations and underpaying them (Satchell, 1994). Since independence, most small island states have had weak governments and, as a result, political and bureaucratic waste and corruption have increased (Satchell, 1994). Low rates of economic growth, combined with high rates of population growth, have resulted in falling living standards in some island states in recent years (ABC, 1994).

In addition to concerns about climate change, deforestation, soil erosion and lagoon pollution are major problems on many small island states (World Resources Institute, 1992). There is a high rate of rural-urban migration in several southwest Pacific island states (Gannicott, 1993). Rapid urbanization in most of the small atoll states, for example, has resulted in growing problems of urban pollution from inadequate sewerage and garbage disposal and overcrowding (Connell & Lea, 1992).

In recent decades, people from the southwest Pacific islands have migrated to Hawaii, Canada, California, New Zealand and increasingly Australia (Anon., 1986; Barkan, 1992; AIDAB, 1993):

In more recent times, the faster growing populations of Polynesia [including Samoa and Tonga] have been able to ease their land pressures by migrating to New Zealand, Australia and the west coast of North America; Micronesians [including Kiribatis and Marshall Islanders] have travelled to work in Nauru and elsewhere, or on ships; while Melanesia [including Papua New Guinea] has had the land mass to sustain increased populations. (Callick, 1993, 2)

These established patterns of migration have also resulted from large numbers of young Pacific island people being attracted by better job prospects overseas. Most island states gained political independence as the age of cheap air travel arrived (Cole, 1993). Modern communications, migration and the remittances of overseas workers have contributed to rising expectations of living standards in many small island states that have not been able to satisfy their citizens' needs. Out-migration has had a dramatic impact on the smaller Polynesian states of Niue, the Cook Islands, American Samoa and Tokelau, as indigenous populations have been more than halved (J. Connell cited in Anon., 1986) In recent years, the remittances of large numbers of Tongans and Western Samoans working overseas have provided the major source of investment funds for these countries (Gannicott, 1993). Migration from the Marshall Islands and the federated states of Micronesia to the United States of America is allowed under the Compact of Free Association (Connell & Lea, 1992). In recent years, immigration into the United States of America from the Pacific region has increased markedly (Anon., 1986; Barkan, 1992).

New Zealand has strong historical ties with several south Pacific states and has had special entry regulations which have resulted in large Pacific island communities now residing in New Zealand. In 1991, New Zealand held over 125,000 Pacific islanders, in addition to its indigenous Maori population of over 320,000 people (NZ Department of Statistics, 1993). Historically, Australia has been more difficult for Pacific island people to migrate to due to criteria for educational qualifications and employment skills for migrant entry (AIDAB, 1993). There were over 50,000 Pacific islanders in Australia in 1986 (AIDAB, 1993). As a consequence of poor economic prospects and population growth in several small island states, Australia is under some pressure from some Pacific island governments, some churches and academics to accept more Pacific islanders either as temporary guest-workers or permanent migrants (AIDAB, 1993). Pointing to population trends in south Pacific countries, Jones notes:

Although their populations are tiny (6.2 million in 1990, almost two-thirds of this in Papua New Guinea), they are obviously of considerable importance to Australia. Fertility remains higher than in Asia and projected population growth is 46 per cent by 2010 according to the United Nations medium projections. If past experience is any guide, this increase will exert great pressure for migration to countries such as Australia and New Zealand. (Jones, 1993b, 6)

Population pressures on the low atoll states of Tuvalu and Kiribati have led to calls on several occasions for consideration of special entry treatment by Australia (L. Langford, Acting Direction, Pacific Islands II Section, AIDAB, personal communication). For example, the Joint Standing Committee on Foreign Affairs, Defence and Trade (1989), which examined Australia's relations with the South Pacific, acknowledged the exceptional problems of Kiribati and Tuvalu and argued for some migration concessions for these countries. Nevertheless, to date the Australian government has refused to introduce special migration schemes for Pacific islanders. In his opening address to a ministerial seminar on population and development in the Asia-Pacific region in 1993, Gordon Bilney, then the Australian Minister for Development Cooperation and Pacific Island Affairs, pointed to high population growth rates in many south Pacific countries and warned: "It should . . . be remembered that the migration safety valve may no longer be an option in a future, more crowded world" (Bilney, 1993, 5).

Kritz (1990) points out that the aspects of greenhouse warming that may be most important for their implications for human migration are changes in temperature, sea level, precipitation and the incidence of extreme climatic events such as cyclones, floods, droughts and climate variability. Warming is expected to be greater at high latitudes (Houghton et al., 1990). Absolute temperatures and temperature increases may not be a major cause of human migration (Kritz, 1990). Humans now cope with seasonal and daily temperature changes greater than predicted greenhouse temperature rises. While most people prefer a temperature around 20°C, human settlements are found in environments characterized by very hot (50°C) to very cold (-60°C) temperatures (Kritz, 1990).

Temperature, humidity and wind speed interact and together determine the degree of comfort that weather conditions afford people. Consequently humidity and wind speed should be taken into account when assessing how people may respond to a temperature rise (Kritz, 1990). In developed countries people may respond to a temperature increase by greater use of air conditioners (Kritz, 1990) and swimming pools. However, equatorial warming of 2°C by the end of the twenty-first century is expected to decrease human comfort in developing countries (McGregor, 1990). As we have said previously, temperature changes may also affect human health (Kritz, 1990; Hashimoto & Nishioka, 1991; McMichael, 1993).

A rise in temperature may cause a sea level increase through thermal expansion of the upper layers of the oceans, some melting of glaciers and changes in the volume of ice and snow in Antarctica and Greenland (Houghton et al., 1990). Rising sea levels may force people living in low-lying coastal areas and on small islands to move (Houghton et al., 1990). The prospect of rising sea levels has caused concern and led to predictions of large numbers of Third World "ecological refugees" (Kritz, 1990). Sea level rise is certainly considered the most potentially dangerous effect of climatic change on human settlements (Tegart et al., 1993). Some small Pacific islands are low-lying and most of them are small. So a rise in sea level has serious implications for some island populations in the southwest Pacific region.

Developed countries generally have the resources, technology and organization to protect major human settlements from rising sea levels (Kritz, 1990). Dams, dykes, levees, flood walls, sea walls, tidal barriers and perhaps building up sand dunes will be options available to developed countries (Madhava Sarma, 1991). In contrast, populations on small islands in the southwest Pacific appear more vulnerable to sea level rise as they may not have the resources to defend their settlements (Roy & Connell, 1989). Affected populations may be forced to relocate. Short-distance relocations due to storm surges have already occurred on the north coast of Papua New Guinea, where a narrow sandy barrier enclosing the Murik Lakes, on the shores of the Sepik delta, has been overwashed by storm surges and driven landward. Villages built on this barrier have been moved back and rebuilt after each storm surge (Bird, 1987). However, populations in Papua New Guinea have higher land to migrate to. By contrast, the Marshall Islands, Tokelau, Tuvalu and Kiribati are threatened by sea level rise (Roy & Connell, 1989). The four island states consist of low-relief atolls. Under a rising sea scenario, atolls, which rarely rise three meters above sea level, appear to be seriously at risk from the drowning of barrier reefs, intrusion of saltwater into ground water supplies and coastal erosion (Roy & Connell, 1989; Connell & Lea, 1992). Possible increased frequency of cyclones and storm overwash due to climatic change may increase salting of soils and wells. The small atoll states appear highly vulnerable to rising sea levels.

Variations in precipitation levels may affect agriculture and human settlements. Droughts and floods have often caused populations to shift (Kritz, 1990). A predicted increase in the intensity and frequency of heavy rainfalls worldwide will cause more frequent flooding (Whetton et al., 1993). Some areas of small island states may be affected by desertification by the end of the twenty-first century. These include the Port Moresby area in Papua New Guinea, parts of Fiji, Vanuatu and the Solomon Islands (Pernetta & Hughes, 1990).

What factors may encourage significant numbers of South Pacific islanders to migrate in response to greenhouse warming? People may migrate for a range of reasons. Traditionally demographers have classed these reasons as either "push" or "pull" factors. Adverse environmental or climatic changes could be potent "push" factors spurring people to abandon present settlement sites in an attempt to seek more favorable locations (Kritz, 1990). Benign destinations may exert a "pull" influence, especially once migration routes and networks are established, with expatriate communities providing information and support to potential migrants in the source country or area, through modern means of communication and with migration flows facilitated by modern means of transport (Barkan, 1992; Massey, 1994). According to Hugo (1989), people have a range of migration choices which is "a continuum ranging from totally *voluntary* migration in which the choice and will of the migrants is the overwhelmingly decisive element encouraging people to move to totally *forced* migration where the migrants are faced with death if they remain in their present place of residence" (Hugo, 1989, 4).

While migration is one possible adaptive response of human populations to the stresses of climatic change, other possible demographic responses to such stresses are lower fertility and higher mortality (Hugo, 1984). For example, more heat stress as a result of climatic change could cause increased mortality in some countries (Tegart et al., 1993). However, populations may be capable of nondemographic adjustments and adaptations to climatic change. What factors would facilitate successful nondemographic adaptations? The scale and severity of climatic impacts are obviously major factors affecting the ability of societies to adjust and adapt effectively, as is the pace of climatic change (Kritz, 1990). For example, while societies may be able to adapt *in situ* to slow changes, rapid ones may stimulate out-migration (Kritz, 1990).

Societies may differ in their vulnerability to adverse impacts of climatic change (Kates, 1985; Gleick, 1989; Kritz, 1990; Houghton et al., 1990; Brookfield, 1990). Small states and those with much land at sea level may be most vulnerable to sea level rises. With the increased frequency of extreme events such as droughts and floods, populations that have little national territory may attempt to migrate to land owned by other nation states (Kritz, 1990). In comparison with developed countries, developing countries appear more susceptible to adverse impacts of climatic shifts (Kates, 1985). Populations in developing countries are likely to be less able to adapt successfully to climatic stresses because they are more likely to lack the organization and resources both to plan and to use technologies to counter the worst effects of climatic change. In comparison with developed countries, a greater proportion of the population of developing countries lives close to the margins of sustenance (Kritz, 1990). Developing countries generally have a larger proportion of their population dependent on agriculture for a livelihood than do more developed countries. The greater the percentage of a country's population engaged in agriculture, the more vulnerable it is to adverse effects of climatic change on agriculture (Harrison, 1992). Commentators have predicted that it is from these more vulnerable countries that waves of "Greenhouse refugees" may come in the future (Kritz, 1990). Will the small south-west Pacific island states, with their often rapidly growing populations, be a source of such "refugees" in future? An attempt to assess the links between climate and migration may be helped by examining some studies of interactions between climate and population.

Recent migration studies indicate that important differences exist in the migration processes that are influenced by climatic factors in developed countries as compared to those in developing countries (Kritz, 1990). Populations in developed countries are largely urbanized and consequently removed from the agricultural activities that are most directly influenced by climatic shifts. Some U.S. studies have found that climate has been a factor in attracting population to the sunbelt region (Svart, 1975; Graves, 1980). In this respect climate has played a positive role in that people have been attracted to the climatic amenity of the sunbelt area rather than being forced to leave their original source area by severe climatic conditions (Kritz, 1990). Growing numbers of retired people and the growth of both the tourism and service industries have contributed to growing economic opportunities in the sunbelt. In Australia, a similar process seems to have occurred in the last decade. The sunbelt coastal area of southeast Queensland has attracted people from the southern States (ABS, 1994c). Queensland's climate has been a major factor in attracting this population (Harris, 1994). Studies have shown that in developed countries several aspects of climate influence migration choices, including very hot or very cold days, mean annual windspeed and mean relative humidity (Svart, 1975; Schachter & Althaus, 1982).

While climate in developed countries may exert a positive "pull" influence on migration, in developing countries climate tends to play a negative "push" role in migration. Kritz argues:

In contrast to the resilience of populations in developed countries to climate and the view of climatic conditions as an amenity that can be improved via migration, climate in developing countries has to be seen as a supply-side variable or as a factor of production. Most people in developing countries live in rural areas . . . and therefore continue to be highly dependent on a predictable climate for their basic sustenance. Thus, climate tends to operate in developing areas as one of several push factors (deteriorating soils, lack of markets and social services . . .) that encourages people to move to other rural areas or to leave rural areas altogether. (Kritz, 1990, 8)

Forced migration flows in response to some combination of climatic or environmental stress, hunger and political conflict in developing countries sometimes cross national borders (Kritz, 1990). This occurs most frequently in Africa. But people often try to adapt to climatic stress in other ways. Populations may be able to adjust and adapt to climatic change through the use of technological means to minimize the unwelcome effects of climatic shifts, changes in consumption and production patterns and political measures to socialize costs such as public assistance to those social groups most disadvantaged by climatic change (Kritz, 1990).

In the southwest Pacific region, there are several documented cases of relocations of small island populations to other nearby islands due to climatic stress and/or population pressure (Knudson, 1977; McKnight, 1977; O'Collins, 1990a). By contrast, there are few documented cases of long-distance migration from a small island society to a Western society as a result of climatic stress. The case of the migration of Tokelauans, Polynesian atolldwellers, to New Zealand following a hurricane warrants consideration.

Tokelau consists of three small atolls, 3,600 kilometers, northeast of New Zealand. In 1948 Tokelauans received New Zealand citizenship rights, including the right to migrate to New Zealand. Before 1965 few Tokelauans migrated to New Zealand (Prior, 1986). After a 1966 hurricane caused major damage in Tokelau, the New Zealand government initiated a resettlement program to move Tokelauans to New Zealand in order to reduce both food shortages and population pressure on the atolls (Prior, 1986). From 1966 to 1982, the population of Tokelau fell from some 2,000 to 1,546 while the number of Tokelauans in New Zealand, including those born in New Zealand, increased from about 600 to 2,762 (Prior, 1986). To what extent Tokelauans migrated in response to "push" factors of climatic stress, food scarcity and population pressure or to the "pull" factor of greater economic opportunities in New Zealand or to some combination of these, is unclear.

In 1967, a longitudinal, multidisciplinary study, the Tokelau Island Migrant Study, was begun in order to investigate the social and health consequences of this migration on the migrants themselves and to examine their adaptation to New Zealand. This study was conducted until 1986. One important finding of the study has been that both adult Tokelauans and their children in New Zealand suffer higher blood pressure than do those on Tokelau (Joseph et al., 1983). Other health indices indicate a lower level of health of Tokelauan migrants in New Zealand in comparison with Tokelauans remaining in Tokelau. The study showed that Tokelauan migrants experienced stress when interacting with New Zealand society. A significant positive association was found between both blood pressure and hypertension and non-Tokelauan social interaction (Beaglehole et al., 1977). Unfortunately, as Roy and Connell (1989) point out, there is little published information on the social consequences of the Tokelauan resettlement program. However, in the light of the Tokelauan Island Migrant Study, it seems clear that in terms of the success or failure of migration as an adaptation to climatic stress, migration is a strategy that can entail significant costs for migrants (Roy & Connell, 1989).

Greenhouse warming may exert one extra stress on some small Pacific island states. Adverse impacts of climatic change may provide a "push" influence on migration from rural areas to urban centers and from smaller outer islands to larger main islands of some small island states (Roy & Connell, 1989). This may increase strains on the provision of services such as housing, sewerage and water supplies, as well as exacerbating existing problems of overcrowding and unemployment in some urban areas.

Adverse impacts of climatic change may exert a significant push influence on migration from small island states to the English-speaking developed countries of the Pacific region. While to date there has been little migration from Melanesian countries such as Papua New Guinea and the Solomon Islands to developed countries, it is possible that in the future there will be growing demand for such migration due to some combination of demographic, environmental and climatic change stresses operating as "push" factors as well as "pull" factors because of better economic and educational prospects available overseas for prospective migrants. There may be growing pressure for migration from the larger Melanesian countries if migration concessions are granted to smaller island states (Hastings, 1994).

The United States of America, Australia and New Zealand are three of only a few countries in the world that still have large immigration programs. These three countries are major net receivers of international migrants with a significant unmet demand for larger intakes. In recent years in all three countries there have been signs of growing public disenchantment with immigration programs. In the United States of America, current immigration policy is being questioned as the impact of large numbers of Third World immigrants on the major cities of Los Angeles, New York and Miami has become visible (Glazer, 1994). Whether American culture, based on European ideals, can survive a continuous wave of migrants from diverse but nondemocratic cultures is being debated.

In Australia lower economic growth in recent years has resulted in historically high levels of long-term structural unemployment (ABS, 1994b). From the 1970s the Australian public's support for the immigration program has declined (Betts, 1988; Morgan Gallup Poll, 1992; Hugo, 1994), perhaps due mainly to economic factors, but also perhaps partly to cultural and environmental concerns. These factors may have contributed to a reduction in the size of the immigration program since 1990 (ABS, 1994a) and to an apparent government commitment to a smaller program (Garran & Sexton, 1994). Indeed, in mid-1996, the Howard Liberal Government cut Australia's immigration intake for 1996-1997 by about 10,000 people, we believe in response to electoral pressure from political forces such as Graeme Campbell (Independent for Kalgoorlie), Australians Against Further Immigration Party and others which now constitute the new Australian nationalist movement, *Australia First*.

In New Zealand there are Maori concerns about immigration and multiculturalism (Carmichael et al., 1993; Walker, 1994). Public skepticism about the benefits of immigration programs may have encouraged both the Australian and New Zealand governments to try in recent years to increase the proportion of wealthy and skilled migrants in their immigration intakes, in an attempt to maximize the economic benefits of immigration to the receiving countries. In New Zealand, unemployment has risen in the 1980s with Maoris and Pacific islanders suffering high unemployment rates (NZ Department of Statistics, 1993). Following public concerns about immigration (Trlin, 1993), there was some reduction in migration to New Zealand from the small Pacific island states of Tonga and Western Samoa in the late 1980s due to a tightening of immigration controls (Bedford, 1990). Within Australia and New Zealand, there appear to be some indicators of declining migration opportunities, especially for unskilled labor. If continued, this tendency could constrain pressures for migration from the small island states to Australia and New Zealand in the future, particularly while domestic unemployment levels remain high. While the pressures for migration may grow partly as a result of adverse impacts of climatic change, it is difficult to assess whether significantly increased out-migration from the small Pacific island states will result over the next few decades. However, if further concessionary migration schemes are offered to Pacific islanders by any of the developed countries in the Pacific region, as climatic change proceeds, out-migration is likely to be substantial.

Will migration that is stimulated by climatic change be a successful strategy of adaptation? Adaptation entails costs, as well as benefits. Costs are likely to be considerable for Pacific island populations vulnerable to climatic change impacts. As Pernetta and Hughes note:

Resettlement and out-migration can be expected to have major social and economic costs both within island states and regionally. For some of the smaller atoll based nations, out-migration may mean resettlement in another country with consequent costs both to the original and the recipient state. (Pernetta & Hughes, 1990, 10)

If, for example, migration to English-speaking developed countries is able to be adopted by significant numbers of Pacific islanders in response to climatic shifts, some Pacific islanders may benefit, while others bear many of the costs. Young unemployed islanders with few educational or economic prospects at home may benefit from access to the educational facilities, the job market and perhaps the greater freedom available in developed countries. Older Pacific islanders and those unwilling to migrate may be losers if forced to migrate. They may experience psychological trauma (Pernetta & Hughes, 1990), perhaps suffering from a sense of cultural crisis which can result from natural disasters (Oliver-Smith, 1982) and experience a loss of cultural identity (O'Collins, 1990b). They may have difficulty in adapting to modern Western market-based culture. This is a small cost, it may be said, to the alternative of drowning! There are, however, other larger social costs.

Racial animosities may create difficulties for both the host country and those attempting to settle in developed countries. The 1992 Los Angeles riots involving African-Americans, Koreans and Hispanics showed that multiracial tension is a major problem in some of the ghettoes of large U.S. cities (Miles, 1992). Racial conflict is also a problem in some poor areas of large New Zealand cities (Hastings, 1994; Smellie, 1994). It is to the larger cities of the United States, New Zealand and Australia, that Pacific islanders tend to move (Anon., 1986; Bedford, 1990; AIDAB, 1993). In Australia, despite what is often claimed to be a successful multicultural society, the government has introduced "racial hatred" legislation to ban racial taunts from the public arena. Growing numbers of Pacific islanders in deprived areas of Western cities may contribute to rising racial frictions. Multiculturalism, the effort of minority groups to retain ancestral ethnic cultures in a new country, has not been shown to be a viable solution to the long-term survival of cultures (Blainey, 1994).

Whether climatic shifts may spur significant population flows from the small southwestern Pacific islands over the next few decades will depend ultimately on the pace of such change, the magnitude of impacts, the ability of affected societies to use a range of adjustments and adaptive strategies to cope with such impacts, people's attitudes toward migration and, in the case of international migration, the willingness of societies to accept migrants and possibly "environmental refugees." Climate change may exert one extra pressure on populations that are already subjected to other stresses. In the southwest Pacific region, the small island states appear vulnerable to adverse impacts of climatic shifts. Low-lying coral atolls appear most threatened by rising sea levels and their populations may in the future be forced to try to migrate.

Where international migration from small island states to developed countries is already well established, adverse impacts of climate change may augment such flows. Climate change may contribute to a widening of source countries in the south Pacific for international migration to the United States, Australia and New Zealand. The migration strategy may entail costs. Adaptation of Pacific islanders to life in the industrialized societies may incur significant medium-term psychological, health and social costs for some migrants. Increased racial friction among the poor of the large Western cities of the Pacific region may also be a significant cost, both to the newcomers and to the receiving countries.

THE STATE OF THE ARGUMENT

The demographer Joel E. Cohen in *How Many People Can the Earth Support?* (1995) says that there are three laws of intellectual honesty which should be applied in demography, and we believe in other intellectual inquiries as well. The first law is the *Law of Information*: 97.6 percent of statistics are made up (including, self-referentially, this statistic) (Cohen, 1995, 21, 369). In other words, statistics are idealizations, theoretical and mathematical constructs that are fallible. His second law is the *Law of Action*: that it is difficult to do just what you intended to do. As a corollary, one can never do only one thing; there are unintended consequences of action (Hardin, 1993). Finally, there is the *Law of Prediction*: the more confidence an expert places in a prediction about humanity's future, the less confidence you should have in it (Cohen, 1995, 369). In this chapter we have attempted to refute the Economist view held by Julian Simon that there are no limits to population growth. We have not, however, followed the usual course of such discussion, swapping statistic for statistic. We began this chapter by observing Cohen's Law of Information and recognizing the fallibility of official statistics about human population growth. These statistics are biased against the Limitationist perspective and it is highly likely that the twenty-first century will see a human population larger than received medium predictions.

Even if this is not so, the world faces an incredible problem in dealing with ten billion people in 2050 if even some of the problems cited in this chapter and the previous chapter by various authorities are real. As Limitationists we believe that the Earth has already exceeded its carrying capacity, although for reasons given in this chapter we cannot tell you what this exact level is. In a world that is nonlinear and chaotic and where both things and concepts are fuzzy (Kosko, 1994) this should not be surprising. It is highly likely on a business-as-usual scenario that a population crash will occur sometime in the twenty-first century. As we shall show in chapter 4, this will be fueled by economic globalization of the world—which Economists like Simon believe will be the saving grace of mankind. We will have more to say about the prospects of ecological and social collapse in the concluding chapter of this book.

In these two chapters we have discussed the ecological crisis. But humanity, tragically, faces other crises of civilization. One of these is economic and we will discuss that in chapter 4. The other crisis is intellectual and philosophical. In another age we would call this crisis *spiritual*, a crisis of sense and meaning. The combined forces of modernization, scientific reductionism and materialism have made such concerns a matter of intellectual embarrassment, and that we believe is a problem in itself. Very few books attempt to investigate the nature and connections between these crises. We will do so here. We propose that there is a common core to the crisis of civilization in the philosophy of modernity which in itself constitutes a flaw in Western civilization. In the next chapter we will attempt to isolate this flaw and relate this discussion to the notion of limits. In doing so we shall attempt to destroy at the most basic and fundamental level the world view of Economists and internationalists such as Julian Simon, and also to make a contribution toward cognitively humbling the forces of modernization, materialism and meaninglessness.

NOTES

1. The demographic transition theory makes a projectionable causal link between affluence and modernization conditions on the one hand and fertility decline on the other. It is most unlikely that any such high-level universal generalization about human populations is true. The fertility decline seen in the West could well be a complex dialectical product arising from technological innovations in contraception, feminism and the social processes that have transformed family life in the later part of the twentieth century.

2. The Danish economist Ester Boserup (1965, 1981) proposes that population growth has determined changes in agriculture and has spurred other changes in technology (Harrison, 1992). We do not deny this. After a certain critical threshold, population growth can create problems that require a technological solution. No doubt this will occur in the future with agricultural technology as the world tries to feed future billions. However, our point against Simon is that the *initial* population pressure arose because technologies (including public health knowledge) allowed it to be sustained in the first place. It is quite possible that a positive feedback situation exists where technological changes → population growth → further technological changes → further population growth . . . (where "→" means "leads to").

3. Simon also gives another progrowth argument in a number of his books. Stated formally, the argument is as follows: (1) an immigrant-swelled population will use more natural resources than otherwise; (2) thus the price of raw materials will rise; (3) this price rise will lead to new technologies and substitutes occurring, thus (4) the price of the resources in question will fall lower than when the scarcity occurred. The problem with this argument is that it conflicts with other arguments in Simon's work. For example, as we recall from chapter 1, for Simon resources are not finite and limited but are increasing inexorably over time. This is due to natural human ingenuity. As humans are the "ultimate resource," on Simon's own premises, the situation occurring in (1) will not occur, even in the shortterm.

4. The theological argument is advanced from time to time that we have a moral obligation to maximize the number of people on Earth—even if this leads to earthly misery—because it will maximize the number of souls that can be "saved" and go to Heaven. However, in a world of overcrowded misery, the most likely result of this soul making is an overcrowding of Hell. If Earth is made unpleasant through overcrowding, then it is likely that more sins will occur than in a quiet, low populated world. How can one even respect people when they are as numerous as rats in a plague? We do not believe that there are any satisfactory theological arguments for population maximization.

5. Exponential growth, either of populations or of debt at compound interest (usury), continued indefinitely will break all bounds and tend toward infinity. Any growth rate that is positive has this property, which lies in the mathematical nature of the simple exponential growth equation $y = ke^{bt}$. If $y = ke^{bt}$, then $dy/dx = kb.e^{bt}$ which means that the exponential rule applies. As long as k and b are positive, as t increases dy/dx increases as well. The natural exponential function is its own derivative. As $e^x > 0$ for all x, e^x is said to be strictly increasing.

A decline in growth rates from 2 to 1.7 percent does not mean that a population doubling will not occur. The growth rate may fall, but a growth in absolute numbers continues.

It should be noted that demographers regard the exponential growth model of human population growth as an idealization and a simplification of a more complex, possibly *chaotic* phenomenon (at least in the long run). This model assumes that growth rates have been constant for long periods, which is not strictly speaking true even of the twentieth century (Lutz et al., 1994). The exponential growth curve does not consider the age structure of the population and the momentum of the population growth. With a young age distribution, populations can still grow significantly with a constant fertility at replacement level. Exponential growth curves thus can make us too *optimistic*. Consequently arguments using exponential growth curves must be regarded as simplifications of a complex reality that may be much worse than we expected (Fischer, 1993).

Another point worth clarifying here is the exact logical form of the Malthusian argument. Cosmologist and physicist Fred Hoyle (1986) has argued that the Malthusian argument can be refuted by a *reductio ad absurdum* argument based on two propositions: (1) a technologically complex society would collapse long before the Malthusian starvation point is reached and (2) a technologically complex society can sustain more people above the starvation level than a technologically inefficient society can sustain at the starvation level. While there could be debate about (2), we will accept it here. Hoyle then argues that once a technologically complex society exceeds primitive starvation conditions, the Malthusian argument is rendered invalid "because a decrease in population is required to reach the Malthusian state, whereas all our expectations are that the population will *increase*" (Hoyle, 1986, 553). The fallacy here is Hoyle's assumption that a decrease in population is required for a population crash. His first premise, in fact, shows that this is not so for technologically complex societies where most people have no food self-sufficiency at all and depend on the smooth operation of society for their survival. All the Malthusian need maintain is that population limits are set by the limits of food resources (as well as other ecological capital). Malthus himself did not say that people necessarily breed themselves into poverty and starvation when a certain level of income and education is reached (Keyfitz & Lindahl-Kiessling, 1994, 23).

6. The concept of an optimum population size has been subjected to some telling philosophical criticism. David Heyd in *Genethics* (1992) argues that the concept of an optimum population size is incoherent because there is no noncircular way of determining the ideal number of people. To solve this problem would require a prior solution to the question of what is "ideal" and at some point in the epistemological regress each of the conflicting responses will beg the question of its own validity (Heyd, 1992, 152).

7. According to Heilig (1994, 236), "there is no foreseeable limitation to the basic natural resources of food production, which are space, water, climate conditions, solar energy, and man-made inputs." These resources are said to be unlimited or may be utilized in such a way as to become unlimited. Heilig's own discussion of the Net Primary Production of the Earth (Heilig, 1994, 210) refutes his own position. As the Earth is (roughly) a sphere, with a finite diameter, it therefore has a finite surface area. Hence there must be space limits, as we also showed early in this chapter (see also Rees, 1996).

8. Cohen (1995) is cautious in his answer to the question that is the title of his book, "how many people can the Earth support?" because of the uncertainty of human knowledge and the fallibility of statistics (Cohen, 1995, 369) but he accepts that "the possibility must be considered seriously that the number of people on the Earth has reached, or will reach within half a century, the maximum number the Earth can support in modes of life that we and our children and their children will choose to want" (Cohen, 1995, 367).

9. A huge iceberg, A24, broke free from the Price Gustav iceshelf early in 1995. Iceberg A24 was 100 kilometers long and consisted of 400 billion tonnes of ice. It

drifted into the South Atlantic Ocean before breaking up. Other icebergs of between fifty and 100 kilometers long have broken off the Larsen Filshner and Ross iceshelves. A major scientific debate exists about the significance of this. The warming trend observed in Antarctica may be a small-scale climatic variation. But the warming trends are consistent with the Greenhouse warming hypothesis that predicts that warming will be most pronounced at the polar latitudes. According to Dr. Joe Jacka of the Co-operative Research Centre for Antarctic Studies (CRCAS) in Hobart, Australia, temperatures have risen in the Antarctic at the rate of 1.3°C per century. This warming trend has been observed in the Southern Ocean. As the first temperature monitoring began in 1945, the data time series is not long enough to determine if this trend is compatible with natural temperature variations.

The once-permanent ice cap at the North Pole is melting. A layer of warmer water—*hypothesized* to have been produced by global warming—collects 200 meters under the ice and gradually melts it. The physical cause of the melt is a rise in temperature of the Gulf Stream, the warm current that flows toward the North Pole from the Atlantic. The Gulf Stream has been weakened due to a disruption of deep water ocean currents around Greenland, in turn caused by the disappearance of an ice tongue known as the *Odden Feature*. It has not appeared for the last three years. This is also hypothesized to be because of global warming. Evidence of the warming of the Arctic Ocean comes from the 1994 journey from Alaska to Iceland by two icebreakers, the U.S. and the Louis St.-Laurent, from Canada.

Dr. Peter Wadhams, Co-ordinator of the European Commission's Sub-Polar Ocean Program (and also for the Scott Polar Research Institute, Cambridge), believes that global warming has raised the temperature of water under the ice at the North Pole by about one degree centigrade in the past five years. In his opinion it is possible that the temperature rise would be enough to melt the now-permanent ice at the North Pole leading to a situation where the ice completely disappears in the summer, but returns in the winter. Note that most of the polar ice is already floating in the sea, so (by Archimedes' Principle) if it melts there will not be a rise in global sea levels. The real problem is, if these trends continue, the melting of icesheets on *land* at both poles.

10. The following material is based on Moore and Smith, (1995). We are grateful to Evonne Moore for permission to use this material here, and to Professor Virginia Abernethy, editor of *Population and Environment* and Myrtle Banness of Human Sciences Press Inc., for permission to reprint this material here.

3

The Unreasonable Silence of the World: Postmodernity and the Crisis of Philosophy, Science and Knowledge

> We live amidst the ruins of the great, five-hundred-year epoch of Humanism. Around us is that "colossal wreck." Our culture is a flat expanse of rubble. It hardly offers shelter from a mild cosmic breeze, never mind one of those icy gales that regularly return to rip men out of the cosy intimacy of their daily lives and confront them with oblivion. Is it surprising that we are run down? We are desperate, yet we don't care much any more. We are timid, yet we cannot be shocked. We are inert underneath our busyness. We are destitute in our plenty. We are homeless in our own homes.
>
> What should be there to hold our hands, is not. Our culture is gone. It has left us terribly alone. In its devastation it cannot even mock us any more, sneer at the lost child whimpering for its mother. That stage too is over. Our culture is past cruelty. It is wrecked. It is dead. (Carroll, 1993, 1)

CLINGING TO THE WRECKAGE

John Carroll begins his remarkable book *Humanism: The Wreck of Western Culture* (1993) with the above words. He maintains that the time is approaching to bury humanism and to make a new beginning. First, however, an analysis must be given of what was wrong with humanism so that the bad choice is not made again. He sees humanism as having put "man" (in the politically correct sense) at the center of the universe, replacing God. He quotes Pico della Mirandola, who in 1486 said, "We can become what we will." Through his/her own individual will, the creative self can move the earth. Humanism replaced the "I" of the premodern Old Testament "I am that I am" with the "I" of the liberal, enlightened self.

The central point of the Renaissance was to do this through showing by example that a diverse array of great men—great scientists, statesmen and artists—could make themselves. They were not in all cases aware of the metaphysical implications of their actions. Even so, in all cases Renaissance man rebelled against the alleged physical and social darkness of the medieval period, a period of disease, warfare and death on earth and of the ever-present possibility of a demonic hell after life. The humanistic response was to propose that through science, technology and "Universal Reason," the physical world could be controlled and the shadows and superstitions of thought could be chased away by the light of reason: dirt, death and darkness would be gone.

Carroll notes that it is not the "physical edifice" built by humanism which is in ruin, but its "cultural metropolis." He accepts that humanism has made a lasting achievement by producing industrial civilization and has scored a triumph over poverty, starvation, disease and brute labor. It has provided, to date, material comfort for the average Western worker that not even the kings and queens of the premodern era could imagine.

Carroll's book is concerned with the spiritual history of the post-Christian West concentrating on High Culture and examining the leading thinkers and masterpieces of each period. As such his work is concerned primarily with literature and culture. It offers a fascinating study of its field, ranging from an examination of Shakespeare's early intimation of the first cracks in the humanist edifice, to an examination of the Westerns of filmmaker John Ford and the myths they created about modern America. However, Carroll does not discuss topics such as philosophy, logic, mathematics, science and ecology—the "physical edifice" of humanism—and it is here we believe that a more convincing case can be made for the failure of "humanism." Rather than speak of "humanism" we shall speak here of "Enlightenmentism" or "the Enlightenment Project." In this book we shall use these terms as many writers have used "modernism." There are complexities and difficulties with "modernism" which we shall discuss below.

The *Renaissance* was the revival of arts and letters under the influence of classical models in the fourteenth to sixteenth centuries. The *Enlightenment*, or "Age of Reason," is typically taken to be an eighteenth-century movement originating in France, emphasizing reason and individualism against tradition, these progressive and liberal ideas leading to the French Revolution. A formulation of Enlightenmentism was given by d'Holbach (1723–1789) in his *Système de la nature* (1770). Human unhappiness stems from an ignorance of nature. A summary of the thesis of this book, in condensed but excellent prose, occurs in Anthony Flew's *A Dictionary of Philosophy*; it will also serve as a first statement of "Enlightenmentism" for us:

Nature, he maintains, is knowable through human experience and thought, and explanations should not be sought in traditional beliefs or the alleged "revelations" of the Church. There is a fundamental continuity between man and the rest of nature, between animal and human behaviour; all natural phenomena, including mental ones, are explicable in terms of the organization and activity of matter. Religion and extranatural beliefs inculcate habits inhibiting enquiry and the acquisition of the knowledge that is necessary to achieve the fundamental aims of man: happiness and self-preservation.

Nature makes men neither good nor evil but malleable by education and experience. Reason shows man's need of others and is the foundation of moral systems determined by what is useful to a society . . . The power of man over man is justifiable only by utility; education and legislation can be effective only when men are convinced that their interests will be served thereby. (Flew, ed., 1979, 99)

The Enlightenment doctrines of materialism and naturalism were opposed by the European "Romanticism" movement, at its peak towards the end of the eighteenth and early part of the nineteenth centuries, especially by German idealist philosophy. It is here that we have problems with Carroll's doctrine of *humanism*, for many of the romantics opposing materialism and naturalism would be "humanists" by Carroll's account, and this is counterintuitive. Carroll's account of humanism, based on the idea that "We can become what we will," would make a late nineteenth-century thinker, such as Nietzsche, a humanist. Nietzsche's superman (*Übermensch*) is a man of the new order, who is able to transcend orthodox morality and adopt a new sense of good. This new sense of good is not a variant of moral goodness which would form part of some ethical theory referring to a moral law. *Übermensch* follows his instincts, regarding his will to power as a suitable foundation for action. For Nietzsche, all that strengthens life and the will to power is good. Again, it seems counterintuitive to classify such a philosophical position as *humanist*. In any case, elsewhere in his book Carroll turns his critical spotlight upon Enlightenmentism and its doctrine of the universality of reason, which he sees as having a self-undermining tendency because unbound reason, which questions everything, knows no certainty (Carroll, 1993, 122–123; Saul, 1992).

Lyons, Moore and Smith argued in *Is the End Nigh?* (Lyons et al., 1995) that the Enlightenment's project of using reason to gain scientific knowledge to intervene into the natural and social world to further human emancipation has backfired. It was held that the progressive mastery of nature would realize the utopian aim of the Enlightenment Project, but this has given rise to the unintended consequences of an enlightening reason becoming entangled in a blind domination of nature (Dutton, 1988; Ellul, 1990; Mander, 1991; Katz, 1992). The fully enlightened Earth now radiates ecological disaster. Many postmodernists would argue that as this is the case, we should dismantle the whole Enlightenment Project as it has come to a dead end.

We also believe that a new beginning is needed and this can be achieved only by the abandonment of "universalism," "cosmopolitanism," "internationalism" and "globalism." In *Is the End Nigh?* (Lyons et al., 1995) we examined this proposal in detail from a largely empirical and ecological perspective arguing that globalist tendencies are hurtling the Earth toward ecological catastrophe. Here we wish to combat internationalism in its most general form by criticizing universalism and the sovereignty of Universal Reason underlying the Enlightenment Project. This will take us on a journey through philosophy, logic, epistemology and physics. Before doing so, however, we need to clarify and elaborate upon the components of the contemporary moral and epistemological crisis.

THE ENLIGHTENMENT PROJECT

The Enlightenment Project promised freedom from the ravages of an unknown and uncontrollable nature and advocated freedom to appropriate and manipulate nature in rational ways which would result in the wealth of nations. Science and technology permit human beings to control nature rather than be controlled by nature, and the side benefit, once nature's mysteries have yielded to scientific reason and capitalist rationality, would be that human beings will be freed from a lifetime of hard and dreary labor and premature death from disease. Francis Bacon, for instance, hoped that the use of science and technology would enable human beings to predict and control natural phenomena and so satisfy human desires better and more rationally. He argued that nature would give up its fruits more easily, they could be extracted with less and less labor power and less and less pain, and nature would become a decent home for human beings. Bacon claimed that science could free us from the bondage of disease and poverty—from the servitude to nature—and theoretical and practical mastery of nature would generate material progress designed to satisfy human desires (Bacon, 1855, 57). René Descartes argued that in knowing the way nature worked and in making ourselves lords and masters of nature, universal scientific reason could be used to master nature for the good of human beings (Descartes [1637], 1985).

This dream developed in the eighteenth and nineteenth centuries into the idea of progress: the onward motion of material progress would produce humanized environments and perfected human beings. The application of the social sciences to the reorganization of society, it was argued, would eradicate those outmoded institutions and authority structures which prevented humankind from reaping the potentially rich harvest that was contingent upon the scientific control of nature.

The Enlightenment dream has turned sour. The powerful mix of a globalized free market, with science and technology being a part of capitalism's mode of production, is destroying nature (Lyons et al., 1995). Science and technology, once regarded as universally good, are now regarded with suspicion, because of the way they have been used to treat nature as sink and drain. The response of the leaders of the nation state is to retain their faith in technological solutions to the global ecological and economic problems. They argue that the revenge of nature, resulting from its disenchantment, domination and exploitation, is the price that human beings have to pay for human freedom from constant labor and disease. Human autonomy, freedom and the good life require economic growth, not the romantic ideal of living in harmony with nature advocated by back-to-the-land here-comes-the-sun enthusiasts. The cost of this project, if indeed it is a cost, is the acceptance of the disenchantment of the world and continuing to use nature as a sink and drain (Whitelock, 1979). What we need, it is argued, is more high-tech industry, scientific research and knowledge-driven projects of technological development to make good on the promise of universal abundance and a more egalitarian distribution of the benefits of economic growth.

It is not difficult to find criticisms of this optimistic view of the progressiveness of the human condition, and we addressed this matter earlier in this book. Anthony Giddens, one of Britain's leading social theorists, in reflecting on left-wing thought as humanity approaches the twenty-first century, writes that the world has "taken us by surprise." It has been contrary to the direction predicted by Enlightenment thinkers who thought that by overcoming dogma, prejudice and tradition, human beings with increased knowledge would become the masters of their own destiny (Giddens, 1994). Giddens sees us as living in a "run-away world," not subject to tight human control. Advancing human knowledge and the increased capacity to manipulate the environment increase rather than decrease the unpredictability of modern life. We are threatened by *manufactured uncertainty* which does not respond to the Enlightenment prescription of more knowledge, more control. Globalization is one of these manufactured uncertainties which is destroying traditional ways of life across the globe and offering, for consolation, consumerism and the market. Globalization itself is a product of technological innovations, such as mass transportation and global electronic communications systems, along with population growth.

The idea of progress, of the world evolving into a better and better state, is a social construction, a product of the industrial revolution (Nitecki, ed., 1988). It has not been universally upheld in all societies throughout history; the ancient Greeks believed in a regressive view of history, that society had declined from a golden age. Christianity also asserted that history was not progressive, but regressive from the fall of man. It would only become progressive with the coming of Christ—which in any case would mark the end of human history. John Gowdy, an economist and author of *Evolutionary Economics* (Gowdy, 1994a), has argued that there is "no convincing argument for past human progress and no reason to believe that it will occur in the future" (Gowdy, 1994b, 41). Following Lasch, he also believes that the "belated discovery that the earth's ecology will no longer sustain an indefinite expansion of productive forces deals the final blow to the belief in progress" (Lasch, 1991, 528).

Gowdy's argument is advanced by considering the criteria for progress used in biology. These include: (1) morphological complexity; (2) adaptive ability; (3) accumulation of genetic information; (4) increasing biomass, and (5) increasing resistance to extinction. He argues, convincingly in our opinion, that because of globalization, modern societies are becoming simpler, not more complex, and more culturally uniform. Modern societies are technologically complex, but as we have seen this is a weakness not an advantage. Gowdy notes that there has been an explosion of technical and scientific knowledge in this century but little of it is relevant to our survival as a species. Outside of survivalist circles, little work has been done on how to survive without modern technology. Increasing biomass (the population problem), is a threat to the human species, so it cannot be taken as a ground for belief in human progress.

What about the criterion of an increasing resistance to extinction? The evidence given in this book justifies a general pessimism about the prospects of long-term human survival if present trends continue. If we are right, then the ideal of progress is an illusion. Being tied to the front of a truck with no brakes, which is hurtling down a mountainous road, is not progress, however technologically sophisticated the truck may be.

The most radical challenge to the ideals of the Enlightenment Project comes from the *postmodernity* tradition. What is postmodernity? It is pointless to attempt any sort of explicit characterization of postmodernism, for as Frodeman observes, "postmodernism is a movement that celebrates its own schizophrenia, embracing pastiche and spontaneity and renouncing self-classification" (Frodeman, 1992, 308). As a broad movement, postmodernism proclaims the death of "metanarratives," used to ground the idea of "universal" human history (Lyotard, 1984; Hassan, 1985; Harvey, 1989; Docherty, ed., 1993). The Enlightenment's project of a progressive emancipation of reason and freedom and the enrichment of humanity through science and technology is bankrupt. Jean-Francois Lyotard, a major postmodernist writer, put this thesis as follows: "there is no longer any horizon of universality, universalisation or general emancipation to greet the eye of postmodern man" (Lyotard, 1992, 89). Postmodernism is thus characterized by *endism*, asserting the end of ideology, art, social class, Marxism and so on. In philosophy, postmodernism is associated with the attack upon *epistemological foundationalism* (the position that knowledge can only be justified by basing it upon secure or justified foundations), *the referential theory of language* (language gains its meaning by representing the objects to which it refers), *atomism/individualism* (the individual is ontologically prior to society) and *the metaphysics of presence* (the objective clarity of the subject to itself). Postmodernism proclaims the end of metaphysics and morality and welcomes the demise of the "tradition" (Cohen & Dascal, eds., 1989; Nielsen, 1991a, b).

Closely associated with postmodernism is the movement of *deconstructionism*, the key figures being Jacques Derrida, Michel Foucault and Roland Barthes. The movement arose in Paris in the late 1960s and has become, arguably, the dominant paradigm in American, British and Australian humanities and social science departments and has taken a hold on legal studies through the critical legal studies movement (Finnis, 1985; Belliotti, 1987a, b). It offers the most radical critique of liberal humanism available today, "arguing" (if it can be called that) that "history is a fiction" and that there is no reality outside of texts, no truth, no falsehood, no good or bad. Language doesn't refer to reality at all, but is only a system of arbitrary signs that are indeterminate with respect to their meaning—any assertion is constituted on the basis of exclusions that bring about its own self-contradiction—hence language is meaningless because it can never refer beyond itself.

The French philosopher Jacques Derrida, born of Sephardic Jewish parents in Algiers, has been concerned since the 1960s with the deconstruction of metaphysics, especially "logocentric" metaphysics. Western philosophy has an affinity for the *presence* of meaning, being and knowledge. The desire for a direct, unmediated access to meaning, being and knowledge is called "logocentrism." Derrida's denial of *presence* is the denial of a non-linguistic entity which determines sense, what he calls the *transcendental* signified—such as essence, being, consciousness and other entities that ground meanings. Metaphysical texts that advocate presence are allegedly shown by Derrida to be self-refuting or self-undermining.

Logocentrism is the quest for certain knowledge of the world obtained by reason and empirical inquiry, a quest which Derrida believes is hopelessly misplaced. The logocentric way of understanding the world involves the use of a *binary structure* in which an *other* is cast for the privileged term by which the primary term can be given positive value. The secondary term, by negative definition, contains all those elements regarded as "waste," "residue" and "corruption" in the primary term. Such oppositional pairs include man/woman, mind/body, reason/passion, speech/writing, being/nothingness, culture/nature, self/other, identity/difference and many others. The two terms are viewed as logically incompatible, such that if one term of the pair is accepted, then necessarily the other must be excluded and there is no middle ground between the pairs.

For Derrida, deconstruction is a "method" for criticizing existing doctrines by showing how arguments often support their negations as well as for offering a critique of conventional interpretations of texts. From what has already been said, we can see that this "method" consists in general of two parts. First, the identification of hierarchical oppositions A and B and their reversal to show that the privileged position of (say) A is "mistaken" as A depends upon B as much as B upon A. Second, Derrida, as we have noted, sees a bias in Western philosophy, called the "metaphysics of presence," using a preferred concept as a basis for an explanation of another concept in a duality. For example, identity depends on difference because an object x cannot be identical to itself unless there is (or could be) an object y such that x is different from y. Identity presupposes difference. Neither concept is fundamental because both are mutually dependent on each other. The concept of goodness presupposes the concept of evil. Derrida speaks of *différance* here: each term in a hierarchy defers to the other, being fundamentally dependent upon the other. *Différance* means both to differ, to be distinct and discernible and to defer, to be present while being omitted with the omission having a significance in what is present. As Derrida puts it in his book *Margins of Philosophy*:

différance has no name in our language. But we "already know" that if it is unnameable, it is not provisionally so, not because our language has not yet found or received this *name*, or because we would have to seek it in another language, outside the finite system of our own. It is rather because there is no *name* for it at all, not even the name of essence or of Being, not even that of *"différance,"* which is not a name, which is not a pure nominal unity, and unceasingly dislocates itself in a chain of differing and deferring substitutions. (Derrida, 1982, 26)

Deconstruction seeks to uncover the implicit hierarchies contained in a text and to exhibit suppressed meanings hidden by such hierarchies. As Derrida has said:

To "deconstruct" philosophy, thus, would be to think—in the most faithful, interior way—the structural genealogy of philosophy's concepts, but at the same time, to determine—from a certain exterior that is unqualifiable or unnameable by philosophy—what this history has been able to dissimulate or forbid, making itself into a history of means of this somewhere motivated repression. (Derrida, 1981, 6)

The end result of this deconstruction of Western metaphysics is the discovery of "racism" of a metaphysical shade:

Metaphysics—the white mythology which reassembles and reflects the culture of the West: the white man takes his own mythology, Indo-European mythology, his own *logos*, that is, the *mythos* of his idiom, for the universal form of that he must wish to call Reason. Which does not go uncontested: White mythology—metaphysics has erased within itself the fabulous scene that has produced it, the scene that nevertheless remains active and stirring, inscribed in white ink, an invisible design covered over in the palimpsest. (Derrida, 1982, 213)

Zygmunt Bauman in *Modernity and the Holocaust* (1989) has continued this theme, arguing that modernist reason, whilst not leading inexorably to the Holocaust, provided a metaphysical context for it as part of the self-sustaining rational order of modernity. The gas chambers were driven by the same principles of rational efficiency that guides modern global capitalism (Docherty, ed., 1993, 13).

Deconstructionism has fallen into hard times, for it has been exposed as having "contaminated roots," having a "Nazi as prophet" and even "more disturbing the theory itself, notably its jargon, has been used to obscure anti-Semitism" (Ellingsen, 1991). Heidegger, for example, had a "deep and long lasting commitment to National Socialism" and "blatant anti-Semitism" (Sheehan, 1993, 30).

The godfather of deconstructionism, Paul de Man, wrote some 170 articles for the Nazi-controlled Belgian newspaper *Le Soir* in 1940–1942 (Lehman, 1991), containing "putrid anti-Semitic" passages such as the following:

> If our civilization had let itself be invaded by a foreign force, then we would have to give up much hope for its future. By keeping, in spite of Semitic interference in all aspects of European life, an intact originality and character, it has shown that its basic nature is healthy. What is more, one sees that a solution of the Jewish problem that would aim at the creation of a Jewish colony isolated from Europe would not entail, for the literary life of the West, deplorable consequences. The latter would lose, in all, a few personalities of mediocre value and would continue, as in the past, to develop according to its great evolutive laws. (de Man, 1941 quoted in Derrida, 1988, 623)

De Man wrote shortly before his death, "It's always possible to excuse any guilt" (Ellingsen, 1991). It has been argued by David Lehman, in his book *Signs of the Times: Deconstruction and the Fall of Paul de Man* (Lehman, 1991), that followers like Derrida used deconstructionism to "absolve the master of guilt." In retrospect it is not surprising that this debate has occurred. The French postmodernism of Jean Baudrillard and Jean Lyotard resembles the "end of history" thesis put forward in Germany in the late 1940s and 1950s by ex-Nazis lamenting the defeat of the Third Reich. Further, if there is no real distinction between history and fiction and memory is a creative fabricator, then why not disbelieve the Holocaust? What is the deconstructive basis for rejecting Nazism and anti-Semitism? Why not regard, from a deconstructive perspective, the Jews as the oppressors of the Nazis? If language really is an arbitrary and indeterminate structure, then aren't anti-Semitic propaganda by Goebbels and the *Talmud* interchangeable? These tough questions, which sensible people would regard as a *reductio ad absurdum* of deconstructionism, have not been adequately answered by deconstructionists. For example, Derrida has said in defense of de Man:

> To judge, to condemn the work or the man on the basis of what was a brief episode, to call for closing, that is to say, at least figuratively, for censuring or burning his books is to reproduce the exterminating gesture which one accuses de Man of not having armed himself against sooner with the necessary vigilance. (Derrida, 1988, 651)

In other words, de Man made a small slip; he should have been more careful! It is grimly ironic that a movement such as deconstructionism, which has been a basis for political correctness and the debunking and degrading of Northern European culture and people and the replacement of the classics of "dead white men" with "pop and porno" culture, should be found to have "vicious racism" at its roots (Gross & Levitt, 1994; Windschuttle, 1994).

Deconstructionism, while claiming that the orthodox philosophy of language undermines itself, suffers as well from self-referential paradoxes, as a number of writers have observed (Scholes, 1985; Ellis, 1989; Parks, 1992). If God/Universal Reason and the self are dead, if the author is absent from his text, if society is really irredeemable and truth and meaning impossible, then there would be nothing to say, nothing worth saying, no one to say it and no one to say it to (Bannet, 1989, 1). In claiming that language has no determinate sense, a claim is made that has determinate sense, and even if Derrida is "right" (whatever that "means"), there is nothing determinate to understand in his works. A. Megill in his book *Prophets of Extremity* says: "To interpret the writings of Jacques

Derrida . . . is already to engage in an act of violence, for Derrida contends that his writings are meaningless—that they are, in the literal sense of the word, nonsensical" (Megill, 1985, 259). Elsewhere in his book Megill observes that in Derrida's writing, "distinctions are grandly postulated, yet simultaneously undermined: in a single movement posed, exposed, deposed, reposed—laid to rest in their very postulation. Yet, Derrida manages to spin out page after page as if he were somehow committed to these distinctions" (Megill, 1985, 259). Megill continues: "One is left with a structure of words haunted by the merest ghost of meaning" (Megill, 1985, 260).

Megill believes that thinkers such as Nietzsche, Heidegger, Foucault and Derrida are "aesthetic" in their sensibility, observing "an enclosure within a self-contained realm of aesthetic objects and sensations, and hence also . . . a separation from the 'real world' of nonaesthetic objects" (Megill, 1985, 2) Megill also uses this term to refer to "an attempt to expand the aesthetic to embrace the whole of reality," a tendency to see "art" or "language" or "discourse" or "text" as constituting the most fundamental realm of human experience (Megill, 1985, 2). For example, Nietzsche in *The Birth of Tragedy* sees existence and the world as "eternally justified" only by virtue of their being aesthetic phenomena; the "ontologically creative potential of art" is also seen in various *Nachlass* fragments where "facts" and "things" are created by the interpreter him/herself. Megill interprets Nietzsche as viewing the "death of God," or the decline in the importance of the transcendent, not as an empirical observation as such, but a declaration of negative faith in nihilism of the present (Megill, 1985, 33). Ross Poole in *Morality and Modernity* (1991) interprets Nietzsche's doctrine of eternal recurrence (that time is circular, and that the past will be repeated endlessly) as a metaphor, rather than as a metaphysical doctrine. Eternal recurrence is nihilism taken to its most extreme, of existence without meaning and without the final curtain of nothingness. From this ultimate negation the free spirit affirms existence by willing that it occurs without "needing any other validation than that which is provided by existence itself" (Poole, 1991, 127–128). To take the hard blow of eternal recurrence on the chin without whimpering for moral and metaphysical certainties is to transcend the mentality of the herd and become an overman, *Übermensch*. For Nietzsche and other deconstructionist thinkers the world is a "text" and textuality exhausts the whole of being.

We reject the idea that the "world is text." This view holds in common with analytic philosophy that all thinking is in or with some language. The so-called linguistic turn in philosophy has dominated Western philosophy, both Anglo-American and continental, for at least a century. It is present as well in postmodernist and deconstructionist writings and in a formalist version dominates logic. D. H. Wrong published what has become a famous paper in the *American Sociological Review* in 1961 entitled "The Oversocialized Conception of Man in Modern Sociology" (Wrong, 1961) in which he argued that humans may be social, but they are never *fully* socialized creatures, for following Freud, the social nature of man is a source of conflicts that create resistance to socialization. Biological determinants of human behavior are often ignored or explained away. The Language-View-of-the-World is a product of the oversocialized view of cognition and epistemology. Dallas Willard, in his 1973 paper in *Southwestern Journal of Philosophy* (Willard, 1973), criticized this view as did Rom Harré in *The Principles of Scientific Thinking* (Harré, 1970). Since the "world as a text" view has led to absurdity, the search should be on for an alternative position. We suggest that linguistic abilities are only possible because of ontologically prior cognitive capacities such as the capacity for thought, and that human thought is not the slave of language any more than a driver is the slave of his car (Willard, 1973).

We also agree with Johan Goudsblom, who argues in *Nihilism and Culture* (1980) that it is the truth imperative or "Socratic command" that is directly related to the emergence of nihilism. The conquest of nihilism was an important theme in the nineteenth century and first half of the twentieth century, but had virtually disappeared until the postmodernism debates of the late 1960s to today (ter Borg, 1988). Nihilism is the state of mind in which nothing appears to have value or point, where the world registers Camus' "unreasonable silence" in a vacuum of meaninglessness (Camus, 1955). Absurdly, one must attempt to obtain the unattainable and search for that which cannot be found (Strong, 1976). Goudsblom claims that according to the truth imperative or Socratic command, for one's actions to be right, one must know what is right, they must be based on firm knowledge. But "consistent obedience to this demand . . . can lead to an endless suspension of judgement" (Goudsblom, 1980, xi). Goudsblom says:

The study of nihilsm directs our attention to one of the traps which people have unwittingly set for themselves, that of demanding a degree of certainty which is incompatible with the social standards of rational and empirical criticism that have come to be generally accepted. The dilemma posed by such a demand is not necessarily inherent in the human condition; rather, it is the product of the way in which people have thus far succeeded in conceptualizing and clarifying the problems arising from their social existence. (Goudsblom, 1980, xi–xii)

Nihilism within the romantic traditions of the last century typically dealt with grand themes such as the growing estrangement between science and religion and science and humanity (Crosby, 1988). Nihilism was seen as a disastrous and inevitable development of the logic of the Enlightenment and modernity. This is also how we see the matter in this book. The epistemological crisis is a product of the Enlightenment's desire for the rigorous justification of everything in an attempt to achieve universality. It is Enlightenmentism which has seen the world as an "unreasonable silence" and Enlightenmentism which has produced the ultimate maxim of domination—beloved of sociologists—that "nature is a social construction." As Christopher Manes remarks in an insightful paper on this theme: "We require a viable environmental ethics to confront the silence of nature in our contemporary regime of thought, for it is within this vast, eerie silence that surrounds our garrulous human subjectivity that an ethics of exploitation regarding nature has taken shape and flourished, producing the ecological crisis that now requires the search for an environmental counter-ethics" (Manes, 1992, 340). Manes does not advocate irrationalism but instead supports

the need to dismantle a particular historical use of reason, a use that has produced a certain kind of human subject that only speaks soliloquies in a world of irrational silences. Unmasking the universalist claims of "Man" must be the starting point in our attempt to reestablish communication with nature, not out of some nostalgia for an animistic past, but because the human subject that pervades institutional knowledge since the Renaissance already embodies a relationship with nature that precludes a speaking world. (Manes, 1992, 350)

Rather than advancing yet one more philosophical, metaphysical or theoretical political system, the acceptance of which will allegedly lead us to a changed relationship with nature, we agree with the postmodernists that philosophy, metaphysics and theoretical politics are exhausted. These intellectual activities soak up too much energy, time and creativity that would best be put toward dealing with pressing practical issues of survival, arising from the crisis of modernity—the destruction of cultures and peoples, the social malaise of globalization and the decimation of local environments by the malevolent greed of capitalism and the Soviet experiment in communism. The *big* philosophical projects—such as interpreting quantum mechanics in a realistic manner, a solution to the problem of induction or of the existence of the external world—seem sterile and somewhat pointless once one has participated in practical political and ecological activism. We are very pleased to replace *Analysis, Journal of Philosophy* and *Australasian Journal of Philosophy,* with *Environmental Ethics* and *Population and Environment*; to write about pollution in our local area for a local newspaper, rather than read what some American philosophical guru writes about the existence of universals or of "possible worlds." We find it difficult to become excited about possible worlds, when our actual world is being destroyed.

John Gray, in his superb book *Beyond the New Right: Markets, Government and the Common Environment* (Gray, 1993a), notes that the rejection of progress and unending economic growth, is a theme common to both green thought and traditional conservatism. Gray summarizes the homely truths of the traditional conservatism of Pascal, Montaigne and Hume as follows:

[traditional conservatism] is the idea of human imperfectability and even of the elusiveness (for merely human understanding) of the idea of perfection itself. We cannot know what is the best human society, if only because the goods that make up good human societies are not always combinable or commensurable, and the idea that there is a definite ranking among them is dubiously coherent. For a traditional conservative, human imperfection and its consequences are intractable and permanent, not to be conjured away by the petty and shallow half-truths of any ideology. (Gray, 1993a, x)

Likewise with respect to political life:

political life is not a project of world improvement in which are invested the transcendental hopes of an age without faith. It is instead an almost desperately humble task of endless improvisation, in which one good is compromised for the sake of others, a balance is sought among the necessary evils of human life, and the ever-present prospect of disaster is staved off for another day. (Gray, 1993a, xi)

We have called the position that combines traditional conservatism and green thought *Limitationism*. Gray (1995) has come to reject conservatism given a confrontation with postmodernity and globalism, but we are quite prepared to accept this much of his former position. Joseph Wayne Smith and his co-workers have developed the Limitationist position with respect to environmental and political issues in a number of works, including *The High Tech Fix* (1991a), *AIDS, Philosophy and Beyond* (1991b), *Is the End Nigh?* (Lyons et al., 1995), *Beyond Economics* (Sauer-Thompson & Smith, 1996) and *Immigration and the Social Contract* (Tanton et al., eds, 1996). The position was advanced earlier by Smith in books such as *Reason, Science and Paradox* (Smith, 1986), *Essays on Ultimate Questions* (Smith, 1988a) and *The Progress and Rationality of*

Philosophy (Smith, 1988b). Although Smith had previously been critical of postmodernism and deconstructionism—and with just cause—we have convinced him that his Limitationist project and his dissatisfaction with orthodox logic and philosophy is really a postmodernist concern. Since the term "postmodernism" is up for grabs, we intend to define it to distinguish our position from Derrida and others, taking postmodernism to involve the rejection of universalism, cosmopolitanism, internationalism and globalism in all of its modernist forms and a recognition of *limits*: the limits of growth, understanding, science and tolerance.

Consequently, we are not at present in any "postmodern" age; on the contrary, modernism rules the wider society even if there are pockets of resistance within some university circles. Worse, universalist and globalist dogmas are pushed by the power elites in Western societies with such a ferociousness that a climate of fear is created so that few thinkers oppose these trends. The push to "Asianize" (internationalize) Australia well illustrates this point (Smith, ed., 1991, 1992b). Where old left intellectuals would have seen this attempt to transform a nation and a people as a cruel new form of imperialism, new left intellectuals support this project because they see Australian culture, institutions and the Australian people themselves as flawed and in need of replacement by a "cosmopolitan" culture (used interchangeably, and incorrectly with the adjective "multicultural"—cosmopolitanism does not preserve cultures, it levels them). Thus, they join hands, usually unknowingly, with "new right" elites who also wish to create a global culture, but for the advancement of capitalism and the maximization of profits. As we saw in *Immigration and the Social Contract* (Tanton et al., 1996), a similar situation exists in the United States. The ideological roots of this open borders view of the world is a universalism grounded on the celebration of Enlightenment ideals, especially unending economic growth. Previously we attacked this ideology on the surface; now we aim to destroy its philosophical, metaphysical and political basis. If a truly authentic *multi-culturalism* is to exist—a pluralism that allows ecosystems, cultures, races, ethnicities and communities to not merely survive, but flourish (but not all in the same locality)—then universalism must be overthrown, not only by people in the so-called "Third World," but also by European people.

In this chapter we shall attack universalism in its most abstract form as found in philosophy, epistemology and physics. The arguments to follow will establish a strong form of *Limitationism* supporting the position argued for in the first two chapters of this book. We will see that there are indeed limits to knowledge, truth, science and understanding and hence, contrary to Julian Simon, limits to development as well as limits to growth. The place to begin is with modern Western philosophy itself. We shall see that there are fundamental, self-refuting dilemmas facing both orthodox analytic philosophy and French-based postmodernism. In the final section in this chapter we sketch an alternative direction for cognitive and scientific inquiry.

POSTMODERNITY AND THE DEMISE OF THE TRADITION

The death of Western philosophy has been proclaimed a number of times in philosophy's past but today it is proclaimed loudly and by many. We see on bookshop shelves titles such as A. Cohen and M. Dascal, eds., *The Institution of Philosophy: A Discipline in Crisis?* (1989) and K. Baynes, J. Bohman and T. McCarthy eds., *After Philosophy: End or Transformation* (1993). Both books have been highly influential texts, presenting criticisms of orthodox philosophy primarily from a postmodernist perspective. This trend was given impetus by Richard Rorty's earlier *Philosophy and the Mirror of Nature* (1979). There he argued that the philosophy of mind and knowledge since the seventeenth century has been dominated by the notion of *representation*. The mind is a mirror that reflects reality, and knowledge is concerned with the accuracy of this reflection. Philosophy attempts to be a general theory of representation by which the claims to knowledge by other segments of the culture can be judged. This view of philosophy, Rorty explained, is mistaken; it has failed and is bankrupt and exhausted. Philosophy should be replaced by hermeneutics, an activity that would be more "satisfactory" in continuing the conversation of humanity (Haack, 1990, 1993). Kai Nielsen also believes that we should bid farewell to the tradition and do without epistemology and metaphysics (Nielsen, 1991a, b). Instead we should work in the direction taken by pragmatists and the Frankfurt school philosophers, reconstructing philosophy as a critical theory of society.

D. R. Hiley, in *Philosophy in Question: Essays on a Pyrrhonian Theme* (Hiley, 1988), views Pyrrhonic skepticism not only as a tradition doubting the possibility of knowledge and its desirability, but also as a tradition that has taken a moral stand against the philosophy of Plato, Descartes and Kant.

Hiley sees the postmodern attempt to overcome philosophy as an attempt to release us from philosophy's Platonic illusion that we can escape from the finitude, fallibility and contingency of the human condition. However, if reason is rejected as a tribunal of our beliefs, then we seem immediately to be flung into an "uncritical unreflective acquiescence in the traditional and customary" (Hiley, 1988, 3). This leaves Hiley, and the postmodernists for that matter, with a skeptical challenge. The skeptical challenge that faces an epistemologist is to (1) justify our commitment to reason itself and justify our ultimate commitments and (2) justify our beliefs and values in the face of alternative beliefs and values.

We will argue that an epistemological and philosophical project committed to answering the skeptic's challenge is a mistake: Universal Reason cannot ground itself and if that is what is required, then skepticism, nihilism and relativism are inevitable. We agree with Benson Mates, who in *Skeptical Essays* wrote that "[t]he principle traditional problems [of philosophy] are genuine intellectual knots; they are intelligible enough, but at the same time they are absolutely insoluble" (Mates, 1981, 1). We also agree with George Santayana, who in *Scepticism and Animal Faith* maintained that commonsense is sounder than the special schools of philosophy: "I am animated by distrust of all high guesses, and by sympathy with the old prejudices and workaday opinions of mankind: they are ill expressed, but they are well grounded" (Santayana, 1955, v). In our opinion "dogmatism" and "prejudice" are unavoidable in cognitive life, just as they are unavoidable in daily life. We do not advocate the abandonment of reason and the adoption of a romantic or "new age" irrationalism"—as if these were exhaustive alternatives—we support the view that there are limits to reason and rationality, limits to science and epistemology and that at some point dogmatism is inevitable. The skeptic and the rationalist/objectivist are wrong to suppose that all prejudices are equal: prejudice itself is highly discriminatory and not all dogmas and prejudices are arbitrary or crazy. At least, this is what we will propose, contrary to the Enlightenment project. Our beliefs in the existence of the external world and the rationality of induction are, from a purely objectivist perspective, unjustified—but this does not make them disposable or arbitrary, as Santayana observed.

Skepticism is the other side of the coin of "absolutism," "objectivism" and the ilk, for both the skeptic and the objectivist accept that any claim that is to be accepted as knowledge must be justified or supported without presupposing unjustified beliefs or untested beliefs (Murphy, 1990). Foundationalists have held that there must be some beliefs, basic beliefs, that are not justified by other beliefs if any beliefs are to be justified at all. Knowledge, although defined as justified true belief, is seen as a whole as a hierarchical system. To prevent an infinite regress of justification, basic beliefs need not be self-evident, but their rational acceptance must not depend on other beliefs (Day, 1988; Black, 1988; Clark, 1988). As H. I. Brown in *Rationality* notes, the classical theory of rationality, which is part of this same framework, assumes *universality*: rational results must be universal, necessary and determined by rules (Brown, 1988, 5). Universality means that rational thinkers must arrive at the same solution to a problem given the same data. If they don't, then they must have different data after all and/or are not proceeding rationally (Brown, 1988, 5-6; Newton-Smith, 1981).

Many aspects of the orthodox account of knowledge came under attack in the post–World War II period. The justified true belief account of knowledge, a view held by many philosophers since Plato's *Theatetus* (e.g., C. I. Lewis, A. J. Ayer and Roderick Chisholm), has been seen to be problematic since Gettier's *Analysis* paper of 1963 (Gettier, 1963). There has been a revival of interest in epistemological skepticism (Nozick, 1981), especially from a fallibilist position (Cohen, 1988).[1] There is also a movement of resistance to a belief account of knowledge led by philosophers who reject the implicit and unexamined methodological individualism of this view and the alleged irrelevance of this view to the study of scientific knowledge. Mario Bunge points out, for example, that most scientific statements would not qualify for knowledge on this view because they are at best only "partially true" (Bunge, 1983, 86). It is also quite possible that our ordinary commonsense account of knowledge used in everyday homely discourse is inconsistent (Reldman, 1983).

Due to these problems with ordinary language analysis, many epistemologists, especially within the Popperian school, chose to work on problems within the philosophy of science and the philosophy of logic. However, within these fields many traditional skeptical problems can be restated, especially concerning the justification of the standards of rationality (Johnson, 1975; Kekes, 1975; Barnes & Bloor, 1982; Rescher, 1988; Wedgwood, 1990). Consider, for example, the ancient problem of the *diallélus* and the vicious circle argument (*circulus vitiosus in probandi*) as stated by Sextus Empiricus in *Outlines of Pyrrhonism*:

The Unreasonable Silence of the World

[I]n order to decide the dispute which has arisen about the criterion we must possess an accepted criterion by which we shall be able to judge the dispute; and in order to possess an accepted criterion, the dispute about the criterion must first be decided. And when the argument thus reduces itself to a form of circular reasoning (*diallélus*), the discovery of the criterion becomes impracticable, since we do not allow them to adopt a criterion by assumption, while if they offer to judge the criterion by a criterion we force them to a regress *ad infinitum*. And furthermore, since demonstration requires a demonstrated criterion, while the criterion requires an approved demonstration, they are forced into circular reasoning. (Sextus Empiricus, 1939, 163-165)

There is an extensive literature attempting to deal with this problem (Coffey, 1917; Rescher, 1980b; Moser, 1991; Chisholm, 1982; Amico, 1988; Westphal, 1988). The best-known form of the vicious circle argument occurs, however, as a *tu quoque* argument against rationality: an attempt to justify a standard of rationality will lead to either *circularity*, in which the standard is used to justify itself, *infinite regression*, in which another standard is used to justify the first standard and so on *ad infinitum*, or the *arbitrary cessation* of the principle of sufficient reason (Albert, 1968; Haller, 1974; Apel, 1976; Kekes, 1976; Berkson, 1979).

In the philosophy of science the vicious circle argument arises in the problem of the justification of induction, the method of reasoning to a universal generalization from its supportive instances. Induction "is understood to include all of our rational devices for reasoning from evidence in hand to objective facts about the world" (Rescher, 1980a). It is well known that most attempts to justify induction lead to circularity. For example, consider the work of Harré and Madden in *Causal Powers* (1975) and Roy Bhaskar in *A Realist Theory of Science* and other works (1978, 1979, 1986, 1989). They argue that the intelligibility of the problem of induction depends on prior acceptance of a Humean atomistic ontology. Harré, Madden and Bhaskar accept that traditional approaches to the problem that seek to justify induction inductively or pragmatically or see the problem as a pseudo-problem beg the question against the skeptic. Harré, Madden and Bhaskar see the problem of induction to be: what warrant have we for supposing that the course of nature will not change? Bhaskar argues that Popper cannot escape this problem, because for an observational statement to refute a general law-like statement (or theory), it must be presupposed that the course of nature will not change so that our best falsified theories (Marxism) do not become true. For Bhaskar, induction is only justified when the generalization concerned is a law of nature (although he is prepared to relax the stringency of this condition in everyday situations). Induction is justified because of the acceptance of necessary connections in nature (Smith, 1982, 1984). But how do we know that a realist philosophy of science is true? Presumably on the basis of experience. However, this will not do, as Bertrand Russell observed:

Experience might conceivably confirm the inductive principle as regards the cases that have been already examined; but as regards unexamined cases, it is the inductive principle alone that can justify any inference from what has been examined to what has not been examined. All arguments which, on the basis of experience, argue as to the future or the unexperienced parts of the past or present, assume the inductive principle; hence we can never use experience to prove the inductive principle without begging the question. (Russell, 1978, 38)

Formulated in this way, the problem of induction is meaningful, but absolutely unsolvable within a justificationist framework. Popperians in fact believe this (Swann, 1988). Popper rejects not only the idea of certain truth, but also probable truth and reliable truth as well. For justificationists, a hypothesis has to pass tests and be confirmed to be accepted as rational; if it does not, it is excluded. Falsificationism inverts the traditional epistemological *status quo* insofar "that it relies on expulsion procedures rather than entrance examinations, as the chief way of maintaining academic standards" (Miller, 1982, 22). Hypotheses are subjected to tests once they have been admitted to science. If the hypotheses fail the tests, then they are expelled from science. If they pass them, they are retained—but that is all. The passing of tests does not make scientific hypotheses more probable, it merely means that the hypotheses are not yet rejected. No falsification is conclusive; all falsifications are conjectural and tentative. The best that we can say about hypotheses that have survived critical tests is that (for the time) they are the ones "that we have the least reason to think to be false (Miller, 1982, 40). Strictly though, for Popperians we have no such *reasons*—that is a slide back into orthodox justificationism (Stove, 1991). Popper himself is inconsistent in this respect; he claims that the aim of science is to discover true laws and theories but he also claims that because of the universality of laws and theories, the truth is as improbable as that of a self-contradiction, zero (Stove, 1982, 5). Equally as absurd is Popper's claim that there can be a growth-of-knowledge yet no accumulation of knowledge. In fact, as David Miller, one of the more consistent Popperians, has said: "Scientific knowledge is everything that a classical epistemologist says it ought not to be: it is unjustified, untrue, unbelief" (Miller, 1980, 129). In one sentence, the fate of the Enlightenment program is sealed. Science does not and cannot give us *knowledge* in the traditional sense.

Popperians are usually criticized by philosophers of science using arguments to the effect that their position makes science impossible. It seems to us that if the problem of induction does establish that all that science is left with is unjustified, untrue, unbelief, then Sextus Empiricus would be happy enough. As well, Popper's flight to deductivism doesn't really evade skepticism because in using test statements in premises in falsifying *deductive* arguments, the falsifying argument must have a valid logical form and true premises. But we cannot assert that the premises of *any* argument involving empirical statements are *true*: that is the very point of Popperianism. So if we accept falsificationism, falsificationism is impossible. There are also problems of justifying *deduction* as severe as those facing the justification of induction (Harris, 1969; Capaldi, 1971; Swartz, 1993).

W. W. Bartley's generalization of Popper's epistemology, the theory of comprehensively critical rationalism (Bartley, 1984), also is subject to skeptical paradoxes. Bartley generalizes on Popper's account of rationality to include all rational positions in logic, philosophy, morality and metaphysics. Here rational positions must be highly criticizable, subject to criticism and to have withstood criticism. Critics have attempted to show that comprehensively critical rationalism has some essential component which is uncriticizable (Bartley, 1988a). This is another long-drawn-out philosophical debate. The most important development in this debate, in our opinion, is that Bartley has produced a "paradox" in his own theory, using no assumptions that are unacceptable to him. The proposition that all positions are open to criticism and are not immune to revision is self-refuting (Chipman, 1974; Wertz, 1987). Bartley considers two propositions:

(A) All positions are open to criticism
(B) (A) is open to criticism

and argues as follows:

Since (B) is implied by (A), any criticism of (B) will constitute a criticism of (A), and thus show that (A) is open to criticism. Assuming that a criticism of (B) argues that (B) is false, we may argue: if (B) is false, then (A) is false; but an argument showing (A) to be false (and thus criticizing it) shows (B) to be true. Thus, if (B) is false, then (B) is true. Any attempt to criticize (B) demonstrates (B); thus (B) is uncriticizable, and (A) is false. (Bartley, 1988b, 320)

Bartley takes this argument as merely another logicosemantic paradox, the solution of which is to be found on Tarskian grounds. He doesn't consider the counterargument to this, that a Tarskian solution would rule out the position of comprehensively critical rationalism as ill-formulated because the position must be self-referential to meet the skeptical challenge of the justification of rationality. In any case, Bartley's argument is not a *paradox* as such but is actually a demonstration that comprehensively critical rationalism is uncriticizable and hence necessarily *false*. Look at the argument again: that is exactly the conclusion which is reached. We conclude that Popperianism does not save us from skepticism: if the problem of induction shows that justificationism is flawed, then the problem of deduction shows that falsification in all its forms is flawed as well.

REASON, TRUTH AND REALISM

The epistemological problem of the justification of the standards of rationality or of truth is well illustrated by the realism/antirealism debate (Worrall, 1982; Smart, 1985; Tennant, 1987; Vision, 1988; Almeder, 1989; Walker, 1989; Hand, 1990; Jackendoff, 1991; Wright, 1992). It is difficult to find even uncontested definitions of these positions, let alone resolve the larger philosophical question as to which, if any, of these positions are correct. For example, Michael Luntley in *Language, Logic and Experience* gives the following definition of realism:

Realism is the belief that the world exists independently of our knowledge of it. What this means is that for any propositions P, to the question "Is P true or false?" the world has a determinate answer irrespective of our ability to calculate the answer. (Luntley, 1988, 1)

Dummett's original view was that a philosopher who was a realist about some class of statements asserted that the principle of bivalence held for these statements and that each statement was determinately either true or false (Dummett, 1978; Wright, 1988). Realism stands or falls with the acceptability of classical logic. Yet surely one could be a realist about, say, the external world and yet reject classical logic, perhaps because of a belief in the existence of objective vagueness (Levin, 1990).

The same problem of definitional inadequacy faces many other accounts of realism. For example, the formulation of realism that takes it to be the position that the world is mind-independent is inadequate because reality and mind independence are distinct; those believing in the existence of mental things are surely "realists." Yet this account of realism seems to place mind either outside or at the limits of the world (Heil, 1989). As another example consider Fine's "natural ontological attitude" (Fine, 1984). Fine believes that scientific realism has been destroyed by criticisms, so he proposes that we accept the "natural ontological attitude," a minimalist core position that is neither realist nor antirealist. The results of science should be accepted as *true* in the same way as the evidence of the senses and other homely truths. Realists and antirealists are distinguished by what they add to the core position. But the natural ontological attitude does not resolve the realism/antirealism dispute because realists and antirealists will have a differing account of even homely truths (Musgrave, 1989).

In recent years Hilary Putnam has distinguished between "internal realism" and "metaphysical or external realism." He has said of metaphysical realism:

On this perspective, the world consists of some fixed totality of mind-independent objects. There is exactly one true and complete description of "the way the world is." Truth involves some sort of correspondence relation between words or thought signs and external things and sets of things. (Putnam, 1981b, 49)

Putnam has said about internal realism that

it is characteristic of this view to hold that *what objects does the world consist of?* is a question that it only makes sense to ask *within* a theory or description. Many "internalist" philosophers, though not all, hold further that there is more than one "true" theory or description of the world. "Truth," in an internalist view, is some sort of (idealized) rational acceptability—some sort of ideal coherence of our beliefs with each other and with our experiences *as those experiences are themselves represented in our belief system*—and not correspondence with mind-independent or discourse-independent "states of affairs." (Putnam, 1981b, 49-50)

Metaphysical realism holds that truth is radically nonepistemic, that an epistemically ideal theory could be false, we could be "brains-in-a-vat" and the external world not exist at all. The truth of a theory is never a function of its degree of epistemic support, even in the limit. To refute this position Putnam advanced a model-theoretic argument against metaphysical realism:

So let T1 be an ideal theory, by our lights. Lifting restrictions on our all-too-finite powers, we can imagine T1 to have every property *except objective truth*—which is left open—that we like. E.g. T1 can be imagined complete, consistent, to predict correctly all observation sentences (as far as we can tell), to meet whatever "Operational constraints" there are (if these are "fuzzy" let T1 seem *clearly* to meet them), to be "beautiful," "plausible," etc. The supposition under consideration is that T1 might be all this *and still* be (in reality) *false*.

I assume THE WORLD has [been] (or can be) broken into infinitely many pieces. I also assume T1 *says* there are infinitely many things (so in *this* respect T1 is "objectively right" about THE WORLD). Now T1 is *consistent* (by hypothesis) and has (only) infinite models. So by the completeness theorem (in its model theoretic form), T1 has a model of every infinite cardinality. Pick a model M of the same cardinality as THE WORLD. Map the individuals of M one-to-one into the pieces of THE WORLD, and use the mapping to define relations of M directly in THE WORLD. The result is a satisfaction relation SAT—a "correspondence" between the terms of L and sets of pieces of THE WORLD—provided we just interpret "true" as TRUE(SAT). So what becomes of the claim that even the *ideal* theory T1 might *really* be false?

...The supposition that even an "ideal" theory (from a pragmatic point of view) might *really* be false appears to collapse into *unintelligibility*. (Putnam, 1978, 125-126)

Alternatively put: consider an ideal theory T1 and a model M. Now relative to the interpretation of the language that yields M, T1 comes out true. As T1 is ideal, there can be no constraints that would rule out M as the intended model, so T1 must be true in any intended model. Therefore, T1 must be true. Further reflection led Putnam to conclude that the skeptical argument that we could just as easily account for the existence of the external world by the "brains-in-a-vat" hypothesis is self-refuting:

"[V]at" refers to vats in the image in vat English or something related (electronic impulses or program features), but *certainly not to real vats* [our emphasis], since the use of "vat" in vat English has no [relevant] causal connection to real vats.... It follows that if [the brains'] "possible world" is really the actual one, and we are really the brains-in-a-vat, then what we now mean by "we are brains-in-a-vat" is that *we are brains-in-a-vat in the image* or something of that kind (if we mean anything at all). But part of the hypothesis that we are brains-in-a-vat is that we aren't brains-in-a-vat in the image (i.e. what we are "hallucinating" isn't that we are brains-in-a-vat). So, if we are brains-in-a-vat, then the sentence "we are brains-in-a-vat" says something false (if it says anything). In short if we are brains-in-a-vat then "we are brains-in-a-vat" is false. So it is (necessarily) false. (Putnam, 1981b, 7)

Putnam's arguments have been extensively criticized in the literature, with counterarguments usually advancing the position that his arguments are either questionbegging or irrelevant to the truth of metaphysical realism (Tuomela, 1979; Tymoczko, 1989; Wright, 1994; Forbes, 1995; Smart, 1995). The model-theoretical argument, for example, has been taken by Bailey to merely amount to the tautology that the "mappings for which a theory is true of the world are not mappings for which a theory is false of the world" (Bailey, 1983). Collier has rejected Putnam's argument, claiming that even given Putnam's argument we can *conceive* being a brain-in-a-vat (Collier, 1990). Collier argues that we can conceive possibilities that we cannot truly state; we can conceive that our best theory of the world could be false, even though we could not truthfully state that it is false. A skeptic could argue that Putnam is assuming in his argument a theory of reference where words have their meaning not because of mental states, but because they actually refer to what they do. Putnam says that the brains in the vat can't use language in a referentially meaningful way. The skeptic could accept this: after all, if one is willing to question the existence of the external world, then why should language be sacrosanct? For Davidson (1977), most of what we believe must be true, or otherwise we could never learn or translate a language. Davidson argues that the idea that there is massive error about the world is unintelligible. The skeptic is not disturbed. Perhaps there is *no* world at all; perhaps we never do learn or translate a language; perhaps language is itself epistemologically corrupt, as some postmodernists believe.

Now let us suppose that Putnam is wrong. It doesn't follow from this that all is well with metaphysical realism. Indeed, how can metaphysical realism be rationally chosen as a better theory than skepticism? If ideal rational justification is not sufficient for the truth of metaphysical realism, then what is? Robert Almeder has noted that the orthodox position in epistemology is that because the truth conditions for knowledge are logically distinct from the evidence conditions, the satisfaction of the evidence condition does not entail the satisfaction of the truth condition (Almeder, 1974). In other words, a person can have evidence sufficient for knowledge, without thereby entailing the truth of what he/she claims to know. But if the evidence condition does not entail the satisfaction of the truth condition, then it is a mystery as to how the truth condition could be satisfied at all. Truth becomes epistemically *inaccessible*, and if it is, then so is the truth of metaphysical realism. So Putnam is right after all; metaphysical realism despite its initial intuitive plausibility is self-undermining. This is after all not surprising, for the correspondence theory of truth, which takes sentences to map appropriately onto the objects of a theory–independent world, has been under attack for some time. Quine, for example, has argued that reference is behaviorally inscrutable, except relativized to a theory of translation. He advances a *reductio ad absurdum* argument against the correspondence theory of truth and concludes on the basis of this *reductio* that the thesis of ontological relativity holds: that to which the sentences of a theory refer and that of which the true sentences of a theory are true, are but theory–relative posits, and we can give alternative, equally satisfactory accounts of the referents of the terms of this theory, so there is no fact of the matter as to which account is "correct" (Quine, 1969; Hauptli, 1979). Putnam's argument against metaphysical realism is Quine's argument in reverse: Putnam assumes that there are theory-independent facts as the correspondence theorist requires and shows that the position is self-refuting.

The indeterminacy of translation and the inscrutability of reference are based on the thesis of the underdetermination of theory by data, which in its strong form says that for *any* theory there is an incompatible rival theory that is evidentially equivalent. The weak form of this thesis asserts that there can be such theories (Newton-Smith, 1981, 40). John Wright has argued, convincingly in our opinion, that given the truth of the strong underdetermination thesis, antirealism or verificationism is false, while realism is compatible with the thesis of the underdetermination of theory by data. Hence we have good reason to prefer realism over verificationism (Wright, 1985). But this leads us to a very interesting position: key Quinean arguments seem to undercut both realism and antirealism. Indeed, we can also find antirealism being defended on the basis of the underdetermination thesis as van Fraassen's constructive empiricism is so defended (van Fraassen, 1980). Both realism and antirealism appear to be incoherent.

There is another reason for rejecting both realism and antirealism that is based on the problem of the criterion. Arguments for realism, especially scientific realism, *assume* that nature is inherently ordered and take good explanations as exhibiting the order and patterns of nature. The antirealist operates from a philosophical cosmology which sees nature as much more chaotic, so that our explanations may be pragmatically useful, but they are not likely to be true. Rational choice between these two philosophical cosmologies leads one to the problem of the criterion, for to rationally support either cosmology would seem to *presuppose* the acceptability of either realism or antirealism. We cannot decide which cosmology should be *accepted* without *first* deciding which cosmology is actually *true*. However, we cannot decide which theory of truth is satisfactory without first deciding which cosmology should be accepted. We are back, and we believe, broken, on "the wheel" argument.

THE SPECTER OF RELATIVISM

Relativism or perspectivism has become a popular position in philosophy and the social sciences in the post–World War II period. Various factors would need to be incorporated into an explanation for why this is so, but in general, relativism has gained followers because objectivism, rationalism and realism have been seen as incapable of resolving their core internal difficulties. There has also been a trend, exemplified by environmentalist thought, which has taken science and technology, the crowning glory of the Enlightenment project, to be oppressive and inherently destructive and exploitative of nature (Manes, 1990). Relativism, then, is one response to the failure of the Enlightenment project and the failure of universalism.

Relativism, like realism, has been variously defined. Larry Laudan in *Science and Relativism* defines relativism as "the thesis that the natural world and such evidence as we have about the world do little or nothing to constrain our beliefs" (Laudan, 1990, viii). Barnes and Bloor note that relativisms employ an equivalence postulate, that all beliefs are on par with one another with respect to some parameter such as truth, falsity and justification (Barnes & Bloor, 1982). Relativism may be reached from the perception of the social causation and historicity of beliefs and ideologies (as in the strong program of the sociology of knowledge) (Dawson, 1985; Meja & Stehr, eds., 1990; Fuller, 1993; Slezak, 1994) or it may be reached by the acceptance of antirealism and a coherence theory of truth and/or knowledge. Here we will consider the latter route to relativism.

The coherence theory of truth is a theory about the nature of truth; for a proposition to be true it must cohere with a certain system of beliefs. Its truth consists entirely in such a coherence. Coherence theorists can consistently speak of "true propositions corresponding to the facts" but the "facts" do not belong to an independent ontological realm—indeed the "facts" themselves are determined by further coherence relationships (Walker, 1989). The coherence theory of knowledge holds that "a sentence is warranted if and only if it can be inferred from, or is otherwise supported by, some system of sentences which speakers hold to be true or, what may be called, a system of beliefs." (Young, 1995, 9). According to James O. Young in *Global Anti-Realism*, global anti-realism is "the view that the truth values of all sentences depend on what can be known" (Young, 1995, 1). Realists hold, as we have seen, to *the principle of transcendence*, that truth may transcend what is known or warrantly asserted; global antirealists deny this, along with the principle of bivalence. Young gives a concise outline of the argument for global antirealism in this passage from his book:

The argument for global anti-realism can be summarized in the following terms. The first premiss is common to all sorts of anti-realism: the meanings of sentences consist in conditions which speakers can recognise, which warrant assertion of the sentence. Next comes the premiss that the conditions under which all sentences are warranted are the conditions under which they cohere with a system of beliefs. From these premisses follows the conclusion that the meaning of any sentence consists in the conditions under which it coheres with a system of beliefs. If the meaning of a sentence consists in recognisable conditions, the sentence is true if and only if these recognisable conditions obtain. Global anti-realists conclude that, since all sentences have recognisable truth conditions, anti-realism provides the correct account of the truth conditions of all sentences. (Young, 1995, 25)

The system in question could be an *ideal* one, that is reached at the ideal limit of inquiry. However, this optimistically assumes that all will be well in the end, and falls in any case into the web of the "pessimistic induction" (our best theories have been false, maybe at the limit of inquiry we will find that our best theories then are also false). If this option is not taken, then the problem now for the global antirealist is that a sentence's truth value is dependent upon coherence with a (strictly) false system of beliefs such as contemporary science. One response to this problem is to take the system to be *any* system of beliefs at all. This would commit global antirealism to relativism. Young embraces relativism as a consequence of global antirealism. A sentence is true, relative only to some system of beliefs with which it coheres.

Such a relativism has often been taken to be self-referentially inconsistent (Siegel, 1987; Harris, 1992). Many such arguments along these lines beg the question against the relativist because these arguments assume an objectivist account of truth. Joseph Wayne Smith has argued that if we take relativism to be *relatively true*, it says that objectivism is relatively true according to its own framework. The relativist does not claim that relativism is objectively true because for the relativist there is no such thing as objective truth because truth is relative. So if relativism is relatively true, objectivism is relatively true. Therefore, objectivism is true relative to its framework. But objectivism's framework is objective and truth is objective according to this framework. So objectivism is objectively true after all. But from the objectivist's framework, relativism is objectively false. Relativism if relatively true is therefore objectively false and not relatively true (Smith, 1985). We cannot take objectivism to be relatively false for relativism because this would mean that there is no perspective from which objectivism can be viewed by which it is even relatively true—and there is. Objectivism is at least relatively true, from its own perspective. So relativism is self-defeating.

Cognitive relativism, by virtue of the equivalence postulate, asserts that all beliefs are on par with respect to truth. Well, if this is so then what about systems of beliefs such as Nazism and Holocaust denial? Are not these pernicious ideologies "relatively true" or on par with respect to truth to any of our beliefs? How can relativism reject Nazism and rule it out of court? Young struggles with this problem:

[A]ny set of beliefs which includes the views of Holocaust-deniers and racists cannot be the maximal coherent set of beliefs. The views of Holocaust-deniers, for example, cannot be retained without rejecting the canons of scientific method and inductive logic, to say nothing of a number of highly confirmed historical theories. If scientific method and inductive logic are rejected, a huge body of beliefs will also have to be excluded from a system of beliefs. In short, the hypothesis that no Holocaust occurred is directly or indirectly inconsistent with virtually every belief held by a community. The attempt to preserve it would result in a system which is more likely to [be] minimal than maximal. (Young, 1995, 119–120)

We don't doubt that this is so. But again, the Nazi who was also a rationality skeptic would not be disturbed and would sadistically point out that contemporary postmodern philosophy of science confirms his views. Rejecting the principle of induction after reading Popper's philosophy of science, he may even challenge us to justify our belief that World War II occurred at all. And he would note, if global antirealists believe that a sentence is true if and only if it coheres with a community's system of beliefs, then that is fine by him. It means that Nazism is true, relative to the Nazi community. Further, if cognitive relativism is accepted, then Nazism is on par with any other system of beliefs. This seems to us to be mistaken, so that there must be something wrong with cognitive relativism and global antirealism. This problem also infects the works of Paul Feyerabend. To see this, let us review albeit briefly, Feyerabend's relativist philosophy of science.

For Feyerabend, in a free society there should be a separation of science and state, just as there is of church and state, because:

1. science is but one of other cultural traditions and ideologies;
2. a free society allows "equality" among cultural traditions and ideologies;
3. Western societies' preferred treatment of science violates the "rights" of other traditions.

Feyerabend argues that science is not "better" than other alternative cultural traditions and ideologies such as magic and Aristotelian science. Science is said to be superior to witchcraft or the voodoo cult of the examination of chicken entrails, by being a *rational enterprise*, whereas other traditions such as magic are not. Science is said to have a rational set of rules, a scientific methodology and it is successful as a cognitive enterprise because it is rational and rational because of its method. Feyerabend argues, in *Against Method* (1975), that in exemplary episodes in science's history, not only were the most basic rules of scientific methodology violated (e.g., "reject hypotheses that conflict with the facts," "avoid *ad hoc* moves"), but they had to be violated for scientific "progress" to occur. Then advancing a *reductio ad absurdum* argument, Feyerabend concludes that there is a necessary conflict between scientific methodology on the one hand, and scientific progress on the other, so that science is either progressive or rational, but it cannot be both. There are thus no universal rules of scientific method, even though there are rules that advance scientific progress in particular contexts. Lakatos' methodology does not involve commitment to rational standards, but rather to long-run progressive research programs (Lakatos, 1978). Feyerabend argues that even degenerating research programs cannot be eliminated, because they may make a comeback. Lakatos gave no idea of how much time constituted "the long run," so his methodology of scientific research programs fails to constitute a satisfactory defense of scientific rationalism.

There is no real distinction, in Feyerabend's opinion, between reason and practice because reason is itself a tradition, and reason cannot serve as a criterion for the assessment of traditions. Indeed, traditions simply exist, they are neither "good" nor "bad." This justifies a social order where "*all traditions are given equal rights, equal access to education and other positions of power*" (Feyerabend, 1978, 30), because choosing one position as the basis for a free society is arbitrary. At present, in Feyerabend's opinion, liberalism only allows "*equality of access to one particular tradition*—the scientific, rationalistic tradition of the White man" (Feyerabend, 1978, 76). In Feyerabend's free society, citizens would have a say in fundamental decisions; if the citizens want their state universities to teach voodoo, then that is what they will teach (Feyerabend, 1978, 87).

One would have thought that in a contest between modern science and the voodoo practice of examining chicken entrails or modern African black magic, science would win hands down because the results of science in terms of explanation and technology are immeasurably greater. Let us see Feyerabendians levitate by "magic"! But in response to this sort of challenge his reply in his work is that non-Western traditions have been suppressed by Western scientific imperialism. Otherwise the techniques of primitive people "are often more adequate and have better results than their Western competitors and describe phenomena not accessible to an 'objective' laboratory approach" (Feyerabend, 1978, 104). Some of these phenomena supposedly conflicting with scientific ideas include fire, the domestication of animals, navigation and crop rotation and the breeding of new types of plants.

However, if anything goes, then Nazism is a "goer," irrespective of Dachau and Auschwitz, as Joseph Agassi notes:

The worst example possible: he defends Nazism too, and merely because it may be interesting and intrigue the best of us. Hence, it too, is a contender, etc. The Nazi, too, can have a human quality now and then. And so we can take the beast as just one other animal in our zoo and shed no tear, especially no tear about our past: no one is perfect, not the Führer who hated the Jews, but also not the Jews who now, except for Hannah Arendt, make such a fuss about matters as if they were perfect. (Agassi, 1991, 385)

This is the stark dilemma that contemporary relativism must face. However, as we have argued that relativism is self-defeating, this problem—the Nazi argument—is not our problem. It is though, we contend, a problem for postmodern philosophy which warmly grasps the glove of relativism without first inquiring whether there are sharp objects inside.

We have been concerned so far in this chapter with the question of the cogency of epistemology or the theory of knowledge. Now we shall examine the cogency of contemporary metaphysics and ontology by examining the coherence of the key metaphysical research program of orthodox Western philosophy: *physicalism*. Physicalism has been taken to be a "scientific" metaphysics, a scientifically grounded and technologically informed philosophy. However, we shall see that it too is a failure.

UNIVERSAL METAPHYSICS: PHYSICALISM

The mind-body problem is traditionally stated with a materialist bias: how can consciousness, subjective awareness, the self and the entire landscape of our mental life arise from a biochemical system such as the human brain? Why should certain brain activities be associated with thoughts, purposes, intentions and ideas (Globus, 1973; Madison, 1976; Segal, 1976; Madell, 1988)? If the mind is nothing but the brain and its associated processes, then how is it possible for matter to reflect not only on itself, but on higher mathematical questions—transfinite numbers, paradoxical objects, things that don't exist in the empirical world and things that could not possibly exist? Of all the philosophical problems that one could choose to discuss, the mind-body problem is one which unquestionably has been examined by the best philosophical minds over the centuries. Further, as this problem lies at the intersection of philosophy and science, the best minds from many disciplines have also tackled this problem. An enormous amount of experimental data has been generated by neurophysiology and an understanding of the functioning of the brain has been achieved in such detail that past materialists such as Hobbes, Leucippus, Democritus and Epicurus would be delighted. However the mind-body/mind-brain problem remains unsolved. Moreover, we can find in the literature expressions of despair by respectable philosophers that this problem cannot be solved, that there is a mind-brain impasse (Schlagel, 1977; McGinn, 1989). We are also of this opinion and have argued for it elsewhere (Smith, 1992a). Here, we will argue for this position again, but for a different reason. The mind-brain impasse demonstrates quite clearly a limit to the Enlightenment Project of scientifically understanding the whole of reality. It also confirms the cynical view of orthodox philosophy and knowledge taken in this book.

Physicalism is the most comprehensive metaphysical research program in Anglo-American philosophy. Physicalism, a contemporary version of the materialism of Leucippus, Lucretius and Hobbes, is the view "that the world contains nothing but the entities recognized by physics" (Armstrong, 1978-79, 268). Physicalists are realists about the theoretical entities of physics. They assert that everything in the universe is "wholly constituted by such entities, their connections and arrangements" (Armstrong, 1978-79, 268). Physicalism is thus a variety of *naturalism*, "the doctrine that reality consists of nothing but a single all-embracing spatiotemporal system" (Armstrong, 1978-79, 261). To prevent physicalism becoming an empty doctrine, "physics" in the above definition means "contemporary physics," because physics in the past (or at least some notable physicists) did refer to occult entities that contemporary physicists and physicalists would reject. Physicists such as J. J. C. Smart maintain that (1) the physics of "ordinary matter" is complete and (2) the properties of mind depend on the properties of "ordinary matter" (Smart, 1978, 341; Smith, 1983). J. J. C. Smart and his fellow Australian David Armstrong championed the doctrine of central state materialism, or the contingent identity thesis, that consciousness is a brain process and that in general mental phenomena are really just brain phenomena (Smart, 1963; Armstrong, 1968; Smith, 1984). It is, unfortunately, Australia's best known philosophical export.

Physicalism has undergone a substantial evolution since the early writings of Smart and Armstrong. Some philosophers have found the reductionism of physicalism problematic and have argued for a non-reductive physicalism (Beckerman et al. eds., 1992). A particularly interesting attempt to construct a nonreductive metaphysics is given by John Post in his book *Faces of Existence* (Post, 1987; House & McDonald, 1992). At the other extreme is *eliminative materialism*. Stephen Stich (1983) and Paul and Patricia (Smith) Churchland (Churchland, P. M., 1981, 1988, 1989, 1991; Churchland, P. S., 1980, 1986; Churchland & Churchland, 1980) argue that our best (future) physicalist theory of cognition, based on connectionist artificial intelligence and neuroscience, will not posit mentalistic phenomena such as beliefs and desires. Propositional attitude psychology, or what they call "folk psychology," is in their assessment a flawed theory which will be ultimately replaced or eliminated just as phlogiston theory has been replaced, and belief-talk will wither away just as phlogiston-talk has done. At present the eliminative materialist finds it difficult to avoid using the concepts of folk psychology because the ultimate physicalist framework for cognition does not exist (Hunter, 1995), but in the future—perhaps not too far off—this framework will exist and problematic propositional attitude talk can be eliminated. (For criticisms cf. Everitt, 1981; Gordon, 1986; Madell, 1986; Baker, 1987; Bogdan, 1988; Graham & Horgan, 1988; Cling, 1989; Preston, 1989; Ramsey, 1990; Reppert, 1991; Egan, 1995.) The Churchlands, like most analytic philosophers in this tradition, devote no time at all to discussing the nature of the social and political transformations that are required for such a radical change of worldview. Yet it would not be far from the truth to propose that they look forward to a technocratic society where humans are treated as the meat machines that they are, as we saw earlier in our discussion of technological optimism in chapter 1. Indeed, as Putnam has recognized, consistent eliminative materialism must also junk "folk logic" as well, including the classical notion of truth and reference (Putnam, 1988a). Along with all this goes classical ethics and morality. Down the neurophilosophical sink will also go all concepts of decency and right. This world sounds very much like the world of the Nazi concentration camp where Jews were treated as sheer meat, as mere animal bodies that could be *eliminated* at will. This time, however, humans may be replaced by racially superior cyborgs. Eliminative materialism is a fitting conclusion to the modernist project.

Ignoring these political questions, as philosophers find easy to do, let us consider whether this materialist project is empirically substantiated. Obviously, to cover the ground that needs to be covered we cannot give the first-hand rigorous discussion beloved of American analytic philosophers. That would take an entire book, and frankly there are more important issues to write books about. Consequently, to conserve space we will argue by way of references, attempting to give a broad outline of the general trends in the body of literature with which we are familiar. Why reinvent the wheel?

First, does neuroscience support the Churchlands' position? Is neuroscience heading in the direction that the Churchlands say it is? The answer to this question is definitely "yes"; neuroscience is strongly committed to reductionist principles. We do not see anything particularly wrong in this, anymore than we would condemn a reductionist approach in cardiology. Surely after a lifetime of the lethal combination of thought, high-cholesterol food, cigarettes and good wines, even the philosopher would wish for his heart surgeon to be an expert cardiomechanic if slicing and cutting must be done? So, as the neurosciences are methodologically committed to reductionism it is obvious that a physicalist would see almost all advances in the neurosciences as supporting her worldview.

Having said this though, a look at the neurosciences is a sobering experience for philosophers. The human brain is the most complex piece of organized matter in the known universe. It consists of 10^{10} neurons with their dendrites and axons in networks, where one neuron may be connected with up to hundreds of thousands of other neurons. The idea that there are neural correlates of subjective human mental experience, such that mental phenomena can be individuated and placed in either a one-one or one-many correspondence with brain states, is known as the *correspondence thesis*. This doctrine, which lies behind the identity theory and other mechanistic accounts of mind, can be criticized on philosophical and neurophysiological grounds (Solomon, 1975; Lurie, 1979; Puccetti & Dykes, 1978). One piece of neurophysiological data that raises problems for this thesis comes from Professor John Lorber's studies of hydrocephalus, or water on the brain. He quotes the case of a highly intelligent mathematics graduate who has "virtually no brain." When a brain scan was performed, "we saw that instead of the normal 4.5 centimeter thickness of brain tissue between the ventricles and the cortical surface, there was just a thin layer of mantle measuring a millimeter or so. His cranium is filled mainly with cerebrospinal fluid" (Lewin, 1980, 1232). Apparently there are scores of similar cases in the neuroscientific literature. Ignoring the possibility of an empirical confirmation of Cartesian dualism, this evidence indicates that there is a massive redundancy in the brain, even at the level of functions. The cerebral cortex may not even be the exclusive domain of higher intellectual functions.

There are debates in neuroscience about what the basic "stuff of thought" is, even within a materialist framework. Neurosurgeon Richard Bergland in his book *The Fabric of Mind* (Bergland, 1988) argues that the stuff of thought is not electricity at all, but hormones. He rejects the view that the brain is an electronic computer; the brain is "wet"—bathed in "wet" molecules such as endocrine hormones. "Thinking," for Bergland, can occur in the ovaries and testicles. He believes that the "brain as a gland" hypothesis will revolutionize the study of mental illness. Computational models of mind contribute little toward this study. An ecological model of the brain has also been developed by Gerald Edelman, who sees the brain as being more like an ecosystem than a computer (Edelman, 1978). In an interview Edelman had this to say about computer models of the mind:

There is a tendency in every age to compare the mind with the toys that excite us. Leibniz . . . thought of the mind as a kind of flour mill; at the turn of the century the notion of a telephone exchange was in vogue. In our own time we have got used to describing the mind as a computer and the world as a piece of computer tape . . . . Unlike computers, we understand ourselves and our world in individual, creative, dynamic and unpredictable ways. We create our outer and inner worlds in a context of unceasing novelty and change. Computer codes simply can't encompass the infinite range of human language, imagination and metaphor; our ability to hold intelligent conversation and create works of art . . . our sense of being individuals. (Cornwell, 1993, 4)

Neuroscience is a purely inductive or empirical science and lacks the theoretical laws expected by physicists and chemists. Consequently there is a tremendous amount of theoretical "slack" in this discipline, so empirical findings can be interpreted in a number of ways (Puccetti, 1974, 162). This makes it difficult for a physicalist or an eliminative materialist to give any really convincing empirical arguments for her position because alternative metaphysical frameworks such as dualism and idealism will be able to incorporate and systematize these empirical findings within their own metaphysical worldview.

In any case, it is highly doubtful whether identity theorists will ever be able to empirically substantiate their metaphysical position, even for a phenomenon such as pain. Hall (1977) has noted that in pain perception, the transmission of an injury message through the gate-control region of the brain is contingent not only upon the arrival of the message, but also upon other events in the periphery and central modulating mechanisms and whether the brain has decided to accept the message in the first place. This introduces an indeterminacy into neurophysiological examination:

[O]ne could need to make simultaneous observations of the state of activity of several structures to understand the origin of the actual transmitted message. As the number of independent observing probes multiplies, the destruction they produce increases. It is theoretically possible to provide a particular solution to a particular "N" body problem but not if the means of observation and manipulation forbid the collection of the data needed to establish a causal chain. (Hall, 1977, 367)

Consequently the search for a "pure pain" center has been a failure because it is highly probable that the pattern is individual to the subject under observation because pain perception depends not only on injury but on present and past circumstances. Further, "if each stimulus changes the pattern of activity by adding memory and recall, the code is a shift code which is uncrackable" (Hall, 1977, 368).

If we turn from the neurosciences to examine artificial intelligence (AI), matters are not substantially better for the physicalist. The strong program of artificial intelligence was to construct a suitably complex computer that could be said to have a mental life. This would give strong inductive support to the thesis that human consciousness arises from the brain's information-processing capacity. Let us ignore here the criticisms by cognitive psychologists of the mechanistic view that the brain is a limited capacity information processor (Neisser, 1980). Ignore all of the philosophical criticisms of orthodox AI (Dreyfus, 1979; Palmer, 1984; Dreyfus & Dreyfus, 1986; Born, ed., 1987; Putnam, 1988a; Weinberger, 1988; Mellor, 1991; Penrose, 1994; McClintock, 1995), including the frame problem (Pylyshyn, ed., 1987; Lormand, 1990). Ignore also that functionalism, essentially the position that psychological states are computational states of the brain, has fallen into philosophically hard times.[2] Now Stich and the Churchlands have argued that psychology and folk psychology as well must reduce to our best mind-brain theory or be eliminated or junked. For such a reduction to occur, they require a *theoretical reduction*, where the terms of folk psychology are identified with the terms of our best mind-brain theory so that the mind-brain theory will explain folk psychology, outlining its underlying generative mechanisms, so to speak. Ignore the obvious again, that this is an exceedingly strong demand for reduction, which in the light of the post-empiricist philosophy of science that the Churchlands accept is seldom achieved even in physics. They then argue that connectionism and folk psychology are incompatible, so that if connectionism is the correct theory of mind, folk psychology must be rejected. Let us again see if this is likely.

Orthodox AI is based on the idea, concisely expressed by Kenneth Craiks, that "thought parallels reality through symbolism" (Cowan & Sharp, 1988, 115). The digital computer is a rule-governed symbol manipulator. Conventional AI attempts to explain cognitive capacities by use of representation and formal computation rules. These computers have been very good at tasks involving precise computations and the processing of large quantities of information. For example, a real number X represented by digits taking up the space of a page of this book can be squared to obtain another real number Y in microseconds. No human could perform the same task for any X beyond more trivial examples (e.g., a page of zeros, etc.). However, for more complex tasks, explicit symbolic descriptions may not exist. Connectionism arose because of commonsense knowledge (Tienson, 1987). Connectionism has not been so progressive as to necessitate a Kuhnian revolution in AI (Bechtel, 1993). It is still stuck with many of the deep problems of AI such as the frame problem, the "folding" problem and the problem of relevance. Tienson is of the opinion that no connectionist system so far devised is complex enough to model or simulate *any* aspect of human cognition (Tienson, 1987, 4). Other researchers are not as pessimistic but see the day of autonomous intelligent robots as a long way off (Cowan & Sharp, 1988, 114). As Schwartz puts it, the largest supercomputer systems likely to be developed in this decade

will probably not attain speeds in excess of 1 trillion arithmetic operations per second, which is about one one-millionth of the computation rate that we have estimated for the brain. Today's large magnetic storage disks hold around 1 billion bytes of digital information each, which is roughly one ten-millionth of the storage capacity that we have ascribed to the brain. Even if we assume continuing rapid advances in storage technology and systems equipped with hundreds of storage disks, supercomputers seem unlikely to achieve more than 1 percent of the brain's storage capacity over the next decade. Clearly, the neuroscientist confronts a system whose workings are difficult to approach physically and whose operations are of awesome complexity. (Schwartz, 1988, 127)

All of this is a far cry from the optimistic scientism of the Churchlands. Indeed, even connectist AI is somewhat limited as long as it ignores vagueness and fuzziness. Kosko, in *Fuzzy Thinking*, outlines fuzzy systems that can be built which implement "rules of thumb" and heuristics, where no mathematical model of the process in question is needed at all (Kosko, 1994). Consequently a model-free estimation can be given. The "fuzzy approximation theorem" (that a fuzzy system can approximate a continuous system as accurately as desired) says that

you can get rid of all the books on physics and chemistry and biology and economics and replace them with new books that have fuzzy systems where equations used to be. (Kosko, 1994, 170)

Kosko quotes the case of Professor Michio Sugeno of the Tokyo Institute of Technology, who has built a fuzzy system that can stabilize a helicopter in flight after it has lost a rotor blade, which no human system and no known mathematical system can do (Kosko, 1994, 170). In the light of philosophical arguments about the long-unsolved problem of the heap (sorites argument) (Priest, 1991), the adoption of a fuzzy logic to model real-world processes seems unavoidable. There is no question that most psychological phenomena are vague.

The essential vagueness of psychological phenomena refutes the idea advanced by a younger Putnam that the psychological states of a human being are Turing machine states or disjunctions of Turing machine states (Putnam, 1960). Turing machines, even with an infinite tape, can only be in exactly one state at a time; they are wholly discrete. Now ignoring for the moment the paradoxes of quantum mechanics, even if it were true that the material world could be conceived in this way, psychological phenomena cannot (Putnam, 1992). The undeniable vagueness of psychological phenomena such as beliefs defeats the correspondence thesis (defined earlier) (Solomon, 1975; Lurie, 1979; Puccetti & Dykes, 1978). The correspondence thesis is presupposed by the Turing machine model of mind. But this argument in itself is hardly decisive. The eliminative materialist could argue that the irreducible vagueness of psychological phenomena constitutes a reason for junking them. However, there are more general arguments that can be brought to bear against mechanism.

First, by Chaitin's incompleteness theorem there are information-theoretic limits of formal systems and fundamental limits to our ability to generate mathematical truths from programs (Chaitin, 1987, 1990a, b; Bennett & Landauer, 1985; Stockmeyer & Chandra, 1979). Second, there are computationally intractable physical problems. Many physical systems are "computationally irreducible," so in some cases questions about the systems can only be answered by potentially infinite computations (Wolfram, 1985). Third, it has been proven that there exists a computable and continuous function $f(x, y, z)$ such that the solution $u(x, y, z, t)$ is continuous but not computable and the value $u(0, 0, 0, 1)$ is a noncomputable real number (Boykan Pour-El & Richards, 1979, 1981). Fourth, "no Turing machine can compute a function whose domain and range are the set of all real numbers, since the set of real numbers in uncountably infinite and the set of all finite strings of symbols (Turing machine tapes) is countably infinite" (Cleland, 1993, 305, 1995; Horsten & Roelants, 1995; Shapiro, 1981). Hence, at least from the perspective of received mathematics, no Turing machine can compute any function that maps the reals onto the reals. The number of functions from the natural numbers onto the natural numbers is, according to received wisdom, also uncountably infinite. Therefore, there are number-theoretic functions which are not computable by any Turing machine. Fifth, as Hillis has argued, models of the computational universe of computing science are vastly different from models of the physical universe by physicists (Hillis, 1982). According to Hillis, orthodox computing science is lacking locality, symmetry and invariance of scale, factors that give the laws of physics their explanatory power. For example, outside of quantum mechanics, the effect that one event has upon another in the physical world tends to decrease with the distance in space and time. But in computation, arbitrarily small events (such as a virus destroying memory) can have decisive or overwhelming effects, so one memory location is just as easily influenced as another. There is, Hillis notes, no principle of distance. So it follows that the mechanistic attempt to regard the whole of reality as a Turing machine is deeply flawed. Finally, the mechanistic paradigm underlying physicalism is under attack from a number of directions. There is the difficulty of giving a mechanistic account of the origin of life on earth (Shapiro, 1977; Fry, 1995), problems of such a magnitude that the molecular geneticist Frances Crick (1981) and cosmologists Fred Hoyle and Chandra Wickramasinghe (1981) have reviewed Svante Arrhenius' panspermist hypothesis, that life came from other worlds. There is also the challenge from chaos theory and complexity theory which seems to support a nonreductionistic metaphysics, one that allows genuine emergence (if only at the property level) to occur (Griffin, ed., 1988; Gleick, 1989; Nicolis & Prigogine, 1989; Davies, 1991; Waldrop, 1992; Lewin, 1993).

The idea that there is an irreducible pluralism in the world is a view that has been championed by John Dupré in *The Disorder of Things: Metaphysical Foundations of the Disunity of Science* (1993) and also by Crane and Mellor as a consequence of their argument that physicalism is ill-defined and that no nonvacuous interpretation is true (Crane & Mellor, 1990; Robinson, 1991; Crane, 1993; Pettit, 1993, 1994, 1995; Daly, 1995). It is arguable that Hilary Putnam is also arriving at such a position in his recognition of the failure of natural metaphysics, the embarrassment to materialists of quantum mechanics (quantum mechanics in Putnam's opinion has no defensible realist interpretation at all) and his criticism of the One-True-Metaphysical-Theory view, held by metaphysical realists (Putnam, 1982, 1984). Philosophical pluralism is implicit in Putnam's internal realism. There is, however, a deeper argument for such a pluralism.

The "underdetermination of theory by data" thesis seems to be generally true of metaphysical theories. There is an essential argumentative slackness in philosophy in general and metaphysics especially, such that empirical considerations alone seldom *decisively* refute any metaphysical thesis. It is possible to pile problem upon problem to try to get a balance of reason against a position, as we have attempted to do in this chapter, but it is most unlikely that any of one's opponents would ever be convinced. For example, ignore all of the conceptual problems facing the thesis of psychophysical identity (Lowe, 1981; Swinburne, 1982). Suppose that a contingent identity of the mind and the brain was asserted. Would it follow that physicalism or materialism was true? Not necessarily—as a few philosophers have noted from time to time, the inverse *idealistic* identity thesis is also established—if the mind is identical to the brain, then the brain is also identical to the mind (Butler, 1972). This has never been taken to be a problem by materialists because they have a prior dogmatic conviction of faith that materialism is right, that it *must* be true. We have seen this conviction displayed by the Churchlands—if connectionism and folk psychology conflict, then so much the worse for folk psychology—junk it! But why not junk connectionism and neuroscience? Why should we accept them as giving us the One-Correct-View-of-the-World? Because they give us deeper, more comprehensive explanations of reality? But why should that be taken to be a criterion of either truth or rationality? Why choose deep and comprehensive explanations of reality? Is this because reality is deep and comprehensive? How do you know? We certainly believe that reality is "deep," but this metaphysical belief requires a defense, and physicalists never give it.

Physicalism is the ruling ideology today among Anglo-American philosophers. There have been some valiant attempts to break this hegemony and defend some nonmaterialist metaphysical theories. John Foster, for example, has contributed two outstanding books in this direction, *The Case for Idealism* (Foster, 1982) and *The Immaterial Self* (Foster, 1990). *The Immaterial Self* is a defense of the Cartesian dualist conception of mind, defending the theory of Descartes that the mental is ontologically separate from the physical (Averill & Keating, 1981; Richardson, 1982; Dilley, 1988). *The Case for Idealism* is just that, an argument that ultimate reality is wholly nonphysical so physical realism is not merely false, but incoherent. T. L. Sprigge in his book *The Vindication of Absolute Idealism* (1983) argues for a psychicalist view of reality in the tradition of Spinoza, Leibniz and Whitehead: "reality . . . is composed of innumerably momentary centres of experience related so as to make subsidiary wholes of various sorts and ultimately the universe" (Sprigge, 1983, 3). We doubt whether in the foreseeable future idealism will get a toehold in Anglo-American philosophy departments. Physicalism is entrenched because physicalists are entrenched. When they die out, perhaps other traditions may be able to flourish. However, the domination of physicalism in Anglo-American philosophy has *not* been because the position has been supported by outstanding logical arguments. In fact, physicalism is not even consistent with modern physics, as we shall now see.

POSTMODERN PHYSICS: QUANTUM MECHANICS AND THE PARADOXES OF REALITY

Bertrand Russell said in his *Autobiography* that physics had driven him to a position "not unlike that of Berkeley, without his God and his Anglican complacency" (Russell, 1967, 233; Nelson, 1982). Elsewhere Russell puts his finger precisely on the metaphysical paradox that quantum mechanics generates:

What we can say, on the basis of physics itself, is that what we have hitherto called our body is really an elaborate scientific construction not corresponding to any physical reality. The modern would-be materialist thus finds himself in a curious position, for, while he may with a certain degree of success reduce the activities of the mind to those of the body, he cannot explain away the fact that the body itself is merely a convenient concept invented by the mind. We find ourselves going round and round in a circle: mind is an emanation of body, and body is an invention of mind. Evidently this cannot be quite right, and we have to look for something that is neither mind nor body, out of which both can spring. (Russell, 1958, 227)

Russell had hoped to have found a resolution of this ontological paradox in his theory of *neutral monism*, but this theory has no champion today and has already become an historical curiosity. Russell's problem has been addressed by Michael Lockwood in *Mind, Brain and Quantum* (Lockwood, 1989). Lockwood notes that philosophers who have examined the mind-body problem have tended to regard matter "as having a conceptual solidity to match its supposed literal solidity" (Lockwood, 1989, ix). The compromise must be on the side of the mind; matter is unproblematic. But quantum mechanics "has robbed matter of its conceptual quite as much as its literal solidity. Mind and matter are alike in being profoundly mysterious, philosophically speaking" (Lockwood, 1989, x). We wish to go further than Lockwood: quantum mechanics has shown that matter is *inscrutable*, perhaps not physically, but certainly philosophically. Again, we cannot argue for this position firsthand and again we must make extensive references to the technical literature.

The difficulties of giving a realist interpretation of quantum mechanics are well known (Wigner, 1970, 1973; Folse, 1978; Trigg, 1980; Cartwright, 1983; Brown, 1985; Daniel, 1989; Mohanty, 1989). A. H. Goldman in *Empirical Knowledge* says that there is "no single, coherent physical analogue for the various models of the theory, from which we could infer to the nature of the subatomic realm" (Goldman, 1991, 245). He notes that the discontinuities in the space-time trajectories (quantum jumps) already violate classical intuitions about the nature of a particle, so a realist interpretation of quantum mechanics was problematic even at this point (Stace, 1932, 381). Schrödinger's wave mechanics did not help realism because the wave function ψ is complex rather than real and in any case for an n-particle system it must be located in 3n dimensional space (Priest, 1989). The collapse of the wave function upon measurement also introduces discontinuities which realists find metaphysically problematic (Goldman, 1991, 246). Wave-particle duality, if it cannot be eliminated, "itself blocks a coherent physical model of the entire domain of quantum mechanics. Particles and waves have incompatible properties" (Goldman, 1991, 246). Further, given both the wave-particle duality and the quantum indeterminacies, "microentities have . . . both too many (incompatible) and too few (defining) properties to fit a single, coherent physical model" (Goldman, 1991, 249). Scharf has also concluded from a study of the quantum-mechanical measurement problem that "quantum mechanics is inconsistent with the program for the unity of science" (Scharf, 1989, 623). Paul Davies, however, goes even further and claims that

> the concept of an independent reality "out there" has been discredited. We see in its place a shifting world of uncertainty in which apparent realities can come and go in seemingly random fashion, and in which even the observer himself has dissolved into something evanescent and insubstantial. The central conclusion is that if reality has any meaning at all, it is only in the context of the observer and the observation itself. There is a kind of continuous creation—a new world every moment—brought into being by our own conscious awareness. Or so it seems. In a world full of uncertainty, who can be sure? (Davies, 1979, 158)

Let us now take up some of these points. First, we seem to be stuck with wave-particle duality whether the Copenhagen interpretation of quantum mechanics is accepted or not. John Gribbin in *Schrödinger's Kittens* notes that in the famous two-slit experiment, experiments have been done with single photons with both holes open (Gribbin, 1995, 5). When millions of photons are allowed to hit the screen, one at a time, the familiar wave inference pattern is generated. A single photon seems to have gone through both holes at once and placed itself so that it makes its own contribution to the overall interference pattern rather than the situation occurring when all photons follow the same path and end up hitting the same spot on the screen. The experiment has been repeated with atoms and the same results have been obtained. Roger Penrose in *The Emperor's New Mind* accepts that the particle "is" indeed in two places at once. On this view, the particle has actually passed through both slits at once (Penrose, 1989, 252). Penrose recognizes that this is logically paradoxical but believes "that the resolution of the puzzles of quantum theory must lie in our finding an improved theory" (Penrose, 1989, 298). This problem is unlikely to be solved by a new theory such as Maxwell's quantum propensiton theory (Maxwell, 1972, 1976a, b, 1982, 1988) because it is an ontological and logical problem generated by experimental data: quantum entities seem to have logically incompatible properties, coexisting simultaneously. In 1992 Japanese researchers observed individual photons exhibiting simultaneously wave-like and particle-like properties (Gribbin, 1995, 115). This problem is not resolvable by quantum logic (Butrick, 1971; Gardner, 1971), and only trivially by paraconsistent quantum logic, for the problem is not how to avoid deducing every proposition from quantum mechanics, but of making metaphysical sense of the situation (Smith, 1990a, b).

Orthodox quantum mechanics views the "collapse of the wave function" as follows. If an electron (for example) is not being observed, it has no precise position, it is spread out in an area of space, and when a measurement is taken, the wave collapses to a single point. Consider a box in which a single electron is placed. According to quantum theory, its quantum wave spreads uniformly through the box. If an impenetrable screen divides the box into two separate parts, the quantum wave is said to be in both chambers. But if the electron is a particle, it is in one or the other chamber. On observation, the electron can be seen to be in one particular chamber. According to quantum mechanics, the quantum wave collapses or disappears from the other chamber, even if the electron was not in that chamber. Prior to observation it is as if the electron didn't really exist, but two potential "electrons" were in each chamber, and the act of observation brought them into being. The chambers could be taken an arbitrary long distance apart and the collapse of the quantum wave would still occur. How does observation do this? How can merely receiving light rays from the experiment into your eyes cause the wave function to collapse? If unobserved electrons are merely potential, how does the world maintain its macroscopic structure? Why doesn't an unobserved world just fall apart? If the only possible observers were to be found on Earth, why don't unobserved stars cease to exist (Mermin, 1981, 1985, 1990; Wigner, 1963)? In a paper too technically complex to summarize here, Fine (1970) has argued that certain macroscopic observables can take on no value whatsoever. Consequently, "no laboratory observations can be cited in support of the quantum theory" (Fine, 1970, 2787). This is indeed a paradoxical situation for a theory that is supposed to offer a foundation for physical reality.

Closely related to the measurement problem is the superposition problem. The result of a measurement is a superposition of vectors. Each vector represents the observed quantity as having one of its possible values. Why, then, do we observe only *one* value? In Schrödinger's cat experiment, the unobserved cat is in a superposition of states, one wave form consisting of "dead cat" and the other wave form consisting of "live cat." If an observation is performed, the cat will be observed to be either alive or dead. But what happens when no one observes the box? Replace the cat by a person. The person will report being alive at all times but quantum mechanics requires that the person was in a live-dead superposition before the box was observed. This paradox has also generated a substantial literature (Krips, 1987; Selleri & van der Merwe, 1990). Putnam has proposed that there is no observer-neutral truth about the matter "is the cat alive or dead?" (Putnam, 1981a). But the idea that there is no observer-neutral truth about the matter "is the cat alive or dead?" is bizarre and unacceptable. Replace the cat by an explosive device, so that if the radioactive particle decays, the entire box is blown to pieces. We sit at a safe distance and watch the (*sealed*) box. Suddenly the box is blown to pieces. Is there really no observer-neutral truth about this?

In the many-worlds view, the universe splits into two parallel universes, one with a live cat and the other with a dead cat (Everett, 1957; DeWitt, 1970). The other universes are inaccessible, with their own space-time. Countless times each second the universe is duplicated. This solution substitutes one mystery for another: it has never been explained how all of this happens and in fact it can't be explained because the universes are by definition inaccessible. We would be better off accepting the mysteries of the original problem. One could justifiably attempt to eliminate the observer from quantum mechanics altogether as the *spontaneous decoherence* position does (Zurek, 1991; Mulhauser, 1995). This will still leave us with another problem, perhaps the most puzzling of all, namely the nonlocalism arising from Bell's work (Vandegrift, 1995).

Perhaps one is prepared to live with the mysterious correlations involved in the nonlocality experiment. Perhaps superluminar communication has not occurred, and the principle of causality, that it is impossible to change the past, is not violated. However, there are other problems which cannot be evaded. One problem is that the quantum theory is inconsistent with special relativity, and the resolution is not made in quantum field theory (Sachs, 1982; Maxwell, 1985). Another problem is that the usual interpretation of ψ as representing the best possible description of the state of a single particle and the Heisenberg uncertainty principle lead to contradiction (Davidson, 1965; Robinson, 1969; Prugovecki, 1982). As well, the standard quantum limit for monitoring the position of a free mass can be breached (Yuen, 1983; Caves, 1985; Maddox, 1988). But the Heisenberg uncertainty principle is a direct logical consequence of the fundamental principles of quantum mechanics. If it can be breached, then quantum mechanics is false.

There is also something of a conceptual clash between quantum mechanics and classical chemistry. Woolley has argued that from the perspective of quantum mechanics, if a molecule is observed in an eigen state of its associate molecular Schrödinger equation, then the classical concept of molecular shape is inappropriately ascribed (Woolley, 1976, 1978; Weininger, 1984). The use of atomic and molecular orbitals in chemistry is strictly inconsistent with quantum mechanics and is certainly not derived from it (Scerri, 1989, 76). As Scerri notes, "the statement of Pauli's principle in terms of quantum numbers for individual electrons of an atom is outdated, and yet it forms the basis for the electronic configurations of atoms used routinely in chemistry. Only the atoms as a whole can be said to possess meaningful quantum numbers. The holistic aspect of quantum mechanics is denied by the use of electronic configuration" (Scerri, 1989, 76). This problem of systematic coherence also raises a difficulty for the physicalist unity of science program because false theories are not supposed to be reducible to true theories (Primas, 1981; Hall, 1986; Scerri, 1991, 1994, 1995). It is likely that both quantum mechanics and classical chemistry are false though, indicating that today's physicalism is also false. For example, according to the chemistry textbooks, a nitrogen atom cannot form more than *four* bonds. Chemists in West Germany have discovered a nitrogen compound that has *five* bonds and is extremely stable. The new compound is made from a chemical called tetrakis (phosphine gold) ammonium tetrafluoroborate, which consists of a nitrogen atom surrounded by four atoms of gold. It was formed when (triphenylphosphine) gold tetrafluoroborate was added to nitrogen. The same chemists have proved that carbon can form six bonds to gold (Baggott, 1990; Emsley, 1990). Molecules have been made with phosphorus and carbon atoms which contravene all conventional bonding theories, having the electrons closer together than these models predict (Emsley, 1989; Hall, 1988).

It is our opinion that the present evidence justifies the position that matter is *inscrutable*, at least at the depth of understanding required for the physicalist unity of science program. The difficulties cited above may be resolved in the future but this is most likely to involve a mathematically more complex theory than both quantum mechanics and relativity. It may be necessary to abandon the concept of space-time or see it as a macroscopic concept (Zimmerman, 1962). If there is to be a theory of everything, it is likely to be virtually an exercise in pure mathematics and one perhaps incomprehensible to us today. At the present state of knowledge it is absurd to make the arrogant predictions that physicalist reductionists and eliminative materialists have made. It is inconsistent with the skeptical humility that most working physicists have, for they are only too aware of the problems, paradoxes and limitations of their discipline. Physicalism, however, is not *scientific* philosophy; it is an ideology of science worship, which dogmatically wishes to reduce or eliminate all which does not fit its simple, neat and tidy worldview. Whatever can be said about "reality," it is far from simple and is messy and chaotic. (Our justification for believing this is based precisely on the failure of simplistic reductionist programs.) Whatever "reality" is, it has not been classified within the confines of some metaphysical theory or world view. Like the great idealist world views which have crumbled before it, physicalism will likewise crumble. Indeed the process of decay has already begun. So will die possibly the last great experiment in philosophy of the building of a world system. Unlike the theist and idealist systems before it, physicalism seemed to be an explication of the metaphysics of science itself. But it has been destroyed, essentially by advances in science itself. Philosophy needs to bury the cruelly impossible task of searching for an epistemological cosmology that will coherently account for the whole of reality.

In conclusion, it can be seen that even given the technological sophistication of modernity, the modernist has failed to produce a unified system of the world which Enlightenment thinkers had hoped for. We certainly know more about the world in a technical sense than the premodernists did, but in terms of arriving at some ultimate coherent metaphysical *Weltanschauung*—we are no more advanced. Indeed, at the deepest level we have no metaphysically coherent picture of reality at all. This, we believe, refutes the epistemological and scientific optimism of Julian Simon (et al.) at the most basic possible level. There are clearly limits to science, limits to knowledge and limits to understanding. What is the philosophical significance of this? That is the subject of the concluding section.

SEARCHING THROUGH THE RUINS

We have argued in this chapter that the Enlightenment Project is bankrupt, that the idea of the creation of a universal culture is self-defeating and in any case is now collapsing. This thesis has recently been defended by John Gray in his book *Enlightenment's Wake* (Gray, 1995). There he argues that all of the intellectual traditions of modernity are variations on the Enlightenment Project of the creation of a universal culture. Gray, in contrast to his previous book *Beyond the New Right* (Gray, 1993a), argues that traditional conservatism is also dead, killed by the hand of neoliberal ideology and policy. Conservatism across the world has become another variant of the Enlightenment project's universal culture, civilization and reason (Gray, 1995, 87). For Gray "neither a return to a pre-modern world view nor the post-modern affirmation of a distinctively modernist project are viable historical options for us" (Gray, 1995, 146–147).

What, then, is the answer? Gray proposes first an abandonment of the universalizing project of Western cultures and an acceptance of pluralism. This may involve allowing new sovereign states or ethnostates, reflecting an underlying national culture to come into existence. This in turn requires an abandonment of internationalism, to be manifested in a resistance to projects such as GATT. Gray also proposes that we abandon the humanist conception of the privileged place of mankind in nature and he looks hopefully to the growth of another way of thinking "found in some varieties of poetry and mysticism" (Gray, 1995, 184) which may assert itself against the Universal Reason of the West. He suggests that hope may lie with Oriental people, who have modernized but not Westernized, but he admits that these cultures may have "nevertheless assimilated too much of the Western nihilist relationship with technology and the earth for a turning in man's relationship with the earth to be any longer a real possibility" (Gray, 1995, 184). Joseph Wayne Smith in *The High Tech Fix* (Smith, 1991a) has argued that this is indeed so. Japanese economic imperialism and Asian capitalism are equally as oppressive as the Western liberal capitalism they have transcended. Gray has not given us any alternative to the Enlightenment Project.

We believe that a substantial contribution to this issue was made by Nicholas Maxwell's *From Knowledge to Wisdom* (Maxwell, 1984). Maxwell argues for an intellectual revolution that will affect to some extent all branches of scientific and technological research and scholarship. It will also have profound effects on the education system. Maxwell's proposed revolution is not a revolution about knowledge of the world, but a change in our overall philosophy, aims and methods guiding science and other intellectual activities. The search for knowledge for knowledge's sake (the philosophy of knowledge), the satisfaction of intellectual curiosity, the pursuit of the eternal "how" and "why" needs to be replaced by a quest for personal and social wisdom and the resolution (if possible) of problems of living (the philosophy of wisdom). We have no such tradition at present and Maxwell argues that many of our social and global problems remain unsolved because of the absence of such a tradition.

At present, rational inquiry in the sciences is geared toward the production of knowledge, which can be applied to solve various problems of living. The aim of science, though, remains to *understand* the world, not to change it, although applied science has changed the world, sometimes for the better and sometimes for the worse. Maxwell regards it as damagingly irrational to give intellectual priority to the task of producing knowledge for knowledge's sake in a world as dangerous, unstable and threatened as our own. Intellectual priority should be given to the task of articulating the nature of our social and global problems, devising solutions and developing proposed solutions. He does not claim that having a tradition of wisdom is a *sufficient* condition for solving our problems of living and the crisis of civilization, but it is, he argues, a *necessary* condition.

Maxwell's basic epistemological objection to the philosophy of knowledge is that it violates the most elementary conceivable requirement for rationality; to state one's problems clearly and critically examine *all* of the proposed solutions. The basic problem that inquiry must solve, according to the philosophy of knowledge, is to promote human welfare. But to do this the primary problems which must be solved are problems of action, and technical and scientific problems are secondary. But according to Maxwell, the philosophy of knowledge does not give intellectual priority to the problems of life. Not only is this inconsistent, but this cognitive bias has undesirable consequences for the general quality of human life. It means in essence that the problems of life, the challenging problems of human existence, are never tackled full-on or by the best minds at the depth at which these problems deserve to be addressed.

The philosophy of wisdom, by contrast, gives "absolute intellectual priority to our life and its problems, to the mystery of what is of value . . . and to the problems of how what is of value is to be realized" (Maxwell, 1984, 64). Wisdom is the desire and the capacity to discover what is of value in life—and what is not—for oneself and for others. Wisdom requires knowledge, why it is worthwhile to have knowledge at all. The philosophy of wisdom is about living wiser, with wiser institutions and social relations in a wiser world. The modern world is technologically sophisticated and knowledgeable, but unwise—for reasons Maxwell lists, but which have also been given in this book. If humanity destroys civilization, then modernity will be seen by the last survivors (for however long they live) as a mistake, a folly and a curse.

John Kekes in a critical review of Maxwell (Kekes, 1985) interprets Maxwell as claiming that the philosophies of knowledge and wisdom are rival interpretations of the Enlightenment program. Maxwell has replied to Kekes (Maxwell, 1986) pointing out that his position is more than a mere advocation of change in the aims and methods of science. It is a radical transformation of the Enlightenment Project itself. Kekes argues that the Enlightenment Project is indefensible and must be rejected because the relativity of values and diversity of cultures indicates that there is no highest or best life for human beings. Enlightenmentism, Kekes argues, is only one particular ranking of the plurality of values but there are others.

Kekes' argument is successful against an internationalist or universalist interpretation of Maxwell's wisdom, but it is a mistake to suppose that Maxwell is advocating an Enlightenment imperialism: the point of his book is exactly the opposite of this. Maxwell does believe that many of our global problems have arisen because of a breakdown in cooperation during the course of human history. Tribal cooperation was easy; for the tribal cooperation of humanity on a global scale, the academic enterprise itself must become an institutional substitute for the tribal discussion of humanity. This internationalism, based on the ideals of the "brotherhood of the races" and the "unity of mankind," is highly dubious in our opinion and was extensively attacked by some of the present authors in *Is the End Nigh?* (Lyons et al., 1995).

One of our major departures from Maxwell relates to the role of reason in the philosophy of wisdom. Reason understood in a theoretical sense is often impotent in the political sphere, especially regarding the big environmental issues. We find that tough issues are increasingly put in the "too-hard basket," or insanely, the very opposite direction to ecological sustainability is taken. Consider once again the case of population growth. As long as the human population continues to grow, energy and resource conservation is ultimately futile. At a growth rate of 1.6 percent per year, a 25 percent reduction in resource use will be eliminated in just over eighteen years.

It would make sense to limit population growth—especially in the West. Australia, for example, is one of the worse offenders per capita for the production of greenhouse gases. It would make sense to limit Australia's population growth rate, at least through controlling immigration (Australia's immigration rate proportional to the population is also one of the highest in the Western world). However, something of a new religion has emerged, supported by the New Right, the New Left and sadly many Greens, where immigration is regarded as a sacred object of devotion beyond rational examination. It is very difficult to argue the case for limiting immigration; even if one could convince the intelligentsia, one still has to face a powerful ethnic movement and big business. The Australian economy is very much geared around increasing numbers of people: it fuels the building industry and keeps housing prices up making the sharks in the real estate business rich. No amount of reasoning or argument can resolve this conflict—especially since the major Australian political parties have bipartisan support for high immigration and do not put the matter on the public agenda—even though survey after survey shows the Australian people's opposition to high immigration (Betts, 1991). If this problem of living cannot be solved short of a bloody revolution or civil war, then how can Australia and other nations, especially large nations such as the United States, make more radical changes such as moving away from consumerism and becoming a conserver society (Trainer, 1995a)? What if the message of environmentalism came down to this: that the capitalist economic system *cannot* ensure ecological sustainability, that this system is necessarily committed to unending economic growth? What then? What happens in the final showdown between the forces of malevolent greed and the forces of life? We have shown in our book *Beyond Economics* (Sauer-Thompson & Smith, 1996) that the moneypower is totally ruthless and is not bound by any ethical respect for life or by any logic other than the economic rationalism of the maximization of profit (or market domination). This, we believe, is one of the strongest grounds for believing that Enlightenmentism is dead: theoretical philosophical reason has lost its binding impact (if it ever had it), leaving us at the mercy of technical instrumental reason. The triumph of this mode of rationality, foreseen by Max Weber, leads to a situation where the wider rationality of narrow economic ends is not critically examined.

In this situation it seems to us utterly pointless to attempt to build complex metaphysical and ethical systems such as deep ecology (McLaughlin, 1993; Mathews, 1991), as these systems will be subject to the postmodern dilemmas examined in this chapter (Gare, 1993). Rather, we see the key task for environmentalism or ecologism is to attack and dismantle the universalizing project of Enlightenmentism and by political action to create a smaller, more fragmented world where genuine pluralism can exist within the framework of an ecologically sustainable autarkic economy. To this aim it is necessary to refute globalism in the field where its influence is the strongest—economics—and to outline an alternative. As Gare has noted, the decline of "grand narratives" has occurred in all areas except economics: "Economists, with the support of the international bourgeoisie, have been able to dominate politics throughout the Western world, and in most of the remainder" (Gare, 1995, 25). It is the aim of the rest of this book to examine this issue.

NOTES

1. The fallibilist rejects the entailment principle:

    (E) S knows that p on the basis of reason r only if r entails p

on the grounds that (E) leads to skepticism. However, other principles cause problems for fallibilism. For example, the set of propositions known by S is closed under entailment:

   (1) If S knows that p and S knows that p entails not-h,
       then S knows that not-h.

Consider a proposition p which we claim to know and let h be a skeptical hypothesis (e.g., S is being deceived by an evil Cartesian demon) whose denial is entailed by p. Then:

(2) S does not know not-h

leading us to infer

(3) S does *not* know that p.

cf. also (Luper-Foy, ed., 1987). For further information on the epistemological issues discussed in the main text cf. (Johnson, 1971; Almeder, 1973, 1987; Wolgast, 1977; Pappas & Swain, eds., 1978; Rosenberg, 1980; Klein, 1981; Chisholm, 1982; Odegard, 1982, 1986; White, 1982; Mates, 1984; Gill, 1985; Grayling, 1985; Schreiber, 1987; Lycan, 1988; Oakley, 1988; Hookway, 1990; Lehrer, 1990; Goldman, 1991).

2. Psychological states were taken to be individuated by the *abstract* causal-functional roles; as psychological states were functional characterizations, they cannot be identified with any specific neurophysiological structures. These abstract states may be realized by physically heterogeneous systems. Although functionalism is generally thought to be consistent with a token-token identity theory of the mind/brain, functionalism is also consistent with a number of other nonmaterialist mind/brain theories such as dualistic interactionism. Functionalism is itself a form of dualism, for the mind itself is an *abstract entity* that is physically realizable or embodied. This metaphysical point is explicitly recognized by A. Kuhn (1977), who identifies the mind with a *pattern*, patterns being relations between two or more concrete or abstract elements. Patterns are nonmaterial as they can be created and destroyed and they are not subject to conservation laws. Kuhn makes this a defining characteristic of pattern (Kuhn, 1977, 91). The pattern may be embodied in matter, but is not itself material. It is itself an abstract entity. Now abstract entities are generally recognized to be a problem for physicalism because they are not physical entities, and in the case of mathematical entities, are presupposed by physics itself. The mind-body problem cannot be satisfactorily solved for physicalism if we substitute problematic Cartesian mind-stuff for problematic Platonistic abstract mind-stuff. Explaining how mathematics and reality "connect" for the Platonist is just as much a problem of explaining how the mind and brain "connect" for the Cartesian dualist.

4

Economic Irrationalism: Against Cosmopolitan Economics

> Economists have become a plague as dangerous as rabbits, prickly pear or cane toads. Economists have become the cultural cane toads of Canberra, oozing over the landscape and endangering myriad indigenous species. Not only the economy but also mental health would be greatly improved if we could lift the fog of obfuscation on things economic. The first step is to take economists from their pedestal and to see them as the curiosities they are. The first step to reducing their power is to reduce their legitimacy. How is this to be achieved? First, economists' outpourings should, as a matter of principle, be met with laughter, derision, benign paternalism. They should cease to be employed as media commentators. In the long term they should cease to be hired. Let them be pensioned off and die out. Extinction is a worthy end for a profession whose brief is rotten to the core. (Jones, 1991, 88)[1]

GLOBAL ECONOMIC CHAOS

Globalism, or economic cosmopolitanism, is the thesis that economic efficiency of production and the maximization of individual marginal utility will most effectively occur if all restraints are removed from capital, technology and labor so that resources can move to those areas where free, unregulated markets can utilize resources most efficiently (that is, maximize profits). Usually globalism is stated as the position that capital and technology should be free to move to areas to be able to exploit the cheapest labor. To do this, all restraints must be removed from the banking and financial systems; they must be deregulated.

An extensive literature has grown up around either the celebration or exploration of globalism and the borderless world (Gill & Law, 1988; Gordon, 1988; Chase-Dunn, 1989; King, ed., 1991; Gilbert, 1992). The mobility of capital, the opening of the information superhighway, the economic integration of national economies are factors that McKenzie and Lee in *Quicksilver Capital*

(1991), Robert Reich in *The Work of Nations* (1991) and Kenichi Ohmae in *The Borderless World* (1990) believe are making nations economically redundant. People see, Reich notes, the public interest served by national economic growth and the common good in turn served by the creation of a strong economy. The metaphor is wrong, Reich says. Citing the case of America, he notes that foreigners are coming to own an ever greater proportion of America's productive assets and American companies are relocating abroad—between 1980 and 1990, he observes, American companies increased their overseas spending on new factories, equipment and R&D at a higher rate than their U.S. internal investments. This and other trends—money, information and goods flowing effortlessly across national borders—lead Reich to reject the idea of a national economy and a common good for a nation. Instead, the good of the United States and other "nations" must be to "increase the potential value of what its citizens can add to the global economy, by enhancing their skills and capacities and by improving their means of linking those skills and capacities to the world market" (Reich, 1991, 8). Hence there is no longer any reason for the United States or any other nation to protect, subsidize or support "its" industries. Talk then of a "Japanese or Asian challenge" is by definition besides the point. There is only one economy— the global economy—which for Reich is a sacred object: "'American' corporations are no longer even American; the core corporation is a facade, behind which teems an array of decentralized groups and subgroups continuously contracting with similarly diffuse working units all over the world" (Reich, 1991, 81).

Reich notes that the shift of routine production jobs to Third World nations has imposed a cost upon American workers who simply no longer have well-paying routine production jobs. As he states: "Twelve thousand people are added to the world's population every hour, most of whom, eventually, will happily work for a small fraction of the wages of routine producers in America" (Reich, 1991, 209). As well, lower- and middle-level management jobs involving routine production have also vanished, although it is good news for "symbolic analysts," who are facing worldwide demand. But Reich admits that there is a darkside to the emergence of the cosmopolitan "global citizen." Cosmoman may resist all solutions involving sacrifice and commitment: "without strong attachments and loyalties extending beyond family and friends, symbolic analysts may never develop the habits and attitudes of social responsibility" (Reich, 1991, 309). Reich notes that for the nationalist, concerned with national problems, personal sacrifice makes sense, but for the cosmopolitan, concerned with the whole of humanity, such sacrifices seem useless (Reich, 1991, 310). Hence Reich concludes that it is not clear that wise cosmopolitanism is in fact superior to "foolish" nationalism (Reich, 1991, 311). Then surely wise nationalism is better than wise cosmopolitanism? In any case, Reich concludes *The Work of Nations* with an assertion of positive economic nationalism, appealing to a sense of "national purpose" to prevent the social disintegration of nations, a sentiment that seems to contradict the fundamental thesis of his book.

Where Reich finds cosmoman problematic, Ohmae welcomes him/her. But none of these authors have taken the globalist/cosmopolitan position to its logical conclusion. Gregory Stock in *Metaman: Humans, Machines, and the Birth of a Global Super-Organism* (1993) does. Human society, according to Stock, is becoming a living being, a global superorganism, where individual humans are like cells, linked by the nerves of modern technology and communication. This global superorganism is called "Metaman," meaning "beyond and transcending humans." Metaman is the economic rationalist equivalent of James Lovelock's idea of Gaia (Lovelock, 1979, 1988).

These positions may be exaggerated and extreme but they do capture a fundamental truth:national economies to an arguable, but significant degree are being broken down (Alexander & Baker, 1994). This is seen most acutely in the promotion of free trade and the construction of regional trading blocs. GATT (General Agreement on Tariffs and Trade) has since its inception in January 1948 promoted the ideal of a global free market in all goods and services, including primary products, with often devastating consequences for the Third World (Gray, 1993b).[2] To achieve, however, a completely deregulated world in one swoop is impossible. Consequently the internationalist money-power has pushed to develop various free trade regions or regional trading blocs that at some future date can be integrated together. The best-known of these trade blocs is the EU (European Union) (Molle, 1991) but others include the Andean Pact (including Bolivia, Columbia, Ecuador, Peru, Venezuela), ASEAN (Brunei, Indonesia, Malaysia, Philippines, Singapore, Thailand), the Central American Common Market, East African Community, Southern Cone Common Market Treaty, NAFTA (North American Free Trade Agreement) and APEC (Asia-Pacific Economic Co-operation). In support of our position that traderegionalism leads ultimately to global free trade, we note that trade ministers from thirty-four nations of the Americas agreed in 1995 to create a Free Trade Area of the Americas (FTAA) by 2005, a super-NAFTA. If the problems plaguing APEC can be sorted out by that time, the world would have moved very close to complete global free trade by early in the next century, all going well for the globalists.

Perhaps the most important aspect of economic globalization (Camilleri & Falk, 1992) is the globalization and consequent deregulation of financial markets (Pecchioli, 1983; Zuhayr, 1987; Reinicke, 1995). The turnover of the London Eurodollar market for the entire year of 1970 was $59 billion. In the mid-1980s on an average day it was turning over $300 billion, which is twenty-five times the value of world trade in merchandise and services per day. By 1990 the average volume of foreign exchange trading had reached $600 billion per day, reaching the $1 trillion per day mark in 1992 (Cerny, ed., 1993, 1). Indeed, global financial markets have taken on a "life" of their own constituting the underlying structure of international trade (Allen, 1994). The globalization of finance has introduced the possibility of instability into the global system (Cerny, ed., 1993, 6). While some international financial economists see open financial markets as highly efficient (money flowing to the most productive use), other economists see these markets as a drag on the productive economy as money can easily be made from the trading of money, so that financial capital flows into rentier capital used for speculative purposes, rather than for productive uses. R. E. Allen, for example, argues in his book *Financial Crisis and Recession in the Global Economy* (Allen, 1994) that for international financial markets to operate efficiently, an increasing amount of money must be absorbed by the financial system leaving less money for nonfinancial and GDP purposes. This leads to a decline in the income velocity of money, which may cause a financial crisis itself, as a "money-liquidity shortage" is created "somewhere in the global economy" (Allen, 1994, p. xvi). Without elaborating upon these technical points, we can already see that there is some debate even within orthodox economic circles about the stability of the modern globalized economy.

All does not go well in the world's economies. Let us begin our discussion by considering America's economic woes. In November 1995 the United States teetered on the brink of defaulting on its national debt—which would have caused the meltdown of the global economy. The U.S. public debt is nearly $5 trillion and in November 1995 for the first time, it became politically impossible to meet debt repayments. The Gramm-Rudman-Hollings Act (Balanced Budget and Emergency Deficit Control Act of 1985) sets a statutory limit on public debt of $4.9 trillion. In a standoff between President Clinton and the Republicans, the U.S. government was partially shutdown with up to 800,000 workers being temporarily laid off. The Republicans would not increase the debt ceiling unless President Clinton agreed to balance the budget within seven years by cutting back on welfare, especially health care programs for the elderly and poor. Clinton agreed (with some qualifications) on November 20, 1995 to the Republican demands.

However, over the next four months, to the time of writing, the Republican demands became substantially watered down due to community pressure and the approaching US elections to the point that they would not pursue their threats. A budget compromise was reached in April 1996. President Clinton agreed to a future balancing of the U.S. budget. The U.S. budget deficit for the 1996 fiscal year was revised downward from $145 billion to $130 billion, which the Clinton adminstration believes will ensure that the deficit will be cut in half before the end of his first term. Clearly, the problem has been avoided, not resolved, and is certain to arise again after the U.S. elections. We believe that this is inevitable because U.S. society is becoming harder, less sympathetic to the poor, adopting a "not in my backyard" approach to life.

Francis Fukuyama, author of *The End of History and the Last Man* (1992) (a celebration of the triumph of liberal democracy over communism), sees the United States becoming a more selfish society. In an interview with *The Australian* he observed that a "whole range of things, like our high rates of violent crime and litigation, and the fall-off in voluntary associations, are symptoms of a lower willingness to abide by the norms and laws of a community" (Wilson, 1996, 1). The United States is now the most economically stratified society in the developed world. At the beginning of the 1990s the richest 1 percent of Americans owned 40 per cent of the nation's wealth. By contrast, in a country such as Britain which is regarded as class-based, the richest 1 per cent own 18 per cent of the wealth (Wilson, 1996, 1). The United States in 1996 has child poverty rates four times those of other developed nations and its poor and lower-income earners are worse off in absolute terms than they were twenty years ago. Unskilled and temporary workers receive much lower wages than in most other developed nations. Although the United States has added twenty-eight million new jobs since 1980, there is a vast population of working poor with eleven million workers making ends meet on a minimum wage of $US4.25 an hour (which has recently been rased since (Wilson, 1996)), with poor benefits. Three-quarters of these workers are adults and 40 percent of these workers are sole bread winners. Professor Seymour Martin Lipset observes that the United States "has the highest proportion of people living in poverty among developed nations" (Wilson, 1996, 1). One in four black men in their twenties are in jail, on probation or on parole. Despite the rise in black education levels, the percentage of blacks living in poverty has remained approximately the same: 33.5 percent in 1970, to 33.1 percent in 1993 (Wilson, 1996, 6).

These social problems are unlikely to be solved by the social democratic method of increasing taxes. Taxes as a percentage of total income have increased every year of the Clinton presidency. Today a typical American family of four pays 38.2 percent of their income in taxes, taking up more than three hours of a eight-hour workday. By contrast, the same families in the 1950s paid on average only 5 percent of their income in taxes (North Dakota Republican Party, Republican Report, April 15, 1996, World Wide Web). Over the last twenty years the living standards of middle class workers have fallen 4.6 percent since 1979, with 2.5 percent of that drop occurring in the first three years of the Clinton presidency (North Dakota Republican Party, Republican Report, April 15, 1996, World Wide Web).

The closedown of the U.S. government is similar to chapter 1 ("The Week from Hell") in H. E. Figgie and G. J. Swanson's book, *Bankruptcy 1995* (1993). Debts for the United States in the period 1994–2000 based on DRI/Grace Commission projections, chart a "hockey stick curve." Figgie and Swanson predicted that in 1995 the current U.S. debt curve would become vertical, not merely because of deficit spending on government programs but because of "the compounding of the annual interest charge . . . together with indexed entitlement spending that will throw the United States into insolvency" (Figgie & Swanson, 1993, 84–87). In 1964 the national debt was $316 billion and the interest charge $10.7 billion; the 1992 interest charges on the debt amounted to $292.2 billion. Eventually the interest charges alone will exceed 100 percent of income tax—one of the marvels of compound interest. On Grace Commission projections the accumulated government debt will reach $13 trillion by the year 2000. This is nine times the amount the government will collect in income tax that year. Debt is growing three times faster than the U.S. economy is growing. The debt is not being used for productive investments but to pay current debt obligations. Without a radical slashing of the welfare system, the United States, in Figgie and Swanson's opinion, will face at some time in the near future economic collapse by either hyperinflation or death by panic as the world's financial markets close America down (Figgie & Swanson, 1993, 96). But a radical slash in social welfare will most likely lead to riots and social chaos.

In recent times a number of writers and analysts have advanced the thesis that America is in decline because the economy upon which it rests is in decline (Kennedy, 1987; Mead, 1987; Friedman, 1988; Kurtzman, 1988; Sharp, 1988). Since 1978 Ravi Batra has predicted the collapse of both communism and capitalism by the year 2000 (Batra, 1978a, b, 1988). So far he has been proven correct on one account. In his book *The Myth of Free Trade* (1993), he argues that laissez-faire economics has wrecked U.S. industry and that international trade is the worse polluter of all economic activities; free trade will destroy local economies and play havoc with the global environment. Concentrating our attention upon the U.S. economy for the moment, Batra notes that until 1970 the United States was a "closed economy." Around 1973 it became a free-trade economy and since that time earnings have declined despite a rise in productivity (Batra, 1993, 53). The erosion of the nation's industrial base occurred as multinational firms relocated in low-wage Asian countries to manufacture goods and then sell them back to the United States. In a closed economy, Batra observes, this would not occur, but the United States is no longer a closed economy.

Batra, who published his book before NAFTA came into force (January 1, 1994), maintained that NAFTA would be the "straw that breaks America's back" (Batra, 1993, 6). On the day that NAFTA came into force, the peasant revolt broke out in Chiapas. By Christmas week of that year, the peso had shed around 40 percent of its value as jittery Wall Street financiers (investment banks and mutual funds), nervous about an artificially high peso and rising current account deficits, pulled the plug on the peso and began a stampede to get their money out of the country. It was only by the swift action of President Clinton—not wishing to have another financial catastrophe after the Orange County bankruptcy in California a week before—that Mexico was saved from financial implosion. President Clinton rescued Mexico by appropriating $US20 billion from the U.S. monetary reserve, and $13 billion from "anonymous sources" and he also insisted that the IMF put up another $US17 billion. The Mexican Treasury was able to pay off the Wall Street banks and inject $US4 billion into the Mexican-owned banks so they could cover their bad debts. Interest rates for the Mexican people rose between 50 and 100 percent. Thousands of businesses collapsed, making another one million Mexicans unemployed. Mexican oil revenues have been appropriated as security and are now being paid into a special U.S. Treasury fund.

What is particularly interesting about this, according to a report by the U.S. Senate Banking Committee, was that the Clinton administration knew about the perilous state of Mexico's economy right through 1994 even while lobbying to get congressional support for NAFTA—which the Clinton administration made on the grounds of the strength of the Mexican economy. American officials had their own private data, Mexican data and CIA data to go on. NAFTA was created to serve the agenda of the global money power, not for any sound national economic reasons. Billions of U.S. dollars were invested in Mexico, but not in establishing an industrial base. The dollars were in high-interest, short-term Mexican bonds, which could be cashed quickly. And they were bringing misery and disaster to the Mexican people.

On the Mexican side, NAFTA benefits elites and gives greater power to multinational companies and foreign banks. Mexican President Salinas offered an attractive package to attract US investors. He collaborated with the economic oligarchy and the union leadership "to force down labour costs, crush independent union initiatives on better wages, conditions and safety standards and make labour more 'flexible and disciplined'" (Morley & McGillion, 1993, 13). In the agricultural sphere peasants have been "shouldered off" their traditional land, which in turn has been taken over by giant agribusinesses. Production of stable foods for local consumption has declined, resulting in the necessity of importing more basic items from abroad. NAFTA's tough economic reform measures involve cuts in spending on housing, health, education and other social service, environmental services and safeguards. Foreign investment in Mexico in recent times has been primarily speculative capital, not productive capital. Investment in assembly-line production has not resulted in a significant investment in human capital, education and training. While Mexican labor productivity rose 41 percent between 1980 and 1992, the wages and benefits of workers are now 68 percent of what they were in 1980 (Morley & McGillion, 1993, 13). We agree with Batra's statement that "eventually, free trade could be more devastating than even the Great Depression" (Batra, 1993, 53).

Australia's economy is in a perilous state, also due to free market, economic rationalist and economic globalist policies. Professor Russell Mathews (Emeritus Professor of Economics, Australian National University) summed up this situation in a CEDA[3] Public Information Paper in these words:

Free market policies are killing the Australian economy and causing hardship and financial ruin for millions of Australians. The economy has been brought to its knees by financial and economic deregulation, the elimination of tariffs, unsuccessful structural reforms in industry, free trade in agriculture, open slather for imports, privatisation, repressive monetary policies, a taxation system that favours consumption over saving and investment and is an administrative nightmare, and budgetary policies that treat surpluses as triumphs of financial management.

The balance of payments on current account is in a permanent state of massive deficit. Overseas debt has reached an exorbitant level and is still growing rapidly. Foreign ownership of Australian assets has increased exponentially. The financial system is in tatters as a result of its own greed and extravagant lending policies, carrying the fortunes of hundreds of thousands of farmers, small businesses, home owners, superannuants and investors with it. Manufacturing and primary industries are being systematically destroyed. The public sector capital stock—the economic infrastructure on which industries depend and the social infrastructure which determines the quality of life—is in a state of chronic decay. The economy has plunged into a recession we were told we had to have but which is so deep-seated that it can reasonably be regarded as a full-scale depression. Homelessness, poverty and despair have become common-place in a country where the majority of the population still lives extravagantly and beyond its means. (Mathews, 1992, 1)

Economic rationalist policies—or what Professor Mathews calls "economic perversity" policies—have placed Australian on the "Mexican road." A respected commentator on economic affairs in Australia, Tom Fitzgerald believes that economic rationalist policies have led to an Australian economy that is "out of control" (Fitzgerald, 1990, 22). The freeing of the exchange rate and exchange controls has created a financial black hole that promotes ever greater deficits in the current balance of payments: "High interest rates attract short-term funds from overseas; the inflow of funds sustains or raises the exchange rate; the high exchange rate, combined with the interest payments on the inflowing funds, increases the deficit in the balance of payments" (Fitzgerald, 1990, 22). High interest rates, used as an instrument of monetary policy by the Australian government to deal with what former Prime Minister Keating called an "overheated economy," then set this cycle in motion again. It is an economic policy that is leading to the self-destruction of the Australian economy. The OECD claims that Australia's current account deficit is the worst in the Western world (English, 1995; Henderson, 1995). As a proportion of the economy it is four times that of Mexico and almost double that of the U.S. deficit. The OECD correctly estimated that Australia's current account deficit would reach 6 percent of its economic output in 1995. Consequently it is unfair to say that Australia is on the "Mexican road," as the British financial magazine *The Economist* predicted in early November 1995: Mexico is on the Australian road (English, 1995; Henderson, 1995). The age of affluence for Australia seems to have ended (Blainey, 1996).

Urban ghettoes of poverty are being created in Australia not seen since the Great Depression. Australian National University economists Bob Gregory and Boyd Hunter have found that the average household income gap between the poorest and richest suburbs has grown by $26,580 since 1976 (Dusevic, 1995; Ellis, 1995). This is leading to the creation of "two-nations"—with the rich living in "fortresses" for protection (Collins, 1993). Gregory maintains that a deregulated labor market will further drive down wages of the poorest sector of Australian society. The structural weakness of the Australian economy, produced by decades of economic mismanagement, has led to Australia adopting what Butcher (1996) calls a "fish and chips" economy. Dwindling supplies of southern blue fin tuna are sold to Japan and native forests are cut down and sold as woodchips overseas or used in the immigration-fueled housing industry (Butcher, 1996).

The deregulation of the Australian economy began in 1973 under the allegedly "nationalistic" Whitlam government, when all import tariffs were cut by 25 percent and the Australian dollar was revalued upward by 20 percent, making imports cheaper and exports dearer than before. Financial deregulation did not occur until 1982 under the Fraser government. The "Campbell Committee" was set up in 1981 by Treasurer John Howard and comprised, among other people, Howard's economic adviser John Hewson and, standing as secretary, Professor Fred Argy. Howard admitted in an interview published on October 31, 1987 in *The Australian* that the program of deregulation of the Australian economy—the floating of the dollar, the dropping of exchange controls, the entry of foreign banks, the establishment of the currency market, the removal of interest controls and the freeing of foreign investment controls—was his responsibility. Howard stated in his interview that he rigged the Campbell Committee "deliberately [setting out] to choose people who believed in free financial markets." To overcome hostility in the government, Howard decided "that the way to get Campbell up was not to say you were getting it up, but to do it bit by bit."[4] The rest is history. John Howard, who is now the Prime Minister of Australia, believes that all Australian tariffs must be eliminated and he will maintain the pace of tariff elimination allowing Australia to be more rigorously penetrated by the free market (Taylor, 1995).

The Australian elites' passion for globalization is seen most clearly in the (Australian) Industry Commission's 1995 annual report where it recommends that Australia should "go it alone" in reducing its barriers to imports, irrespective of whether other countries reciprocate. This it believes, contrary to a wide body of historical evidence (Goldsmith, 1995), will maximize the benefits for Australians from domestic microeconomic reform. Australia from 1953 to 1972 had greater economic growth than in the period 1983 to 1993 (5 percent change in real GDP versus 3.3 percent); less than half the rate of inflation (2.5 percent versus 5.7 percent change in the CPI); less than one-quarter of the unemployment (1.9 percent versus 8.6 percent of the labor force); less than half the level of interest rates (5.0 percent versus 11.5 percent, five-year bonds) and one-half the deficit on the balance of current accounts. "Old Australia" had a rise in the level of average earnings, while "new Australia" had a fall. There was no privatization of state or federal publicly owned enterprises. The era of economic internationalization involved the removal of government control over banks, interest rates, the import and export of currency and a reduction of tariff protection (Santamaria, 1996). As

Santamaria correctly notes, the transformation from good results to bad results is clear, making nonsense of the idea that free market economics necessarily yields better results than "controlled capitalism." Over the last twenty years Australian industrial productivity has risen by 35 percent and manufactured exports by 400 percent. But over the same period Australian manufacturing's share of the GDP has fallen from 24 percent to 14 percent. While manufactured exports have risen by $14 billion since 1986, manufactured imports have risen by $37.5 billion.

The disastrous effects of free market economic policies are felt very strongly in the Australian car manufacturing industry. With the value of the yen rising 20 percent against the dollar by mid-1995, Australian car manufacturers no longer saw the Japanese as a competitive danger. Now another Asian invasion is occurring, being led by the South Koreans. Imported cars now account for over half of the Australian car market and as import tariffs are reduced, this market share will rise ever higher. In the twelve months to May 1995, sales of locally produced cars fell 16 percent and imports rose by 35 percent. If tariff protection drops below 15 percent, Ford will cease to produce cars in Australia—and zero tariffs are likely to operate within APEC by 2010. Mike Quinn of Mitsubishi Australia has summed up the perverse genius of economic rationalism in these words: "If Australia continues the move towards eliminating all forms of assistance to our local industry, well in advance of any comparable moves overseas, we may be able to boast about a domestic level playing field—but we will no longer be able to field a team in the international competition" (Grennan, 1996).

Financial deregulation throughout the Western world has produced a world capital market consisting in the main of capital flights that are pure gambling transactions in a global casino. This thesis is well known and is the only real explanation of the critical state of both the global economy and local economies. For yet another example consider the savings and loans (S&L) disaster in the United States where the U.S. government inadvertently lost $250 billion. The S&L institutions before the 1980s loaned money to individuals to buy houses. Deregulation in 1982 allowed the S&L institutions to invest in anything which they desired. The Reagan administration believed in the myth of deregulated market efficiency; they did not believe that it would be a license for high rollers and global thieves. It was.

Economic rationalists often cite the New Zealand economy (which has had an economic growth rate of 6.1 percent) as the correct model of economic rationalism in practice. It has been argued that economic rationalism has failed elsewhere because it has not been ruthless enough. However, even in pure economic terms this argument is doubtful, as John Quiggin has argued:

New Zealand today looks much like Britain in 1988. The economy is on the upswing, but it has a long way to go to catch up the losses accrued between 1984 to 1991, when real GDP per capita actually declined. This period of economic contraction is defended on the basis that New Zealand was an economic basket case in 1984, exactly the rationalisation used by British advocates of the "Thatcher miracle" for ignoring the economic devastation of the early '80s.

The fact that New Zealand's recovery is heavily dependent on favourable movements in the terms of trade is ignored, just as was Thatcher's dependence on North Sea oil. The New Zealand economic miracle could end just as abruptly in the late '90s as Thatcher's did in the late '80s. (Quiggin, 1995, 11; also Carroll, 1995)

Further, even if we do grant that economic rationalism can achieve its aims if practiced ruthlessly, the social costs of this in New Zealand have been enormous (Rees et al., eds., 1993). The New Zealand commissioner for children, Dr. Ian Hassall, stated on June 22, 1994 that economic reforms since the mid-1980s have contributed to New Zealand having the highest youth suicide rate in the world (Smellie & Weekes, 1994). There has also been an increase in racial tension in Maori and Pacific Islander communities due to the slashing of social welfare, a violent tension well captured in Lee Tamahori's film *Once Were Warriors*. By 2031 Maori and Pacific Islanders will constitute 40 per cent of New Zealand's population; eight out of ten people are Maori (53.6 percent) in Otara or Pacific Islander (27.8 percent) and one-third of Otara's adults are unemployed, primarily from these racial groups (Smellie, 1994). It does not take much insight to be able to see that as a result of deprivation these groups may become warriors again— and who could blame them? Even in pure economic terms, there is no greater inefficiency than unemployment. The rise of Winston Peters' anti-immigration, nationalist party, New Zealand First, which has essentially given Peters the balance of power (Smellie, 1996), indicates that there is substantial community resistance to the globalization of New Zealand. New Zealand's economy therefore cannot be considered to be efficient and New Zealand cannot be considered to be a success story for economic rationalism.

Another economy in bad shape is Japan. Its productive sphere remains strong but its financial sector is unstable (Johnson, 1995). Christopher Wood, *The Economist's* Tokyo-based Far East finance editor, describes Japan's economy as a "bubble economy," a gossamer that can and will burst (Wood, 1993). Along with the instability of the yen seen in 1995, a series of bank and financial institution crashes have occurred, including Kizu Credit Co-op and Hyogo Bank. It was only the Japanese government's support of the financial system—contrary to the logic of economic rationalism—which prevented its collapse, according to D. Snoddy of Jardine Fleming Securities in Tokyo (Hartcher, 1995). Japan's banks are now facing the consequences of Japan's debt-based capital spending boom of the 1980s. Wood argues that a crash in the Japanese property market would be the final step in Japan's economic implosion. Most Japanese businesses and the Japanese themselves have borrowed money using land as collateral. This potentially catastrophic situation involves the world's biggest commercial banks, accounting for approximately 40 percent of all international cross-nation lending.

The same global forces that ended the 1950s/1960s boom in Western economies have ended Japan's phenomenal growth. The economy has had four years of stagnation. Even given the likelihood of a short-term recovery, many Japanese economic experts believe that the economy may revert back to low growth in 1997 or 1998 (Wood, 1995). Professor Ueda of Tokyo University believes that Japan will average only 1 percent growth for the next five to ten years (Wood, 1995). Along with this problem of sustaining growth, a survey by Asia Pacific Economic Group, headed by Dr. Ross Garnaut and Dr. Peter Drysdale of the Australian National University, has found that East Asia's current account surplus will sharply fall from $US106.5 billion in 1995 to $US73.2 billion in 1996. The East Asian current account surplus has been a source of capital for deficit countries such as Australia and the United States, which will be required to further tighten budget policies (Hiscock, 1996).

Some writers have gone still further and have identified what they believe is a critical instability in the global financial system. James Dale Davidson and Sir William Rees-Mogg in their book *Blood in the Streets* (Davidson & Rees-Mogg, 1989) recognize that the world banking system is collectively insolvent and in danger of economic collapse.[5] In *The Great Reckoning* they say:

> The end, when it comes, will not only reveal the insolvency of many individuals and corporations, it may also bring bankruptcy to the welfare state and widespread breakdown of authority within political economies. More than you may now imagine, you are vulnerable to financial, economic, and political collapse. (Davidson & Rees-Mogg, 1992, 12–13)

In conclusion, it is highly likely that there is an instability present in the heart of the global financial system and in particular within orthodox capitalist financial systems. We will turn now to outline a theoretical case against free trade theory and economic internationalism/globalism. To do so we need an understanding of the intellectual history of ideas behind the free trade debate. We will then advance further criticisms.

AGAINST FREE TRADE AND ECONOMIC GLOBALIZATION

Francois Quesnay (1694–1774) was the first political economist to advance the idea of universal free trade and to argue that political economy should be concerned with the affairs of the entire human race, rather than taking the nation as its unit of analysis. Hence the title of his work:*Physiocratie ou du Gouvernement le plus avantageux au Genre Humain*. He proposed that the merchants of all nations be considered in such a way as to form, if only theoretically, one commercial republic. Quesnay's *Tableau Économique* (1758) laid the basis for the physiocrat economic school of thought, which held that land was the single source of wealth and income in the economy, the only source of society's "new product." The physiocrats believed in the idea of a natural order of society in which the interests of the individual were harmonized with the interests of society as a whole. The state's role was merely to preserve private property and defend and uphold the natural order. Consequently, the physiocrats were strong proponents of individual liberty and strong opponents of government regulation and intervention. The expression *"Laissez-faire, laissez-passer"* originated from the physiocrats.

While rejecting the physiocratic idea that land was the only source of income (the only "factor of production"), Adam Smith was strongly influenced by physiocracy and took over much of the physiocrat's theoretical and metaphysical baggage. He accepted their individualism and social atomism and their idea of a "natural order," which in his *An Inquiry into the Nature and Causes of the Wealth of Nations*, first published in 1776, became the "invisible hand" by which unregulated "free markets" ensured efficiency in the production and distribution of goods and services.

What is of interest to us here is not Smith's outline and defense of *laissez-faire*, but his view that political economy should be concerned with the study of all nations of the entire human race, rather than with the affairs of a particular nation at a particular period of its history. Up until the time of Quesnay and

Smith, political economy was concerned with the functioning of particular nations or societies because it was firmly believed that the economy was only a part of society's social structure and that it was not possible to study all societies, or society in general, because different societies had different political and social structures. For Smith though, national or political economy must be replaced by "cosmopolitan or world-wide economy."

Jean-Baptiste Say (1767-1832) was even more explicit in his cosmopolitanism than Smith: for general free trade to operate we should aim for the creation of a *universal republic*. Say did not deny the existence of nations in a metaphysical sense, but other advocates of free trade did. Thomas Cooper, President of Columbia College and the first public intellectual in the United States to advocate free trade, saw the nation as a "grammatical fiction" created by the mind of politicians. It has no ontological existence beyond that. Liberalism with its atomistic view of the social world, somewhat paradoxically, inevitably leads to globalism, internationalism or cosmopolitanism because if societies and nations do not exist in the way that holists believe, then it is arbitrary to stop politics and ethics at national borders. It is natural then to collect together, in a set-theoretical way, these raceless, placeless liberal social atoms into a convenient unit of study:the "global village," the "international community" and the like.

There have been alternative schools of economic thinking that have opposed (to varying degrees) cosmopolitanism economics. Generally speaking, *protectionists* have opposed free trade because they felt that it was in some way damaging to the interests of the nation and the common good, even if it did allow some consumers to consume goods not produced in the country (e.g., tropical fruit in the Nordic countries). Alexander Hamilton, who along with James Madison and John Jay authored *The Federalist or, The New Constitution* ([1787/1788], 1948), submitted a report written in 1790 (*Report on the Subject of Manufactures*) (Cole, ed., 1968) in favor of temporary protection of infant American industries. However, he believed that once America had achieved industrial strength, by establishing a strong industrial infrastructure, free trade could be adopted.

Hamilton's idea was elaborated by Fredrich List, who was an active participant in the free trade/protection debates in both Germany and the United States in the first half of the nineteenth century. List was an early critic of the classical school of economics of Adam Smith and his disciples. He called this position the "cosmopolitan school," which he opposed with what he first described as a "natural" and then a "national" school of economics (List [1837], 1983, [1840], 1885]). Although a critic of free trade, like Hamilton, he recognized that in the distant future free trade may be desirable and achievable. However, at the time, when he wrote *The Natural System of Political Economy* ([1837], 1983), it was undesirable because France, Germany, Russia and the United States had not achieved the industrial efficiency of Britain.[6] While advocating protection for manufactured goods, List did not do so for agricultural products and raw materials. Departing in his works from the usual topics discussed by classical political economy (such as stages of economic growth), List elaborated a theory of the "powers of production." Productive powers included not only manpower, animal power and technology, but also the administrative, political and social infrastructure and institutions. The point of protection was the establishment of an industrial base; productive powers were developed by prohibitions and import duties. This, he noted, may lead to higher prices for consumers but it is a sacrifice that the public should bear to aid in nation building and to promote the future economic security of the nation. Sacrifices in exchange value can be made to increase productive power in the future. If it is always foolish to make short-term sacrifices for long-term gains, then it would be preferable to always buy pears rather than plant pear trees (List [1837], 1983, 38). List did not carry his argument through to its logical conclusion:if everybody acted in this way, being concerned with *immediate* utility satisfaction, no pear trees would have been planted by anybody at all.

List's position on free trade can be summarized by quoting a particularly powerful passage in *The Natural System of Political Economy*:

We regard ourselves as citizens of the world, but our faith in humanity rests upon the solid basis of nationalism. We can certainly envisage a situation in which a country would find freedom of trade preferable to a restrictive fiscal policy. We are citizens of a nation before we are citizens of the world. We devote our facilities to the energetic pursuit of the culture, welfare, fame, and security of the nation to which we belong. We strive towards the same goal for humanity. But the fortunes of humanity must be compatible with the fortunes of our country. We cannot support any policy that would harm our country in order to benefit the whole world. This is because we owe to our country our culture, our language, our livelihood, and our intellectual values. Nature has implanted in our hearts the desire that future generations should enjoy the same benefits from the nation as we enjoy today. (List [1837], 1983, 122)

Continuing this tradition of nationalistic economics in the nineteenth century were a number of political economists whose works today lie locked away in dusty library storage rooms. Daniel Raymond's *The Elements of Political Economy* in two volumes (Raymond [1823], 1964) launched an attack on the economic orthodoxy of his day. Raymond was the first American to write a systematic political economy treatise, *Thoughts on Political Economy* published in 1820. In 1822, Matthew Carey published *Essays on Political Economy*, which included a defense of protectionism. John Rae, in his 1834 *Statement of Some New Principles on the Subject of Political Economy, Exposing the Fallacies of the System of Free Trade, and Some Other Doctrines Maintained in the "Wealth of Nations"* (Rae [1834], 1964), presented a critique of Adam Smith. He argued that individual and national interests are not identical; individuals grow rich by the acquisition of previously existing wealth, nations by the creation of wealth that did not yet exist. Horace Greeley, in *Essays Designed to Elucidate the Science of Political Economy* (Greeley, 1869), attacked Smithian economics and free trade, saying: "I consider the Free Trade premise fallacious, pestilent, and utterly mistaken" (Greeley, 1869, 129). Such a statement was also accepted by Henry Carey, who supported permanent protection on nation-building grounds (Carey, [1851], 1967).

John B. Clark's *The Philosophy of Wealth* (1887) was in this same period criticizing Smith's model of economic man, arguing that it was based on a "degraded conception of human nature" (Clark, 1887, v). He attacked Adam Smith's extreme individualism: "The assumed man is too mechanical and too selfish to correspond with reality; he is actuated altogether too little by higher psychological forces" (Clark, 1887, 35). Further, Smith's political economy was flawed because "competition is no longer adequate to account for the phenomena of social industry" (Clark, 1887, 203). David Syme, in *Outlines of an Industrial*

Science (Syme, 1876), also developed a comprehensive critique of English political economy. He rejected the idea of self-interest as the great regulator leading to social harmony. Those who advocate this view "seem to forget that some people desire to prosper, and appear indeed for a while to prosper, at other people's expense; that, in fact, there are thieves and cheats in the world". (Syme, 1876, 34). He also rejected the idea that unrestricted competition was necessary for the orderly functioning of the economy. Syme pointed out that common sense alone tells us that "excessive competition produces enormous waste, and that it leads to the perpetuation of fraud, the extent of which is generally in proportion to the intensity or keenness of the competition" (Syme, 1876, 56). Competitors do not desire to lower prices, but to gain possession of something someone else has; sellers to secure a market, buyers to secure possession of some commodity— "the successful competitor attains his end at the expense of his rival" (Syme, 1876, 57). Syme also criticized English political economy for its "deductivism," a complaint that many contemporary critics in this century have made of the orthodox economics of their day.

This is not the place for a detailed analysis of what has been called "national systems economics."[7] Our aim has been to save some important works of political economy from disappearing down the "memory hole." We recommend that readers of this book should read the texts listed above. This should be done not for the purpose of gaining knowledge about the workings of present-day economy but as part of a deprogramming exercise. Economics has come to occupy a dominating role over our lives. National identity, freedom, truth, dignity—all of the values that make humans more than low-grade fleshy machines—must be sacrificed on the altar of economic rationality. For example, if there is a conflict between capitalism and democracy, as Samuel Brittan believes there is, then democracy must go (Jones, 1993a, 260). If there is a conflict between the laws and policies of the nation (being a member of GATT) and World Trade Organization (WTO) rules, then it is national rules which must bend. The national systems economists would never accept this loss of freedom:they would rebel against what they would see as a tyrannical system— and also an unstable one—hurtling toward destruction. There must be more to life than the grubby pursuit of money.

In the modern period John Gray's book *Beyond the New Right* goes, we believe, a long way toward capturing the spirit of resistance that is needed if communities are to survive the onslaught of the global economic juggernaut (Gray, 1993a). Gray notes that *Conservatism* holds to the imperfectibility of all human projects and the ultimate vanity of all the "great" political projects. Conservatism is skeptical of all ideologies, especially the rationalist doctrines of the Enlightenment. It is particularly opposed to the modernist version of political thought where an appeal is made to first principles of justice or some set of basic human rights. For the Conservative this gives to political discourse a certainty that it cannot have. The neoliberalism of the New Right ignored or forcefully denied the dependence of market institutions upon civil society and a common culture. Obsessed with economic reductionism, market institutions were conceived as spontaneous outcomes of natural human propensities, rather than legal, social and cultural products. The market is as fallible and imperfectible as any other human institution, including government. Indeed, champions of market liberalism such as Hayek accept that market economies inevitably involve large measures of *inequality*, yet the fundamental argument for market liberalism in the first place is its alleged contribution to individual well-being (positive freedom)—which we believe is (arguably) self-contradictory (Smith, 1991b).

We now turn to the task of outlining some theoretical objections to the free-trade doctrine and to economic globalization. Perhaps the best place to start is with comparative cost considerations. The British economist Brian Hindley has maintained that Ricardo's comparative cost theory is the major intellectual obstacle to the critics of free trade (Goldsmith, 1995, 17). David Ricardo's argument from comparative advantage is that countries export and specialize in the production of goods for which they have a comparative advantage in those products for which labor is relatively productive. Ricardo argued, taking labor as the sole factor of production, that trade would take place even if one country had as *absolute* advantage in productivity in all goods because of relative price differences between countries. Therefore, each country should specialize in the production of those goods in which it holds a comparative advantage (Ricardo, 1951, 135). This argument is both simple and compelling, but rests on the assumption of the immobility of capital and labor flows. Ricardo in *Principles of Political Economy and Taxation* (1951) explicitly recognized this in his discussion of why the principle of comparative advantage cannot work within a country (Ricardo, 1951, 136). If capital and labor freely flowed across national boundaries, then the international situation would be like that within a single country. Trade in this case would be governed, Ricardo notes, by *absolute* advantages in labor (and other factor endowments) rather than comparative advantages (Ricardo, 1951, 136–137). This argument has been advanced against the free trade position by H. E. Daly (Daly & Cobb, 1989; Daly, 1991, 1993; Daly & Goodland, 1994a, b). William Hixson (1994) has noted that although labor is relatively mobile through migration, there is no similar mobility of labor to rival capital's capacity to be electronically transferred from place to place. It is *physically impossible* for workers to *simultaneously* live in different countries with different benefits, so fairness requires that the mobility of capital also be severely restricted.

MacDonald and Markusen (1985) have noted that the comparative advantage model implies that identical economies will not trade, but there is empirical evidence to indicate that countries with approximately the same technologies and factor endowments do trade. We shall see shortly that this "non-comparative advantage trade" forms a basis for an environmental criticism of free trade. Other critics of the comparative advantage model have seen the model as being of limited importance. Yoffie notes that comparative advantages may be of importance initially, but comparative advantages quickly fade. For example, American semiconductor firms lowered costs by moving to low-wage Asian countries but Japan moved to automation, which increased reliability and lowered costs even more (Yoffie, ed., 1993, 433).

The U.S. economist J. M. Culbertson (1984, 1985, 1989, 1991) has also rejected the comparative advantage argument. International free trade is not trade between nations, but trade across the borders of nations by individuals and firms in pursuit of profit. Unregulated trade will lead, in Culbertson's opinion, to a decline in the wage level of Western countries and the standard of living. He supports this claim by an appeal to the factor-price equalization theorem and also less technically by the rule of "one price": in open trading, by virtue of the dynamics of supply and demand, a good tends to sell for one price (Hardin, 1993; Swartout, 1993). A mathematical model produced by Krugman and Venables (1995) confirms the view that globalization does not always benefit all nations, but is in fact responsible for inequalities between nations.

James Goldsmith has also noted that global free trade with a high degree of labor mobility will prove disastrous for Western workers:

If 4 billion people enter the same world market for labour and offer their work at a fraction of the price paid to people in the developed world, it is obvious that such a massive increase in supply will reduce the value of labour. Also, organized labour will lose practically all its negotiating power. When trade unions ask for concessions, the answer will be:If you put too much pressure on us, we will move offshore where we can get much cheaper labour, which does not seek job protection, long holidays, and all the other terms that you want to negotiate.

Global free trade will shatter the way in which value-added is shared between capital and labour . . . In mature societies, we have been able to develop a general agreement as to how it should be shared . . . . Overnight that agreement will be destroyed by the arrival of huge populations willing to undercut radically the salaries earned by our workforces. The social divisions that this will cause will be deeper than anything ever envisaged by Marx. (Goldsmith, 1994, 25–26)

By way of empirical illustration of Goldsmith's argument, let us briefly consider the case of Indonesia, cited as having the growth rate that the West should aspire to. In a speech to the Association of Indonesian Economists Conference in Surabaya, Indonesia's Minister for Manpower, Abdul Latief, said in November 1993 that 38 percent of Indonesia's workforce (being twenty-nine million people) cannot find full-time work. The official unemployment rate is 2.6 percent, unemployment being defined as people who work less than one hour a week or not at all. The Indonesian workforce grows by about 2.9 percent a year, or 2.3 million people, and this requires an economic growth rate of at least 6 percent. Most of the unemployed are aged between fifteen and thirty-four years with 125,000 jobless university graduates; 60 percent of graduates from Indonesia's universities are not expected to find work in the next five years (Walters, 1993). The primary textile industry hourly labor rate in Indonesia in 1995 was \$US0.50 an hour compared to \$US12.48 in Australia and \$12.18 in the United States (Ford, 1996).

Ethan B. Kapstein (1996) has published a surprising article in the journal *Foreign Affairs*. He is the director of studies at the U.S. Council on Foreign Relations, an organization that certain right-wing writers see as being part of a global "conspiracy" to bring about a world government. (Such right-wing writers have little understanding of the processes that are happening around them, for the globalized world that they so fear has already been assembled around them by the forces of international finance, technology and mass migration.) The Kapstein paper is surprising because he does not celebrate the triumph of one-worldism. On the contrary, Kapstein states that the global economy is resulting in great inequality, unemployment and "endemic poverty." Globalism was not supposed to have led to this. Kapstein is alarmed at a rise of nationalism, xenophobia and protectionist sentiments within communities across the world. A global social crisis is dawning, he warns. Kapstein as an internationalist puts the blame for this upon the nation-state, which should have acted as a buffer between working people and the world economy. We believe that the blame should be put firmly on the shoulders of the internationalists.

Economic globalization has led to a situation where international financiers now dictate to nations that they shall have balanced budgets and labor reforms. The World Economic Forum in Davos, Switzerland, held in early 1996, brought together industrialists, central bankers, financiers and politicians from around the world (Gottliebsen, 1996). The message of the Forum was that the days of the welfare state are numbered, allegedly because the system of providing a social security safety net and providing income distribution through taxation is the cause of huge unemployment gripping the West! The Central Bankers of Germany and France pointed this out strongly at the Forum. Politicians are in a dilemma. Their constituents want a return to job security and a stable standard of living. This cannot be delivered in the present globalized world, the Central Bankers argue, because financial markets require balanced or much lower deficits. The globalization of capitalism and the use of advanced technology and information transfer, all require a global free market and deregulation. This reality is a long way from the neoclassical economic fantasy (backed by the mathematics of the Coarse Theorem (Coarse, 1960) that free trade will provide maximum satisfaction of an individual's consumption schedules (Hillman, 1989). There is something desperately wrong when considerations of corporate efficiency, competition and profitability lead to a free-market attitude of "to hell with the effects on society." This defeats the sole point of having economies at all.

The environmental costs of free trade have been extensively discussed in the literature, so we shall not redocument them here (Batra, 1993). Transportation costs alone in international trade account for approximately one-eighth of world oil consumption. This trade is often in the same or similar products. Such intraindustry trade in 1978 alone made up almost 60 percent of the trade of the G-7 countries and 56 percent of world trade (Batra, 1993, 227). Batra concludes that

> international trade comes out as the worse villain in the destruction of the environment. It is the most diabolical polluter in the world and offers a precious lesson in the desirability of economic diversification versus specialization. In other words, in order to meet human wants, local production is preferable to imports so that trade and hence pollution are minimized. (Batra, 1993, 226)

We believe that these considerations give us good reason for rejecting the doctrines of free trade and economic globalization. Readers who are convinced may skip the next section and proceed to the section on ecological economics. Readers who are either not convinced or require more theoretical argument should now read the next section. There we shall attempt to supply a theoretical justification for the autarky position.

THE NAKED ECONOMIST: UTILITARIANISM AND THE MYTH OF THE MAXIMUM

In the first part of this chapter a critique was made of economic rationalism and economic internationalism. In advancing our defense of autarky and nationalism, we believe that ways must be parted with orthodox economics or neoclassical economics (Lyons et al., 1995). Economics, but also philosophy and decision theory, has been long dominated by maximization or optimization models which take rational choice to involve maximizing/optimizing one's preference-satisfaction (Slote, 1989). Neoclassical economics still operates with a model of "rational economic man," *homo economicus*, whose sole purpose is the maximization of his own selfish welfare based on utilitarian calculations. Rational economic man has fully ordered preferences, perfect information and omnipotent computing power. For the neoclassical economist, unfettered markets generate the best social decisions because they are the free expressions of people's preferences. Stated more precisely, market prices are the expression of consumers' *marginal preferences* because price levels in competitive or free markets show the tradeoffs people are willing to make between one good and others. Neoclassicism holds that:

(N1) the free market is a self-regulating system which is in equilibrium, or tending toward equilibrium at any point in time (supply equals demand), and over time evolves from equilibrium to equilibrium;
(N2) in a free market, prices are set by the free play of supply and demand;
(N3) free markets are an expression of individual freedom and sovereignty (consumer sovereignty).

It is our aim to now show the untenability of the neoclassical position.

Arnis Vilks, in an insightful paper (Vilks, 1992), notes that the concept of equilibrium is central to neoclassical economics in the sense of "simultaneous optimization" (Vilks, 1992, 52).[8] Vilks has argued, on the basis of very general axioms, that (a) actual states must be equilibrium states and (b) the existence of equilibria is a necessary and sufficient condition for the logical consistency of neoclassical models. Thus those who accept the neoclassical axioms of Vilks (assuming that his argument is correct, which we believe it to be) must reject an economic model if it has no equilibrium (Vilks, 1992, 53).

There have been a number of attempts to formulate axioms of neoclassical economics. Weintraub, working on the basis of a Lakatosian metascience of economics, lists six "hard core propositions":

(W1) There exist economic agents.
(W2) Economic agents have preferences over outcomes.
(W3) Economic agents independently optimize, subject to constraints.
(W4) Choices are made by economic agents in interrelated markets.
(W5) Economic agents have full relevant knowledge of markets.
(W6) Observable economic outcomes are coordinated, so they must be discussed with reference to equilibrium states. (Weintraub, 1985a, b)

Vilks objects to Weintraub's axioms on a number of grounds. First, the propositions do not establish a conceptual link between the terms "optimization," "preference" and "choice" other than trivially ascribing these to "agents." Vilks believes that his own axioms characterize more adequately the logical structure of optimization. Second, "equilibrium" is taken as a primitive, whereas Vilks believes that it can be defined. Third, axiom (W5) does not apply to the model of temporary equilibrium (Hicks, 1939), so this axiom fails in generality (Vilks, 1992, 55). Vilks offer the following axioms, which he takes to be basic axioms of neoclassical economic theory:

(A1) Whether an agent believes an action to be possible (for him), may depend on the situation he is in (but on nothing else).

Economic Irrationalism

(A2) Whether an agent prefers an action to another one, may depend on the situation he is in (but on nothing else).

(A3) Whether agents' actions are physically possible, may depend on the situation they are in (but on nothing else).

(A4) If, in a given situation, an agent carries out an action, then there is no other action that he, in that situation, believes to be possible and that he prefers to the one he carries out.

(A5) If, in a given situation, an agent carries out an action, then he, in that situation, believes this action to be possible (for him).

(A6) If, in a given situation, agents carry out actions, then these actions are, in that situation, physically possible.

(A7) Some situation obtains, and every agent carries out some action.

(A8) A situation that obtains is a situation, and an action that is carried out is an action. (Vilks, 1992, 57)[9]

We accept the above axioms as a reasonable characterization of neoclassical economic theory. These axioms clearly express the individualistic and reductionist nature of the theory, basing economic explanations on the actions of individual agents (Vilks, 1992, 58) However, these axioms do not in themselves entail that in the absence of exogenous disturbances, markets will tend toward some "state of rest" or efficient allocation of resources. Vilks notes that one can even accept these axioms and also believe that the future is largely "unknowable and unpredictable" as some "chaotic" models do (Vilks, 1992, 80; Benhabib & Day, 1982). Consequently propositions (N1), (N2) and (N3) must be supported on some independent basis if they can be supported at all.

Although not intended as axioms of neoclassical economics in any formal sense, Mario Bunge's "Psychoeconomic Decalogue" is a convenient characterization of neoclassical economics for critics:

(i) The individual, in particular the consumer, is sovereign.

(ii) Man is insatiable with regard to wants.

(iii) Man is naturally acquisitive.

(iv) All persons have preferences and can order them consistently.

(v) The more anyone has of something the less he values any increase in the quantity of it (law of diminishing marginal utility).

(vi) Everybody is willing to do a spot of work to satisfy his or her needs and some of his or her wants.

(vii) Man attempts to minimize the effort spent in satisfying his needs and wants. (Shorter:Man dislikes work).

(viii) Man is naturally competitive (or even aggressive) rather than cooperative.

(ix) Man is constantly confronted with choices, and is thus forced to make decisions.

(x) Man is a maximizer:he makes the decisions most likely to maximize his utility (or pleasure or gain). (Bunge, 1985, 188–189)

So much, then, for a characterization of neoclassical economics. The material to follow will be concerned with attacking the utilitarian decision theoretical structure of neoclassical economics as it is this which directly challenges the theoretical cogency of *autarky*. Autarky is a philosophy of moderation and *satisficing*; it is not necessarily irrational from the perspective of autarkism to choose not to maximize one's greatest good; a satisficer does not necessarily seek to maximize/optimize his/her good—near enough may be good enough. Likewise autarkic societies do not strive to maximize output, GDP or population levels;

they strive for ecological balance, sustainability, conservation and the "steady state."

However, before moving toward a critique of utilitarianism and the myth of the maximum, it is important to note that neoclassical economics is subject to philosophical and empirical criticisms on all fronts. Its individualistic ontology has been criticized since the time of Adam Smith and new books continue to criticize it (Kaldis, 1993; Radnitzky & Bouillon, eds., 1995). Likewise for the questions of the methodological, theoretical and empirical adequacy of this alleged science (Shackle, 1972; Galbraith, 1973; Hollis & Nell, 1975; Katouzian, 1980; Bell & Kristol, eds., 1981; Dyke, 1981; Black, 1982; Eichner, ed., 1983; Leemer, 1983; Thurow, 1983; Wiles & Routh, 1984; Zadek, 1993). Nicholas Kaldor sums up this situation as follows:

[U]nlike any scientific theory, where the basic assumptions are chosen on the basis of direct observations of the phenomena the behaviour of which forms the subject-matter of the theory, the basic assumptions of economic theory are either of a kind that are unverifiable—such that producers "maximise" their profits or consumers "maximise their utility"—or of a kind which are directly contradicted by observation—for example, perfect competition, perfect divisibility, linear-homogeneous and continually differentiable production functions, wholly impersonal market relations, exclusive role of prices in information flows and perfect knowledge of all relevant prices by all agents and perfect foresight. There is also the requirement of a constant and unchanging set of *products* (goods) and of a constant and unchanging set of *processes of production* (or production functions) over time—though neither category, goods nor processes, is operationally defined:in other words, no attempt is made to show how these axiomatic concepts are to be defined or recognised in relation to empirical material. (Kaldor, 1972, 1238)

Competitive equilibrium theory has viewed rational economic man as being fully aware of his preferences and the full workings of the economy, both now and in the future (although, as we have noted, there are some models where this is not so, but in the main, it is true). Dasgupta and Heal (1981) have shown that a fully informative price system is impossible: that it is not possible to prove the existence of a price system that reflects all of the information necessary to prevent a resource from being exhausted. David Newbery and Joseph Stiglitz (1982; Ormerod, 1995) have shown that under conditions of uncertainty, competitive equilibrium is not in general Pareto optimal.[10]

Another problem, uncovered through the work of Arrow, concerns the existence of futures markets. *Futures* are contracts made for the purchase or sale of commodities or financial assets in "future markets," at some specified date in the future. These markets exist for some commodities, such as primary products and raw materials, which allow traders to hedge against changes in price. However, in general it is not possible to agree to buy goods in the future at prices that are fixed today, not only because such markets do not exist, but also because sellers fear that inflation and rising costs may erode profitability. Competitive equilibrium theory requires that there are a very large number of futures markets, certainly more than exist in reality (Ormerod, 1995, 81).

Some economic theories, such as *monetarism* (increases in the money supply are a necessary and sufficient condition for inflation), have been soundly refuted theoretically and empirically[11]—yet are still reheated and served to a long-suffering public. Criticisms are ignored. Indeed, one of the most interesting areas where a decisive refutation of an important part of neoclassical economics has occurred is capital theory. Here the presentation of special models of *capital reversing* challenged the idea of the neoclassicists that investment increases as the required rate of return falls. (The rate of return is net profit after depreciation as a percentage of average capital employed in the firm.) Neoclassical economics holds that as the required rate of return falls, firms switch from less to more capital-intensive methods of production. Therefore, the rate of investment should increase. Models were constructed which showed that the rate of return could reach a level where *capital reswitching* would occur, where firms would reswitch from more to less capital-intensive production methods. Therefore, contrary to neoclassicism, investment would fall as the required rate of return also fell (Harcourt, 1975a; Yeager, 1976; Hausman, 1981).

M. C. Howard has argued that the neo-Ricardian critique of capital theory, particularly that embodied in Piero Sraffa's *Production of Commodities by Means of Commodities* (Sraffa, 1960), is itself subject to limitations. He says:

[T]he neo-Ricardians do not have a coherent theory which is both contrary to the neoclassicism they seek to overthrow and capable of overcoming the limitations of Marx's work which they themselves have been partially responsible for uncovering. Even where they have achieved success against neoclassical theory, it has been only on the periphery. Those forms of neoclassicism that Sraffian economists undermined are precisely those which failed to rigorously follow through that theory of action on which this economics ultimately takes its stand. Consequently, contemporary neoclassical general equilibrium theorists have had no difficulty in accepting such criticisms. (Howard, 1987, 332–333)

Even if Sraffa's own position is subject to internal problems, as Joan Robinson has noted, Sraffa's work demonstrates that there is no such thing as a "quantity of capital" existing independently of the rate of profit for a capitalist economy (Robinson, 1973a, 203). Commodities are necessary to produce commodities. If capital cannot be reduced to a single quantity, then it is not theoretically possible to calculate the effect of varying it by a unit amount. The claim that the single quantity is money is a circular claim because one has to assume a rate of interest to show how the equilibrium rate of return is decided. Why is a "quantity of capital" needed anyway? As Harcourt concisely explains, it is needed because the neoclassical view holds:

that the relative supplies of "capital" and labour, and their accompanying marginal products are *determinants* of the returns to and shares of "capital" and labour *in the national income*. . . . In order for this to be so, the amount of "capital" must be measured *prior* to the start of the analysis (as labour may be, making certain approximations, in terms of, say, man hours), even though the prices of the products and of the services of the factors themselves may be determined simultaneously as the equilibrium solutions of a general equilibrium analysis. That is to say, the technical conditions of production, whereby total output is regarded as a function of "capital" and labour, formally expressed in terms of an aggregate production function, must exist *before* the equilibrium solutions are derived, in the same way as the subjective preferences of individual consumers, the other set of determinants in a general equilibrium analysis and the focal point of the neoclassical marginalist revolution, exist prior to and independently of, the ultimate equilibrium solutions. Only in this way can the relative supplies of "capital" and labour be regarded as ultimate determinants of the shares of profits and wages as capital goods are accumulated over time. But aggregate "capital" on which the capitalist class earns a uniform rate of profit in competitive conditions must be valued in terms of prices that, themselves, contain the rate of profits as an element. The fact that the prices *and* the rate of profits, and, therefore, the value of "capital", can be obtained as the *end* results of analysis at each point in "time" is thus besides the point. (Harcourt, 1975a, 5)

If no meaning can be given to the concept of a "quantity of capital" apart from the rate of profit, then the neoclassical proposition that the "marginal product of capital" is a determinant of the rate of profit (ignoring in this argument, the other factors of production) is meaningless. Further, as Joan Robinson has stated (Robinson, 1973a), when the marginal productivity of labor is defined, either the physical inputs other than labor are kept constant, or the rate of profit on capital is. Robinson notes that this refutes the doctrine that wages are regulated by marginal productivity (Robinson, 1973b, 234). To try and avoid these problems by arbitrarily identifying some substance to which heterogeneous capital goods can be reduced, which can be converted into any type of capital good which one desires—is not a solution to the problem of the epistemological circularity in capital theory. This "unit of capital" needs to be common to both physical, financial and knowledge-information capital, an economic substance common to both physical and nonphysical productive resources. It seems to us that it is metaphysically impossible to say what this common substratum is; it is something of which one knows not what; it is nothing at all (Meade, 1961).

UTILITARIANISM, DECISION THEORY AND THE PROBLEM OF PREFERENCES

The theoretical and philosophical dilemmas of capital theory pose embarrassing foundational problems for orthodox economics, although the orthodox economist blissfully ignores these problems. Equally severe problems face orthodox decision theory primarily because of its utilitarian maximization foundation. First, however, let us consider a general problem facing economics as a science, based on the preferences of individuals.

We observed earlier in our quotation from Harcourt that the neoclassical position assumes that the subjective preferences of individual consumers exist prior to and independent of equilibrium solutions. This is so because it is on the basis of such subjective preferences that indifferent curves can be constructed, and in turn demand curves. But is this so? E. J. Mishan and others have argued that the concept of consumer sovereignty (the preprice existence of preferences) is a myth used to show that consumer wants ultimately control the output produced (Mishan, 1967; Galbraith, 1971; Gintis, 1976). Mishan maintains that modern markets are *want-creating*, rather than want-satisfying. Producers determine the range of goods that consumers choose from and, by advertising, mold their choices. The market preexists preferences, so the subjective preferences of individual consumers do *not* exist independently of equilibrium solutions. This is so even if consumers have a moderate degree of rationality and freedom and are not fully influenced by advertising. An individual by virtue of being a social and cultural being is inevitably shaped by his/her environment, so it would be absurd to suppose that preferences for goods and services are not. This, we feel, raises a problem for orthodox economics as severe as the epistemological problem confronting capital theory.

The theoretical cogency of orthodox economics, along with liberal social choice theory, is challenged by a number of logical arguments, the most important of which is Arrow's Impossibility Theorem (Arrow, 1951). Arrow's work establishes the limitations of liberal social theory just as Gödel's work establishes the limitations of Hilbert's formalist foundations of mathematics (Kelly, 1976, 1978; Strasnick, 1976; Resnik, 1987). The proof depends on these conditions:

(A1) *Collective Rationality*: For any given set of orderings, the social choice function is derivable from an ordering.

(A2) *Pareto Principle*: If alternative *x* is preferred to alternative *y* by every single individual according to his ordering, then the social ordering also ranks *x* above *y*.

(A3) *Independence of Irrelevant Alternatives*: The social choice made from an environment depends only on the orderings of individuals with respect to the alternatives in that environment.

(A4) *Nondictatorship*: There is no individual whose preferences are automatically society's preferences, independent of the preferences of all other individuals.

Arrow showed that no social choice function can fulfill all four conditions.[12] Amartya Sen has shown that under weaker conditions than Arrow, namely acyclicity and the Pareto Principle, it is impossible to have a social choice function that allows an individual an absolute choice over any pair of choice options:the so-called "impossibility of a Paretian liberal."[13] There have been developments of Sen's work. Weale (1980) has shown that egalitarianism is inconsistent with the Pareto Principle and McLean (1980) has shown that liberalism is inconsistent with egalitarianism. Richard Routley (1979, 1980) has restated and generalized Arrow's Impossibility Theorem, arguing that the theorem is a problem for conventional economic assessment in general. Neoclassical economics is a form of optimization theory where choices are made between competing alternatives. Routley's generalization involves replacing individuals by factors and removing individual reduction assumptions. Thomas Schwartz (1972) has also criticized maximization decision theory, using a refinement and development of Arrow's Impossibility Theorem. Forming a social choice function from individual preferences seems to be impossible.[14]

There are other so-called paradoxes that also refute the view of neoclassical economists that each rational economic man pursuing his own selfish interests best serves the interests of all in the long run. The "tragedy of the commons," first stated by William Forster Lloyd in 1833 and developed by Garrett Hardin in 1968, shows otherwise (Hardin, 1968). Hardin states this paradox as follows:

Let a number of herdsmen turn their cattle loose in a pasture that is jointly owned and soon the common will be ruined. Why? Because the pasture has a limited "carrying capacity" . . . and each herdsman gets the full benefit of adding to his herd, while the disbenefits arising from over-exploitation of the resource (eg soil erosion) are shared by all the herdsmen. Fractional losses are not enough to deter aggressive cattle owners, so all the exploiters suffer in an *unmanaged commons*. (Hardin, 1994, 199)

Individual exploiters make doubly wrong decisions: wrong for themselves and wrong for society in the long run. *Laissez-faire* leads to ecological disaster. The individual pursuit of self-interest does not necessarily lead to social order.

The famous "Prisoner's Dilemma" can also be interpreted to be a refutation of the individualist, egoist foundations of decision theory (Ions, 1977). The

Prisoner's Dilemma shows that the pursuit of individual rational self-interest (personal utility maximization, if you like) can lead to collective ill. It also shows that this simple form of utilitarianism is self-refuting because the unconstrained pursuit of rational self-interest leads to the ultimate frustration of that self-interest (Sen, 1977). In a market context it shows that neoclassical market forces can't guarantee the best result. Combined with Arrow's Impossibility Theorem, we can conclude that the neoclassicist cannot justify in *general* (or *a priori*) the free market's theoretical claim to optimality or efficiency (Dyke, 1981). Arguments can also be found in the literature which indicate that utilitarianism can generate individual obligations that are *collectively*, not merely *individually*, irrational to fulfill. It has been argued that it is *not* necessarily true that if each member of a group fulfills his or her individual obligations, the group is better off than in the situation when some or all members had failed to fulfill their individual obligations.[15]

Expected utility theory is a cornerstone of neoclassical economics. It has been used to give a foundation to the market demand schedule, to justify the claim that the demand curve expresses a law-like relationship between price and quantity demanded and that this relationship is not merely a correlation, but can tell us what would occur counterfactually (Samuelson, 1975; Fishburn, 1982; Haslett, 1990; Broome, 1991). Classical Bayesian decision theory holds that a rational agent has degrees of confidence, represented by a probability function, and value judgments, represented by a utility function. A choice is rational for the Bayesian if it maximizes expected utility.

In the classic writings of Bentham and Mill, utilitarianism is defined as the position that the purpose of all action should be to bring about the greatest happiness of the greatest number of people. Pleasure and happiness of the individual or mankind in general is the end and criterion of moral good and right. This position is untenable, as von Neumann and Morgenstern have shown (von Neumann & Morgenstern, 1994, 11). In general, two or more functions cannot be maximized at once, as one function may have a maximum while the other does not. However, Yunker notes in his defense of utilitarianism, the social welfare function need not be linear; more complex social welfare functions exist including the Rawlsian maximin-utility rule and the Nash product-of-utility rule (Yunker, 1986). We will not consider these different utilitarian accounts of the social welfare function here, because orthodox neoclassical economics is not based on them.

Is maximization possible at all? Shackle argues that for maximization to occur, the knowledge necessary for choosing the best alternative must be acquired so that a calculation of which alternative maximizes utility or profit can be made (Shackle, 1973; Tintner, 1941; Alchian, 1950). Shackle denies that such knowledge acquisition is possible, so maximization is impossible. The argument that the possession of the necessary knowledge is impossible, as Boland notes (Boland, 1981), is based on *induction* and there are notorious problems in justifying inductive inferences when information is finite or incomplete. Shackle's skepticism about the possibility of obtaining the necessary knowledge to maximize utility under conditions of uncertainty, when a potentially infinite amount of information is needed, is not refuted by an appeal to inductive skepticism. On the contrary, if inductive skepticism is true, then rational economic man cannot function as neoclassical theory requires him to, because he cannot have the necessary knowledge to make fully rational decisions. Much of rational economic man's knowledge is based on induction.

Boland denies that true knowledge is necessary for maximization; for neoclassical economics all that is necessary is that the consumer believe that his theory of what is the shape of the utility function is true (Boland, 1981, 1032). However, as the consumer is a "rational economic man," this does not solve Shackle's problem as the argument can be restated using "rational belief" rather than "true knowledge." Consumers are unlikely to have rational beliefs about the *best* alternatives because of the underdetermination of evidence.

Both Leibenstein (1979) and Simon (1979) argue against the maximization thesis by denying that consumers are maximizers. Boland notes that an attempted empirical refutation of the utility maximization thesis faces the methodological difficulty that survey reports are suspect and direct observations of the agent's decision making is impossible. Behavioral maximization is not directly testable. One may then try to test the utility maximization thesis by testing logically derived consequences but the same methodological problems regarding observations will remain (Boland, 1981, 1033).

Boland maintains that the neoclassical maximization thesis is beyond criticism: "no logical criticism of maximization can ever convince a neoclassical theorist that there is something intrinsically wrong with the maximization hypothesis" (Boland, 1981, 1035). The argument advanced here is that the maximization thesis is an "all-and-some-statement": "For all decision-makers there is something they maximize." All-and-some-statements are neither verifiable nor refutable Boland says, because as universal statements claiming to be true for all decision makers they are unverifiable. Thus it should be logically possible to prove that such a statement is false when it is false by providing a counterexample, but because an existential statement is involved, any alleged counterexample is unverifiable even if the counterexample is true. The verification of the counterexample requires the refutation of a strictly existential statement and standard classical logic holds that one cannot refute existential statements.

It is possible to challenge the claim that one cannot refute existential statements, as Harré has done in *The Principles of Scientific Thinking* (1970). But let us follow through Boland's argument. He maintains that the maximization thesis should be viewed not as a tautology (or mere logical truth) but as a metaphysical thesis much like others such as determinism, realism, theism and materialism. The difference between the maximization thesis and all of these other theses is that even though they are metaphysical, and thus not refutable by experimental evidence, they are purported to be true of the world and capable of being supported by argument. They are also capable of critical evaluation. Thus, for example, in metaphysics we have well-known debates such as determinism versus freedom (or libertarianism) and realism versus nominalism. The strategy taken by Boland would prevent empirical counterexamples from refuting the maximization thesis and empirical evidence from supporting it. Metaphysical the statement may be, but it is a metaphysical statement that is utterly lacking in epistemic warrant by definition. There is no reason at all for a critic to rationally accept the maximization thesis. If it is true, we can't know that it is true. This in itself is sufficient reason for rejecting the maximization thesis in favor of, say, Simon's position that economic agents satisfice.

We should, however, reject the view that an existential statement is irrefutable. Whether or not an existential statement is refutable depends on whether or not there is an infinite or, for practical purposes, indefinitely large domain, for which the variable in the existential statement ranges over. In may cases if the domain is infinite, an existential statement cannot be falsified. Many existential statements referring to finite domains and finite space-time regions can be refuted. For example, "There is an elephant in my room at (this) time t" is false. This can be empirically verified. Likewise, existential statements can be falsified because they conflict with general scientific principles such as the second law of therodynamics. The statement:

There is a perpetual motion machine in my room

is false because there are no perpetual motion machines. We believe that a statement such as:

There is a decision maker who satisfies rather than maximizes

is not only verifiable, but from Simon's work, *true*. We believe, then, that Boland's defense of the maximization thesis is flawed.

Traditionally neoclassical economists have defined utility (U) as a function $U = U(W)$ of a single variable wealth, which is a proxy for all that constitutes the individual's true utility function. But this simplification has led to paradoxes such as simultaneous gambling and insurance (Friedman & Savage, 1948; Markowitz, 1952) and the Allais and Ellsberg paradoxes (Allais & Hagen, 1979; Levi, 1986). Kemp (1988) proposes that the traditional utility function should be modified to include another variable to recognize the fact that when individuals receive increments or decrements in wealth, this is unlikely to be independent of the manner in which the change was brought about. Expected utility theory has treated equal money gains and losses as equivalent but this is not psychologically correct. Thus Kemp formulates a more general utility function for which money per se cannot act as a proxy. He reasons, knowing his Beatles, that money can't buy one love, so letting this metaphysical quality be L:

$$U = U(W, L).$$

The problem though with this approach is that it is impossible to generate information empirically about the nature of this utility surface. A von Neumann cardinal utility function is said by the neoclassicists to be constructible from experimental observations. This is done by offering individuals bets at various odds and observing the probabilities at which bets are accepted or rejected. On this basis it is claimed that a utility function of the form $U(W)$ can be constructed. However, putting "love" as an argument within a utility function prevents this because "love" varies with the size of the bets. I may be indifferent about a ten-cent bet on the toss of a coin, but not about $100. Therefore, rational economic man does not have a single $U(W)$ curve, but rather a number of different $U(W)$ curves. Kemp concludes: "We are forced reluctantly to the conclusion that experiments can provide no confirmation or falsification of any hypotheses about the nature of the utility function. Because of the existence of love, observed behavior might be consistent with any assumption about attitudes towards risk. The assumption of risk aversion is then an act of faith" (Kemp, 1988, 159). The discussion ends at that point without facing the fact that this is a serious objection to his entire approach, which must in turn be seen as empirically empty.

Contrary to Boland, the neoclassical maximization hypothesis can be criticized and, we believe, refuted. Decision problems can be described where none of the available options maximize expected utility (Gibbard & Harper, 1978). One of us has argued elsewhere (Smith, 1986) that Newcomb's Problem (Nozick, 1969) is a major problem for utilitarianism and received decision theory. The unsolvability of this problem, recently conceded by Nozick (Nozick, 1993), well supports our skepticism.

In situations where paradoxes such as this occur, it is well recommended that one examine fundamentals and, in this case, the basic axioms of revealed preference theory and utility theory—the completeness, transitivity and reflexivity of preferences. An indifference curve is associated with each commodity, each point of the curve representing commodity combinations such that the consumer is indifferent to the specified goods. If either completeness, transitivity or reflexivity fails, then there would be no way of connecting increasing consumer satisfaction with the movement away from the origin of an indifference curve. It is well known that counterexamples can be presented to the transitivity axiom (Loomes et al., 1991). This was admitted by Luce and Raiffa in *Games and Decisions*, an early, yet still authoritative text on decision theory. They recognized that there were counterexamples to basic axioms such as transitivity, continuity and monotonicity, but accepted these axioms because they were "mathematically tractable" (Luce & Raiffa, 1957, 27). Mathematical tractability does not imply truth or correctness.

Hilary Putnam has argued that the assumptions of decision theory are more dubious than is usually recognized (Putnam, 1986). The von Neumann axioms for rational preference imply that all choices (including "incomparable alternatives") can be rank-ordered. Any two commodities x and y are such that (i) x is preferred to y or (ii) the subject is indifferent between x and y. As Putnam notes, there are *incomparable* alternatives and choosing between them is *not* the same as choosing between alternatives that are indifferent. Putnam supplies a counterexample. The general point to be made is that people may claim that it does not make sense to say in general that they prefer one object to another or that they are indifferent to both. Objects may fail to enter into the preference relation at all. The subject, through ignorance or uncertainty, may not have a defined preference structure for a wide range of goods, but may not be indifferent to choice. Choices may be made on noneconomic grounds.

In received decision theory if two alternative courses of action have the same expected utility, then the choice between them is a matter of indifference, so that a small chance is compensated for by a large return, and conversely. However, as Bunge has concluded from a survey of the empirical literature, decision theory (DT) has been empirically refuted:

[W]hen the outcomes are non-negative, subjects show a strong risk aversion:they prefer sure gains over gambling, even if the expected utility of the latter is greater than that of the former. On the other hand, when the outcomes are nonpositive, subjects show a strong aversion to sure-things:they prefer gambling even if its expected utility is smaller than that of the sure loss. These results contradict DT. Worse, they show that, though people have preferences, they have no utility functions. (Bunge, 1985, 304–305)

Another, little-talked-about result in social choice theory seals the fate of orthodox economics. The theory of the "second best," proposed by Lipsey and Lancaster (1956–57), states that in a situation where there is a deviation from a social optimum, the implementation of policy measures that eliminate only some of the departures from the optimum may result in a net decrease in social welfare. If an optimum cannot be achieved, a move toward it is not necessarily better than a move away. For example, even if perfect competition was not attainable in all markets, it would not follow that it was rational to establish it in some because it might result in effects diametrically opposed to those desired.

The attainment of a Paretian optimum requires the simultaneous fulfillment of all the optimum conditions:

> The general theorem for the second base optimum states that if there is introduced into a general equilibrium system a constraint which prevents the attainment of one of the Paretian conditions, the other Paretian conditions, although still attainable, are, in general, no longer desirable. (Lipsey & Lancaster, 1956–57, 11)

If one of the Paretian optimum conditions cannot be fulfilled, optimality can only be reached by departing from the other Paretian conditions, to reach a "second-best optimum." There is no *a priori* way to decide between situations where some of the Paretian optimum conditions are satisfied, while others are not.

Ng (1985) notes that orthodox economics assumes in an optimality analysis that the first-best optimality conditions prevail in other sectors of the economy. Ng cites the case of a general equilibrium-type analysis of externality, which usually assumes that problems of, say monopolistic power or government interference and other market-distorting affects do not occur. But:

> From the theory of second best, it seems that all these analyses are useless. By adjusting the economy to take account of externalities alone, we may be making matters worse if there exist other distortions in the system. Similarly, by studying a (proper) subset of the economy, even considering all problems including externality, monopoly, etc., the resulting policy recommendation may be worse than doing nothing unless the complicated interrelationships of this subset and the rest of the economy are taken into consideration. It seems that, to make any improvement at all, we must analyse the whole economy and take every problem into account. We must leap right to the summit to be sure of an improvement. But it is clear that this task is epistemologically, administratively, and politically impossible. (Ng, 1985, 224)

The theory of the second best poses for orthodox economics a problem similar in some respects to the n-body problem in physics. Ng tries to "soften the blow" of the second-best theorem by pointing out that constraints used in many economic analyses are not the complicated ones giving rise to "second-best" conditions, they may take the form of simple linear inequalities (Ng, 1985, 224–225). This exit is not likely to be successful. If Ormerod (1995) is right in believing that economics needs to be understood in nonlinear terms, then any mathematical representation of a real economy will be much more complicated than the formulation used by Lipsey and Lancaster and certainly by Ng in his theory of the "third best."

This is especially so, given the difficulty of achieving Pareto optimality in an economy. Pareto optimality is reached if, and only if, there is an *optimal* distribution of goods between consumers, an *optimal* allocation of inputs in production and *optimal* amounts of output. In the last case, for example, for two goods X and Y and consumers A and B, optimal output occurs when the ratio of marginal cost to marginal utility is the same for each good. This must hold for *all* goods and *all* individuals in the economy. If it doesn't, the neoclassicist says that consumers could benefit if more of the good that has the higher marginal utility per unit of marginal cost is produced. No doubt it would. But the neoclassicist cannot establish in a noncircular way that this preestablished harmony actually exists and it is incredible to suppose that it does for all individuals and all goods. The aim of a capitalist economy is not to satisfy consumers or maximize their expected utility functions, but to sell commodities at a profit. Consequently, Pareto optimality is unlikely ever to be achieved in a modern capitalist economy (and under conditions of uncertainty, the Newbury-Stiglitz result is that competitive equilibrium is not, in general, Pareto optimal). Thus, the theory of the second best not only applies outright, but applies as well to "third best," "fourth best," . . . options. Contrary to Ng, we should throw away the texts of received economics.

BEYOND OPTIMIZING

Maurice Allais in his critique of economics, "Theories of General Economic Equilibrium and Maximum Efficiency" (Allais, 1978), notes that General Equilibrium Theory assumes continuity and convexity of fields of choice and fields of production at all points. Other unrealistic assumptions are also made, such that the quantity of any good can be any real number—the assumption of perfect divisibility. The demand function is assumed to be single-valued and continuous and that for every commodity bundle there are a set of prices for which that bundle will be demanded for a given income level. Allais is concerned primarily with convexity assumptions, but it seems to us that the *continuity* assumption is the Achilles' heel of orthodoxy.

Consider, for example, the transformation curve. This is a graph in Euclidean two-space representing a real valued concave curve, showing the maximum amount of one good or service that an economy can produce by reducing production of another good and transferring the resources saved to the production of the other good. In many cases this idea of a transformation of resources is logical; for example, in wartime there is a tradeoff between consumer goods such as cars and military vehicles because of resource shortages. But it is utterly absurd to suppose, as Bannock, Baxter and Davis (1987) do, that one could compare battleships and food. They say, by way of example, that an economy might be capable of producing fifty battleships if it produces no food, or no battleships if it produces a million tons of food.

Now for the point of the model, we assume that there are no exports of food and no food stockpiles—for we are, after all, considering the production possibility curve of only *one* society. If a society produced no food, it would produce *no* battleships—this is an ecological fact, people need food to live and work. There are no ready mechanical *transfers* of resources between high-technology industries such as military weapon production and agricultural and food production. In the case of labor resources, technicians to a limited extent could perhaps do manual labor work on farms, but farmhands would not be able to do electronics without training to become electronics experts.

A frontier mapping all of the possible combinations of any goods can, of course, be drawn, dividing the possible from impossible situations. However, there is no guarantee that such a curve will be concave or continuous. It will not be a "transformation curve," but only a curve mapping maximum efficient situations in a preference index space. There is no reason at all to believe that such a curve would be continuous.

The standard explanation of concavity is based on the notion of the rate of technical substitution declining the more of a commodity that is produced. (The role of technical substitution is the increase in production of one commodity, achieved by decreasing the production of another commodity by one unit.) Bannock, Baxter and Davis state that:

> a large amount of food can be made for the sacrifice of one battleship if no food is being made to start with, because the best fields can be used and the people good at farming but poor at battleship building can be transferred to farming productively. However, suppose that only one battleship is being built and the rest of the economy is geared to food production; transferring resources from the battleship to food will have hardly any effect on food output. Thus, the rate at which battleships can be transformed into food declines as food production rises. (Bannock et al., 1987, 406)

In fact, Allais has shown that there is a logical inconsistency between the standard marginal and average cost curves (the average cost is at a minimum at the intersection of the two curves) and the production possibility curve. The production possibility curve must be composed of juxtaposed curvilinear elements, which are discontinuous at some points (Allais, 1978).

The arguments given above indicate to us that economics and decision theory based on the view that rational decision making involves maximizing one's own greatest good or greatest preference satisfaction is flawed. Slote in *Beyond Optimizing* (1989) has argued that the optimizing individual as a matter of conceptual necessity is lacking in *autarkeia*, self-sufficiency. Slote defends the commonsense position of *satisficing* (Simon, 1955). In this view it often makes sense *not* to pursue one's own greatest good or desires. A modesty of desire, rational moderation, is a view that accepts *limits*. The acceptance of limits—*Limitationism*—is ultimately what inclines a reasonable person to reject utilitarianism, and orthodox economic and decision theory. If these doctrines fail to help us to understand even individual behavior, then they are quite impotent when applied on the national and individual level. Orthodox economics operates with a subjectivist theory of value, which denies that the contents of preferences can be rationally assessed (Gauthier, 1986). However, it *is* appropriate to examine the rationality of preferences. The technical results reviewed in this chapter show that individual welfare is not all that counts in policy choices (Boulding, 1979; Sagoff, 1986). We must therefore look for an alternative economic framework, which, because of the ecological truth of Limitationism, is consistent with *autarkeia*. This is the aim of the next part of this chapter.

ECOLOGICAL ECONOMICS: THE SEARCH FOR ALTERNATIVES

I sympathise, therefore, with those who would minimise, rather than those who would maximise, economic entanglement between nations. Ideas, knowledge, art, hospitality, travel—these are the things which should of their nature be international. But let goods be homespun whenever it is reasonably and conveniently possible; and, above all, let finance be primarily national. Yet, at the same time, those who seek to disembarrass a country of its entanglements should be very slow and wary. It should not be a matter of tearing up roots but of slowly training a plant to grow in a different direction. For these strong reasons, I am inclined to the belief that, after the transition is accomplished, a greater measure of national self-sufficiency and economic isolation between countries than existed in 1914 may tend to serve the cause of peace, rather than otherwise. At any rate the age of economic internationalism was not particularly successful in avoiding war; and if its friends retort that the imperfection of its success never gave it a fair chance, it is reasonable to point out that a greater success is scarcely probable in the coming years. (Keynes, 1982, 236–237)

In the previous section we argued that neoclassical economics fails to provide us with a satisfactory theoretical foundation for the understanding of economic life. Others have argued that neoclassical economics has a totally inadequate and misplaced view of the environment (Hamilton, 1994). Economic orthodoxy is particularly ignorant of basic ecology, physics and biophysical realities such as the second law of thermodynamics. This point has been argued through in some detail by Herman Daly (Daly & Cobb, 1989). For the moment, though, let us consider the objection that our point seems to be refutable by only a cursory knowledge of the history of the marginalist revolution. For example, Mirowski in one historical study has argued that "neoclassical economic theory is bowdlerised nineteenth century physics" (Mirowski, 1984, 377). However, neoclassical economic theory itself was *not* given a physical rationale or justification; it was merely interpreted within the mathematical formalism of energetics. For example let $\mathbf{F}$ be under the vector of prices of a set of traded goods and q be the vector of the quantity of those goods purchased, then the integral $\int \mathbf{F}.dq = T$ is the total expenditure on those goods (Mirowski, 1984, 368). If the integrand is an exact differential, then a scalar function of the goods x and y can be defined by a function of the form $U = U(x, y)$, which is the utility function. This concept parallels the concept of potential energy. But the use of a common mathematical formalism implies nothing beyond that. It does not imply an isomorphism in reality. The utility and power of mathematics arise precisely because it allows such modeling to occur.

Juan Martinez-Alier in *Ecological Economics: Energy, Environment and Society* has presented us with a very scholarly survey of a number of theorists who believed that orthodox economics lacked an adequate biophysical grounding (Martinez-Alier, 1993). Thinkers discussed include Patrick Geddes, Frederick Soddy, William Kapp, Josef Popper-Lynkeus, Serhii Podolinsky, Lancelot Hogben, Lewis Mumford, Otto Neurath, Leopold Pfaundler, Henry Adams, Karl Ballod-Atlanticus, Nicholas Georgescu-Roegen, Kenneth Boulding and Herman Daly. They are united in believing that political economy should be based, not on the psychological dispositions of individuals, but on physical and biological laws (Peshine Smith, 1897, ii).

This tradition can be called the *ecological economic* tradition. We would include in this tradition as well Thomas Malthus (Hardin, 1993) and the works of many of the so-called *Humanistic economic* school (Goodwin, 1991; Lutz, 1990, 1992; Lutz & Lux, 1979, 1988). According to Lutz, humanistic economics is part of a general social economics movement where "the market is rejected as a final arbiter of social values and instead priority is given to a non-reductionistic, holistic ethos intrinsically related to a concept of society as an organic whole" (Lutz, 1992, 112). This, as we shall see, is essentially an ecological concept of society, because human values cannot be excluded from the domain of economics. Also, it is impossible to understand the work of ecological economists such as Herman Daly without understanding the social/humanistic foundations to his work. Let us examine this tradition as we search for an alternative to orthodox economics.

Humanistic economics is traced by Lutz in his historical survey to the Swiss political economist Jean C. L. S. Sismondi (1773–1842). He was originally a follower of Adam Smith, but broke with the classical orthodoxy in 1815. He began an attack upon the doctrine of *laissez-faire* in support of state intervention. In 1819 he published *Nouveaux Principes d'Économie Politique (The New Principles of Political Economy)* (Sismondi, [1819], 1991). Political economy, rather than being exclusively concerned with the nature and causes of the wealth of nations, "has, or ought to have, the purpose of striving for the welfare of all people united in society. It pursues this highest end by exploring all means and opportunities compatible with human nature; at the same time it aims at securing the greatest possible sharing of all persons in this welfare" (Sismondi, [1819], 1991, 21). In other words, the point of an economy for Sismondi is to serve the happiness of the people, not production for production's sake and the unlimited growth of wealth.

Sismondi was a very early critic of industrialization, emphasizing its alienated nature and the social dislocation caused by it. His work influenced Thomas Carlyle, who called the mainstream political economy of Adam Smith "the dismal science" and "pig philosophy" (Lutz, 1992, 93). Sismondi also influenced John Ruskin, whose most important work, *Unto This Last* ([1864], 1988), attacked the view of human nature held by utilitarian political economists such as John Stuart Mill. His point was that wealth or economic utility is incommensurable with social utility. Rational economic man has "no other moral influences than those which affect the rat or swine" (quoted from Lutz, 1992, 94).

John Hobson (1885–1940) was in turn influenced by Ruskin (Hobson, 1914, 1929). He likewise believed that economic systems needed to be judged by reference to a value standard. He had, Lutz notes, "a programme of building a new economics centred on the whole person with an inborn capacity for self-fulfilment, a social economics that counts both economic and non-economic costs and benefits in the assessment of alternative institutions and policies" (Lutz, 1992, 97). Hobson was also a critic of internationalism and universalism. In his book *Imperialism: A Study* (1902) he argued that imperialism arose from the view that there was an ideal system suitable for all humanity. He observed that "there may be many paths to civilization, that strong racial and environmental differences preclude a hasty grafting of alien institutions, regardless of continuity and selection of existing agencies and forms" (Hobson, 1902, 245). Richard

Tawney (1880–1962) held to a similar humanistic economics as Hobson (Tawney, 1920, 1926, [1931], 1964). M. K. Gandhi (1869–1948) was also influenced by Ruskin's *Unto This Last*. Gandhi's advocacy of self-reliance and his critique of modernism and Westernization influenced E. F. Schumacher (1973, 1977). Schumacher had an undeniable influence on work in the broad fields of political ecology and ecological economics. His emphasis upon the need for small-scale development and the construction of "conserver societies" constitutes one of the most important postmodern economic critiques of modernity and scientism. More important, though, Schumacher's work tied together two schools of criticism of modernity—the ecological and the humanistic economic schools.

"Ecological economics," as defined by Robert Costanza in his 1991 edited book and (his edited) journal of the same name (Costanza et al., 1991), is founded on the proposition that the world's environment is endangered and that decisions made on the basis of conventional economic criteria are primarily short-run and can lead to disasterous long-run consequences. Traditional economic and ecological models and concepts are inadequate for the task of creating a sustainable world system. Consequently there needs to be a new transdisciplinary field which addresses economic and ecological issues in the widest sense. Traditional intellectual boundaries need to be transcended. Further, problems need to be approached as problems in themselves, rather than as phenomena viewed by the preconceived categories of orthodox economic theory. Existing theoretical tools from economics should be used if they are judged to be adequate, but if not, new tools should be used.

Ecological economics differs from both conventional ecology and orthodox economics by virtue of "the breadth of its perception of the problem, and the importance it attaches to environment-economy interactions" (Costanza et al., 1991, 3). This wider and longer view is taken in terms "of space, time and the parts of the system to be studied" (Costanza et al., 1991, 3). The environment within the framework of conventional environmental economics is viewed merely as a resource, so the attention of study is on optimal resource depletion and optimal rates of pollution. The tastes and preferences of consumers are theoretical givens and the resource base is regarded as unlimited:there are no limits to growth or limits to environmental degradation. Ecological economics takes a wider view, seeing humans as but one species in the biosphere, albeit a very important one. Consequently, nature is not regarded as a limitless pollution sink and the ecological economics tradition maintains that there are limits to growth. It rejects the view of neoclassical economics that natural and man-made capital are substitutes for each other, seeing them rather as complements. Technology and machines can to some degree substitute for some aspects of natural capital—such as sunlight, plant and animal biomass, forests, genetic information, water and even petroleum—but the proposition that they are in general substitutes is absurd. It is only because conventional economists are purely urban creatures, pampered by modern technology and society, and because of a general disinterest in biology, chemistry and ecology that such an idea was entertained in the first place. Indeed, ecological economics, unlike conventional economics, is skeptical about the ability of technology and scientific progress to solve the general problem of resource constraints. If we gamble that technology will save the day and do not take other action—and are proved wrong—the results will be disastrous, being no less than the destruction of our resource base and civilization itself (Costanza, et al, 1991, 7).

Ecological economics, like environmental economics, attempts to place economic value on intangibles such as human life, forests and ecosystems. The argument for this is that this is done everyday in the construction of bridges, highways and so on. However, ecological economics differs from conventional economics in that it does not hold that ecological goods and services are an outcome of individual human preferences, for ecological goods are long-term and are not traded in well-defined markets, or in markets at all. The relationship of many ecological goods and services to individual well-being is often not understood by individuals at all. Individuals are often not informed about the true cost of ecological goods and services and there may be conflicts between short-term benefits and long-term costs.

Future individuals are also not free to bid in these markets, so their preferences are not represented. As an alternative basis of ecological valuation Costanza, Daly and Bartholomew propose the following:

[T]he economic value of ecosystems is connected to their physical, chemical, and biological role in the long-term, global system—whether the present generation of humans fully recognizes that role or not. If it is accepted that each species, no matter how seemingly uninteresting or lacking in immediate utility, has a role in natural ecosystems (which *do* provide many direct benefits to humans), it is possible to shift the focus away from our imperfect short-term perceptions and derive more accurate values for long-term ecosystem services. Using this perspective we may be able to better estimate the values contributed by, say, maintenance of water and atmospheric quality to long-term human well-being. Obviously, these services are vital and of infinite value at some level. The valuation question relates to marginal changes, incremental tradeoffs between, say, forested land and agricultural land on a scale of hundreds of acres rather than hundreds of square miles. (Costanza et al., 1991, 10–11)

While we find much of value in the ecological economics position, we do not believe that advocates of the position are fully aware of the philosophical ramifications of their views. In the above quotation, for example, it is recognized that our life-support systems are of "infinite value" at some level. But what level? The next sentence in the quotation seems to indicate, by stating that the level is one of the scale of hundreds of square miles rather than hundreds of acres, that "minor" exploitations of the environment are acceptable to maintain present consumption standards. Yet it has been the sum total of these "minor" development which has led, day by day, year by year, to the degradation and destruction of many of the ecosystems of the Earth. Ecological economics still wishes to trade and negotiate on issues that rationally should not be a matter of negotiation *if* the biosphere is in the perilous state that leading proponents of ecological economics inform us that it is (Goodland, 1992). If the world has reached limits, if the business-as-usual view is leading us to the abyss of ecological catastrophe, then our goal should not be to obtain an economic value of ecosystems to see how much more can be traded and exploited—but to work out ways to control human population growth and scale down production. In general, ecological economics, represented by the contributions published in the journal *Ecological Economics*, has not attempted to do this, nor has there been a serious attempt to think through the political and philosophical consequences of their worldview. Work published in the American journal *Population and Environment*, in our opinion, is more satisfactory in this respect.

The exception to this criticism is the work of Herman Daly. Perhaps no modern writer has contributed more high-quality work—to the level of deserving an alternative Nobel Prize in economics—to a critical understanding of his discipline. His criticism of orthodox economics is that it comprehensively and consistently commits the "fallacy of misplaced concreteness," which in Whitehead's words involves "neglecting the degree of abstraction involved when an actual entity is considered merely so far as it exemplifies certain categories of thought" (Whitehead, 1929, 11). In other words this fallacy involves theoreticians forgetting the level of abstraction involved and mistaking the model for reality. Whitehead himself said of classical economics:

It is very arguable that the science of political economy, as studied in its first period after the death of Adam Smith (1790), did more harm than good. It destroyed many economic fallacies, and taught how to think about the economic revolution then in progress. But it riveted on men a certain set of abstractions which were disastrous in their effect on modern mentality. It dehumanized industry. This is only one example of a general danger inherent in modern science. Its methodological procedure is exclusive and intolerant, and rightly so. It fixes attention on a definite group of abstractions, neglects everything else, and elicits every scrap of information and theory which is relevant to what it has retained. The method is triumphant provided the abstractions are judicious. But, however triumphant, the triumph is within limits. The neglect of these limits leads to disastrous oversights. (Whitehead, 1925, 200)

We have seen in previous chapters examples of this fallacy; Daly has documented many others. The ignorance of biophysical reality in the orthodox economic assumption that man-made capital is a near-perfect substitute for natural capital is an example (Daly, 1992). In our opinion, cosmopolitanism and economic globalism also embrace the fallacy of "misplaced concreteness." Operating with abstract philosophical and economic models of "one world," it is assumed that the actual world, and indeed even extant nations, will operate in accordance with the model. This, as we have seen earlier in this book, is simply not so.

Daly and Cobb in *For the Common Good* (Daly & Cobb, 1989) follow Dudley Seers (1983) in believing that social and political positions should be examined not only on a scale from "left" to "right," but also on a scale that incorporates a "nationalist" and "antinationalist" axis. Daly and Cobb believe that this scale should in turn be modified to incorporate "communitarian" and "anti-communitarian" dimensions, as nations are only one form of community. They reject cosmopolitanism as a viable and sustainable geopolitical philosophy and in turn advocate the protection of local communities from the acidic affects of globalism and hope for the development of communities of regional communities. Decentralization of economies will allow a decentralization of political power and avoid the need for the establishment of a world government (Daly & Cobb, 1989, 178). This theme is seen especially acutely in Daly and Cobb's critique of free-trade theory in chapter 11 of *For the Common Good* and in other essays by Daly and co-workers discussed earlier in this chapter. Cosmopolitanism and economic globalism threaten the existence of communities and traditions. Further, cosmopolitanism and globalism threaten the possibility of *autarky* or *self-sufficiency*: "There can be no effective national economy if a people cannot feed themselves and otherwise meet their essential needs. Hence a national economy for community will be a relatively self-sufficient economy." (Daly & Cobb, 1989, 173). This does not mean that no trade will occur, Daly and

Cobb note, but it will preclude countries becoming dependent on trade. It will certainly preclude manias of cargo cultism such as Australia's present economic fetish in becoming a part of Asia, regardless of the wishes of local communities.

Since the publication of *For the Common Good*, a number of other works have criticized globalism and advocated autarky, or autarky of varying degrees. By way of outlining and defending the autarky position, we will now examine the arguments of these works.

THE METAPHYSICS OF AUTARKY

Brecher, Childs and Culter, editors of *Global Visions: Beyond the New World Order* (1993), in their introduction to their book distinguish between "globalization-from-above"—known as the *New World Order*, based on transnational business and political elites—and "globalization-from-below," producing a one-world community of human rights. The editors and contributors give what we believe are a devastating series of objection to the New World Order. The New World Order is creating a homogenizing global supermarket that "transfers power and resources from the natural world to human domination, from communities to elites, and from local societies to national and transnational power centers" (Brecher et al., 1933, xi). Globalism is destroying communities and environments, proceeding under the banner of free-market liberalism. It promises riches for all, but supplies only a growing disparity between the rich and the poor both within nations and between nations. This has resulted in a massive migration of people from the Third World to the West, where cheap migrant labor serves the need and greed of industrial capitalism (Brecher et al., 1993, xiii). The New World Order is eroding the power of national governments to control their own societies. Muto Ichiyo of the Pacific-Asian Resource Center in Tokyo is quoted as saying that "people are divided into a multitude of groups with their respective identities: gender, ethnic, religious, geographical, cultural, class, nation-state." However, "these groups are being forced to live together under conditions imposed upon them" by a "state-supported global capitalism" aiming to create "a system of international and hierarchical division of labour." Resistance is "rooted in each group's identity" (quoted from Brecher et al., 1993, xvi; see also Ekins, 1992). The editors conclude:

Proposals for a New World Order are often actually efforts to institutionalize and legitimate globalization-from-above through the United Nations. Guinean political scientist Siba Grovogui notes that "many Western policymakers have called for a reactivation of the UN in a manner that increases the policing role of the Security Council." They use images of "international cooperation, peace, and stability," but in practice, the New World Order they describe is "dominated by the West, in which the Security Council, and the UN in general, lends legitimacy to Western interests and hegemony." Meanwhile, war and turmoil continue throughout much of what Francis Deng has dubbed "The New World Disorder." (Brecher et al., 1993, xiv)

Skepticism about UNCED (the United Nations Conference of Environment and Development) has also been expressed by a number of contributors to *Global Ecology: A New Arena of Political Conflict*, edited by Wolfgang Sachs (Hildyard,

1993; Sachs, ed., 1993). Matthias Finger voices such a skepticism about even this seemingly sensible form of globalism:

> UNCED has served to accelerate the process towards global management, in which the environmental crisis is used as a pretext to further hasten the build-up of a world technocracy managing resources and so-called "environmental" risks, stemming generally from industrial development. In this view, global environmental problems such as resource depletion and pollution are seen as being caused by micro-actors, general individuals in the South, but which, nevertheless, need to be managed globally. This will take the form of so-called global crisis management: environmental threats, along with individual fears and anxieties, will be used in order to legitimize a militaristic and technocratic approach, curing symptoms rather than causes and assembling power in the process. What remains is a profound absence of vision and leadership. No project is in sight to get us out of the crisis. It will need some time and catastrophes to get beyond UNCED. Further ecological degradations will be proof enough that UNCED has failed to deal with the crisis . . . but people, then, will only be more atomized, feel more insecure, and probably ready to accept more planetary technocracy. (Finger, 1993, 47–48)

Sachs in his introduction to *Global Ecology* and other contributors argue that the sustainable society can only be constructed at the local grassroots level—not by working at the global level. These writers also attack the views of a rising "ecocracy," which is attempting to manage nature and people worldwide, that is aiming for an international rationalization of life-styles and the elimination of cultural diversity: "the invitation to think globally inadvertently paves the way for worldwide surveillance and management" (Sachs, ed., 1993, xvii).

The rejection of globalism and the advocacy of autarky was made by Schumacher and writers influenced by Leopold Kohr (1978) such as Kirkpatrick Sale (1980). Schumacher's work is very well known and will be only briefly discussed. He argued in *Small Is Beautiful* that the modern industrial system consumes the very basis on which it is supported, namely the endowment of natural capital, and it treats irreplaceable capital as income. Schumacher's concept of "Buddhist economics" (or "Catholic economics" or "Muslim economics") gives emphasis to production from local resources for local needs. Global free trade is therefore seen as uneconomical, for to satisfy needs by use of resources from afar is a failure, not a success. The advocacy of small-scale economies of self-reliance, self-sufficiency—in short autarky—is supported on scale considerations (Kirk, ed., 1983; McRobie, 1985). Kirkpatrick Sale's *Human Scale* is one of the most detailed defenses of this idea—that the present crisis of the environment and civilization is the product of *bigness*—and can only be solved by a return to the human scale, by the decentralization of institutions, the devolution of power, and by the slow dismantling of the large-scale systems and their replacement by smaller, community-based, people-sized units. (See also Morris, 1982; Drengson, 1989, 1995; Naess, 1991; Goldsmith, 1992; McLaughlin, 1993; Berry, 1995.)

Pierre-André Julien and Christian Lafrance have given a formal defense of the Schumacherian position (Julien & Lafrance, 1983). They note that economic efficiency criteria are based on considerations of centralization, standardization and concentration and that these may ignore internal and external *diseconomies*. Julien and Lafrance argue for a reconsideration of the economic criterion of efficiency and the theory of economies of scale. This notion they regard as questionable: "economies of scale originate from the neglect of multiple internal and external diseconomies associated with any growth process" (Julien & Lafrance, 1983,

212). Such diseconomies are usually part of a social cost that is frequently ignored because of their diffuse and collective nature.

Economies of scale are typically discussed in a static and product-oriented context, rather than in a systemic, dynamic and person-oriented perspective. Neoclassical economics conceives of efficiency as private efficiency; for firms or businesses it is the maximization of profits and for individual consumers it is the maximization of marginal utility. Concentrating on firms here, economic efficiency means the minimalization of costs of production, management and distribution costs. Profit maximization means the maximization of revenue and the construction of a set of strategies to dominate the market. For a given technological state profit maximization requires achieving economies of scale in production by obtaining an optimal size compatible with a given level of profitability.

Against the orthodox concept of *private efficiency* Julien and Lafrance introduce the notion of *collective efficiency*, defined as the process of minimizing social costs, these social costs being externalities such as pollution and congestion, the planned accelerated obsolescence of goods, the overutilization of nonrenewable resources, the alienation of labor and structural and cyclical unemployment. The private efficiency criteria reflected in the economies of scale argument ignores these by-products of business activity. Indeed, "at a given state of technology, state of nature and a given state-of-the-art in management and social institutions (factors which are fixed), the by-product of any growth in the production process generate increasing costs of an environmental and social nature" (Julien & Lafrance, 1983, 213–214). Why is this so? They argue their case through with the example of pollution:

> Concentration decreases the ability of a small ecosystem to self-correct the damaging. Thus natural local equilibria are less disturbed and can cope with pollution more easily when productive organizations are more scattered territorially. More often, pollution increases more than proportionally to population or economic growth. A large organization is often the source of more than one negative externality, and although the results of studies of this phenomenon are still preliminary, most suggest that increasing the diverse types of toxicity produce[s] effects which are not necessarily linear and independent, but interactive, resulting in greater negative effects. These results more rapidly affect the ability of nature to assimilate pollution by decreasing the threshold of equlibrium through the phenomenon of congestion. (Julien & Lafrance, 1983, 214; Scitovsky, 1966; Ayres & Kneese, 1969)

Efficiency thus involves private efficiency within the confines of wider collective efficiency, in short the minimization of social costs arising from the pursuit of private efficiency. Introducing social costs into the calculation of economic efficiency reduces, in both the short and long run, the optimal size of many large firms. Julien and Lafrance note that small organizations have many advantages over large organizations. Small organizations can adjust their equipment more readily than big organizations in the face of technological and market change. Small organizations have greater "flexibility" with shorter lines of communication in their information systems; they have a greater adaptability to change so that small firms are more innovative than large firms. Large firms often suffer from an inertia effect because of their sheer size, and in the case of failure, failure of a large organization may be socially disastrous.

Johan Galtung has also championed the autarky position (what he calls "self-reliance") in a number of publications (Galtung, 1979; Galtung et al., 1980). Self-reliance, Galtung states, challenges received economics preoccupation with specialization, the national and international division of labor and the theory of comparative advantage. He thus outlines some basic principles of self-reliance:

(1)   Some mechanisms in addition to the market must be found for the satisfaction of basic human needs. However, economic activity should not necessarily be limited to the basics.
(2)   A strategy for producing what is needed relying upon ourselves and our own productive resources, must be adopted. This involves a total rejection of the international division of labour, producing what we consume and consuming what we produce.

In short:

produce what you need using your own resources, internalising the challenges this involves, growing with the challenges, neither giving the most challenging tasks (positive externalities) to someone else on whom you become dependent, nor exporting negative externalities to somebody else to whom you do damage and who may become dependent on you. (Galtung, 1986, 101)

By following this principle, externalities, both positive and negative, are kept to ourselves. Negative externalities such as pollution are best controlled *locally* rather than globally. Galtung suggests, somewhat sardonically, that pollution of rivers by riverside factories would be prevented by forcing the management to drink downstream water! The serious point here is that ease of pollution control is best tackled locally. Self-reliance preserves the positive externalities by trading much less "up" and protects against the negative externalities by trading much less "down," embracing both enlightened egoism and enlightened altruism.

Complete self-reliance is, of course, in many situations impossible due to scarcity of certain resources. In such a situation trade is necessary. Trade should be conducted, according to Galtung, in accordance with two rules. First, net balance of costs and benefits, including externalities for both parties, should be as equal as possible involving intrasectional rather than intersectional trade. Thus primary products will be exchanged for primary products (raw materials, agriculture), secondary products (e.g., manufactured items) for secondary products and tertiary products (services) for tertiary products. When exchange goes beyond exchange in a single sector, an imbalance of externalities is likely to occur, especially if services and manufactured goods are exchanged for primary products, such as, for example, agricultural products (Galtung, 1986, 102).

Second, production for basic needs should be carried out in a fashion such that the country is at least potentially self-sufficient and not merely self-reliant. Fields of production include food, clothing, shelter, energy and whatever is needed for the maintenance of health care systems, education and national defense. These principles of self-reliance are applicable not only for nations, but for local communities as well, in a quest for "transcending the nakedness of economic relations." As Galtung notes:

There is a strong normative injunction, based on a feeling of compassion and a will to resist threats and the actual exercise of violence, direct or structural from the outside. At the same time, it puts some limitations on the kinds of contractual relations that should legitimately be entered into. Self-reliance is psycho-politics as much as economics; it presupposes and builds, self-respect. It does not mean more or less splendid isolation, but spins a web of interaction that is mainly horizontal rather than vertical. (Galtung, 1986, 102–103)

Galtung suggests that the world may be viewed as a series of Chinese boxes: first as a set of regions of the globe and inside these regions are the national states or countries. Inside the countries are the local communities. Global interdependence is concerned primarily with horizontal interaction so that the principles of self-reliance are practical for regions, nations and local communities. Self-reliance, then, should be practiced regionally, nationally and locally so that center-periphery exchange is reduced and periphery-periphery exchange increased. Local communities will not be able to become self-reliant if the nation is not self-reliant because they will not be able to have sufficient strength to resist external economic penetration. However, exchange is secondary; the raison d'être of self-reliance is to produce goods oneself in a spirit of pride and independence:

I see no reason at all why the rest of the world should be dependent on Japan for electronics of all kinds, cameras, watches, cars and motorcycles. Why should others deny themselves the growth they could obtain through their own production of these challenging goods? And even those at the very top may contemplate whether it is not also in their interests to seek arrangements with some built-in stability, being neither dependent on somebody, nor threatened by somebody dependent on them in a situation from which, sooner or later, they may want to withdraw, possibly in a very violent manner. Ultimately, dependency is very unpleasant to everyone involved. Yet it is the consequence of conventional economic theory and practice. A new economic practice based on self-reliance has to be based on a whole new economic theory. (Galtung, 1986, 106)

We mentioned Wolfgang Sachs' work previously in the context of presenting a critique of globalism. Sachs, like Galtung, has a positive theory of autarky, or what he calls *eco-decentralism* (Sachs, 1986). Eco-decentralism will revitalize the self-reliance of local communities so that people are no longer at the mercy and caprice of international capitalism. Sachs says that local self-reliance involves an inversion of market relations on two levels: first, to strengthen the local economy by downscaling the range of exchange relations and second, to encourage noneconomic activities such as unpaid work. Sachs also stresses that a different type of economic security is advocated:

one where wealth is not derived from specialising in export for distant markets, and sending the earned money to distant producers in order to import a large percentage of food, energy, materials, insurance, health care, but rather from reducing people's involvement in the national and international economy and providing more locally. In the long run, what we might call a market-enhanced self-reliant economy should enable people to live gracefully with less money, less consumption and less wage labour, because an infrastructure which is geared towards self-sufficiency will compensate for losses in income. (Sachs, 1986, 333)

Would autarkic policies economically marginalize countries with declining international competitiveness? Sachs replies to this objection by maintaining that scaling down export-import relations will decrease the vulnerability of countries to crises and crashes abroad which will enrich domestic development and drastically reduce unemployment. Further, he would agree with our analysis of the dangerous state of the global economy outlined earlier:

The cosmopolitan idea of one world based on free trade has fallen to pieces. It rested on the doctrine of comparative advantage, claiming that the general well-being would be enhanced if each nation specialised in doing the things which nature and history had made it relatively most proficient: coffee beans from Guatemala in contrast to pharmaceuticals from Holland. This might be true from a static point of view; in the long run, however, it is the economy offering more complex products which benefits by internalising the spin-off effects of more sophisticated production: pharmaceuticals stimulate research and complete processing technologies, whereas coffee beans don't! Thus the weaker party finds itself at a cumulative disadvantage, a downward spiral which can be only be overcome, even under the condition of "equal" terms of trade, by partially retreating from the free-trade arena. (Sachs, 1986, 337)

The other major argument for autarky—and we believe the strongest argument—is based on the limits to growth (*Limitationist*) position. Autarkists who are Limitationists not merely support self-reliance but advocate national and even local *self-sufficiency*. Ted Trainer's "conserver society" is a society where nonaffluent life-styles are lived with small-scale, decentralized, zero-growth economies comprising maximum levels of local self-sufficiency. Most of the goods and services used in a town or suburb would be required to be produced nearby using local resources. Trainer has detailed how this can be done in ways that would improve our lives and eliminate much of the alienation and angst that is an inevitable product of modernity (Trainer, 1995a).

However, more likely self-sufficiency may well be forced upon us—or those of us who survive, if David Price and other ecological pessimists whose views were considered earlier in this book are right. As we have seen, Price argued in his 1995 paper in *Population and Environment* (Price, 1995) that the exhaustion of fossil fuels will lead to the collapse of industrial society because there is no other energy source that is abundant and cheap enough to replace it. The combination of a growing world population and an increased demand for energy merely to heal some of the existing environmental wounds of the world will seal our fate, in Price's opinion. The collapse of the human population will occur through the apocalyptic forces of starvation, social strife and disease. Civilization will come to an end and survivors will by necessity adopt life-styles similar to the subsistence economies of our ancestors. They may stare at the decaying cities and the rusty technological wonders of modernity, while burning philosophy books for fuel, and wonder about the fate of the gods who built such strange objects. If humanity can survive such a desperate situation, it will only be because it is capable of regaining the primal autarky that has been lost. We will have more to say about the collapse of civilization in the last chapter.

Even if one rejects out of hand such pessimistic scenarios of ecological collapse, evidence and theoretical arguments have been presented in this book which indicate that global economic collapse is even more probable than ecological collapse. As we have argued above, there is an inherent contradiction within economic globalism which renders the system economically unsustainable. This economic mess, moving in tandem with the environmental crisis, will ensure disaster. Autarky is the alternative. It is a way of obtaining control of our lives and destinies and ending the age of the internationalization of everything. Its achievement will be as difficult as the achievement of the ecologically sustainable society. It will involve "turning back the clock," a dreaded reactionary notion. Almost all nations (if the nation-state survives) will have to reduce population numbers to obtain a much greater food self-reliance than they already have. But if survival and sanity, if the survival of cultures, traditions, races and people require this, then so be it. While time travel may be impossible, we can "turn back the clock." Society, like a clock, is a human construction and is thus subject to human intervention. With sufficient force it can be changed in any direction one desires. The international economic system is already beginning to break up and these cracks will widen as the environmental crisis deepens—contrary to the views of the technological and economic optimists considered earlier. Autarky is inevitable, by either design or default.

NOTES

1. Evan Jones is senior lecturer in economics at the University of Sydney.
2. John Gray (1993b, 17) observes that the

globalisation of market forces has already undermined local and regional ways of life in many parts of the world. For the Third World, global free trade means the destruction of agrarian communities and peasant traditions, as local farming practices are undercut by mechanised western agribusiness. This in turn means the accelerated migration of impoverished agricultural workers to swollen mega-cities.

3. CEDA—Committee for the Economic Development of Australia—includes most major Australian businesses. This big-business organization advocates the dictatorship of capital over labor and supports markets to determine the "price" of labor, so that labor is a deregulated commodity. The world of CEDA is a world where capital and resources can be freely moved to where the greatest profit can be earned, where there are vast markets for consumer goods. They proclaim the virtues of an Asianized multicultural Australia not for the same reasons as the socialist-internationalists (a sense of guilt and hatred of European culture and people), but on the grounds of profit maximization and power to further the cancer of cosmopolitan consumerism of a raceless, rootless rational economic man. The rapidly expanding market of consumers is to be imported largely from South East Asia because of their infinite consumer potential and Australian industry must be reorientated to supply the northern imperialists with resources. It was precisely such a form of neocolonialism that the old *Labour* Party (by contrast to the new cosmopolitan *Labor* Party) was formed to fight. In supporting immigration restriction by way of the White Australia Policy, it prevented, until the 1970s, cheap labor slavery on the Australian continent and a capitalist class dominating a Eurasian coolie class.
4. These quotes have been taken from the editorial of the *Economic Reformer* (Monthly Newsletter of Economic Reform Australia), no. 121, June 1995. The same article cites the case of Professor Fred Argy, secretary of the Campbell Committee. In an ABC television interview on the *7:30 Report* (New South Wales, Australia), April 26, 1995, he stated that financial deregulation was largely driven by the ideology of financial globalization. He is now skeptical of both processes. He said:

[T]he benefits of financial deregulation are not what they were expected to be, or what they're even now made out to be. They [are becoming] increasingly perverse, erratic, inconsistent, and extremely arrogant . . . [we have] increasing volatility [in financial markets] which has a significant effect on the real interest rates we have to pay, and there are effects on business confidence and long-term economic and employment growth.

Economic Irrationalism 143

The financiers, the money-power, are to be feared, Argy goes on to say in this interview, because they have "the power to make an awful mess of the key indicators ... and governments know that, and basically they're afraid of them."

President Clinton has been widely quoted in the media as saying, when told by his economic advisors that his future depended on his accommodation of the financial markets: "Do you mean to tell me that the success of the program and my re-election hinges on the Federal Reserve and a bunch of fucking bond traders" (Santamaria, 1995). Clinton obviously doesn't understand the forces that rule America.

5. Logically, when some countries have pluses in their balance of payments, others have corresponding minuses. Calculations since the late 1970s have given rise to paradoxical situations. In the early 1980s, for example, the world was running an annual balance-of-payments deficit with itself of around $100 billion. The International Monetary Fund calls these statistical holes "asymmetries." These "asymmetries" include the growth of "hot" and "homeless" money of speculative funds, which seeks a home across the globe. It also includes the money of supercrooks and other white-collar criminals. G. Dauncey in *After the Crash* (1988) says of this *hot money*: "Instability breeds instability, adding to the risk that the whole charade will tumble" (Dauncey, 1988, 3).

6. List claimed that Adam Smith's "cosmopolitan economics" was based on the principle of "universal peace." The editor of *The Natural System of Political Economy*, W. O. Henderson (List [1837], 1983), says that List was wrong to suppose that Adam Smith had ignored the fact that the world was divided into many nations. It is true that Smith recognized that the primary duty of a sovereign was to protect a country from external invasion. List did not deny this, he was merely noting a logical consequence of Smith's free trade position. List in this book did in fact state that Adam Smith "recommended that internal peace should be established as well as security for commerce and transport in order to secure the maximum welfare of a State" (List [1837], 1983, 22). In chapter 1 of *The Natural System of Political Economy*, List goes on to note that for holders of Smith's position:

conflicts between nations—whether settled by force of arms or by other means—must be replaced by an alliance of all peoples governed by laws of universal application. A world republic, as envisaged by J. B. Say, is necessary to secure the fulfilment of the dreams of the free traders. (List [1837], 1983, 29)

7. We will have more to say on this topic in a future book, *The Bankruptcy of Economics* (forthcoming, Macmillan, London).

8. On general equilibrium theory see Arrow & Debreu, 1954; Debreu, 1959; Arrow & Hahn, 1971; Hahn, 1973; Balasko, 1988.

9. An approach similar to that of Vilks in characterizing neoclassical economics is taken by P. S. Dasgupta and G. M. Heal, *Economic Theory and Exhaustible Resources* (1981), chapter 2. Using the concepts of the *viability* of states of affairs, and the *upsetting* of a vector of feasible acts, the following equilibrium concepts can be defined:

(a) If a feasible vector of acts **a** cannot be upset by the grand coalition of all individuals, then **a** is said to be *Pareto efficient*;
(b) If a feasible vector of acts cannot be upset by any single-membered coalition, then it is said to be a *Nash equilibrium*;
(c) If a feasible vector of acts cannot be upset by *any* coalition than it is said to be a *strong equilibrium*. (Dasgupta & Heal, 1981, 13–14).

10. This in itself is not a surprising result as there are few situations where improvements in the welfare of one group does not affect the welfare of another group (Hunt, 1977, 25).

11. Monetarism is theoretically refuted by economic models where inflation occurs with a constant stock of money (Hahn, 1983). This is not unreasonable as inflation is not *caused* by rising prices, inflation *is* such a phenomenon. Nor is inflation rising wages, as wages are just another set of prices. Modigliani studied the U.S. economy between 1953 and 1975 and found that the most economically unstable periods coincided with periods of relative monetary stability (Modigliani, 1977). The same situation was observed in the United Kingdom (Hendry & Ericson, 1983). (These references have been taken from Bunge 1985, 187.)

12. Schmeidler and Sonnenschein (1978) have shown that Arrow's result follows without the assumption of the independence of irrelevant alternatives and they conclude that "the theorem demonstrates that all mechanisms for passing from individual preferences (over three or more alternatives) to a social choice are vulnerable to strategic play" (Schmeidler & Sonnenschein, 1978, 227). Fishburn (1974) argued that *any* reasonable procedure for aggregating individual preferences to arrive at a social choice will be objectionable to someone.

13. See: (Sen, 1970, 1983; Pressler, 1987, 1988; Kelly, 1988; Kelsey, 1988.) A. Gibbard (1974) has shown that individual liberties can be internally inconsistent even if Pareto optimality is not demanded, such as in the case of individuals who have preferences that refer to the relationship between their own personal sphere and that of other people; e.g., my main concern is that my preference p should be the same as yours, whilst your preference q is that it be different from mine. Another interesting result is the *Probability Agreement Theorem*: if each person has coherent preferences, preferences that conform to the axioms of expected utility theory, then social preferences cannot be both coherent and Paretian unless everyone agrees about the probability of every event—and that will seldom occur (Broome, 1989).

14. This was shown, in our opinion, by the Marquis de Condorcet in the eighteenth century in his famous voting paradox:

> One-third of the voters prefer A to B to C.
> One-third of the voters prefer B to C to A.
> One-third of the voters prefer C to A to B.
> Therefore, if A vs. C, C wins, then C vs. B, B wins.
> Therefore, if B vs. C, B wins, then B vs. A, A wins.
> Therefore, if A vs. B, A wins, then A vs. C, C wins.

Any outcome is thus possible depending on the order of the vote.

15. See: (Gibbard, 1965; Barnes, 1971; Feldman, 1980, 1986; Regan, 1980; Sobel, 1985; Almeida, 1994.) Almeida tries to show that there are *no* circumstances in which utilitarian theories violate either (P1) or (P2):

(P1) If any member of a group G fulfills her actual obligations, then the result is at least as good for G as it would have been had some or all of the members of G failed to fulfill their actual obligations.

(P2) If some or all members of a group G fail to fulfill their actual obligations, then the result is at least as bad for G as it would have been had every member of G fulfilled her actual obligations.

It is difficult, if not impossible, to show that no counterexamples to a philosophical proposition exist, and Almeida doesn't succeed in his defense. There are situations where every member of a group fulfills his or her actual obligations but where the group would have been better off if some or all failed to do so. There are also circumstances in which some or all members of a group fail to fulfill their actual obligations, but where the group would have done even worse if every member had fulfilled his or her actual obligations. Such situations arise in "tragedy of the commons" situations involving immigration to countries that have already exceeded their ecological carrying capacity. Excessive moralism and altruism can also lead to the destruction of all (Hardin, 1995).

Shelly Kagan in *The Limits of Morality* (1989) gives us another reason for rejecting consequentialism in general and utilitarianism (in its social rather than individual guise [Harsanyi, 1985]) in particular. Commonsense suggests that there are limits *on* morality, limits to what morality can demand of us—"we are not morally required to make our greatest possible contribution to the overall good" (Kagan, 1989, xi). Kagan rejects this, indirectly defending consequentialism ("agents are morally required to perform the act that will lead to the best results overall" [Kagan, 1989, xi]). As well, "there is simply no limit to the sacrifices that an agent might be required to make in the pursuit of the greater good" (Kagan, 1989, xi–xii). The problem with this position is that it would make normal social life impossible. In a finite and chaotic world such as ours there must be limits to sacrifices, because of time and biological constraints. Kagan's position is simply unrealistic and the response of most people would be: to hell with the greater good!

5

Endgame: Healing a Wounded World

PREPARING FOR DISASTER

We have completed the main argument of this book and consider Economism refuted and Limitationism defended. By way of conclusion and as a lead-in to our next book, *Global Meltdown: Immigration, Multiculturalism, and National Breakdown in the New World Disorder*, we would like to compare the different philosophies of two of the most important books to be published in recent years: Paul Kennedy's *Preparing for the Twenty-First Century* (1993) and Garrett Hardin's *Living within Limits* (1993). This comparison will serve as a critical springboard for outlining our own position on the prospects of human survival as well as setting the scene for our next book.

Kennedy and Hardin both note that discussion of the full social, political and philosophical ramifications of human population expansion, and the related issue of immigration, remains taboo. Both authors, however, bravely confront these taboos. In sweeping, yet detailed analyses, Kennedy and Hardin portray a world battered by savage tempests of social and environmental upheavals, stretching over the next thirty years. The human population explosion, the revolutions in biotechnology and robotics, together with global warming and ecological degradation, confront us with a future world that seems to be relentlessly racing to an abyss. Although both authors are in agreement about the general nature of the problems plaguing humanity, as would be expected, they differ in matters of emphasis of the degree of severity of particular problems and ultimately in their response to the fundamental question of what should be done. Kennedy opts for what we have called a "globalist" or "internationalist" perspective and Hardin for a "localist" or "nationalist" perspective. Nevertheless, the common moral of both books is that without immediate action and a sincere attempt to change the present direction in which the modern world is heading, the "end" may be nigh: not with a bang but with a whimper, and a painful, miserable one at that.

Kennedy argues that the population explosion in the poor regions of Africa, Central America, the Middle East, India and China, combined with the technological revolution in the richer countries, creates a dilemma. The people lack access to the new technologies which, on the one hand, could help feed them, but may, on the other hand, harm them by destroying their source of employment. For example, he sees biotechnology as displacing traditional farming and robots replacing factory labor.

Stressing "regional disparities" between richer and poorer countries, he maintains that migrant flows are now, and will be increasingly, generated from areas of high pressure (poor, young and fast-growing populations) to areas of low pressure (rich, older slow-growing or declining populations). Here Kennedy points to Australia, with a likely population of 22.7 million by 2025, which lies next to the population giant Indonesia, whose population is expected to grow from 180 million to 263 million in the same time. (Estimates given in chapter 2 of this book, put Indonesia's population in the year 2030 at 275.7 million.) Similarly, he argues that the United States faces a growing influx of migrants from Central America and that central European countries will continue to be reluctant recipients of migrants from the former communist Eastern bloc countries. France, Spain and Italy face an even bigger problem, he believes, in their proximity and attractiveness to the exploding populations of North Africa.

Kennedy argues that the rich nation states which are geographically close to major Third World population centers are unlikely to be capable of staunching this immigrant flow. "Enhanced efforts to control migration . . . are unlikely to succeed in the face of the momentous tilt in the global demographic balances" (Kennedy, 1993, 45). He acknowledges that this invasion scenario assumes continuing Third World poverty. If, however, developing countries do manage to lift their standard of living, the power and influence of the Western democracies will decline throughout the world, being overwhelmed by Third World population numbers. Will liberal values survive, he asks, in "a world overwhelmingly peopled by societies which did not experience the rational scientific and liberal assumptions of the Enlightenment" (Kennedy, 1993, 46)?

Kennedy states that if his invasion scenario eventuates, large inflows of Third World migrants will harm the developed countries both socially and environmentally: "A migratory flood from the poorer and more troubled parts of the globe to the richer more peaceful will bring not only social costs but also rising racial antagonisms. The effects of the population explosion on the ecosystem might threaten national interests" (Kennedy, 1993, 128). Viewing the governments of the richer countries as being unable to staunch this flow, Kennedy never considers the possibility that a firm refusal to accept migrants by the developed countries could stimulate a drop in fertility in high-population-growth countries. A clear message could be made to high-fertility countries that excess populations can no longer be shipped or jetted around the globe to fill up less densely populated countries, or at least, an attempt could be made to encourage a more realistic and responsible attitude among Third World governments, to their own population problems. Of course, the developed countries should assist the poorer countries with appropriate aid and technology (as Kennedy later details), but the occasional stick, along with the carrots, could be effective. It is one of the strengths of Garrett Hardin's book *Living within*

Limits that he develops this "hardline" response to the global problem of immigration and the mass movement of people in great detail.

Kennedy denies that he contends that change is necessarily a good thing. Nevertheless, the overall thrust of his text is that we must all be prepared for radical changes, whether we like them or not. He views efforts to resist the global forces for change as reactionary and counterproductive. The future looks bleak. Kennedy sees the main actors as multinational corporations, nation states and the dispossessed growing masses of the Third World. The only role for the citizens of the developed countries is either to accept the inevitable decline of their societies as developing nations outstrip them in numbers and wealth, or to cope with waves of impoverished migrants sweeping over their borders. Reflecting his ambivalence about immigration controls, Kennedy refers, in the closing pages of his book, to the developed societies resorting to "the cruel if necessary policy of blocking the rising migratory floods from over-populated impoverished lands" (Kennedy, 1993, 335). The enormous social, political and moral consequences of this are not explored.

Of course there will be winners and losers in the twenty-first century, Kennedy argues. Japan, for example, is likely to be least harmed by global overpopulation, mass migration and ecological decline. Japan's strengths include, in Kennedy's opinion, a utilitarian education system, its creditor status among nations and its "social and racial coherence" (Kennedy, 1993, 138). Other winners are likely to be the newly industrializing countries such as Korea and perhaps the European Community. These countries are high savers and big investors in plant and equipment; they have good education systems, a skilled workforce, a manufacturing culture and "cultural homogeneity and ethnic coherence" (Kennedy, 1993, 334). Kennedy thinks that Latin America and Africa are likely to be losers. India and China, the two most populous nations, are involved in a race against time.

So what is to be done? While stressing that he does not see his task as providing solutions, Kennedy's message is that we must support the continuing integration of the global economy and embrace new technologies, the "globalist" or "internationalist" response. He suggests that developed countries should help developing countries with technology and capital, literacy programs, the provision of cheap, reliable birth control measures and support attempts to upgrade the status of women in poorer countries to reduce fertility. Measures to reduce environmental damage should be encouraged. People know the world is changing, Kennedy points out, despite their frequent reluctance to accept change. He argues that preparation for the next century comes at the price of changing the national infrastructure and even the governmental structure to suit the global economy. The message here is for rich and poor countries alike. The rich have a lot to lose. The poor have little to lose.

Kennedy's scenario of population explosion, mass migrations and ecological collapse is a frightening one. He sees himself as an advocate of prudent and realistic measures to lessen population growth and to ameliorate environmental problems. His assessment of the severity of our population and ecological problems contains much truth. However, his enthusiasm for embracing an ever-increasing integration of the global economy, dominated by multinational corporations, as a solution is, as we have demonstrated, misplaced and unwarranted. Similarly his support for all new forms of technology should be viewed with caution. Certainly we need new technologies to protect the environment and to try to feed eight to ten billion people, but we hope that we have presented in this book sufficiently detailed arguments and references to give the open-minded reader grave doubts about the tenability of technological fixes for the major social and environmental problems of our age.

Hardin offers a more radical critique of population growth than Kennedy. He argues that over the past three hundred years Western societies have been caught up in a "delusion of limitlessness" (Hardin, 1993, 6), a fatal hubris awaiting Nature's nemesis. The rise of modern science and technology was accompanied by a steady assault on the age-old view that resources were limited. The ideology of "progress" sanctioned never-ending population increase and economic growth. Hardin explores possible avenues for our deliverance from the dilemma of exponential population growth in a finite natural world, developing the argument put forward by Malthus that overpopulation produces "misery and vice," which subsequently lowers fertility and reduces population size. Hardin describes his Malthusian sequence as "a cybernetic control system" or "demostat" and argues that the Malthusian demostat is a necessary result of exponential population growth in a world of real limits. This demostat is, he believes, the central concept of population theory. "Misery and vice," Hardin explains, "are Malthus's terms for such negative feedbacks as premature death caused by famine, epidemics, infant neglect, criminal violence and the mortality of war" (Hardin, 1993, 105).

This is a hard message which many would find difficult to accept. For most intellectuals, the inheritors of Enlightenment ideals and defenders of the rights of individuals, the message of Malthus and Hardin is unacceptable. Hardin appreciates the difficulty many people have in accepting the argument that misery reduces reproduction. It offends "the admirable humanitarian spirit that has grown up during the past two centuries" (Hardin, 1993, 163). Hardin by no means advocates war, famine and plague as methods of population control. Rather, Hardin argues that unless a concerted attempt is made by humanity to live within ecological limits, then war, famine and plague are the evils that will be reaped as part of the remorseless working of things. If we do not solve the population problem, nature will solve it for us. The wounds of the world will heal, with us or without us. If it is with us, then sheer ecological necessity will force us to live within limits.

Hardin believes that the disciplines of economics and ecology should be brought together to develop a more viable approach to a sustainable society. However, before any such synthesis can be accomplished, some tough philosophical problems must be grappled with, the most important being the dispute between the "globalist" and the "localist," or the "internationalist" and the "nationalist." "Globalism," "internationalism" and "universalism" are vague terms used to describe the *moral* view expressed aptly by a now-forgotten poet at the end of World War I: "Let us no more be true to boasted race or clan/But to our highest dream, the brotherhood of man" (Hardin, 1993, 235). Globalists, internationalists and universalists believe that discrimination with respect to kinship, race, shared ethnicity or culture, propinquity in time or space is in general unjustified in most (but not necessarily all) matters of social policy because these parochial qualities are morally irrelevant characteristics. Only in very special circumstances (e.g., race or sex in the case of affirmative action) are such qualities morally relevant. Moral justification requires *universalization*, applicability to all relevant people without discrimination. Hardin is opposed to this "one world" philosophy, which he describes as a form of "promiscuous" altruism. Universalism, despite its noble and lofty sentiments, will lead to the tragedy of the commons. The goods of this world are limited and whenever either matter or energy is redistributed, the result is a zero-sum game, where that which one person or group gains is lost by others. Emma Lazarus' words added to the Statue of Liberty seems to invite all of the "poor," the "huddled masses" and the "wretched refuse" of the world to come to America. In fact the poem was added to the statue, officially called "Liberty Enlightening the World," seventeen years after the statue was erected, without the blessings of either Congress or the American people (Koed, 1992). Lady Liberty promised only to enlighten the world with the knowledge of freedom, not to feed the world. This represents in essence the real dilemma posed today by mass immigration: intellectuals and the *literati* tend to favor mass immigration because they regard themselves as citizens of the world. Anything short of this smacks of "extremism," "racism," and "parochialism" and any intellectual renegades who dare to question internationalist values are strongly censored. To choose an Australian example, this was the fate of Professor Geoffrey Blainey, our leading historian, who questioned the legitimacy of the Australian policy of Asianization: the abandonment of European culture and people and the adoption instead of Asian culture and people ultimately to fit Australia into a regional trade bloc as part of an economic "New World Order." Blainey was censored and punished for raising essentially an embarrassing question for intellectuals: you claim to be the defenders of representative democracy, but on a question such as the composition of the immigration quota where opinion polls clearly show overwhelming public opposition (Smith, ed., 1991) the will of the people can be ignored—how can this constitute a representative democratic policy?

The arguments given in this book support Hardin's hard-nosed environmentalism and his opposition to internationalism. We do not deny that cooperation between nations will be needed to protect the ozone layer and the global commons, if they can be protected at all, yet because this is precisely cooperation *between nations* it does not constitute *internationalism* in any strict sense. The internationalist looks to either a world government or an abstract entity such as a global deregulated free market to solve humanity's problems. Neither entity is capable of doing this in the ecological zero-sum game that is our world. Professor Jonathan Stone, Challis Professor of Anatomy at the University of Sydney, in his 1992 Australian Foundation for Science Lecture (Stone, 1992) has also recognized this terrible existential dilemma at the heart of our crisis of civilization. He notes that a major cause of the environment crisis is the reduction in infant mortality. When a child is saved, we save its children, and their children, and so on. Steps taken to save human life by medicine have led to the human population explosion and a resulting environmental crisis. But this crisis has been generated in part, Stone maintains, by the warm, fuzzy values of enlightened liberalism—human caring, altruism and charity. We have become a plague on the planet, Stone maintains, by our own good works. Ideals of civil rights are contradicted by the reality that we are a plague whose numbers are destroying the planet and ourselves. Stone is also an ecological hardliner: no species has ever lived in harmony with nature; they have lived and reproduced until nature culled them. The harmony of nature is an illusion. Further: "there would be nothing unnatural about a sudden crash of our population, or even our extinction" (Stone, 1992).

Warren M. Hern, an anthropologist at the University of Colorado, shares Stone's stark biopessimistic vision of the human condition (Hern, 1990). Following a number of other biological and medical writers, Hern compares human population growth to the growth of a malignant neoplasm, a planetary cancer (Gregg, 1955; Odum, 1989; Russell, 1983). Malignant neoplasms involve four characteristics: (1) rapid, uncontrollable growth; (2) the invasion and destruction of healthy tissue; (3) dedifferentiation (cancer cells, unlike other cells, tend to have no specific structure that identifies them as a cell from a specific site, such as a cell from the bowel); and (4) metastasis to different sites (that is, the establishment in different sites from the place of origin) (Hern, 1990, 22). Hern argues that human population growth, economic and industrial growth, interracial breeding (miscegenation) (Hern, 1990, 25) and mass migration satisfy the above criteria for a malignant neoplasm. Consequently, in final diagnosis, the "human species, *homo ecophagus*, is a ubiquitous, predatory, omniecophagic species that is a malignant epiecopathologic process engaged in the conversion of all planetary material into human biomass or its support system with coincident terminal derangement of the global ecosystem" (Hern, 1990, 35). It is rare for cancers to stop being cancers, so the most likely fate for humanity is self-destruction.

Hern's position has some interesting philosophical ramifications. Deep ecologists and animal rights ethicists such as Peter Singer (1975) reject a form of so-called "racism" known as "speciesism," arguing that it is morally arbitrary to give preferential discrimination in favor of the human species over other species. They base their position on a generalization of antisexism and antiracism. Some deep ecologists take this view a fraction further, arguing for *biocentric egalitarianism*, wherein all species have an equal right to life. But if this is so, Hern's argument would lead us to conclude that it would be better for the planet were humanity to be extinguished quickly but painlessly (to satisfy Singer's utilitarianism) and in some nonenvironmentally damaging way. It could be seen as a form of planetary self-defense.

In our opinion, this is environmentalism gone mad. If human beings are a cancer or a plague on the planet, and we are to see their scientific, technological and cultural products as lethal to Gaia, Mother Earth (Lovelock, 1979), then why should cultural products such as deep ecology be of value? Such products are, after all, the products of diseased minds! As a matter of evolutionary fact, we cannot avoid speciesism and we cannot see ourselves as a planetary disease. We have a built-in biological xenophobia which has enabled us to survive thus far (we will elaborate on this thesis in *Global Meltdown*). No scientific argument, however rational, can convince us of this at a deep practical level any more than a philosophical argument concluding that induction is unjustified will prevent us from using induction in daily life. We do not feel such feelings when holding our babies or children in our arms. Humans have survived precisely because they are creatures of habit and prejudice; dogmatism and discrimination have had survival value. However, in the world in which we now live this may well be dysfunctional. Humanity is now caught in an ecological "Catch-22": our desire for economic growth was to ensure our survival, but a further increase in economic growth to maintain the global system and raise poor countries to Western standards is ecologically unsustainable (Rees, 1996, 211).

Ecological writers when reaching this point, after staring over the precipice, usually recoil in horror and out of fear (and in some cases, economic self-interest) like to leave their readers with hope: if we change our ways in time, there will be a chance to avert the coming cataclysm. This allows us all to relax and not close the book in a state of anxiety. Such optimism is irrational and dishonest in the face of the evidence and arguments of environmentalism. It is better to face the truth that humanity is *not* going to change its ways because it *cannot*: we are caught in an ecological Catch-22 that is fully integrated into the modern way of life under global capitalism. A major crash in human numbers is likely to occur sometime in the next century (Duncan, 1993). The physicist and cosmologist Fred Hoyle (1986), although critical of Malthusian arguments, believes that a collapse of civilization could occur merely because of an overloading of a technologically complex society with too many people, resulting in a systems breakdown (Hoyle, 1986, 554). He also believes that a sudden discontinuous drop in human numbers will occur.

Hoyle speculates about the reorganization of society after the crash. He foresees the biological evolution of a new species of man—a cooperative, highly intelligent being who will be able to sift through the rubble of civilization and rebuild. High intelligence will be of selective value in the times of coming chaos, as these intellects and scholars will be able to understand the accumulated knowledge of the ages. In our opinion this is all most unlikely. If a crash or breakdown of civilization does occur, it is more likely to be streetwise cunning and Rambo-style survival ability which wins the day over bookish knowledge. There are not likely to be many books around to read in Hoyle's postapocalyptical world in any case. Roaming gangs would have burned them long before for fuel. The scholars, with their hoplophobia and pacifism, would have been hunted down for sport and eliminated. Readers who believe that this is scientific fiction are advised to consult our next book, *Global Meltdown*. This situation of "coming anarchy" (Kaplan, 1994) already exists in some parts of the world. So in conclusion, it is highly improbable that any ecological overman will evolve to manage the planet in a wiser way than humans. Indeed, Hoyle in his book *Of Men and Galaxies* (1964) seems to, quite unknowingly, furnish a refutation of his own postapocalypse scenario:

> It has been often said that, if the human species fails to make a go of it here on Earth, some other species will take over the running. In the sense of developing intelligence this is not correct. We have, or soon will have, exhausted the necessary physical prerequisites so far as this planet is concerned. With coal gone, oil gone, high-grade metallic ore gone, no species however competent can make the long climb from primitive conditions to high-level technology. This is a one-shot affair. If we fail, this planetary system fails so far as intelligence is concerned. The same will be true of other planetary systems. On each of them there will be one chance, and one chance only. (Hoyle, 1964, 64)

If Limitationism is correct, and Hoyle does appear to embrace it here, the very evolutionary conditions that would allow a rise in intelligence or even cultural advances (Duncan, 1993) would be precluded. The future is indeed a grim one—and we have only considered part of the human problem. Our next book, *Global Meltdown: Immigration, Multiculturalism, and National Breakdown in the New World Disorder*, will take this argument even further.

The conclusion of our study is unfortunately a negative one: the basic minimum conditions for a healthy, ecologically sustainable life for all people on Earth cannot be met. Sadly, the technological and economic optimists are wrong. We are entering a new dark age; an age of the great dieback in the exuberant growth of the human species.

Bibliography

Abbott, R. J. (1994). Ecological Risks of Transgenic Crops. *Trends in Ecology and Evolution* 9: 280–282.
ABC (1994). *Lateline*. Australian Broadcasting Commission, August 1.
Abernethy, V. (1993). *Population Politics: The Choices that Shape Our Future*. New York & London: Plenum Press.
Abernethy, V. (1995). Editorial. The Demographic Transition Model: A Ghost Story. *Population and Environment* 17: 3–6.
Abernethy, V. (1995). Editorial: The Four Horsemen. *Population and Environment* 16: 299–300.
ABS (1994a). *Australian Demographic Statistics. Catalogue no. 3101.0 March quarter* 1994. Canberra: Australian Bureau of Statistics.
ABS (1994b). *Australia's Long-Term Unemployed: A Statistical Profile. Catalogue no. 6255.0.* Canberra: Australian Bureau of Statistics.
ABS (1994c). *Population Growth and Distribution in Australia. Catalogue no. 2822.0.* Canberra: Australian Bureau of Statistics.
AFP News Service (1995). Report, June 6.
Agassi, J. (1991). As You Like It. In: G. Munévar ed. *Beyond Reason: Essays on the Philosophy of Paul Feyerabend*. Dordrecht: Kluwer: 379–387.
AIDAB (1993). *Migration to Australia from the South Pacific*. Canberra: Australian International Development Assistance Bureau.
Albert, H. (1968). *Traktat über kritische Vernunft*. Tübingen: Mohr.
Alchian, A. A. (1950). Uncertainty, Evolution and Economic Theory. *Journal of Political Economy* 58: 211–221.
Alexander, K. L. & Baker, S. (1994). Borderless Management. *Business Week* May 23: 24–26.
Allais, M. (1978). Theories of General Economic Equilibrium and Maximum Efficiency. In: G. Schwödiauer ed. *Equilibrium and Disequilibrium in Economic Theory*. Dordrecht: D. Reidel: 129–201.
Allais, M. & Hagen, O. eds. (1979). *Expected Utility Hypotheses and the Allais Paradox*. Dordrecht: D. Reidel.

Allen, R. E. (1994). *Financial Crisis and Recession in the Global Economy*. Aldershot: Edward Elgar.
Allen, T. F. H. & Hoekstra, T. W. (1992). *Toward a Unified Ecology*. New York: Columbia University Press.
Almeder, R. (1973). The Invalidity of Gettier-Type Counterexamples. *Philosophica* 13: 67–74.
Almeder, R. (1974). Truth and Evidence. *Philosophical Quarterly* 24: 365–368.
Almeder, R. (1987). On Being Justified in Believing False Propositions. *Philosophica* 15: 271–285.
Almeder, R. (1989). Scientific Realism and Explanation. *American Philosophical Quarterly* 26: 173–185.
Almeida, M. J. (1994). Collective Rationality and Simple Utilitarian Theories. *Dialogue* 33: 363–375.
Almendares, J. et al. (1993). Critical Regions, A Profile of Honduras. *The Lancet* 342: 1400–1402.
Amico, R. P. (1988). Roderick Chisholm and the Problem of the Criterion. *Philosophical Papers* XVII: 217–236.
Anon. (1986). Reasons for Leaving. *Pacific Islands Monthly* 57 (7): 11–14.
Anon. (1993). Tests Needed to Fight TB, Doctor Warns. *The Advertiser* (Adelaide, South Australia) June 7: 12.
Anon. (1994). Economic Mayday in the Pacific. *The Australian* August 2: 12.
Anon. (1994). Spoon-Fed Days Are Over, Islands Told. *The Advertiser* (Adelaide, South Australia) June 16: 13.
ANZEC (1990). *Towards a National Greenhouse Strategy for Australia*. Canberra: Australian and New Zealand Environment Council.
Apel, K. O. (1976). The Problem of (Philosophical) Ultimate Justification in the Light of a Transcendental Pragmatic of Language (An Attempted Metacritique of "Critical Rationalism"). *Ajatus* 36: 142–165.
Armstrong, D. M. (1968). *A Materialist Theory of Mind*. London: Routledge & Kegan Paul.
Armstrong, D. M. (1978–79). Naturalism, Materialism and First Philosophy. *Philosophia* 8: 261–276.
Arrow, K. J. (1951). *Social Choice and Individual Values*. New York: Wiley.
Arrow, K. J. & Debreu, G. (1954). Existence of an Equilibrium for a Competitive Economy. *Econometrica* 22: 265–270.
Arrow, K. J. & Hahn, F. H. (1971). *General Competitive Analysis*. Amsterdam: North-Holland.
Ascher, W. (1989). Limits of "Expert Systems" for Political-Economic Forecasting. *Technological Forecasting and Social Change* 36: 137–151.
Attewell, P. (1996). The Productivity Paradox. *The Australian* March 27: 25.
Averill, E. & Keating, B. F. (1981). Does Interactionism Violate a Law of Classical Physics? *Mind* XC: 102–107.
Avery, D. (1995). *Saving the Planet with Pesticides and Plastic*. Indianapolis: Hudson Institute.
Ayres, R. V. & Kneese, A. V. (1969). Production, Consumption and Externalities. *American Economic Review* 59: 282–297.
Bacon, F. (1855). *Novum Organon*. Oxford: Oxford University Press.
Baggott, J. (1990). Unimolecular Reaction Breaks the Chemical Rules. *New Scientist* January 6: 13.

Bailey, G. (1983). Putnam and Metaphysical Realism. *International Studies in Philosophy* 15: 11–14.
Bailey, R. (1993). *Eco-Scam: The False Prophets of Ecological Apocalypse.* New York: St. Martin's Press.
Bailey, R. ed. (1995). *The True State of the Planet.* New York: Free Press.
Baker, L. R. (1987). *Saving Belief: A Critique of Physicalism.* Princeton, New Jersey: Princeton University Press.
Balasko, Y. (1988). *Foundations of the Theory of General Equilibrium.* Boston: Academic Press.
Banks, B. E. C. & Vernon, C. A. (1990). The Greenhouse Effect and Human Population. *Journal of the Royal Society of Medicine* 83: 284.
Bannet, E. T. (1989). *Structuralism and the Logic of Dissent: Barthes, Derrida, Foucault, Lacan.* London: Macmillan Press.
Bannock, G., Baxter, R. E. & Davis, E. (1987). *The Penguin Dictionary of Economics* (4th edition). London: Penguin Books.
Barkan, E. R. (1992). *Asian and Pacific Islander Migration to the United States.* Westport, Connecticut: Contributions in Ethnic Studies 30: Greenwood Press.
Barnaby, F. (1986). *The Automated Battlefield.* New York: Free Press.
Barnes, B. & Bloor, D. (1982). Relativism, Rationalism and the Sociology of Knowledge. In M. Hollis and S. Lukes eds. *Rationality and Relativism.* Oxford: Blackwell: 21–47.
Barnes, G. (1971). Utilitarianisms. *Ethics* 82: 56–64.
Bartlett, A. A. (1994). Reflections on Sustainability, Population Growth, and the Environment. *Population and Environment* 16: 5–35.
Bartley, W. W. (1984). *The Retreat to Commitment.* La Salle, Illinois: Open Court.
Bartley, W. W. (1988a). Theories of Rationality. In: G. Radnitzky & W. W. Bartley eds. *Evolutionary Epistemology, Rationality, and the Sociology of Knowledge.* La Salle, Illinois: Open Court: 205–214.
Bartley, W. W. (1988b). A Refutation of the Alleged Refutation of Comprehensively Critical Rationalism. In: G. Radnitzky & W. W. Bartley eds. *Evolutionary Epistemology, Rationality, and the Sociology of Knowledge.* La Salle: Open Court: 313–341.
Bates, D. (1938). *The Passing of the Aborigines.* London: John Murray.
Batra, R. (1978a). *The Downfall of Capitalism and Communism.* London: Macmillan.
Batra, R. (1978b). *The Great Depression of 1990.* New York: Simon & Schuster.
Batra, R. (1988). *Surviving the Great Depression of 1990.* New York: Simon & Schuster.
Batra, R. (1993). *The Myth of Free Trade: A Plan for America's Economic Revival.* New York: Charles Scribner's Sons.
Bauman. Z. (1989). *Modernity and the Holocaust.* Oxford: Polity Press.
Baynes, K., Bohman, J. & McCarthy, T. (1993). *After Philosophy: End or Transformation?* Cambridge, Massachusetts: MIT Press.
Beaglehole, R., Salmond, C. E., Hooper, A., Huntsman, J., Stanhope, J. M., Cassell, J. C. & Prior, I. A. M. (1977). Blood Pressure and Social Interaction in Tokelauan Migrants in New Zealand. *Journal of Chronic Diseases* 30: 803–812.

Bechtel, W. (1993). Currents in Connectionism. *Minds and Machines* 3: 125–153.

Beckerman, W. (1995). *Small Is Stupid: Blowing the Whistle on the Greens.* London: Duckworth.

Beckermann, A., Flohr, H. & Kim, J. eds. (1992). *Emergence or Reduction? Essays on the Prospects of Nonreductive Physicalism.* Berlin: Walter de Gruyter.

Bedford, R. (1990). Ethnicity, Birthplace and Nationality: Dimensions of Cultural Diversity. *New Zealand Population Review* 16: 34–55.

Bell, D. & Kristol, I. eds. (1981). *The Crisis in Economic Theory.* New York: Basic Books.

Bellini, J. (1987). *High Tech Holocaust.* Richmond, Victoria: Greenhouse Publications.

Belliotti, R. A. (1987a). Is Law a Sham? *Philosophy and Phenomenological Research* XLVIII: 25–44.

Belliotti, R. A. (1987b). Critical Legal Studies: Paradoxes of Indeterminacy and Nihilism. *Philosophy and Social Criticism* 13: 145–154.

Benhabib, J. & Day, R. H. (1982). A Characterization of Erratic Dynamics in the Overlapping Generations Model. *Journal of Economic Dynamics and Control* 4: 37–55.

Bennett, C. H. & Landauer, R. (1985). The Fundamental Physical Limits of Computation. *Scientific American* 253: 38–46.

Bequai, A. (1987). *Technocrimes.* Lexington, Massachusetts: Lexington Books.

Bergland, R. (1988). *The Fabric of Mind.* Harmondsworth: Penguin Books.

Berkson, W. (1979). Skeptical Rationalism. *Inquiry* 22: 281–320.

Berry, W. (1995). *Another Turn of the Crank.* Washington DC: Counterpoint.

Bessant, J. & Cole, S. (1985). *Stacking the Chips: Information Technology and the Distribution of Income.* London: Frances Pinter.

Betts, K. (1988). *Ideology and Immigration.* Carlton, Victoria: Melbourne University Press.

Betts, K. (1991). The Politics of Growth. In: J.W. Smith ed. *Immigration, Population and Sustainable Environments: The Limits to Australia's Growth.* Bedford Park, South Australia: Flinders Press: 353–369.

Bhaskar, R. (1978). *A Realist Theory of Science.* Brighton, Sussex: Harvester Press.

Bhaskar, R. (1979). *The Possibility of Naturalism.* Brighton, Sussex: Harvester Press.

Bhaskar, R. (1986). *Scientific Realism and Human Emancipation.* London: Verso.

Bhaskar, R. (1989). *Reclaiming Reality.* London: Verso.

Bilney, G. (1993). Opening Address. *Ministerial Seminar on Population and Development in the Asia-Pacific Region.* Canberra: Australian Academy of Science.

Bird, E. (1987). The Effects of a Sea Level Rise on the World's Coastline. In: *Environmental and Health Effects of Atmospheric and Associated Climate Change.* Conference, Adelaide, South Australia.

Bita, N. (1996). Erosion, Habitat Destruction Trigger Red Alert. *The Australian* June 28: 4.

Black, F. (1982). The Trouble with Econometric Models. *Financial Analysts Journal* 35: 3–11.
Black, O. (1988). Infinite Regresses of Justification. *International Philosophical Quarterly* 28: 421–437.
Blainey, G. (1994). Melting Pot on the Boil. *The Bulletin*, August 30: 22–25.
Blainey, G. (1996). The End (as We Briefly Knew It) of Prosperity. *The Independent Monthly* May: 30–35.
Blank, R. H. (1984). *Redefining Human Life*. Boulder, Colorado: Westview Press.
Body, R. (1991). *Our Food, Our Land*. London: Rider.
Bogdan, R. J. (1988). Mental Attitudes and Commonsense Psychology: The Case Against Elimination. *Nous* 22: 369–398.
Boland, L. A. (1981). On the Futility of Criticizing the Neoclassical Maximization Hypothesis. *American Economic Review* 71: 1031–1036.
Born, R. ed. (1987). *Artificial Intelligence: The Case Against*. London: Croom Helm.
Bos, L. (1994). Environment and Disease: Ever-Growing Concern. *Environmental Conservation* 21: 99–102.
Boserup, E. (1965). *The Conditions of Agricultural Growth*. London: Allen & Unwin.
Boserup, E. (1981). *Population and Technology*. Oxford: Blackwell.
Botkin, D. B. (1990). *Discordant Harmonies: A New Ecology for the Twenty-First Century*. New York: Oxford University Press.
Boulding, K. E. (1979). Ethics of the Critique of Preferences. In: W. M. Finnin & G. A. Smith eds. *The Morality of Scarcity: Limited Resources and Social Policy*. Baton Rouge & London: Louisiana State University Press: 9–23.
Boyden, S., Dovers, S. & Shirlow, M. (1990). *Our Biosphere Under Threat: Ecological Realities and Australia's Opportunities*. Melbourne: Oxford University Press.
Boykan Pour-El, M. & Richards, I. (1979). A Computable Ordinary Differential Equation which Possesses No Computable Solution. *Annals of Mathematical Logic* 17: 61–90.
Boykan Pour-El, M. & Richards, I. (1981). The Wave Equation with Computable Initial Data Such that Its Unique Solution Is Not Computable. *Advances in Mathematics* 39: 215–239.
Brain, R. (1965). The Neurological Approach. In: R. J. Hirst ed. *Perception and the External World*. New York: Macmillan: 40–50.
Brecher, J., Childs, J. B. & Culter, J. eds. (1993). *Global Visions: Beyond the New World Order*. Boston: South End Press.
Briscoe, D. (1995). 30,000 Species at Risk: UN. *The Australian*. November 15: 10.
Bronner, M. E. (1996). The Road to Q-Infinity. *Population and Environment* 17: 373–390.
Brookfield, H. (1990). Vulnerable Places; Vulnerable People: Human Science Approaches to Problems of Adaptation. In: H. Brookfield & L. Doube eds. *Global Change: The Human Dimensions*. Report on a symposium at the 59th ANZAAS Congress, Hobart, Australia 1990. Canberra: Research School of Pacific Studies, Australian National University.

Broome, J. (1989). Should Social Preferences Be Consistent? *Economics and Philosophy* 5: 7–17.
Broome, J. (1991). Utility. *Economics and Philosophy* 7: 1–12.
Brown, D. (1992). Population Does Count. *New Scientist.* August 8: 47.
Brown, H. I. (1988). *Rationality.* London and New York: Routledge.
Brown, J. R. (1985). Von Neumann and the Anti-Realists. *Erkenntnis* 23: 149–159.
Brzezinski, Z. (1993). *Out of Control: Global Turmoil on the Eve of the 21st Century.* New York: Charles Scribner's Sons.
Bunge, M. (1983). *Treatise on Basic Philosophy, Volume 5, Epistemology and Methodology I: Exploring the World.* Dordrecht: D. Reidel.
Bunge, M. (1985). *Treatise on Basic Philosophy vol. 7, Epistemology and Methodology III: Philosophy of Science and Technology Part II, Life Science, Social Science and Technology.* Dordrecht: D. Reidel.
Butcher, D. (1996). "Fish and Chip" Attitude Sells Us Short. *The Weekend Australian* April 20–21: 25.
Butler, C. (1972). The Mind-Body Problem: A Nonmaterialist Identity Thesis. *Idealistic Studies* 2: 229–248.
Butler, C. (1994). Overpopulation, Overconsumption, and Economics. *The Lancet* 343: 582–584.
Butrick, R. (1971). Putnam's Revolution. *Philosophy of Science* 38: 290–292.
Callick, R. (1993). A Doomsday Scenario? In: R.V. Cole ed. *Pacific 2010: Challenging the Future.* Canberra: National Centre for Development Studies.
Callicott, J. B. (1989). American Indian Land Wisdom? Sorting Out the Issues. *Journal of Forest History* 33: 35–42.
Camilleri, J. A. & Falk, J. (1992). *The End of Sovereignty? The Politics of a Shrinking and Fragmenting World.* Aldershot: Edward Elgar.
Campbell, D. & Connor, S. (1986). *On the Record.* London: Michael Joseph.
Camus, A. (1955). *The Myth of Sisyphus.* London: Hamish Hamilton.
Cannon, G. (1995). *Superbug, Nature's Revenge: Why Antibiotics Can Breed Disease.* London: Virgin Publishing.
Capaldi, N. (1971). Why There Is No Problem of Induction. *Journal of Critical Analysis* 3: 9–12.
Capra, F. (1982). *The Turning Point.* New York: Simon & Schuster.
Carey, H. C. (1872). *The Past, The Present and the Future.* Philadelphia: Henry Carey Baird.
Carey, H. C. ([1851], 1967). *The Harmony of Interests Agricultural, Manufacturing and Commercial.* New York: Augustus M. Kelley.
Carey, M. ([1822], 1968). *Essays on Political Economy or the Most Certain Means of Promoting the Wealth, Power, Resources and Happiness of States Applied Particularly to the United States.* New York: Augustus M. Kelley.
Carmichael, G., Buetow, S. & Farmer, R. (1993). Policy and Data. In: G. A. Carmichael ed. *Trans-Tasman Migration: Trends, Causes and Consequences.* Canberra: Australian Government Publishing Service.
Carroll, J. (1993). *Humanism: The Wreck of Western Culture.* London: Fontana Press/HarperCollins Publishers.
Carroll, J. (1995). Failure of Rationalism. *The Weekend Australian* July 8–9: 26.

Cartwright, N. (1983). *How the Laws of Physics Lie.* Cambridge: Cambridge University Press.
Casati, R. & Varzi, A. C. (1994). *Holes and Other Superficialities.* Cambridge, Massachusetts: A Bradford Book, MIT Press.
Catton, W. R. & Dunlap, R. E. (1980). A New Ecological Paradigm for Post-Exuberant Sociology. *American Behavioral Scientist* 24: 15–47.
Catton, W. R. (1982). *Overshoot: The Ecological Basis of Revolutionary Change.* Urbana: University of Illinois Press.
Caves, C. M. (1985). Defense of the Standard Quantum Limit for Free-Mass Position. *Physical Review Letters* 54: 2465–2468.
Ceresa, M. (1994). Africa Dissolves in Dusty Mirage. *Sydney Morning Herald* September 29: 9.
Cerny, P. G. ed. (1993). *Finance and World Politics: Markets, Regimes and States in the Post-Hegemonic Era.* Aldershot: Edward Elgar.
Chaitin, G. J. (1987). *Algorithmic Information Theory.* Cambridge: Cambridge University Press.
Chaitin, G. J. (1990a). *Information, Randomness and Incompleteness: Papers on Algorithmic Information Theory* (2nd edition). Singapore: World Scientific.
Chaitin, G. J. (1990b). A Random Walk in Arithmetic. *New Scientist* March 24: 30–32.
Chamberlin, P. (1995). Grim River Report Brings Water Ban. *The Age.* July 1: 2.
Chambers, A. (1986). *Reproduction in Nanumea/(Tuvalu): An Ethnography of Fertility and Birth.* University of Auckland, Department of Anthropology Working Paper no. 72.
Chapman, P. F. & Roberts, F. (1983). *Metal Resources and Energy.* London: Butterworths.
Chase-Dunn, C. (1989). *Global Formation: Structures of the World-Economy.* Oxford: Basil Blackwell.
Chipman, L. (1974). A Hole in Quine's Holism. *Philosophical Papers* 3: 46–47.
Chisholm, R. M. (1982). *The Foundations of Knowing.* Brighton, Sussex: Harvester Press.
Chivian, E. et al. eds. (1993). *Critical Condition: Human Health and the Environment.* Cambridge, Massachusetts: MIT Press.
Chown, M. (1996). Bright Light, Black Hole. *New Scientist* June 8: 30–33.
Churchland, P. M. (1981). Eliminative Materialism and Propositional Attitudes. *Journal of Philosophy* 78: 67–90.
Churchland, P. M. (1988). *Matter and Consciousness.* Cambridge, Massachusetts: MIT Press.
Churchland, P. M. (1989). *A Neurocomputational Perspective.* Cambridge, Massachusetts: MIT Press.
Churchland, P. M. (1991). A Deeper Unity: Some Feyerabendian Themes in Neurocomputational Form. In: G. Munévar ed. *Beyond Reason: Essays on the Philosophy of Paul Feyerabend.* Dordrecht: Kluwer: 1–23.
Churchland, P. S. & Churchland, P. M. (1980). Stalking the Wild Epistemic Engine. *Nous* 17: 5–22.

Churchland, P. S. (1980). Language, Thought, and Information Processing. *Nous* 14: 147–170.

Churchland, P. S. (1986). *Neurophilosophy: Toward a Unified Science of the Mind-Brain.* Cambridge, Massachusetts: MIT Press.

Clark, J. B. (1887). *The Philosophy of Wealth: Economic Principles Newly Formulated.* Boston: Ginn & Company.

Clark, R. (1988). Vicious Infinite Regress Arguments. In: J. E. Tomberlin ed. *Philosophical Perspectives 2, Epistemology.* Atascadero: Ridgeview Press: 369–380.

Clark, W. (1989). Managing Planet Earth. *Scientific American* 261: 47–54.

Cleland, C. E. (1993). Is the Church-Turing Thesis True? *Minds and Machines* 3: 283–312.

Cleland, C. E. (1995). Effective Procedures and Computable Functions. *Mind and Machines* 5: 9–23.

Cleland, J. (1994). Different Pathways to Demographic Transition. In: F. Graham-Smith ed.. *Population—The Complex Reality: A Report of the Population Summit of the World's Scientific Academies.* Golden, Colorado: The Royal Society/North American Press: 229–247.

Clery, D. (1992). Nanotechnology Rules, OK! *New Scientist* March 7: 38–42.

Cling, A. D. (1989). Eliminative Materialism and Self-Referential Inconsistency. *Philosophical Studies* 56: 53–75.

Clunies-Ross, T. & Hildyard, N. (1992). The Politics of Industrial Agriculture. *The Ecologist* 1992: 65–71.

Coarse, R. H. (1960). The Problem of Social Cost. *Journal of Law and Economics* 3: 1–44.

Cobb, J. B. & Daly, H. E. (1990). Free Trade Versus Community: Social and Environmental Consequences of Free Trade in a World with Capital Mobility and Overpopulated Regions. *Population and Environment* 11: 175–191.

Coffey, P. (1917). *Epistemology or The Theory of Knowledge.* London: Longmans, Green and Co.

Cohen, A. & Dascal, M. eds. (1989). *The Institution of Philosophy: A Discipline in Crisis?* La Salle, Illinois: Open Court.

Cohen, J. E. (1995). *How Many People Can the Earth Support?* New York: W.W. Norton.

Cohen, N. (1970). *The Pursuit of the Millennium.* New York: Oxford University Press.

Cohen, N. (1993). *Cosmos, Chaos and the World to Come.* New Haven & London: Yale University Press.

Cohen, S. (1988). How to be a Fallibilist. In J.E. Tomberlin ed. *Philosophical Perspectives 2, Epistemology.* Atascadero: Ridgeview Press: 91–123.

Cohn, M. (1989). *Health and the Rise of Civilization.* New Haven: Yale University Press.

Cole, A. H. ed. (1968). *Industrial and Commercial Correspondence of Alexander Hamilton.* New York: Augustus M. Kelley.

Cole, R. (1993). Foreword in R.V. Cole, ed. *Pacific 2000: Challenging the Future.* Canberra: National Centre for Development Studies.

Collier, J. D. (1990). Could I Conceive Being a Brain in a Vat? *Australasian Journal of Philosophy* 68: 413–419.

Collins, C. (1993). Fort Paradise. *The Weekend Australian, Weekend Review* August 14–15: 3.
Connell, J. & Lea, J. (1992). My Country Will Not Be There. *Cities* 9: 295–310.
Connell, J. (1988). *Sovereignty and Survival: Island Microstates in the Third World.* Department of Geography, Monograph No. 2, University of Auckland.
Connor, S. (1995). Wars Will Be Fought Over Water, World Bank Warns. *Sydney Morning Herald* August 8: 10.
Cornwell, H. (1987). *Datatheft: Computer Fraud, Industrial Espionage and Information Crime.* London: Heinemann.
Cornwell, J. (1993). Just Who Do We Think We Are? *The Weekend Australian Review*, August 21–22: 4.
Costanza, R. (1987). Social Traps and Environmental Policy. *BioScience* 37: 407–412.
Costanza, R., Daly, H. E. & Bartholomew, J. A. (1991). Goals, Agenda, and Policy Recommendations for Ecological Economics. In: R. Costanza ed. *Ecological Economics: The Science and Management of Sustainability.* New York: Columbia University Press: 1–20.
Coulborn, R. (1954). The Rise and Fall of Civilizations. *Ethics* 64: 205–216.
Coulborn, R. (1966). Structure and Process in the Rise and Fall of Civilized Society. *Comparative Studies in Society and History* 8: 404–431.
Cowan, J. D. & Sharp, D. H. (1988). Neural Nets and Artificial Intelligence. *Daedalus* 117: 84–121.
Crane, T. & Mellor, D. H. (1990). There Is No Questions of Physicalism. *Mind* 99: 185–206.
Crane, T. (1993). Reply to Pettit. *Analysis* 53: 224–227.
Crawford, A. & Edgar, R. (1995). Apocalypse Culture, *21 C* 4: 44–45.
Cribb, J. (1993a). Bitter Harvest. *The Australian* April 16: 8.
Cribb, J. (1993b). Hunger the Grim Forecast for Asia. *The Australian* April 17–18: 9.
Cribb, J. (1994). Death of a Lifeline. *The Weekend Australian Review* May 21–22: 3.
Cribb, J. (1995a). World Faces Water Shortage, Refugee Crisis in 21st Century. *The Australian* June 15: 8.
Cribb, J. (1995b). Future Shock: "Humanoids" on March. *The Weekend Australian* March 9–10: 46.
Cribb, J. (1995c). Grow or Die. *The Weekend Australian* July 1–2: 26.
Cribb, J. (1995d). Starved for Attention on a Diminished Planet. *The Australian* June 14: 13.
Cribb, J. (1995e). Muscle-Bound Robots Signal Synthetic "Nerves" of Steel. *The Weekend Australian* March 9–10. 46.
Cribb, J. (1995f). Environmental Damage Hurting Health: AMA. *The Weekend Australian* October 21–22: 10.
Cribb, J. (1996). Water Wars. *The Australian* January 15: 12.
Crick, F. (1981). *Life Itself, Its Origin and Nature.* New York: Simon and Schuster.
Crosby, D. A. (1988). *The Specter of the Absurd: Sources and Criticisms of Modern Nihilism.* Albany: State University of New York Press.

Culbertson, J. M. (1984). *International Trade and the Future of the West.* Madison: 21st Century Press.
Culbertson, J. M. (1985). *The Dangers of "Free Trade."* Madison, Wisconsin: 21st Century Press.
Culbertson, J. M. (1989). *The Trade Threat and US Trade Policy.* Madison, Wisconsin: 21st Century Press.
Culbertson, J. M. (1991). US "Free Trade" with Mexico: Progress or Self-Destruction? *The Social Contract* Fall: 7–11.
da Silva, W. (1995). Plague Fears. *21 C* 4: 62–67.
Daily, G. C. & Ehrlich, P. R. (1992). Population, Sustainability, and Earth's Carrying Capacity. *BioScience* 42: 761–771.
Daily, G. C., Ehrlich, A. H. & Ehrlich, P. R. (1994). Optimum Human Population Size. *Population and Environment* 15: 469–475.
Daly, C. (1995). Does Physicalism Need Fixing? *Analysis* 55: 135–141.
Daly, H. E. (1987). The Economic Growth Debate: What Some Economists Have Learned But Many Have Not. *Journal of Environmental Economics and Management* 14: 323–336.
Daly, H. E. (1991). Growth, International Trade, and Destruction of Community. *The Social Contract* Fall: 24–27.
Daly, H. E. (1992). *Steady-State Economics.* London: Earthscan.
Daly, H. E. (1993). The Perils of Free Trade. *Scientific American* November: 24–29.
Daly, H. E. & Cobb, J. B. (1989). *For the Common Good: Redirecting the Economy Toward Community, the Environment and a Sustainable Future.* Boston: Beacon Press.
Daly, H. E. & Goodland, R. (1994a). An Ecological-Economic Assessment of Deregulation of International Commerce Under GATT Part I. *Population and Environment* 15: 395–427.
Daly, H. E. & Goodland, R. (1994b). An Ecological-Economic Assessment of Deregulation of International Commerce Under GATT Part II. *Population and Environment* 15: 477–503.
Daniel, W. (1989). Bohr, Einstein and Realism. *Dialectica* 43: 249–261.
Dasgupta, P. S. (1993). *An Inquiry into Well-Being and Destitution.* Oxford: Oxford University Press.
Dasgupta, P. S. (1994). The Population Problem. In: F. Graham-Smith ed. *Population—The Complex Reality: A Report of the Population Summit of the World's Scientific Academies.* Golden, Colorado: The Royal Society/North American Press: 151–180.
Dasgupta, P. (1995). Population, Poverty and the Local Government. *Scientific American* 272, February: 26–31.
Dasgupta, P. S. & Heal, G. M. (1981). *Economic Theory and Exhaustible Resources.* Cambridge: Cambridge University Press.
Dauncey, G. (1988). *After the Crash: The Emergence of the Rainbow Economy.* Basingstoke: Green Print.
Davidson, D. (1977). The Method of Truth in Metaphysics. *Midwest Studies in Philosophy* 1977: 244–254.
Davidson, F. R. (1965). On Derivations of the Uncertainty Principle. *Journal of Chemical Physics* 42: 1461–1462.

Davidson, J. D. & Rees-Mogg, W. (1989). *Blood in the Streets: Investment Profits in a World Gone Mad.* London: Sidgwick & Jackson.
Davidson, J. D. & Rees-Mogg, W. (1992). *The Great Reckoning: How the World Will Change in the Depression of the 1990s.* London: Sidgwick & Jackson.
Davies, P. (1979). Reality Exists Outside Us? In: R. Duncan and M. Weston-Smith eds. *Lying Truths.* Oxford: Pergamon Press: 144–158.
Davies, P. (1991). Is the Universe a Machine? In: N. Hall ed. *The "New Scientist" Guide to Chaos.* London: Penguin Books: 213–221.
Davies, P. (1995). The Accidental Impact. *21 C* 4: 72–76.
Davies, S. (1992). *Big Brother: Australia's Growing Web of Surveillance.* East Roseville, New South Wales: Simon & Schuster.
Dawson, G. (1985). Perspectivism in the Social Sciences. *Philosophy* 60: 373–380.
Day, T. J. (1988). Infinite Regress Arguments. *Philosophical Papers* 16: 155–164.
de Garis, H. (1990). The 21st Century Artilect: Moral Dilemmas Concerning the Ultra-Intelligent Machine. *Revue Internationale de Philosophie* 172: 131–138.
de Man, P. (1941). Les Juifs dans la litterature actuelle. *Le Soir* March 4.
de Marchi, N. ed. (1992). *Post-Popperian Methodology of Economics: Recovering Practice.* Dordrecht: Kluwer Academic.
Debreu, G. (1959). *Theory of Value.* New York: Wiley.
Demeny, P. (1991). Tradeoffs between Human Numbers and Material Standards of Living. In: K. Davis & M. Bernstam eds. *Resources, Environment, and Population: Present Knowledge, Future Options.* New York: Oxford University Press: 408–422.
Derrida, J. (1981). *Positions.* Chicago: University of Chicago Press.
Derrida, J. (1982). *Margins of Philosophy.* London: Harvester.
Derrida, J. (1988). Like the Sound of the Sea Deep within a Shell: Paul de Man's War. *Critical Inquiry* 14, Spring: 590–652.
Descartes, R. ([1637], 1985). *Discourse on Method.* Volume 1 of *The Philosophical Writings of Descartes* (in two volumes), translated by J. Cottingham, R. Stoothoff & D. Murdoch. Cambridge: Cambridge University Press.
DeWitt, B. S. (1970). Quantum Mechanics and Reality. *Physics Today* 23: 30–35.
Diamond, J. (1990). Playing Dice with Megadeath. *Discover* April: 55–59.
Diamond, J. (1991). *The Rise and Fall of the Third Chimpanzee.* London: Vintage.
Dilley, F. B. (1988). Mind-Body Interaction and Psi. *Southern Journal of Philosophy* 1988: 469–480.
Dobson, A. (1993). Biodiveristy. *The Lancet* 342: 1096–1099.
Docherty, T. ed. (1993). *Postmodernism: A Reader.* New York: Harvester Wheatsheaf.
Döös, B. R. (1994). Environmental Degradation, Global Food Production, and Risk for Large-Scale Migrations. *Ambio* 23: 124–130.
Douthwaite, R. (1992). *The Growth Illusion.* Bideford, Devon: Resurgence.

Drengson, A. (1989). *Beyond Environmental Crisis.* New York: Peter Lang Publishers.
Drengson, A. (1995). *The Practice of Technology: Exploring Technology, Ecophilosophy, and Spiritual Disciplines for Vital Links.* Albany: State University of New York Press.
Drexler, K. E. (1990). *Engines of Creation.* London: Fourth Estate.
Dreyfus, H. L. (1979). *What Computers Can't Do: The Limits of Artificial Intelligence.* New York: Harper and Row.
Dreyfus, H. L. & Dreyfus, S. E. (1986). *Mind over Machine.* New York: Free Press.
Dummett, M. (1978). *Truth and Other Enigmas.* Cambridge, Massachusetts: Harvard University Press.
Duncan, R. C. (1993). The Life-Expectancy of Industrial Civilization: The Decline to Global Equilibrium. *Population and Environment* 14: 325–357.
Dupré, J. (1993). *The Disorder of Things: Metaphysical Foundations of the Disunity of Science.* Cambridge, Massachusetts: Harvard University Press.
Dusevic, T. (1995). Unemployment Trap Breeds "Poverty Ghettoes." *The Australian* April 27: 2.
Dutton, D. B. (1988). *Worse than the Disease: The Pitfalls of Medical Progress.* Cambridge: Cambridge University Press.
Dyke, C. (1981). *Philosophy of Economics.* New Jersey: Prentice-Hall.
Dyson, F. J. (1978). Pilgrim Fathers, Mormon Pioneers, and Space Colonists: An Economic Comparison. *Proceedings of the American Philosophical Society* 122: 63–68.
Easterbrook, G. (1995). *A Moment on the Earth: Why Nature Needs Us.* New York: Viking.
Edelman, G. M. (1978). Group Selection and Phasic Reentrant Signalling: A Theory of Higher Brain Function. In G.M. Edelman & V.B. Mountecaste. *The Mindful Brain.* Cambridge, Massachusetts: MIT Press: 51–100.
Egan, F. (1995). Folk Psychology and Cognitive Architecture. *Philosophy of Science* 62: 179–196.
Ehrlich, P. R. (1968). Eco-Catastrophe. *Ramparts* 8: 24–28.
Ehrlich, P. R. & Ehrlich, A. (1990). *The Population Explosion.* New York: Simon and Schuster.
Ehrlich, P. R., Ehrlich, A. H. & Daily, G. C. (1993). Food Security, Population, and Environment. *Population and Development Review* 19: 1–32.
Eichner, A.S . ed. (1983). *Why Economics Is Not Yet a Science.* London: Macmillan.
Ekins, P. ed. (1986). *The Living Economy.* London: Routledge & Kegan Paul.
Ekins, P. (1991). The Sustainable Consumer Society: A Contradiction in Terms? *International Environmental Affairs* 314: 243–258.
Ekins, P. (1992). *A New World Order: Grassroots Movements for Global Change.* London: Routledge.
Elgin, D. (1981). *Voluntary Simplicity.* New York: Morrow.

Ellingsen, P. (1991). The Question of Validity. *The Age* (Australia), August 13: 11.
Ellis, J. M. (1989). *Against Deconstructionism*. Princeton: Princeton University Press.
Ellis, S. (1995). Job Gap a Threat to Social Stability. *Australian Financial Review*. April 27: 5.
Ellul, J. (1990). *The Technological Bluff*. Grand Rapids, Michigan: W. B. Eerdmans Publishing Company.
Emsley, J. (1989). Phosphorus Upsets the Chemical Theories. *New Scientist* November 25: 15.
Emsley, J. (1990). The Nitrogen Molecule that Shouldn't Exist. *New Scientist* May 26: 16.
English, B. (1995). Australia's Deficit "the Worst." *The Advertiser* (Adelaide, South Australia) June 22: 11.
Epstein, P. R. & Sharp, D. (1993). Medicine in a Warmer World. *The Lancet* 342: 1003–1004.
Epstein, P. R. et al. (1993). Marine Ecosystems. *The Lancet* 342: 1216–1219.
Ermann, M. D., Williams, M. B. & Gutierrez, C. (1990). *Computers, Ethics, and Society*. New York: Oxford University Press.
Everett, H. (1957). "Relative State" Formulation of Quantum Mechanics. *Reviews of Modern Physics* 29: 454–462.
Everitt, N. (1981). A Problem for the Eliminative Materialist. *Mind* 90: 428–434.
Ewan, C. E. et al eds (1993). *Health in the Greenhouse: The Medical and Environmental Health Effects of Global Climate Change*. Canberra: Australian Government Publishing Service.
Feldman, F. (1980). The Principle of Moral Harmony. *Journal of Philosophy* 77: 166–179.
Feldman, F. (1986). *Doing the Best We Can*. Dordrecht: D. Reidel.
Fenner, F. (interview) (1996). Threats to the Human Species. *Australians for an Ecologically Sustainable Population Newsletter* 30: 7.
Ferrari, J. (1996a). Bacterial Resistance to Antibiotics Increases. *The Australian* January 15: 3.
Ferrari, J. (1996b). Germ Warfare. *The Weekend Australian Review* April 6–7: 5.
Ferry, L. (1993). *The New Ecological Order*. Chicago: University of Chicago Press.
Feyerabend, P. K. (1975). *Against Method*. London: New Left Books.
Feyerabend, P. K. (1978). *Science in a Free Society*. London: New Left Books.
Figgie, H. E. & Swanson, G. J. (1993). *Bankruptcy 1995: The Coming Collapse of America and How to Stop It*. Boston: Little Brown & Company.
Fine, A. (1968). Logic, Probability, and Quantum Theory. *Philosophy of Science* 35: 101–111.
Fine, A. (1970). Insolubility of the Quantum Measurement Problem. *Physical Review D* 2: 2783–2787.
Fine, A. (1984). The Natural Ontological Attitude. In: J. Leplin ed. *Scientific Realism*. Berkeley: University of California Press: 83–107.
Finger, M. (1993). Politics of the UNCED Process. In: W. Sachs ed. *Global Ecology: A New Arena of Political Conflict*. London: Zed Books: 36–48.

Finley, M. I. (1968). *Aspects of Antiquity: Discoveries and Controversies*. New York: Viking Press.
Finney, B. R. & Jones, E. M. eds. (1985). *Interstellar Migration and the Human Experience*. Berkeley: University of California Press.
Finnis, J. M. (1985). On "The Critical Legal Studies Movement." *American Journal of Jurisprudence* 30: 21–42.
Fischer, G. (1993). The Population Explosion: Where Is It Leading? *Population and Environment* 15: 139–153.
Fishburn, P. C. (1974). Paradoxes of Voting. *American Political Science Review* 68: 537–546.
Fishburn, P. C. (1982). *The Foundations of Expected Utility*. Dordrecht: D. Reidel.
Fitzgerald, T. (1990). *Between Life and Economics: Boyer Lectures, 1990*. Crows Nest, New South Wales: Australian Broadcasting Corporation.
Flannery, T. (1995). *The Future Eaters*. Port Melbourne: Reed Books.
Flew, A. ed. (1979). *A Dictionary of Philosophy*. London: Pan Books.
Folse, H. I. (1978). Quantum Theory and Atomism: A Possible Ontological Resolution of the Quantum Paradox. *Southern Journal of Philosophy* 16: 629–640.
Forbes, G. (1995). Realism and Skepticism: Brains in a Vat Revisited. *Journal of Philosophy* XCII: 205–222.
Ford, S. (1996). How Jobs Are Going (from the) West. *The Independent Monthly* (Australia) May: 36.
Forester, T. & Morrison, P. (1990). *Computer Ethics: Cautionary Tales and Ethical Dilemmas in Computing*. Oxford: Blackwell.
Forester, T. ed. (1989). *Computers in the Human Context*. Oxford: Blackwell.
Foster, J. (1982). *The Case for Idealism*. London: Routledge & Kegan Paul.
Foster, J. (1990). *The Immaterial Self: A Defense of the Cartesian Dualist Conception of the Mind*. London: Routledge.
Foster, M. (1996). No Way to Fight Brain-Eating Bug. *The Advertiser* (Adelaide, South Australia) January 9: 1, 2.
Fowler, C. & Mooney, P. (1990). *Shattering: Food, Politics, and the Loss of Genetic Diversity*. Tucson: University of Arizona Press.
Freier, J. E. (1993). Eastern Equine Encephalomyelitis. *The Lancet* 342: 1281–1282.
Frejka, T. (1994). Long-Range Global Population Projections: Lessons Learned. In: W. Lutz (ed.). *The Future Population of the World*. London: Earthscan: 3–15.
Friedman, B. M. (1988). *Day of Reckoning*. New York: Random House.
Friedman, M. & Putnam, H. (1978). Quantum Logic, Conditional Probability, and Interference. *Dialectica* 32: 305–315.
Friedman, M. & Savage, L. J. (1948). The Utility Analysis of Choices Involving Risk. *Journal of Political Economy* 56: 279–304.
Frith, L. (1994). *Society, Dichotomies and Resolutions: An Inquiry into Social Synthesis*. Aldershot: Avebury.
Frodeman, R. (1992). Radical Environmentalism and the Political Roots of Postmodernism: Differences that Make a Difference. *Environmental Ethics* 14: 307–319.

Fry, I. (1995). Are the Different Hypotheses on the Emergence of Life as Different as They Seem? *Biology and Philosophy* 10: 389–417.
Fukuyama, F. (1992). *The End of History and the Last Man*. London: Hamish Hamilton.
Fuller, S. (1993). *Philosophy of Science and Its Discontents*. New York: Guilford Press.
Galbraith, J. K. (1971). *A Contemporary Guide to Economics, Peace and Laughter*. London: Andre Deutsch.
Galbraith, J. K. (1973). *Economics and the Public Purpose*. Boston: Houghton Mifflin.
Galtung, J. (1979). *Development, Environment and Technology: Towards a Technology for Self-Reliance*. New York: United Nations.
Galtung, J. (1986). Towards a New Economics: On the Theory and Practice of Self-Reliance. In: P. Ekins ed. *The Living Economy: A New Economics in the Making*. London: Routledge & Kegan Paul: 97–109.
Galtung, J., O'Brien, P. & Preiswerk, R. eds. (1980). *Self-Reliance: A Strategy for Development*. London: Bogle-L'Ouverture Publications.
Gannicott, K. (1993). Population, Development and Growth. In: R.V. Cole ed. *Pacific 2000: Challenging the Future*. Canberra: National Centre for Development Studies.
Gardner, M. R. (1971). Is Quantum Logic Really Logic? *Philosophy of Science* 38: 508–529.
Gare, A. E. (1993). *Nihilism Incorporated: European Civilization and Environmental Destruction*. Bungendore, New South Wales: Eco-Logical Press.
Gare, A. E. (1995). *Postmodernism and the Environmental Crisis*. London and New York: Routledge.
Garran, R. & Sexton, J. (1994). Bolkus Signals Permanent Brake on Migration. *The Weekend Australian* June 18-19: 1.
Garrett, L. (1994). *The Coming Plague: Newly Emerging Disease in a World out of Balance*. London: Virago Press.
Gauthier, D. (1986). *Morals by Agreement*. Oxford: Oxford University Press.
Georgescu-Roegen, N. (1971). *The Entropy Law and the Economic Process*. Cambridge, Massachusetts: Harvard University Press.
Gettier, E. (1963). Is Justified True Belief Knowledge? *Analysis* 23: 121–123.
Giampietro, M., Bukkens, S. G. F. & Pimentel, D. (1992). Limits to Population Size: Three Scenarios of Energy Interaction between Human Society and Ecosystem. *Population and Environment* 14: 109–131.
Gibbard, A. (1965). Rule Utilitarianism: Merely an Illusory Alternative? *Australasian Journal of Philosophy* 43: 211–220.
Gibbard, A. (1974). A Pareto-Consistent Libertarian Claim. *Journal of Economic Theory* 7: 388–410.
Gibbard, A. & Harper, W. (1978). Counterfactuals and Two Kinds of Expected Utility. In: C.A. Hooker et al (eds). *Foundations and Applications of Decision Theory*, vol. 1. Dordrecht: D. Reidel: 125–162.
Gibbins, P. F. (1984). Why the Distributive Law Is Sometimes False. *Analysis* 44: 64–67.
Giddens, A. (1994). Brave New World: The New Context of Politics. In: D. Miliband ed. *Reinventing the Left*. Cambridge: Polity Press: 21–38.

Gilbert, A. (1992). Must Global Politics Constrain Democracy? Realism, Regimes and Democratic Internationalism. *Political Theory* 20: 8–37.
Gill, J. H. (1985). Knowledge as Justified Belief, Period. *International Philosophical Quarterly* 25: 381–391.
Gill, S. & Law, D. (1988). *The Global Political Economy*. Brighton, Sussex: Harvester/Wheatsheaf.
Gill, S. (1990). *American Hegemony and the Trilateral Commission*. Cambridge: Cambridge University Press.
Gintis, H. (1976). Consumer Behavior and the Concept of Sovereignty: Explanations of Social Decay. In: E. L. Wheelwright & F. J. Stilwell eds. *Readings in Political Economy* vol. 2. Sydney: ANZ Books: 15–28.
Gladwell, M. (1995). A Plague of Fear. *The Weekend Australian* July 22-23: 26.
Glazer, N. (1994). Golden Door Closes on the Tired, Huddled Masses. *The Australian* January 11: 9.
Gleick, J. (1988). *Chaos: Making a New Science*. London: Cardinal/Sphere Books.
Gleick, P. H. (1989). Climate Change and International Politics: Problems Facing Development Countries. *Ambio* 18: 333–339.
Globus, G. G. (1973). Unexpected Symmetries in the 'World Knot'. *Science* 180: 1129–1136.
Goeller, H. E. & Zucker, A. (1984). Infinite Resources: The Ultimate Strategy. *Science* 223: 456–462.
Goeller, H. E. (1995). Trends in Nonrenewable Resources. In: J. L. Simon (ed.). *The State of Humanity*. Oxford & Cambridge, Massachusetts: Blackwell: 313–322.
Goldman, A. H. (1991). *Empirical Knowledge*. Berkeley: University of California Press.
Goldsmith, E. (1988). *The Great U-Turn*. Hartland, Bideford: Green Books.
Goldsmith, E. (1992). *The Way: An Ecological World View*. London: Rider.
Goldsmith, J. (1994). *The Trap*. London: Macmillan.
Goldsmith, J. (1995). *The Response*. London: Macmillan.
Goodland, R. (1992). The Case that the World Has Reached Limits. In: R. Goodland, H.E. Daly & S.E. Serafy eds. *Population, Technology, and Lifestyle: The Transition to Sustainability*. Washington D.C.: Island Press: 3–22.
Goodland, R., Daly, H. E. & Serafy, S. E. eds. (1992). *Population, Technology, and Lifestyle: The Transition to Sustainability*. Washington D.C.: Island Press.
Goodwin, N. (1991). *Social Economics: An Alternative Theory*. London: Macmillan.
Gordon, D. M. (1988). The Global Economy: New Edice or Crumbling Foundations? *New Left Review* 168: 24–64.
Gordon, K. (1986). Folk Psychology as Simulation. *Mind and Language* 1: 158–171.
Gottliebsen, R. (1996). Davo's Brutal Reality Check. *Business Review Weekly* March 4: 38–42.
Goudsblom, J. (1980). *Nihilism and Culture*. Oxford: Basil Blackwell.

Gould, C. C. ed. (1989). *The Information Web: Ethical and Social Implications of Computer Networking.* Boulder, Colorado: Westview Press.
Gowdy, J. M. (1994a). *Evolutionary Economics.* Dordrecht: Kluwer.
Gowdy, J. M. (1994b). Progress and Environmental Sustainability. *Environmental Ethics* 16: 41–55.
Graham, G. & Horgan, T. (1988). How to be Realistic about Folk Psychology. *Philosophical Psychology* 1: 69–81.
Graham-Smith, F. ed. (1994). *Population—The Complex Reality: A Report of the Population Summit of the World's Scientific Academies.* Golden, Colorado: The Royal Society/North American Press.
Graves, J. C. (1971). *The Conceptual Foundations of Contemporary Relativity Theory.* Cambridge, Massachusetts: MIT Press.
Graves, P. (1980). Migration and Climate. *Journal of Regional Science* 20: 227–237.
Gray, J. (1993a). *Beyond the New Right: Markets, Government and the Common Environment.* London & New York: Routledge.
Gray, J. (1993b). When No GATT Deal Is Probably a Good Deal. *Guardian Weekly* November 17 1993: 17.
Gray, J. (1995). *Enlightenment's Wake: Politics and Culture at the Close of the Modern Age.* London & New York: Routledge.
Grayling, A. C. (1985). *The Refutation of Scepticism.* London: Duckworth.
Greeley, H. (1869). *Essays Designed to Elucidate the Science of Political Economy While Servicing to Explain and Defend the Policy of Protection to Home Industry, as a System of National Cooperation for the Elevation of Labor.* Philadelphia: Porter and Coates.
Gregg, A. (1955). A Medical Aspect of the Population Problem. *Science* 121: 681–682.
Grennan, H. (1995). Driven into the Ground. *The Bulletin* May 30: 70–72.
Gribbin, J. (1995). *Schrödinger's Kittens and the Search for Reality.* London: Weidenfeld & Nicolson.
Griffin, D. R. ed. (1988). *The Reenchantment of Science: Postmodern Proposals.* Albany: State University of New York Press.
Gross, P. & Levitt, N. (1994). *Higher Superstition: The Academic Left and Its Quarrels with Science.* Baltimore: John Hopkins University Press.
Haack, S. (1990). Recent Obituaries of Epistemology. *American Philosophical Quarterly* 27: 199–222.
Haack, S. (1993). *Evidence and Inquiry: Towards Reconstruction in Epistemology.* Oxford: Blackwell.
Hahn, F. H. (1973). *On the Notion of Equilibrium in Economics.* Cambridge: Cambridge University Press.
Hahn, F. H. (1983). *Money and Inflation.* Cambridge, Massachusetts: MIT Press.
Hailstone, B. & Starick, P. (1995). Mutant Bugs Major Threat to Health. *The Advertiser* (Adelaide, South Australia) October 9: 5.
Hailstone, B. (1995). More Potent Strains of AIDS Hits Australia. *The Advertiser* (Adelaide, South Australia) November 29: 3.
Haines, A. et al. (1993). Global Health Watch: Monitoring Impacts of Environmental Change. *The Lancet* 342: 1464–1469.

Haines, M. R. (1995). Disease and Health through the Ages. In: J. L. Simon ed. *The State of Humanity*. Oxford and Cambridge, Massachusetts: Blackwell: 51–60.
Hall, N. (1988). The Shape of Nuclear Models. *New Scientist* March 31: 40–43.
Hall, P. D. (1977). Why Do We Not Understand Pain? In: R. Duncan & M. Weston-Smith eds. *The Encyclopaedia of Ignorance*. Oxford: Pergamon Press: 361–368.
Hall, P. J. (1986). The Pauli Exclusion Principle and the Foundations of Chemistry. *Synthese* 69: 267–272.
Hall, R. J. (1979). Seeing Perfectly Dark Things and the Casual Conditions of Seeing. *Theoria* XLV: 127–134.
Hallam, N. (1984). An Argument in Favour of Non-Classical Logic for Quantum Theory. *Analysis* 44: 61–64.
Hallam, N. (1987). Quantum Logic and Indeterminacy. *Philosophical Papers* 16: 53–58.
Haller, R. (1974). Concerning the So-Called "Münchhausen Trilemma." *Ratio* 16: 125–140.
Hamilton, A., Madison, J. & Jay, J. ([1787/1788], 1948). *The Federalist or, The New Constitution*. Oxford: Basil Blackwell.
Hamilton, C. (1994). *The Mystic Economist*. Fyshwick (Australia): Willow Park Press.
Hand, M. (1990). Anti-Realism and Holes in the World. *Philosophy* 65: 218–224.
Harcourt, G. (1975a). Capital Theory: Much Ado about Something. *Thames Papers in Political Economy*. Autumn.
Harcourt, G. (1975b). *Some Cambridge Controversies in the Theory of Capital*. Cambridge: Cambridge University Press.
Hardin, G. (1959a). *Nature and Man's Fate*. New York: Rinehart.
Hardin, G. (1959b). Interstellar Migration and the Population Problem. *Journal of Heredity* 50: 68–70.
Hardin, G. (1968). The Tragedy of the Commons. *Science* 162: 1243–1248.
Hardin, G. (1993). *Living within Limits: Ecology, Economics, and Population Taboos*. New York & Oxford: Oxford University Press.
Hardin, G. (1994). The Tragedy of the Unmanaged Commons. *Trends in Ecology and Evolution* 9: 199.
Hardin, G. (1995). *The Immigration Dilemma: Avoiding the Tragedy of the Commons*. Washington DC: Federation for American Immigration Reform.
Harding, J. (1995). Worldwide Water Crisis a Threat to Food Stocks. *The Australian* August 8: 12.
Hardison, O. B. (1989). *Disappearing through the Skylight*. London: Penguin Books.
Harré, R. (1970). *The Principles of Scientific Thinking*. London: Macmillan.
Harré, R. & Madden, E. H. (1975). *Causal Powers*. Oxford: Basil Blackwell.
Harries, O. (1993). Clash of Civilizations. *The Weekend Australian* April 3–4: 19.
Harries, O. (1995). Realism in a New Era. *Quadrant* 39: 11–18.
Harris, E. E. (1965). *The Foundations of Metaphysics in Science*. London: George Allen & Unwin.

Harris, J. F. (1969). Achilles Replies. *Australasian Journal of Philosophy* 47: 322–324.
Harris, J. F. (1992). *Against Relativism: A Philosophical Defence of Method*. La Salle, Illinois: Open Court.
Harris, T. (1994). Cash Gap Turns Holiday Capital into Divided City. *The Australian* September 2: 5.
Harrison, J. (1983). Against Quantum Logic. *Analysis* 43: 83–85.
Harrison, P. (1992). *The Third Revolution: Environment, Population and a Sustainable World*. London: I. B. Tauris.
Harsanyi, J. C. (1985). Does Reason Tell Us What Moral Code to Follow and, Indeed, to Follow Any Moral Code at All? *Ethics* 96: 42–55.
Hartcher, P. (1995). Sceptics Jeer at Bank's Claim. *Australian Financial Review* September 1: 24.
Harvey, D. (1989). *The Condition of Postmodernity: An Enquiry into the Origins of Cultural Change*. Oxford: Basil Blackwell.
Hashimoto, M. & Nishioka, S. (1991). Potential Impacts of Climate Change on Human Settlements; the Energy, Transport and Industrial Sectors; Human Health and Air Quality. In: J. Jäger & H.L. Ferguson eds. *Climate Change: Science, Impacts and Policy: Proceedings of the Second World Climate Conference*. Cambridge: Cambridge University Press.
Haslett, D. W. (1990). What Is Utility? *Economics and Philosophy* 6: 65–94.
Hassan, I. (1985). The Culture of Postmodernism. *Theory, Culture and Society* 2: 119–131.
Hastings, P. (1994). Door May Open for Rush from Pacific Slums. *The Sydney Morning Herald* March 19: 8.
Hauptli, B. W. (1979). Inscrutability and Correspondence. *Southern Journal of Philosophy* 17: 199–212.
Hausman, D. M. (1981). *Capital, Profits and Prices: An Essay in the Philosophy of Economics*. New York: Columbia University Press.
Hawkes, N. (1995). Academic Warns of Bad New World. *The Australian* March 9: 11.
Hayes, D. (1990). *Behind the Silicon Curtain: The Seductions of Work in a Lonely Era*. Montréal: Black Rose Books.
Haynes, R. ed. (1991). *High Tech: High Co$t? Technology, Society and the Environment*. Chippendale: Pan Macmillan.
Heft, R. (1994a). Californians Back Moves on Immigration, Crime. *The Australian* November 10: 7.
Heft, R. (1994b). Mexican Flag a Red Rag for Angry Californian Voters. *The Weekend Australian* November 12–13: 14.
Heil, J. (1989). Recent Work in Realism and Anti-Realism. *Philosophical Books* 30: 65–73.
Heilig, G. K. (1994). How Many People Can Be Fed on Earth? In: W. Lutz ed. *The Future Population of the World: What Can We Assume Today?* London: Earthscan: 207–261.
Henderson, I. (1995). Mexican Banana Republic: Our Latest Warning. *The Australian* November 6: 5.

Hendry, D. F. & Ericson, N. R. (1983). Assertion without Empirical Basis. *Bank of England Panel of Academic Consultants*. Panel paper No. 22: 45–101.

Hern, W. M. (1990). Why Are There So Many of Us? Description and Diagnosis of a Planetary Ecopathological Process. *Population and Environment* 12: 9–39.

Heyd, D. (1992). *Genethics: Moral Issues in the Creation of People*. Berkeley: University of California Press.

Hicks, J. (1939). *Value and Capital*. Oxford: Clarendon Press.

Higgins, E. (1992). Crisis of Our Rivers. *The Weekend Australian Review* November 28–29: 3.

Hildyard, N. (1993). Foxes in Charge of the Chickens. In: W. Sachs ed. *Global Ecology: A New Arena of Political Conflict*. London: Zed Books: 22–35.

Hiley, D. R. (1988). *Philosophy in Question: Essays on a Pyrrhonian Theme*. Chicago: University of Chicago Press.

Hill, S. (1988). *The Tragedy of Technology: Human Liberation Versus Domination in the Late Twentieth Century*. London: Pluto Press.

Hillis, W. D. (1982). New Computer Architectures and their Relationship to Physics or Why Computer Science Is No Good. *International Journal of Theoretical Physics* 21: 255–262.

Hillman, A. L. (1989). *The Political Economy of Protection*. Chur: Harwood Academic Publishers.

Hindmarsh, R. (1991). The Flawed "Sustainable" Promise of Genetic Engineering. *The Ecologist* 21: 196–205.

Hiscock, G. (1996). Upward Pressure on Global Rates. *The Australian* May 6: 17.

Hixson, W. (1994). The Mobile and the Immobile of the World. *Economic Reform* June: 7.

Hobbelink, H. (1991). *Biotechnology and the Future of World Agriculture*. London: Zed.

Hobson, J. (1902). *Imperialism: A Study*. London: Nisbet.

Hobson, J. (1914). *Work and Wealth*. London: Macmillan.

Hobson, J. (1929). *Economics and Ethics*. London: D. C. Heath.

Hodell, D. A., Curtis, J. H. & Brenner, M. (1995). Possible Role of Climate in the Collapse of Classic Maya Civilization. *Nature* 375: 391–394.

Hoffman, L. J. & Moran, L. M. (1986). Societal Vulnerability to Computer System Failures. *Computers and Security* 5: 211–217.

Hollis, M. & Nell, E. (1975). *Rational Economic Man*. Cambridge: Cambridge University Press.

Homer-Dixon, T. F. et al. (1993). Environmental Change and Violent Conflict. *Scientific American* 270, February: 16–23.

Honeysett, S. (1996). Murray-Darling a Disgrace: ACF. *The Australian* April 18: 2.

Hookway, C. (1990). *Scepticism*. London: Routledge.

Horsten, L. & Roelants, H. (1995). The Church-Turning Thesis and Effective Mundane Procedures. *Minds and Machines* 5: 1–8.

Houghton, D. (1995). Reasonable Doubts About Rational Choice. *Philosophy* 70: 53–68.

Houghton, J. T., Jenkins, G. J. & Ephraums, J. J. eds. (1990). *Climate Change: The IPCC Scientific Assessment.* Cambridge: Cambridge University Press.
House, D. V. & McDonald, M. I. (1992). Post-Physicalism and Beyond. *Dialogue* 31: 593–622.
How, A. (1995). *Habermas–Gadamer and the Nature of the Social.* Aldershot: Avebury.
Howard, M. C. (1987). Economics on a Sraffian Foundation: A Critical Analysis of Neo-Ricardian Theory. *Economy and Society* 16: 317–340.
Hoyle, F. (1964). *Of Men and Galaxies.* Seattle: University of Washington Press.
Hoyle, F. (1986). On the Argument of Malthus. *Population and Development Review* 12: 547–562.
Hoyle, F. & Wickramasinghe, C. (1981). *Evolution from Space: A Theory of Cosmic Creationism.* London: Dent.
Hubbert, M. K. (1962). *Energy Resources.* Washington DC: National Academy of Sciences National Research Council.
Hueting, R. (1990). The Brundtland Report: A Matter of Conflicting Goals. *Ecological Economics* 2: 109–117.
Hughes, J. D. (1975). *Ecology in Ancient Civilizations.* Albuquerque: University of New Mexico Press.
Hugo, G. (1984). The Demographic Impact of Famine. In: B. Currey & G. Hugo eds. *Famine as a Geographical Phenomenon.* Dordrecht: Reidel.
Hugo, G. (1989). Changing Famine Coping Strategies under the Impact of Population Pressure and Urbanization: The Case of Population Mobility. Paper presented to the First Workshop of the International Geographical Union Study Group on Famine Research and Food Production Systems, Freiburg University.
Hugo, G. (1994). Introduction. In: M. Wooden, R. Holton, G. Hugo & J. Sloan, *Australian Immigration: A Survey of the Issues.* 2nd edition. Canberra: Australian Government Publishing Service.
Humphries, R. (1992). Without a Drop to Drink. *Greenpeace Australia News* 3: 4–6.
Hunt, E. K. (1977). The Ideal Foundations of Welfare Economics. In: J. G. Schwartz ed. *The Subtle Anatomy of Capitalism.* Santa Monica, California: Goodyear Publishing Company: 22–35.
Hunter, G. (1995). The Churchlands' Eliminative Materialism: Or the Result of Impatience. *Philosophical Investigations* 18: 13–30.
Huntington, S. P. (1993a). The Clash of Civilizations. *Foreign Affairs* 72, Summer: 22–49.
Huntington, S. P. (1993b). If Not Civilizations, What? Paradigms of the Post-Cold War World. *Foreign Affairs* 72, November/December: 186–194.
Hutzler, C. (1996). China's Growth May Shrivel for Lack of Water. *The Australian* May 20: 33.
Ions, E. (1977). *Against Behaviouralism: A Critique of Behavioural Science.* Oxford: Basil Blackwell.
Jackendoff, R. (1991). The Problem of Reality. *Nous* 25: 411–433.
Jacobson, J. L. (1989). Environmental Refugees: Nature's Warning System. *Populi* 16: 29–41.
Jaroff, L. (1996). A Shot across the Earth's Bow. *Time* June 3: 65–66.

Jeevan, A. & Kripke, M. L. (1993). Ozone Depletion and the Immune System. *The Lancet* 342: 1159–1160.
Johnson, C. (1995). Intellectual Warfare. *The Atlantic Monthly* January: 99–104.
Johnson, O. A. (1971). Is Knowledge Definable? *Southern Journal of Philosophy* 9: 227–286.
Johnson, O. A. (1975). Scepticism and the Standards of Rationality. *Philosophical Quarterly* 25: 336–339.
Joint Standing Committee on Foreign Affairs, Defence and Trade (1989). *Australia's Relations with the South Pacific*. Canberra: Australian Government Publishing Service.
Jones, E. (1991). Down with Economists. *The Bulletin* (Australia) October 8: 86–88.
Jones, E. (1993a). Economic Language, Propaganda and Dissent. In: S. Rees, G. Rodley & F. Stilwell (eds). (1993). *Beyond the Market: Alternatives to Economic Rationalism*. Leichhardt, New South Wales: Pluto Press: 253–269.
Jones, G. W. (1993b). Population Trends in the Asia-Pacific Region. *Ministerial Seminar on Population and Development in the Asia-Pacific Region*. Canberra: Australian Academy of Science.
Joseph, J. G., Prior, I. A. M., Salmond, C. E. & Stanley, D. G. (1983). Elevation of Systolic and Diastolic Blood Pressure Associated with Migration: The Tokelau Island Migrant Study. *Journal of Chronic Diseases* 36: 507–516.
Julien, P-A. & Lafrance, C. (1983). Towards the Formalization of "Small is Beautiful": Societal Effectiveness Versus Economic Efficiency. *Futures* 15: 211–221.
Kadaba, L. S. (1995). World of Difference. *The Advertiser* (Adelaide, South Australia) August 29: 13.
Kagan, S. (1989). *The Limits of Morality*. Oxford: Clarendon Press.
Kaiser, R. (1987). "A Fifth Gospel, Almost": Chief Seattle's Speech (es): American Origins and European Reception. In: C. F. Feest ed. *Indians and Europe: An Interdisciplinary Collection of Essays*. Aachen: Rader Verlag: 505–526.
Kaldis, B. (1993). *Holism, Language and Persons: An Essay on the Ontology of the Social World*. Aldershot: Avebury.
Kaldor, N. (1972). The Irrelevance of Equilibrium Economics. *Economic Journal* 82: 1237–1255.
Kalkstein, L. S. (1993). Direct Impacts in Cities. *The Lancet* 342: 1397–1399.
Kaplan, R. D. (1994). The Coming Anarchy. *The Atlantic Monthly* 273, February: 44–76.
Kapstein, E. B. (1996). Workers and the World Economy. *Foreign Affairs* 75: 16–37.
Karlen, A. (1995). *Plague's Progress: A Social History of Man and Disease*. London: Victor Gollancz.
Kates, R. W. (1985). The Interaction of Climate and Society. In: R. W. Kates, J. H. Ausubel & M. Berberian, eds. *Climate Impact Assessment*. New York: John Wiley & Sons.
Katouzian, H. (1980). *Ideology and Method in Economics*. London: Macmillan.

Katz, E. (1992). The Call of the Wild: The Struggle against Domination and the Technological Fix of Nature. *Environmental Ethics* 14: 265–273.
Kaufman, W. (1994). *No Turning Back: Dismantling the Fantasies of Environmental Thinking*. New York: Basic Books.
Keighery, G. (1995). The Ecological Consequences of Genetic Engineering. *Search* 26: 274–276.
Kekes, J. (1975). The Case for Scepticism. *Philosophical Quarterly* 25: 28–29.
Kekes, J. (1976). *A Justification of Rationality*. Albany: State University of New York Press.
Kekes, J. (1985). The Fate of the Enlightenment Program. *Inquiry* 28: 388–398.
Kelly, J. S. (1976). The Impossibility of a Just Liberal. *Economica* 43: 67–75.
Kelly, J. S. (1978). *Arrow Impossibility Theorems*. New York: Academic Press.
Kelly, J. S. (1988). Rights and Social Choice: Comment. *Economics and Philosophy* 4: 316–325.
Kelsey, D. (1988). What Is Responsible for the "Paretian Epidemic"? *Social Choice and Welfare* 5: 303–306.
Kemp, J. (1988). "Money Can't Buy Me Love." Paradoxes and Expected Utility Theory: A Clarification. *Scottish Journal of Political Economy* 35: 149–161.
Kennedy, P. (1987). *The Rise and Fall of the Great Powers*. New York: Random House.
Kennedy, P. (1993). *Preparing for the Twenty-First Century*. New York: Random House.
Kerr, R. A. (1995). It's Official: First Glimmer of Greenhouse Warming Seen. *Science* December 8: 1565, 1567.
Keyfitz, N. (1981). The Limits of Population Forecasting. *Population and Development Review* 7: 579–593.
Keyfitz, N. & Lindahl-Kiessling, K. (1994). The World Population Debate: Urgency of the Problem. In: F. Graham-Smith ed. *Population–The Complex Reality: A Report of the Population Summit of the World's Scientific Academies*. Golden, Colorado: The Royal Society/North American Press: 21–51.
Keynes, J. M. (1982). National Self-Sufficiency. In: *The Collected Writings of John Maynard Keynes* vol. XXI edited by D. Moggeridge. London: Macmillan/Cambridge University Press for the Royal Economic Society: 233–246.
King, A. D. ed. (1991). *Culture, Globalisation and the World-System*. Basingstoke: Macmillan.
King, M. & Elliott, C. (1993). Legitimate Double-Think. *The Lancet* 341: 669–672.
Kipnis, D. (1990). *Technology and Power*. New York: Springer-Verlag.
Kirk, G. ed. (1983). *Schumacher on Energy*. London: Abacus.
Klein, P. D. (1981). *Certainty: A Refutation of Scepticism*. Brighton, Sussex: Harvester Press.
Knudson, K. E. (1977). Sydney Island, Titiana and Kamaleai: Southern Gilbertese in the Phoenix and Solomon Islands. In: M.D. Lieber, ed. *Exiles and Migrants in Oceania*. Honolulu: University of Hawaii Press.

Koed, E. (1992). A Symbol Transformed: How "Liberty Enlightening the World" Became "The Mother of Exiles." *The Social Contract* 2, Spring: 134–143.
Kohr, L. (1978). *The Breakdown of Nations*. New York: E. P. Dutton.
Koshland, D. (1992). The Microbial Wars. *Science* 257: 1021.
Kosko, B. (1994). *Fuzzy Thinking: The New Science of Fuzzy Logic*. London: Harper Collins.
Kraushaar, J. J. & Ristinen, R.A. (1993). *Energy and Problems of a Technical Society*. New York: Wiley.
Krieger, M. (1995). Could the Probability of Doom be Zero or One? *Journal of Philosophy* XCII: 382–387.
Krimsky, S. (1982). *Genetic Alchemy: The Social History of the Recombinant DNA Controversy*. Cambridge, Massachusetts: MIT Press.
Krips, H. (1987). *The Metaphysics of Quantum Theory*. Oxford: Clarendon Press.
Kritz, M. M. (1990). *Climate Change and Migration Adaptations.* Working Paper Series 2.16: Ithaca: Cornell University.
Kroeber, A. L. (1944). *Configurations of Cultural Growth*. Berkeley: University of California Press.
Kroeber, A. L. (1957). *Style and Civilizations*. Ithaca: Cornell University Press.
Krugman, P. (1994). *Peddling Prosperity: Economic Sense and Nonsense in the Age of Diminished Expectations*. New York: W.W. Norton.
Krugman, P. & Venables, A. J. (1995). Globalization and the Inequality of Nations. *Quarterly Journal of Economics* CX: 857–880.
Kuhn, A. (1977). Dualism Reconstructed. *General Systems* 22: 91–97.
Kumar, K. (1995). Apocalypse, Millennium and Utopia Today. In: M. Bull, ed. *Apocalypse Theory and the Ends of the World*. Oxford: Blackwell: 200–224.
Kurtzman, J. (1988). *The Decline and Crash of the American Economy*. New York: W.W. Norton.
Lakatos, I. (1978). *The Methodology of Scientific Research Programmes.* Cambridge: Cambridge University Press.
Lasch, C. (1991). *The True and Only Heaven*. New York: W.W. Norton.
Laudan, K. C. (1986). *Dossier Society*. New York: Columbia University Press.
Laudan, L. (1990). *Science and Relativism: Some Key Controversies in the Philosophy of Science*. Chicago: University of Chicago Press.
Laura, R. S. & Ashton, J. F. (1991). *Hidden Hazards: The Dark Side of Everyday Technology and How It Affects Your Health and Environment*. Sydney: Bantam Books.
Leakey, R. & Lewin, R. (1996). *The Sixth Extinction: Biodiversity and Its Survival*. London: Weidenfeld & Nicolson.
Leemer, E. E. (1983). Let's Take the Con Out of Econometrics. *American Economic Review* 73: 31–43.
Lehman, D. (1991). *Signs of the Times: Deconstruction and the Fall of Paul de Man*. London: Andre Deutsch.
Lehrer, K. (1990). *Theory of Knowledge*. London: Routledge.
Leibenstein, H. (1979). A Branch of Economics Is Missing: Micro-Micro Theory. *Journal of Economic Literature* 17: 477–502.
Leslie, J. (1989). *Universes*. London & New York: Routledge.

Leslie, J. (1992). Time and the Anthropic Principle. *Mind* 403: 521–540.
Leslie, J. (1994). Testing the Doomsday Argument. *Journal of Applied Philosophy* 11: 31–44.
Leslie, J. (1996). *The End of the World: The Science and Ethics of Human Extinction.* London & New York: Routledge.
Levi, I. (1986). The Paradoxes of Allais and Ellsberg. *Economics and Philosophy* 2: 23–53.
Levin, M. (1990). Realisms. *Synthese* 85: 115–138.
Lewin, R. (1980). Is Your Brain Really Necessary? *Science* 210: 1232–1234.
Lewin, R. (1993). *Complexity: Life at the Edge of Chaos.* London: Phoenix.
Lewis, D. & Lewis, S. (1970). Holes. *Australasian Journal of Philosophy* 48: 206–212.
Lewis, M. W. (1992). *Green Delusions: An Environmentalist Critique of Radical Environmentalism.* Durham: Duke University Press.
Lines, W. J. (1991). *Taming the Great South Land: A History of the Conquest of Nature in Australia.* North Sydney: Allen & Unwin.
Lipsey, R. G. & Lancaster, K. (1956–57). The General Theory of Second Best. *Review of Economic Studies* 23: 11–32.
List, F. ([1837], 1983). *The Natural System of Political Economy.* Translated and edited by W.O. Henderson. London: Frank Cass.
List, F. ([1841], 1885). *The National System of Political Economy.* Translated by S.S. Lloyd. London: Longmans, Green & Co.
Lloyd, S. A. (1993). Stratospheric Ozone Depletion. *The Lancet* 342: 1156–1158.
Lockwood, M. (1989). *Mind, Brain and Quantum: The Compound "I."* Oxford: Basil Blackwell.
Loomes, G., Starmer, C. & Sugden, R. (1991). Observing Violations of Transitivity by Experimental Methods. *Econometrica* 59: 425–439.
Lormand, E. (1990). Framing the Frame Problem. *Synthese* 82: 353–374.
Lovelock, J. (1979). *Gaia: A New Look at Life on Earth.* Oxford: Oxford University Press.
Lovelock, J. (1988). *The Ages of Gaia: A Biography of Our Living Earth.* London: Norton & Company.
Low, J. W. G. (1985). *The Dynamics of Apocalypse.* Albuquerque: University of New Mexico Press.
Lowe, E. J. (1981). Against an Argument for Token Identity. *Mind* XC: 120–121.
Luce, R. D. & Raiffa, H. (1957). *Games and Decisions.* New York: Wiley.
Lumholtz, C. (1980). *Among the Cannibals.* Canberra: Australian National University Press.
Luntley, M. (1988). *Language, Logic and Experience: The Case for Anti-Realism.* La Salle, Illinois: Open Court.
Luper-Foy, S. ed. (1987). *The Possibility of Knowledge: Nozick and his Critics.* Totowa, New Jersey: Rowman and Littlefield.
Lurie, Y. (1979). Correlating Brain States with Psychological Phenomena. *Australasian Journal of Philosophy* 57: 135–144.
Luten, D. B. (1991). Population and Resources. *Population and Environment* 12: 311–329.

Lutz, M. & Lux, K. (1979). *The Challenge of Humanistic Economics*. Palo Alto, California: Benjamin/Cummings.
Lutz, M. & Lux, K. (1988). *Humanistic Economics: The New Challenge*. New York: Bootstrap Press.
Lutz, M. (1990). *Social Economics: Retrospect and Prospect*. Boston: Kluwer.
Lutz, M. (1992). Humanistic Economics: History and Basic Principles. In: P. Ekins & M. Max-Neef eds. *Real-Life Economics: Understanding Wealth Creation*. London: Routledge: 90–120.
Lutz, W., Goldstein, J. R. & Prinz, C. (1994). Alternative Approaches to Population Projection. In: W. Lutz, ed. *The Future Population of the World*. London: Earthscan: 17–50.
Lycan, W. G. (1988). *Judgement and Justification*. Cambridge: Cambridge University Press.
Lyon, D. (1990). *The Information Society: Issues and Illusions*. Cambridge: Polity Press.
Lyons, G., Moore, E. & Smith, J. W. (1995). *Is the End Nigh? Internationalism, Global Chaos and the Destruction of the Earth*. Aldershot: Avebury.
Lyotard, J. F. (1984). *The Postmodern Condition: A Report on Knowledge*. Manchester: Manchester University Press.
Lyotard, J. F. (1992). *The Postmodern Explained to Children: Correspondence 1982–1985*. Sydney: Power Publications.
Lyytinen, K. & Hirschheim, R. (1987). Information Systems Failures—A Survey and Classification of the Empirical Literature. *Oxford Surveys in Information Technology* 4: 257–309.
MacDonald, G. M. & Markusen, J. R. (1985). A Rehabilitation of Absolute Advantage. *Journal of Political Economy* 93: 277–297.
Maddox, B. (1995). Tales of Doom Backfire on Greens. *The Australian* April 5: 8.
Maddox, J. (1988). Beating the Quantum Limits (Cont'd). *Nature* 331: 559.
Madell, G. (1986). Neurophilosophy: A Principled Sceptic's Response. *Inquiry* 29: 153–168.
Madell, G. (1988). *Mind and Materialism*. Edinburgh: University of Edinburgh Press.
Madhava Sarma, K. (1991). Adaptation Measures. In: J. Jäger & H.L. Ferguson eds. *Climate Change: Science, Impacts and Policy: Proceedings of the Second World Climate Conference*. Cambridge: Cambridge University Press.
Madison, G. B. (1976). The Possibility and Limits of a Science of Man. *Philosophy Forum* 14: 351–366.
Maley, B. (1994). *Ethics and Ecosystems*. St. Leonards, New South Wales: Centre for Independent Studies.
Mander, J. (1991). *In the Absence of the Sacred*. San Francisco: Sierra Club Books.
Manes, C. (1990). *Green Rage: Radical Environmentalism and the Unmaking of Civilization*. Boston: Little Brown and Co.
Manes, C. (1992). Nature and Silence. *Environmental Ethics* 14: 339–350.
Mann, C. C. (1991). Extinction: Are Ecologists Crying Wolf? *Science* 253: 736–738.

Markowitz, H. (1952). The Utility of Wealth. *Journal of Political Economy* 60: 151–158.
Martinez-Alier, J. (1993). *Ecological Economics: Energy, Environment and Society.* London: Blackwell.
Maskell, K. et al (1993). Basic Science of Climate Change. *The Lancet* 342: 1027–1031.
Massey, D. S. (1994). The Social and Economic Origins of Immigration. *The Social Contract* 4: 183–185.
Mates, B. (1981). *Skeptical Essays.* Chicago: University of Chicago Press.
Mates, B. (1984). On Refuting the Skeptic. *American Philosophical Association* 58: 21–35.
Mathews, F. (1991). *The Ecological Self.* Savage, Maryland: Barnes & Noble Books.
Mathews, R. (1992). Is There An Alternative Economic Policy? *CEDA Public Information Paper* 38, March.
Maxwell, N. (1972). A New Look at the Quantum Mechanical Problem of Measurement. *American Journal of Physics* 40: 1431–1435.
Maxwell, N. (1976a). Toward a Micro-Realistic Version of Quantum Mechanics Part I. *Foundations of Physics* 6: 275–292.
Maxwell, N. (1976b). Toward a Micro-Realistic Version of Quantum Mechanics Part II. *Foundations of Physics* 12: 661–676.
Maxwell, N. (1982). Instead of Particles and Fields: A Microrealistic Quantum "Smearon" Theory. *Foundations of Physics* 12: 607–631.
Maxwell, N. (1984). *From Knowledge to Wisdom: A Revolution in the Aims and Methods of Science.* Oxford: Basil Blackwell.
Maxwell, N. (1985). Are Probabilism and Special Relativity Incompatible? *Philosophy of Science* 52: 23–43.
Maxwell, N. (1986). The Fate of the Enlightenment: Reply to Kekes. *Inquiry* 29: 79–92.
Maxwell, N. (1988). Quantum Propensiton Theory: A Testable Resolution of the Wave/Particle Dilemma. *British Journal for the Philosophy of Science* 39: 1–50.
May, R. (1974). Biological Populations with Nonoverlapping Generations. *Science* 186: 645–647.
Mazzarino, S. (1966). *The End of the Ancient World.* London: Faber & Faber.
McClintock, A. (1995). *The Convergence of Machine and Human Nature.* Aldershot: Avebury.
McDermott, J. (1987). *The Killing Winds: The Menace of Biological Warfare.* New York: Arbor House.
McGinn, C. (1989). Can We Solve the Mind-Body Problem? *Mind* 98: 349–366.
McGinn, C. (1991). *The Problem of Consciousness.* Oxford: Blackwell.
McGregor, G. (1990). Possible Consequences of Climatic Warning in Papua New Guinea with Implications for the Tropical Southwest Pacific Area. In: J. C. Pernetta & P. J. Hughes eds. *Implications of Expected Climate Changes in the South Pacific Region: An Overview.* Nairobi, Kenya: United Nations Environment Program Regional Seas Reports and Studies No. 128.

McKenzie, R. B. & Lee, D. R. (1991). *Quicksilver Capital: How the Rapid Movement of Wealth Has Changed the World.* New York: Free Press.
McKnight, R. E. (1977). Commons in Microcosm: The Movement of Southwest Islanders to Palau, Micronesia. In: M. D. Lieber, ed. *Exiles and Migrants in Oceania.* Honolulu: University of Hawai'i Press.
McLaren, D. J. (1996). Population Growth—Should We be Worried? *Population and Environment* 17: 243–259.
McLaughlin, A. (1993). *Regarding Nature: Industrialism and Deep Ecology.* Albany: State University of New York Press.
McLaughlin, W. I. (1983). Human Evolution in the Age of the Intelligent Machine. *Interdisciplinary Science Reviews* 4: 307–319.
McLean, I. (1980). Liberty, Equality and the Pareto Principle: A Comment on Weale. *Analysis* 40: 212–213.
McMichael, A. J. (1993). *Planetary Overload: Global Environmental Change and the Health of the Human Species.* Cambridge: Cambridge University Press.
McNeill, W. (1985). *Plagues and Peoples.* Harmondsworth: Penguin.
McNicoll, G. (1992). The United Nations' Long-Range Population Projections. *Population and Development Review* 18: 333–340.
McRobie, G. (1985). *Small Is Possible.* London: Abacus.
Mead, W. R. (1987). *Moral Splendor: The American Empire in Transition.* Boston: Houghton Mifflin.
Meade, J. (1961). *A Neoclassical Theory of Economic Growth.* London: Allen & Unwin.
Meadows, D. H. et al. (1972). *The Limits to Growth.* New York: Universe Books.
Meadows, D. H. et al. (1992). *Beyond the Limits: Global Collapse or a Sustainable Future.* London: Earthscan.
Megill, A. (1985). *Prophets of Extremity: Nietzsche, Heidegger, Foucault, Derrida.* Berkeley: University of California Press.
Meja, V. & Stehr, N. eds. (1990). *Knowledge and Politics: The Sociology of Knowledge Dispute.* London & New York: Routledge.
Melko, M. (1969). *The Nature of Civilizations.* Boston: Porter Sargent.
Mellor, D. H. (1991). How Much of the Mind Is a Computer? In: *Matters of Metaphysics.* Cambridge: Cambridge University Press: 61–81.
Mermin, N. D. (1981). Quantum Mysteries for Anyone. *Journal of Philosophy* 78: 397–408.
Mermin, N. D. (1985). Is the Moon There When Nobody Looks? Reality and the Quantum Theory. *Physics Today* April: 38–47.
Mermin, N. D. (1990). What's Wrong with These Elements of Reality? *Physics Today* June: 9–11.
Michie, D. & Johnston, R. (1985). *The Knowledge Machine: Artificial Intelligence and the Future of Man.* New York: William Morrow and Company.
Miles, J. (1992). Blacks vs. Browns. *The Atlantic* 270, October: 41–68.
Miller, D. (1980). Can Science Do Without Induction? In: L. J. Cohen and M. B. Hesse eds. *Applications of Inductive Logic.* Oxford: Clarendon Press: 109–129.

Miller, D. (1982). Conjectural Knowledge: Popper's Solution to the Problem of Induction. In: P. Levinson ed. *In Pursuit of Truth*. Atlantic Highlands, New Jersey: Humanities Press: 17–49.
Miller, J. A. (1991). Paul Ehrlich: The Bombardier Returns. *Population Research Institute Review* 1, January/February: 1–4.
Miller, R. W. (1987). *Fact and Method*. Princeton: Princeton University Press.
Mirowski, P. (1984). Physics and the "Marginalist Revolution." *Cambridge Journal of Economics* 8: 361–379.
Mishan, E. J. (1967). *The Costs of Economic Growth*. London: Staples Press.
Modigliani, F. (1977). The Monetarist Controversy or, Should We Forsake Stabilization Policies? *American Economic Review* 67: 1–19.
Mohanty, I. N. (1989). Idealism and Quantum Mechanics. *History of Philosophy Quarterly* 6: 381–391.
Molle, W. (1991). *The Economics of European Integration: Theory, Practice, Policy*. Aldershot: Dartmouth.
Moore, E. & Smith, J. W. (1995). Climatic Change and Migration from Oceania: Implications for Australia, New Zealand and the USA. *Population and Environment* 17: 105–122.
Morgan Gallup Poll (1992). Finding No. 2263. Melbourne: Roy Morgan Research Centre Pty. Ltd.
Morgan, H. (1996). Rabbit Industry Claiming Millions. *The Advertiser* (Adelaide, South Australia) January 22: 3.
Morley, M. & McGillion, C. (1993). A Trade Treaty for the Millionaires, Not the People. *Sydney Morning Herald* December 6: 13.
Morris, D. (1982). *Self-Reliant Cities: Energy and the Transformation of Urban America*. San Francisco: Sierra Club Books.
Moser, P. K. (1991). *Knowledge and Evidence*. Cambridge: Cambridge University Press.
Mosley, G. (1994). Goodbye Global Trade—Hello National Self-Sufficiency. *Enveco* 1, February: 4–5, 7.
Mulhauser, G. R. (1995). Materialism and the "Problem" of Quantum Measurement. *Minds and Machines* 5: 207–217.
Murphy, N. (1990). Scientific Realism and Postmodern Philosophy. *British Journal for the Philosophy of Science* 41: 291–303.
Murray-Darling Basin Commission (October 1992). *The Impact of River Regulation on the National Flows of the Murray-Darling Basin*. Sydney: Murray-Darling Basin Commission.
Musgrave, A. (1989). NOA's Ark—Fine for Realism. *Philosophical Quarterly* 39: 383: 398.
Myers, N. & Simon, J. L. (1994). *Scarcity or Abundance? A Debate on the Environment*. New York: W.W. Norton.
Naess, A. (1991). *Ecology, Community and Lifestyle*. Cambridge: Cambridge University Press.
Naylor, R. T. (1987). *Hot Money and the Politics of Debt*. London: Unwin Paperbacks.
Neisser, U. (1980). The Limits of Cognition. In: P. W. Jusczyk & R. M. Klein eds. *The Nature of Thought*. Hillsdale, New Jersey: Lawrence Erlbaum Associates: 115–132.
Nelson, J. O. (1982). Does Physics Lead to Berkeley? *Philosophy* 57: 91–103.

Nesse, R. M. & Williams, G. C. (1995). *Evolution and Healing: The New Science of Darwinian Medicine*. London: Weidenfeld & Nicolson.
Newbery, D. M. G. & Stiglitz, J. E. (1982). The Choice of Techniques and the Optimality of Market Equilibrium with Rational Expectations. *Journal of Political Economy* 90: 223–246.
Newton-Smith, W. H. (1981). *The Rationality of Science*. Boston: Routledge and Kegan Paul.
Ng, Y.-K. (1985). *Welfare Economics: Introduction and Development of Basic Concepts* (Revised edition). London: Macmillan.
Nicholls, N. (1993). El Niño-Southern Oscillation and Vector-Borne Disease. *The Lancet* 342: 1284–1285.
Nicolis, G. & Prigogine, I. (1989). *Exploring Complexity*. New York: W. H. Freeman.
Nielsen, K. (1991a). *After the Demise of the Tradition: Rorty, Critical Theory and the Fate of Philosophy*. Boulder, Colorado: Westview Press.
Nielsen, K. (1991b). Farewell to the Tradition: Doing without Metaphysics and Epistemology. *Philosophica* 20: 363–376.
Nitecki, M. ed. (1988). *Evolutionary Progress*. Chicago: University of Chicago Press.
North, R. D. (1995a). End of the Green Crusade. *New Scientist* March 4: 38–41.
North, R. D. (1995b). *Life on a Modern Planet: A Manifesto for Progress*. Manchester & New York : Manchester University Press.
Nozick, R. (1969). Newcomb's Problem and Two Principles of Choice. In: N. Rescher et al. eds. *Essays in Honor of Carl G. Hempel*. Dordrecht: D. Reidel: 114–146.
Nozick, R. (1981). *Philosophical Explanations*. Oxford: Clarendon Press.
Nozick, R. (1993). *The Nature of Rationality*. Princeton, New Jersey: Princeton University Press.
Nuttall, N. (1995). 100 Years of Drought Forecast for Africa. *The Australian* October 19: 8.
NZ Department of Statistics (1993). *New Zealand Official Yearbook*. Auckland: Department of Statistics.
Oakley, I. T. (1988). Scepticism and the Diversity of Epistemic Justification. *Philosophical Quarterly* 38: 263–279.
O'Collins, M. (1990a). Carteret Islanders at the Atolls Resettlement Scheme: A Response to Land Loss and Population Growth. In: J.C. Pernetta & P.J. Hughes eds. *Implications of Expected Climate Changes in the South Pacific Region: An Overview*. Nairobi, Kenya: United Nations Environment Program Regional Seas Reports and Studies No. 128.
O'Collins, M. (1990b). Social and Cultural Impact: A Changing Pacific? In: J. C. Pernetta & P. J. Hughes eds. *Implications of Expected Climate Changes in the South Pacific Region: An Overview*. Nairobi, Kenya: United Nations Environment Program Regional Seas Reports and Studies No. 128.
Odegard, D. (1982). *Knowledge and Scepticism*. Totowa, New Jersey: Rowman and Littlefield.
Odegard, D. (1986). Demon Scepticism. *American Philosophical Quarterly* 23: 209–216.

Odum, E. P. (1989). *Ecology and Our Endangered Life-Support Systems.* Sunderland, Massachusetts: Sinauer Associates, Inc.
Ohmae, K. (1990). *The Borderless World: Power and Strategy in the Interlinked Economy.* London: Fontana/HarperCollins.
Oliver-Smith, A. (1982). Here There Is Life: The Social and Cultural Dynamics of Successful Resistance to Resettlement in Post Disaster Peru. In: A. Hansen & A. Oliver-Smith eds. *Involuntary Migration and Resettlement: The Problems and Responses of Dislocated People.* Boulder, Colorado: Westview Press.
Olson, M. (1982). *The Rise and Decline of Nations: Economic Growth, Stagflation, and Social Rigidities.* New Haven & London: Yale University Press.
Omran, A. R. (1971). The Epidemiologic Transition. *Milbank Memorial Fund Quarterly* 49: 509–538.
Ormerod, P. (1995). *The Death of Economics.* London: Faber & Faber.
Palmer, A. (1984). The Limits of AI: Thought Experiments and Conceptual Investigations. In: S. B. Torrance ed. *The Mind and the Machine: Philosophical Aspects of Artificial Intelligence.* Chichester: Ellis Harwood Publishers: 43–50.
Pappas, G. S. & Swain, M. eds. (1978). *Essays on Knowledge and Justification.* Ithaca: Cornell University Press.
Parker, M. (1995). *The Growth of Understanding: Beyond Individuals and Communities.* Aldershot: Avebury.
Parks, W. (1992). Deconstruction: The New Nihilism. *The World and I*, April: 547–561.
Parry, M. L. & Rosenzweig, C. (1993). Food Supply and Risk of Hunger. *The Lancet* 342: 1345–1347.
Pearce, F. (1992). Grain Yields Tumble in Greenhouse World. *New Scientist* 134, April 18: 4.
Pearce, F. (1995). Fiddling while Earth Warms. *New Scientist* 137, March 25: 14–15.
Pecchioli, R. M. (1983). *The Internationalization of Banking: The Policy Issues.* Paris: OECD.
Penrose, R. (1989). *The Emperor's New Mind.* New York: Oxford University Press.
Penrose, R. (1994). *Shadows of the Mind.* Oxford: Oxford University Press.
Perelman, L. J. (1980). Speculations on the Transition to Sustainable Energy. *Ethics* 90: 392–416.
Pernetta, J. C. & Hughes, P. J. eds. (1990). *Implications of Expected Climate Changes in the South Pacific Region: An Overview.* Nairobi, Kenya: United Nations Environment Program Regional Seas Reports and Studies No. 128.
Peshine Smith, E. (1897). *A Manual of Political Economy.* Philadelphia: Henry Carey Baird & Co.
Pettit, P. (1993). A Definition of Physicalism. *Analysis* 53: 213–223.
Pettit, P. (1994). Microphysicalism without Contingent Micro-Micro Laws. *Analysis* 54: 253–257.
Pettit, P. (1995). Microphysicalism, Dottism and Reduction. *Analysis* 55: 141–146.

Pillett, G. (1993). *Towards an Inquiry into the Carrying Capacity of Nations. What Does Over-Population Mean?* (2nd edition). Berne: Report to the Coordinator for International Refugee Policy, Federal Department of Foreign Affairs.
Pimentel, D., et al. (1994). Natural Resources and an Optimum Human Population. *Population and Environment* 15: 347–369.
Pimm, S. (1995). Seeds of Our Own Destruction. *New Scientist.* April 8: 31–35.
Platt, J. (1973). Social Traps. *American Psychologist* 28: 641–651.
Poincelot, R. P. (1990). Agriculture in Transition. *Journal of Sustainable Agriculture* 1: 9–40.
Poleman, T. T. (1995). Population: Past Growth and Future Control. *Population and Environment* 17: 19–40.
Pontifical Academy of Sciences (1994). Considerations of the Pontifical Academy of Sciences on the Occasion of the Population Summit. In: F. Graham-Smith ed. *Population—The Complex Reality: A Report of the Population Summit of the World's Scientific Academies.* Golden, Colorado: The Royal Society/North American Press: 387–390.
Poole, R. (1991). *Morality and Modernity.* London: Routledge.
Post, J. (1987). *Faces of Existence: An Essay in Nonreductive Metaphysics.* Ithaca: Cornell University Press.
Postman, N. (1985). *Amusing Ourselves to Death: Public Discourse in the Age of Show Business.* London: Methuen.
Pressler, J. (1987). Rights and Social Choice: Is There a Paretian Libertarian Paradox? *Economics and Philosophy* 3: 1–22.
Pressler, J. (1988). How to Avoid a Paretian Libertarian Paradox. *Economics and Philosophy* 4: 326–332.
Preston, J. M. (1989). Folk Psychology as Theory or Practice? The Case for Eliminative Materialism. *Inquiry* 32: 277–303.
Preston, S. H. (1994). Population and Environment: The Scientific Evidence. In: F. Graham-Smith ed. *Population—The Complex Reality: A Report of the Population Summit of the World's Scientific Academies.* Golden, Colorado: The Royal Society/North American Press: 85–92.
Price, D. (1995). Energy and Human Evolution. *Population and Environment* 16, March: 301–319.
Priest, G. (1989). Primary Qualities Are Secondary Qualities Too. *British Journal for the Philosophy of Science* 40: 29–37.
Priest, G. (1991). Sorites and Identity. *Logique and Analysis* 135–136: 293–296.
Primas, H. (1981). *Chemistry, Quantum Mechanics and Reductionism.* New York: Springer Verlag.
Prior, I. (1986). Immigrants and Health: A Selective Review and Suggestions for Future Research. In: A.D. Trlin & P. Soonley eds. *New Zealand and International Migration.* Palmerston North, New Zealand: Department of Sociology, Massey University.
Prugovecki, E. (1982). Time-Energy Uncertainty and Relativistic Canonical Commutation Relations in Quantum Space-Time. *Foundations of Physics* 12: 555–564.
Puccetti, R. (1974). Neural Plasticity and the Location of Mental Events. *Australasian Journal of Philosophy* 52: 154–162.

Puccetti, R. & Dykes, R.W. (1978). Sensory Cortex and the Mind-Brain Problem. *Behavioral and Brain Sciences* 3: 337–375.
Putnam, H. (1960). Minds and Machines. In: S. Hook ed. *Dimensions of Mind*. New York: New York University Press: 148–179.
Putnam, H. (1978). *Meaning and the Moral Sciences*. Boston: Routledge and Kegan Paul.
Putnam, H. (1981a). Quantum Mechanics and the Observer. *Erkenntnis* 16: 193–219.
Putnam, H. (1981b). *Reason, Truth and History*. Cambridge: Cambridge University Press.
Putnam, H. (1982). Why There Isn't a Ready Made World. *Synthese* 51: 141–167.
Putnam, H. (1984). Is the Causal Structure of the Physical Itself Something Physical? *Midwest Studies in Philosophy* 9: 3–16.
Putnam, H. (1986). Rationality in Decision Theory and in Ethics. *Critica* 18: 3–16.
Putnam, H. (1988a). Are There Such Things as Reference and Truth? In: *Representation and Reality*. Cambridge, Massachusetts: MIT Press: 57–71.
Putnam, H. (1988b). *Representation and Reality*. Cambridge, Massachusetts: MIT Press.
Putnam, H. (1988c). Why Functionalism Didn't Work. In: *Representation and Reality*. Cambridge, Massachusetts: MIT Press: 73–89.
Putnam, H. (1992). *Renewing Philosophy*. Cambridge, Massachusetts: Harvard University Press.
Pylyshyn, Z. W. ed. (1987). *The Robot's Dilemma: The Frame Problem in Artificial Intelligence*. Norwood, New Jersey: Ablex Publishing Corporation.
Quiggin, J. (1995). The Unacceptable Legacy of Thatcherite Economics. *Sydney Morning Herald* June 27: 11.
Quine, W. V. (1969). *Ontological Relativity and Other Essays*. New York: Columbia University Press.
Radnitzky, G. & Bouillon, H. eds. (1995). *Values and the Social Order; vol. 1: Values and Society*. Aldershot: Avebury.
Rae, J. ([1834], 1964). *Statement of Some New Principles on the Subject of Political Economy*. New York: Augustus M. Kelley.
Ramsey, W. (1990). Where Does the Self-Refutation Objection Take Us? *Inquiry* 33: 453–465.
Ray, D. L. & Guzzo, L. R. (1993). *Environmental Overkill: Whatever Happened to Common Sense?* Washington DC: Regnery Gateway.
Raymond, D. ([1823], 1964). *The Elements of Political Economy* (2 volumes). New York: Augustus M. Kelley.
Redhead, M. (1994). Logic, Quanta, and the Two Slit Experiment. In: P. Clark & B. Hale eds. *Reading Putnam*. Oxford: Blackwell: 161–175.
Rees, S., Rodley, G. & Stilwell, F. eds. (1993). *Beyond the Market: Alternatives to Economic Rationalism*. Leichhardt, New South Wales: Pluto Press.
Rees, W. E. (1990). The Ecology of Sustainable Development. *The Ecologist* 20: 18–23.

Rees, W. E. (1996). Revisiting Carrying Capacity: Area-Based Indicators of Sustainability. *Population and Environment* 17: 195–215.
Rees-Mogg, W. (1992). Is This the End of Life as I Know It? *The Independent* December 21: 17.
Reeve, S. et. al (1996). Countdown to Armageddon. *The Australian* June 25: 53.
Regan, D. (1980). *Utilitarianism and Co-Operation*. Oxford: Clarendon Press.
Reich, R. B. (1991). *The Work of Nations: Preparing Ourselves for 21st Century Capitalism*. New York: Alfred A. Knopf.
Reinecke, I. (1984). *Electronic Illusions: A Skeptic's View of our High-Tech Future*. Harmondsworth: Penguin.
Reinicke, W. (1995). *Banking, Politics and Global Finance: American Commercial Banks and Regulatory Change, 1980–1990*. Aldershot: Edward Elgar.
Reldman, R. (1983). Review of Benson Mates, *Skeptical Essays*. *Nous* 17: 508–514.
Renfrew, C. (1979). Systems Collapse as Social Transformation: Catastrophe and Anastrophe in Early State Societies. In: C. Renfrew & K. L. Cooke eds. *Transformations: Mathematical Approaches to Cultural Change*. New York: Academic Press: 481–506.
Reppert, V. (1991). Ramsey on Eliminativism and Self-Refutation. *Inquiry* 34: 499–508.
Rescher, N. (1980a). *Induction*. Oxford: Basil Blackwell.
Rescher, N. (1980b). *Scepticism: A Critical Reappraisal*. Oxford: Basil Blackwell.
Rescher, N. (1988). *Rationality*. Oxford: Clarendon Press.
Resnik, M. D. (1987). *Choices*. Minneapolis: University of Minnesota Press.
Revelle, R. (1971). Paul Ehrlich: New High Priest of Ecocatastrophe. *Family Planning Perspectives* 2: 66–70.
Ricardo, D. (1951). *Principles of Political Economy and Taxation*. Cambridge: Cambridge University Press.
Richardson, R. C. (1982). The "Scandal" of Cartesian Interactionism. *Mind* XCI: 20–37.
Rifkin, J. (1984). *Algeny: a New Word—A New World*. Harmondsworth: Penguin.
Rifkin, J. (1985). *Declaration of a Heretic*. Boston: Routledge & Kegan Paul.
Robertson, R. (1992). *Globalization*. London: Sage.
Robinson, D. (1991). On Crane and Mellor's Argument Against Physicalism. *Mind* 100: 135–136.
Robinson, J. (1973a). Prelude to a Critique of Economic Theory. In: E. K. Hunt & J. G. Schwartz eds. *A Critique of Economic Theory*. Harmondsworth: Penguin: 197–204.
Robinson, J. (1973b). Capital Theory Up to Date. In: E. K. Hunt & J. G. Schwartz eds. *A Critique of Economic Theory*. Harmondsworth: Penguin: 233–244.
Robinson, M. C. (1969). A Thought Experiment Violating Heisenberg's Uncertainty Principle. *Canadian Journal of Physics* 47: 963–967.
Rodman, J. (1980). Paradigm Change in Political Science. *American Behavioral Scientist* 24: 49–78.

Rogers, D. J. & Packer, M. J. (1993). Vector-Borne Diseases, Models, and Global Change. *The Lancet* 342: 1282–1284.
Rogers, R. A. (1995). Doing the Dirty Work of Globalization. *Capitalism, Nature, Socialism* 6: 117–134.
Rolls, E. (1993/94). Poisoning Paradise. *The Independent Monthly* (Australia) December–January: 36–41.
Rorty, R. (1979). *Philosophy and the Mirror of Nature*. Princeton: Princeton University Press.
Rosen, J. (1974). *G.W.F. Hegel: An Introduction to the Science of Wisdom*. New Haven: Yale University Press.
Rosenberg, J. F. (1980). *One World and Our Knowledge of It*. Dordrecht: D. Reidel.
Routley, R. (1979). Repairing Proofs of Arrow's General Impossibility Theorem and Enlarging the Scope of the Theorem. *Notre Dame Journal of Formal Logic* 10: 879–890.
Routley, R. (1980). On the Impossibility of an Orthodox Social Theory and of an Orthodox Solution to Environmental Problems. *Logique et Analyse* 89: 145–166.
Routley, V. & Routley, R. (1980). Social Theories, Self Management, and Environmental Problems. In: D. S. Mannison, M. A. McRobbie & R. Routley eds. *Environmental Philosophy*. Canberra: Australian National University: 217–332.
Roy, P. & Connell, J. (1989). *"Greenhouse": The Impact of Sea Level Rise on Low Coral Islands in the South Pacific*. Research Institute for Australia and the Pacific, Occasional Paper No. 6, University of Sydney.
Rubin, C. T. (1994). *The Green Crusade: Rethinking the Roots of Environmentalism*. New York: Free Press.
Ruelle, D. (1991). *Chance and Chaos*. Princeton: Princeton University Press.
Ruskin, J. ([1864], 1988). *Unto This Last*. New York: John Wiley & Sons.
Russell, B. (1958). *In Praise of Idleness and Other Essays*. London: George Allen and Unwin.
Russell, B. (1967). *The Autobiography of Bertrand Russell, II*. Boston: Little Brown.
Russell, B. (1978). *The Problems of Philosophy*. Oxford: Oxford University Press.
Russell, P. (1983). *The Global Brain: Speculations on the Evolutionary Leap to Planetary Consciousness*. Los Angeles: J. P. Tarcher Inc.
Sabloff, J. A. (1995). Drought and Decline. *Nature* 375: 357.
Sachs, M. (1982). On the Incompatibility of the Quantum and Relativity Theories and a Possible Resolution. *Hadronic Journal* 5: 1781–1801.
Sachs, W. (1986). Delinking from the World Market. In: P. Ekins ed. *The Living Economy: A New Economics in the Making*. London: Routledge & Kegan Paul: 333–344.
Sachs, W., ed., (1993). *Global Ecology: A New Arena of Political Conflict*. London: Zed Books.
Sagoff, M. (1986). Values and Preferences. *Ethics* 96: 301–316.
Sale, K. (1980). *Human Scale*. New York: Coward, McCann & Geoghegan.
Samuelson, P. (1975). Maximum Principles in Analytical Economics. *Synthese* 31: 323–344.

Santamaria, B. A. (1995). Who Rules Australia Anyway? *The Weekend Australian*. (Focus) December 30–31: 9–10.
Santamaria, B. A. (1996). Economic Irrationalism. *The Weekend Australian* May 18–19: 23.
Santayana, G. (1955). *Scepticism and Animal Faith*. New York: Dover Publications.
Sassone, R. L. (1994). *Handbook on Population*. Fifth edition. Stafford, Virginia: American Life League Inc.
Satchell, T. (1994). Crisis in paradise. *The Advertiser* (Adelaide, South Australia) August 9: 13.
Sauer-Thompson, G. & Smith, J. W. (1996). *Beyond Economics: Postmodernity, Globalization and National Sustainability*. Aldershot: Avebury.
Saul, J. R. (1992). *Voltaire's Bastards: The Dictatorship of Reason in the West*. London: Sinclair-Stevenson.
Savory, A. (1994). Will We Be Able to Sustain Civilization? *Population and Environment* 16: 139–147.
Scerri, E. R. (1989). Quantum Failure. *New Scientist* February 11: 76.
Scerri, E. R. (1991). The Electronic Configuration Model, Quantum Mechanics and Reduction. *British Journal for the Philosophy of Science* 42: 309–325.
Scerri, E. R. (1994). Has Chemistry Been at Least Approximately Reduced to Quantum Mechanics? *Philosophy of Science Association* 1: 160–170.
Scerri, E. R. (1995). The Exclusion Principle, Chemistry and Hidden Variables. *Synthese* 102: 165–169.
Schachter, J. & Althaus, P. G. (1982). Neighbourhood Quality and Climate as Factors in US Migration Patterns 1974–76. *American Journal of Economics and Sociology* 41: 387–400.
Scharf, D. C. (1989). Quantum Measurement and the Program for the Unity of Science. *Philosophy of Science* 56: 601–623.
Schlagel, R. H. (1977). The Mind-Brain Identity Impasse. *American Philosophical Quarterly* 14: 231–237.
Schmeidler, D. & Sonnenschein, H. (1978). Two Proofs of the Gibbard-Satterthwaite Theorem on the Possibility of a Strategy-Proof Social Choice Function. In: H.W. Gottinger & W. Leinfellner eds. *Decision Theory and Social Ethics: Issues in Social Choice*. Dordrecht: D. Reidel: 227–234.
Schnaars, S. P. (1989). *Megamistakes: Forecasting and the Myth of Rapid Technological Change*. New York: Free Press.
Schneider, S. H. (1989). The Changing Climate. *Scientific American* September: 38–47.
Scholes, R. (1985). *Textual Power*. New Haven: Yale University Press.
Schreiber, D. S. G. (1987). The Illegitimacy of Gettier Examples. *Metaphilosophy* 18: 49–54.
Schumacher, E. F. (1973). *Small Is Beautiful*. New York: Harper & Row.
Schumacher, E. F. (1977). *A Guide for the Perplexed*. New York: Harper & Row.
Schumacher, E. F. (1993). The Age of Plenty: A Christian View. In: H. E. Daly & K. N. Townsend eds. *Valuing the Earth: Economics, Ecology, Ethics*. Cambridge, Massachusetts: MIT Press: 159–172.

Schwartz, J. G. ed. (1977). *The Subtle Anatomy of Capitalism*. Santa Monica: Goodyear Publishing Company.
Schwartz, J. T. (1988). The New Connectionism: Developing Relationships Between Neuroscience and Artificial Intelligence. *Daedalus* 117: 123–141.
Schwartz, T. (1972). Rationality and the Myth of the Maximum. *Nous* 6: 97–117.
Scitovsky, T. (1966). External Diseconomies in the Modern Economy. *Western Economic Journal* 3: 197–202.
Seers, D. (1983). *The Political Economy of Nationalism*. Oxford: Oxford University Press.
Segal, E. F. (1976). Mind-Body: What Is the Question? *Philosophy Forum* 14: 325–360.
Selleri, F. & van der Merwe, A. (1990). *Quantum Paradoxes and Physical Reality*. Dordrecht: Kluwer.
Sen, A. (1970). The Impossibility of a Paretian Liberal. *Journal of Political Economy* 78: 152–157.
Sen, A. (1977). Rational Fools: A Critique of the Behavioral Foundations of Economic Theory. *Philosophy and Public Affairs* 6: 317–344.
Sen, A. (1983). Liberty and Social Choice. *Journal of Philosophy* LXXX: 5–28.
Sen, A. (1994). Population: Delusion and Reality. *The New York Review of Books*. XLI: 62–71.
Sextus Empiricus (1939). *Outlines of Pyrrhonism*. Translated by R. G. Bury. London: Leob Classical Library, Heinemann.
Shackle, G. L. S. (1973). *Epistemics and Economics: A Critique of Economic Doctrines*. Cambridge: Cambridge University Press.
Shaker, S. M. & Wise, A. R. (1988). *War without Men: Robots on the Future Battlefield*. Washington: Pergamon-Brassey's.
Shallis, M. (1984). *The Silicon Idol*. Oxford: Oxford University Press.
Shapiro, R. (1977). *Origins: A Sceptic's Guide to the Creation of Life on Earth*. New York: Bantam Books.
Shapiro, S. (1981). Understanding Church's Thesis. *Journal of Philosophical Logic* 10: 353–365.
Sharp, D. A. (1988). America Is Running Out of Time. *New York Times* February 7: 2.
Sheehan, T. (1993). A Normal Nazi. *New York Review of Books* January 14: 30–35.
Short, A. D. (1988). Areas of Australia's Coast Prone to Sea-Level Inundation. In: G. I. Pearman ed. *Greenhouse: Planning for Climate Change*. East Melbourne, Victoria: CSIRO.
Short, R. (1994). Australia: A Full House. *People and Place* 2: 1–5.
Siegel, H. (1987). *Relativism Refuted*. Dordrecht: D. Reidel.
Simkhovitch, V. G. (1916). Rome's Fall Reconsidered. *Political Science Quarterly* 31: 201–243.
Simon, H. (1955). A Behavioral Model of Rational Choice. *Quarterly Journal of Economics* 69: 99–118.
Simon, H. (1979). Rational Decision Making in Business Organizations. *American Economic Review* 69: 493–513.

Simon, J. L. (1981). *The Ultimate Resource*. Princeton: Princeton University Press.
Simon, J. L. (1990). *Population Matters: People, Resources, Environment, and Immigration*. New Brunswick: Transaction Publishers.
Simon, J. L. & Kahn, H. eds. (1984). *The Resourceful Earth: A Response to Global 2000*. Oxford: Blackwell.
Simon, J. L. & Wildavsky, A. (1995). Species Loss Revisited. In: J. L. Simon ed. *The State of Humanity*. Oxford & Cambridge, Massachusetts: Blackwell: 346–361.
Simon, J. L. ed. (1995). *The State of Humanity*. Oxford & Cambridge, Massachusetts: Blackwell.
Singer, F. S. ed. (1971). *Is There an Optimum Level of Population?* New York: McGraw-Hill.
Singer, P. (1975). *Animal Liberation: A New Ethics for Our Treatment of Animals*. New York: Avon Books.
Sismondi, J. C. L. S. ([1819], 1991). *The New Principles of Political Economy*. Translated by R. Hyse. New Brunswick: Transaction.
Skinner, B. J. & McClaren, D. J. eds. (1987). *Resources and World Development*. New York: Wiley.
Slezak, P. (1994). The Social Construction of Social Constructionism. *Inquiry* 37: 139–157.
Slote, M. (1989). *Beyond Optimizing: A Study of Rational Choice*. Cambridge, Massachusetts: Harvard University Press.
Smart, J. J. C. (1963). *Philosophy and Scientific Realism*. London: Routledge & Kegan Paul.
Smart, J. J. C. (1978). The Content of Physicalism. *Philosophical Quarterly* 28: 339–341.
Smart, J. J. C. (1985). Laws of Nature and Cosmic Coincidences. *Philosophical Quarterly* 35: 272–280.
Smart, J. J. C. (1995). A Form of Metaphysical Realism. *Philosophical Quarterly* 45: 301–315.
Smellie, P. & Weekes, P. (1994). NZ Suicide Rate Linked to Economy. *The Australian* June 23: 6.
Smellie, P. (1994). Fruitless Kiwis. *The Australian* October 17: 10.
Smellie, P. (1996). Peters Aims for a NZ First. *The Weekend Australian* May 25–26: 26.
Smil, V. (1991). Population Growth and Nitrogen: An Exploration of a Crucial Existential Link. *Population and Development Review* 17: 569–601.
Smil, V. (1994). How Many People Can The Earth Feed? *Population and Development Review* 20: 255–292.
Smith, C. W. & Best, S. (1989). *Electromagnetic Man: Health and Hazard in the Electric Environment*. London: J.M. Dent.
Smith, J. W. (1982). A Reply to Frankel's Criticism of Harré's Theory of Causality. *Philosophy of Science* 49: 282–289.
Smith, J. W. (1983). The Contentlessness of Physicalism. *Darshana International* 23: 1–9.
Smith, J. W. (1984). *Reductionism and Cultural Being*. The Hague: Martinus Nijhoff.

Smith, J. W. (1984). Woller on Harré and Madden's Account of Natural Necessity. *Kinesis* 13: 777–786.
Smith, J. W. (1985). Meiland and the Self-Refutation of Protagorean Relativism. *Grazer Philosophische Studien* 23: 119: 128.
Smith, J. W. (1986). *Reason, Science and Paradox: Against Received Opinion in Science and Philosophy.* London: Croom Helm.
Smith, J. W. (1988a). *Essays on Ultimate Questions.* Aldershot: Avebury.
Smith, J. W. (1988b). *The Progress and Rationality of Philosophy.* Aldershot: Avebury.
Smith, J. W. (1990a). Logic, Contradiction and Quantum Theory. *Gnosis* 3: 17–27.
Smith, J. W. (1990b). Time, Change and Contradiction. *Australasian Journal of Philosophy* 68: 178–188.
Smith, J. W. ed. (1991). *Immigration, Population and Sustainable Environments*, Bedford Park, South Australia: Flinders Press.
Smith, J. W. (1991a). *The High Tech Fix: Sustainable Ecology or Technocratic Megaprojects for the 21st Century.* Aldershot: Avebury.
Smith, J. W. (1991b), *AIDS, Philosophy and Beyond: Philosophical Dilemmas of a Modern Pandemic.* Aldershot: Avebury.
Smith, J. W. (1992a). The Recent Case Against Physicalist Theories of Mind: A Review Essay. In: D. Lamb ed. *New Horizons in the Philosophy of Science.* Aldershot: Avebury: 49–65.
Smith, J. W. (1992b). *The Remorseless Working of Things.* Kalgoorlie, Western Australia: Kalgoorlie Press.
Sobel, J. H. (1985). Everyone's Conforming to a Rule. *Philosophical Studies* 48: 375–387.
Solomon, R. C. (1975). Doubts About The Correlation Thesis. *British Journal for the Philosophy of Science* 26: 27–39.
Sorokin, P. A. (1957). *Social and Cultural Dynamics.* Boston: Porter Sargent.
Soule, M. ed. (1987). *Viable Populations for Conservation.* Cambridge: Cambridge University Press.
Spengler, O. (1962). *The Decline of the West.* New York: Modern Library.
Speth, J. G. (1989). A Luddite Recants: Technological Innovation and the Environment. *The Amicus Journal* 11: 3–5.
Sprigge, T. L. (1983). *The Vindication of Absolute Idealism.* Edinburgh: Edinburgh University Press.
Sraffa, P. (1960). *Production of Commodities by Means of Commodities: Prelude to a Critique of Economic Theory.* Cambridge: Cambridge University Press.
Stace, W. T. (1932). *The Theory of Knowledge and Existence.* Oxford: Clarendon Press.
State of the Environment Advisory Committee (1996). *Australia: State of the Environment.* Collingwood, Victoria: CSIRO Publishing.
Stewart, C. (1994). Harsh Words Could Help Pacific Stay Afloat. *The Australian* August 3: 9.
Stewart, I. (1989). *Does God Play Dice? The Mathematics of Chaos.* London: Penguin Books.
Stich, S. (1983). *From Folk Psychology to Cognitive Science: The Case Against Belief.* Cambridge, Massachusetts: MIT Press.

Stock, G. (1993). *Metaman: Humans, Machines, and the Birth of a Global Super-Organism.* London and New York: Bantam Press.
Stockmeyer, L. J. & Chandra, A. K. (1979). Intrinsically Difficult Problems. *Scientific American* 240: 124–133.
Stoll, C. (1996). *Silicon Snake Oil: Second Thoughts on the Information Highway.* London: Pan Books.
Stone, J. (1992). Environment, Plague and the Problem of Charity. "Ockham's Razor," ABC Radio Australia, April 5, 12 & 19.
Stove, D. (1982). *Popper and After: Four Modern Irrationalists.* Oxford: Pergamon Press.
Stove, D. (1991). *The Plato Cult.* Oxford: Basil Blackwell.
Strasnick, S. (1976). The Problem of Social Choice: Arrow to Rawls. *Philosophy and Public Affairs* 5: 241–273.
Strong, T. B. (1976). Language and Nihilism: Nietzsche's Critique of Epistemology. *Theory and Society* 3: 239–264.
Stycos, J. M. (1995). Population, Projections, and Policy: A Cautionary Perspective. *Population and Environment* 16: 205–219.
Suzuki, D. & Gordon, A. (1990). *It's a Matter of Survival.* Toronto: Stoddart.
Svart, L. M. (1975). Environmental Preference Migration: A Review. *The Geographical Review* 65: 314–330.
Swann, A. J. (1988). Popper on Induction. *British Journal for the Philosophy of Science* 39: 367–373.
Swartout, J. G. (1993). The Free Trade Charade. *The Social Contract* Fall: 27–38.
Swartz, N. (1993). Getting from P to Q: Valid Inferences and Heuristics. *Dialogue* 32: 689–702.
Swinburne, R. (1982). Are Mental Events Identical with Brain Events? *American Philosophical Quarterly* 19: 173–181.
Syme, D. (1876). *Outlines of an Industrial Science.* London: Henry S. King & Co.
Tainter, J. A. (1988). *The Collapse of Complex Societies.* Cambridge: Cambridge University Press.
Tanton, J., McCormack, D. & Smith, J. W. eds. (1996). *Immigration and the Social Contract: The Implosion of Western Society.* Aldershot: Avebury.
Tate, M. (1991). Whose 100th Birthday? Australian Democracy and "Rerum Novarum" 1891–1991. Occasional Paper No. 9. Adelaide: Australian Catholic Social Justice Council.
Tawney, R. H. (1920). *The Acquisitive Society.* New York: Harcourt Brace Jovanovich.
Tawney, R. H. (1926). *Religion and the Rise of Capitalism.* New York: Harcourt Brace Jovanovich.
Tawney, R. H. ([1931], 1964). *Equality.* London: George Allen & Unwin.
Taylor, G. R. (1970). *The Doomsday Book.* London: Thames & Hudson.
Taylor, L. (1995). Howard Will Maintain Pace of Tariff Reform. *The Australian* July 18: 4.
Tegart, W. J., Sheldon, G. W. & Hellyer, J. H. eds. (1993). *Climate Change 1992: The Supplementary Report to the IPCC Impacts Assessment.* Canberra: Australian Government Publishing Service.

Tennant, N. (1987). *Anti-Realism and Logic.* Oxford: Oxford University Press.
Ter Borg, M. B. (1988). The Problem of Nihilism: A Sociological Approach. *Sociological Analysis* 49: 1–16.
Thurow, L. C. (1983). *Dangerous Currents: The State of Economics.* New York: Random House.
Tienson, J. L. (1987). An Introduction to Connectionism. *Southern Journal of Philosophy* 26: 1–6.
Tintner, G. (1941). The Theory of Choice Under Subjective Risk and Uncertainty. *Econometrica* 9: 298–304.
Tirman, J. ed. (1984). *The Militarization of High Technology.* Cambridge, Massachusetts: Ballinger Publishing Company.
Toynbee, A. J. (1962). *A Study of History.* Oxford: Oxford University Press.
Traber, M. ed. (1986). *The Myth of the Information Revolution.* Beverly Hills, California: Sage Publications.
Trainer, F. E. (1985). *Abandon Affluence!* London: Zed Books.
Trainer, F. E. (1986). A Critical Examination of "The Ultimate Resource" and "The Resourceful Earth." *Technological Forecasting and Social Change* 30: 19–37.
Trainer, F. E. (1989). *Developed to Death.* London: Greenprint.
Trainer, F. E. (1991). The Conserver Society: The Sustainable Alternative. *Habitat Australia* August: 31–33.
Trainer, F. E. (1995a). *The Conserver Society: Alternatives for Sustainability.* London: Zed Books.
Trainer, F. E. (1995b). The Basic Problem: The Commitment to Growth. In: J. Hermann et al. *Towards a New Economic System: Balancing Equity, Economics and the Environment.* Proceedings of the 3rd National T.O.E.S. 1995 and The Other Economic Summit Conference. Adelaide: The University of Adelaide: 23–42.
Trainer, F. E. (1995c). Can Renewable Energy Sources Sustain Affluent Society? *Energy Policy* 23: 1009–1026.
Trigg, R. (1980). *Reality at Risk.* Brighton, Sussex: Harvester.
Trlin, A. D. (1993). The Social Effects and Institutional Structure of Immigration in New Zealand in the 1980s. *Asian and Pacific Migration Journal* 2: 1–25.
Tuomela, R. (1979). Putnam's Realisms. *Theoria* 45: 97–113.
Tymoczko, T. (1989). Mathematical Skepticism: Are We Brains in a Countable Vat? *Philosophica* 43: 31–47.
United Nations Population Fund (1995). *The State of World Population.* New York: United Nations Population Fund.
United Nations, Department for Economic and Social Information and Policy Analysis, Population Division (1995). *World Population Prospects: The 1994 Revision.* New York: United Nations.
United Nations, Department of International Economic and Social Affairs (1992). *Long-Range World Population Projections: Two Centuries of Population Growth 1950–2150.* New York: United Nations.
Van Fraassen, B. C. (1980). *The Scientific Image.* Oxford: Clarendon Press.
Vandegrift, G. (1995). Bell's Theorem and Psychic Phenomena. *Philosophical Quarterly* 45: 471–476.

Verkuyl, D. A. A. (1993). Two World Religions and Family Planning. *The Lancet* 342: 473–475.
Vilks, A. (1992). A Set of Axioms for Neoclassical Economics and the Methodological Status of the Equilibrium Concept. *Economics and Philosophy* 8: 51–82.
Vision, G. (1988). *Modern Anti-Realism and Manufactured Truth.* London and New York: Routledge.
Vitousek, P. M. et al. (1986). Human Appropriation of the Products of Photosynthesis. *BioScience* 34: 368–373.
Von Neumann, J. & Morgenstern, O. (1944). *Theory of Games and Economic Behavior.* Princeton: Princeton University Press.
Waldrop, M. M. (1992). *Complexity: The Emerging Science at the Edge of Order and Chaos.* London: Penguin Books.
Walker, R. (1994). New Zealand Immigration and the Political Economy. *The Social Contract* 4: 86–97.
Walker, R. C. S. (1989). *The Coherence Theory of Truth: Realism, Anti-Realism, Idealism.* London: Routledge.
Walters, P. (1993). Indonesia Warns of Jobs Crisis. *The Australian* November: 8.
Waltz, D. L. (1988). The Prospects for Building Truly Intelligent Machines. *Daedalus* 117: 191–211.
Wark, M. (1995). Black Thunder. *21 C* 4: 46–52.
Weale, A. (1980). The Impossibility of Liberal Egalitarianism. *Analysis* 40: 13–19.
Webster, F. & Robins, K. (1986). *Information Technology: A Luddite Analysis.* Norwood, New Jersey: Ablex Publishing.
Wedgwood, R. (1990). Scepticism and Rational Belief. *Philosophical Quarterly* 40: 45–65.
Weinberger, D. (1988). Artificial Intelligence and Plato's Cave. *Idealistic Studies* 18: 1–9.
Weininger, S. J. (1984). The Molecular Structure Conundrum: Can Classical Chemistry be Reduced to Quantum Chemistry? *Journal of Chemical Education* 61: 939–944.
Weintraub, E. R. (1985a). Appraising General Equilibrium Analysis. *Economics and Philosophy* 1: 23–37.
Weintraub, E. R. (1985b). *General Equilibrium Analysis: Studies in Appraisal.* Cambridge: Cambridge University Press.
Wertz, S. K. (1987). Quine's Revisionism: Re-Entry into Immunity. *International Logic Review* 35: 37–39.
Wesphal, K. R. (1988). Hegel's Solution to the Dilemma of the Criterion. *History of Philosophy Quarterly* 5: 173–188.
Westerway, R. (1990). *Electronic Highways.* Sydney: Allen & Unwin.
Wheale, P. R. & McNally, R. M. (1988). *Genetic Engineering: Catastrophe or Utopia?* Hampstead: Harvester Wheatsheaf.
Whetton, P. H., Fowler, A. M., Haylock, M. R. & Pittock, A. B. (1993). Implications of Climate Change Due to the Enhanced Greenhouse Effect on Floods and Droughts in Australia. *Climatic Change* 25: 289–317.
White, A. R. (1982). *The Nature of Knowledge.* Totowa, New Jersey: Rowman and Littlefield.
Whitehead, A. N. (1925). *Science and the Modern World.* New York: Macmillan.

Whitehead, A. N. (1929). *Process and Reality.* New York: Harper Brothers.
Whitelock, J. (1979). The Problem of Nature in Habermas. *Telos* 40, Summer: 41–69.
Wigley, T. M. L. & Raper, S. C. B. (1992). Implications for Climate and Sea Level of Revised IPCC Emissions Scenarios. *Nature* 357: 293–300.
Wigner, E. P. (1963). The Problem of Measurement. *American Journal of Physics* 31: 6–15.
Wigner, E. P. (1970). Physics and the Explanation of Life. *Foundations of Physics* 1: 35–45.
Wigner, E. P. (1973). Epistemological Perspectives of Quantum Theory: In: C. A. Hooker ed. *Contemporary Research in the Foundations and Philosophy of Quantum Theory.* Dordrecht: D. Reidel: 369-385.
Wildavsky, A. (1995). *But Is It True? A Citizen's Guide to Environmental Health and Safety Issues.* Cambridge, Massachusetts: Harvard University Press.
Wiles, P. & Routh, G. eds. (1984). *Economics in Disarray.* Oxford: Basil Blackwell.
Willard, D. (1973). The Absurdity of Thinking in Language. *Southwestern Journal of Philosophy* 4: 125–132.
Wilson, E. O. ed. (1988) *Biodiversity*: Washington DC: National Academy Press.
Wilson, E. O. (1993). *The Diversity of Life.* New York: W.W. Norton.
Wilson, P. (1996). The "Me"Society. *The Weekend Australian Review* May 18–19: 1, 6.
Windschuttle, K. (1994). *The Killing of History: How a Discipline is Being Murdered by Literary Critics and Social Theorists.* Sydney: Macleay Press.
Winner, L. ed. (1992). *Democracy in a Technological Society.* Dordrecht: Kluwer Academic.
Wolfram, S. (1985). Undecidability and Intractability in Theoretical Physics. *Physical Review Letters* 54: 124–133.
Wolgast, E. H. (1977). *Paradoxes of Knowledge.* Ithaca: Cornell University Press.
Wood, A. (1995). Why Japan Has Stopped Growing. *The Weekend Australian* December 3–2: 26.
Wood, C. (1993). *The Bubble Economy: The Japanese Economic Collapse.* Tokyo: Charles E. Tuttle.
Wood, J. (1995). Murray-Darling Water Use Limited. *Sydney Morning Herald* July 1: 4.
Woodford, J. (1995). Sydney Faces Water Crisis, Say Officials. *Sydney Morning Herald* August 18: 1–2.
Woolley, R. G. (1976). Quantum Theory and Molecular Structure. *Advances in Physics* 25: 27–52.
Woolley, R. G. (1978). Must a Molecule Have a Shape? *Journal of the American Chemical Society* 100: 1073.
World Commission of Environment and Development (1988). *Our Common Future.* Oxford: Oxford University Press.
World Health Organization (1990). *Potential Health Effects of Climatic Change: Report of a WHO Task Group.* Geneva: World Health Organization.

World Health Organization (1996). *World Health Report.* Geneva: World Health Organization.
World Resources Institute et al. (1990). *World Resources 1990–91.* New York: Oxford University Press.
World Resources Institute (1992). *The 1992 Environmental Almanac.* Boston; Houghton Mifflin Co.
World's Scientific Academies (1994). Population Summit of the World's Scientific Academies. In: F. Graham-Smith ed. *Population—The Complex Reality: A Report of the Population Summit of the World's Scientific Academies.* Golden, Colorado: The Royal Society/North American Press: 377–384.
Worrall, J. (1982). Scientific Realism and Scientific Change. *Philosophical Quarterly* 32: 201–231.
Worster, D. (1993). The Shaky Ground of Sustainability. In: W. Sachs ed. *Global Ecology: A New Arena of Political Conflict.* London: Zed Books: 132–145.
Wright, C. (1988). Realism, Antirealism, Irrealism, Quasi-Realism. *Midwest Studies in Philosophy* 12: 25–49.
Wright, C. (1992). *Truth and Objectivity.* Cambridge, Massachusetts: Harvard University Press.
Wright, C. (1994). On Putnam's Proof that We Are Not Brains in a Vat. In: P. Clark & B. Hale eds. *Reading Putnam.* Oxford: Blackwell: 216–241.
Wright, J. (1985). Realism, Verificationism and Underdetermination. *Southern Journal of Philosophy* 23: 503–529.
Wrong, D. H. (1961). The Oversocialized Conception of Man in Modern Sociology. *American Sociological Review* 26: 183–193.
Yeager, L. (1976). Toward Understanding Some Paradoxes in Capital Theory. *Economic Inquiry* 14: 313–346.
Yoffie, D. B. ed. (1993). *Beyond Free Trade: Firms, Governments, and Global Competition.* Boston: Harvard Business School Press.
Young, J. O. (1995). *Global Anti-Realism.* Aldershot: Avebury.
Yuen, H. (1983). Contractive States and the Standard Quantum Limit for Monitoring Free-Mass Positions. *Physical Review Letters* 51: 719–722.
Yunker, J. A. (1986). In Defense of Utilitarianism: An Economist's Viewpoint. *Review of Social Economy* 44: 57–79.
Zadek, S. (1993). *An Economics of Utopia: Democratising Scarcity.* Aldershot: Avebury.
Zimmerman, E. J. (1962). The Macroscopic Nature of Space-Time. *American Journal of Physics* 30: 97–105.
Zimmerman, M. E. (1994). *Contesting Earth's Future: Radical Ecology and Postmodernity.* Berkeley: University of California Press.
Zuhayr, M. ed. (1987). *International Banking.* New York: St. Martin's Press.
Zurek, W. H. (1991). Decoherence and the Transition from Quantum to Classical. *Physics Today* 44: 36–44.

Index

Abernethy, V., 31, 60
Absolutism, 74
Absurdism, 69–70
Adams, H., 131
Africa, 3, 5, 6–7, 30, 33, 36, 46, 53, 148
Agassi, J., 84
Agriculture, 9
AIDS, 22, 24
Allais, M., 129, 130
Allais paradox, 126
Allen, R. E., 103
Almeida, M. J., 144
American Association for the Advancement of Science, 44
Angell, I., 26
Antibiotics, 20
Antimicrobial resistance, 21, 22
Antiracism, xi
Antirealism, 77
Anti-Semitism, 67–68
Apocalyse, 10
Argy, F., 142–143
Armageddon, 30
Armstrong, D., 85
Arrow's Impossibility Theorem, 123
Artificial intelligence, xiv, 19, 20, 88–90

Asia, xiii, 1, 2–3, 4, 5, 6, 7, 28, 46, 142
Asian capitalism, 97
Asianization, 1–2, 142, 151
Asia-Pacific, 1–2
Asteroids, xiii–xiv, xvi
Aum Supreme Truth cult, vii
Australia, 2, 3, 4, 7, 8, 21–22, 27, 30, 47, 48, 49, 50, 54, 72, 85, 98–99, 107–109, 142, 148, 151
Australia First, 55
Australian Aborigines, xi–xii
Australian Conservation Foundation, 8
Australian Medical Association (AMA), 47
Australians Against Further Immigration, 55
Autarky, xi, xv, 25, 99, 119–120, 130–131, 136–142
Avery, D., x, xi
Aziz, S., 3

Bacon, F., 64
Bailey, R., x, 11, 12, 27
Ballod-Atlanticus, K., 131
Banks, B. E. C., 46
Bannock, G., 129–130

Barthes, R., 66
Bartholomew, J. A., 134
Bartlett, A. A., 44
Bartley, W. W., 76–77
Batra, R., 105, 106, 117
Baudrillard, J., 68
Bauman, Z., 67
Baxter, R. E., 129–130
Bayesian decision theory, 124
Baynes, K., 73
Beckerman, W., x, xiv, 12, 13, 17
Bentham, J., 124
Bergland, R., 87
Bhaskar, R,. 75
Bilney, G., 50
Biodiversity decline, 4, 5, 8, 45
Biomass conversion, 10
Biotragedy, 25
Black holes, xvi
Blackmore, D., 8
Blainey, G., 151
Bohman, J., 73
Boland, L. A., 124–125
Borderless world, 100–104
Boserup, E., 36, 39, 58
Botkin, D. B., xii
Boulding, K., 131
Brazil, 27
Brazilian purperic fever, 21
Brecher, J., 136
Brittan, S., 114
Bronner, M. E., 15
Brown, H., 34
Brown, H. I., 74
Brzezinski, Z., viii
Bunge, M,. 74, 119, 127

Campbell, G., 55
Camus, A., xv, 70
Cannibalism, xi, xiii, 24
Capitalism, x, 2
Capital reswitching, 120–121
Capital reversing, 120–121
Carey, H., 113
Carey, M., 113
Carlyle, T., 132
Carroll, J., 61–62, 63
Carrying capacity, 44
Catholicism, 33–34

Central America, 3
Chaitin, G. J., 89
Chaos, 45, 59
Chaos theory, xii, 90
Chief Seattle, xii
Childs, J. B., 136
China, 6, 30, 36
Cholera, 22
Christianity, 33, 65
Churchland, P., 85, 86
Churchland (Smith), P., 85, 86
Clark, J. B., 113
Cleland, J., 31
Clinton, B., 104, 105, 143
Club of Rome, ix
Coarse theorem, 117
Cobb, J. B., 131
Cognitive relativism, 77–79, 81–84
Cohen, A., 73
Cohen, J. E., 45, 57
Coherence theory of truth, 77–80
Collapse of civilization, xii, xiii, 1, 2, 5, 9, 10
Collapse of the wave function, 93–94
Collective rationality principle, 123
Collier, J. D., 79
Collingnon, P., 21
Committee for the Economic Development of Australia (CEDA), 107, 142
Compact of Free Association, 50
Comparative advantage, 115
Competitive equilibrium theory, 120
Complexity, xii
Complexity theory, xii, 90
Computational intractability, 90
Computers, 18
Connectionism, 88–89
Connell, J., 54
Conservatism, 71, 114
Conserver Society, 141
Conspiracy, global, 116
Constanza, R, 133, 134
Consumerism, viii, xv
Cooper, T., 112
Cornucopianism, x, xi, 39
Correspondence thesis, 86

Cosmopolitanism, xv, 63, 72, 101–103, 111, 112, 135
Craiks, K., 88
Crane, T., 90
Creutzfeldt-Jakob disease (CJD), 23
Crisis of civilization, viii
Culbertson, J. M., 115–116
Cullen, P., 8
Culter, J., 136
Cultural homogeneity, 149

Daily, G. C., 44
Daly, H. E., 115, 131, 134, 135–136
Dascal, M., 73
Dasgupta, P. S., 40–41, 120, 143
Dauncey, G., 143
Davidson, D., 79
Davidson, J. D., 111
Davies, P., 93
Davis, E., 129–130
Death of God, 69
Decision theory, 122–129
De Condorcet, M., 144
Deconstructionism, 66–69
Deep ecology, 152
Deforestation, 37, 38, 49
De Man, P., 68
Demeny, P., 41
Democritus, 85
Demographic transition thesis, 31, 58
Dengue fever, 22
Deregulation, 108
Derrida, J., 66–69
Descartes, R., 64, 73
Desertification, 36, 46
Différance, 67
Diminishing returns, 16
Diphtheria, 22
Disease, 20–25, 47
DNA, 24
Dogmatism, 73
Downer cow syndrome (DCS), 27
Drexler, K. E., 20
Drysdale, P., 110
Dummett, M., 77
Dupré, J., 90

Easterbrook, G., x, xi
Easter Island, xiii
Eco-decentralism, 140
Ecological collapse, xiii, 5, 35
Ecological economics, 131–136
Ecological sustainability, 6, 8, 30, 41–47
Ecological traps, 46
Ecology, xii, xiii
Economic collapse, 111
Economic development, viii
Economic globalization, 101–117
Economic growth, viii, ix, 9, 10, 12, 32
Economicism, xi, xiv, xv, 2, 11, 26, 39
Economic rationalism, 14, 24, 107, 109
Economic reductionism, 114
Ecosystems, xii
Ecosystems collapse, 13
Edelman, G., 87
Egypt, 6
Ehrlich, P. R., xiii, 2, 11, 14, 41, 44
Eliminative materialism, 85, 95
Ellsberg paradox, 126
Ellul, J., 14
Emergence, 90
Enhanced greenhouse effect, 46, 47–56, 60
Enlightenment, xv, 62–65, 70
Enlightenmentism, 62–65, 99
Enlightenment Project, xv, 17, 62–72, 81, 96–99
Environmental degradation, 1, 3, 5, 7, 35–36
Environmental impact equation, 41–44
Environmentalism, x, xi, xii, xiv, 12, 13, 17, 25
Epicurus, 85
Equilibrium, 118
Eschatology, xvi
Ethiopia, 6
Ethnic coherence, 149
Ethnic conflict, viii, 48, 49, 56
Ethnocentrism, xi

Europe, 24, 31
European Union (EU), 24
Evolution, xii
Expected utility theory, 124–127
Exponential growth, 58–59
Extinction, xii
Extinction rate, 5

Fallacy of misplaced concreteness, 16
Fallibilism, 99
Famine, 4, 5, 21, 46
Feminists, xi
Feyerabend, P., 83–84
Figgie, H. E., 105
Financial deregulation, 103, 108, 109, 142–143
Financial globalization, 142
Fine, A., 78
Finger, M., 137
First International Conference of Phytogenic Resources, 4
Flew, A., 62
Folk psychology, 85
Food resources, 44–45
Food scarcity, 44–45
Food shortages, 4, 5, 21, 44–45
Ford, J., 62
Fornos, W., 29
Fossil fuels, 9, 10, 14
Foucault, M., 66
Foundationalism, 74
France, 31, 144
Free market, 36, 117
Free trade, xi, 105, 106, 111–117
Fukuyama, F., 104
Functionalism, 100
Future eating, ix
Futures, 120
Fuzzy logic, 89

Gaia, 103, 148
Galtung, J., 139–140
Gandhi, M. K., 133
Gare, A., 99
Garnaut, R., 110
Garrett, L., 25
Geddes, P., 131

General Agreement on Tariffs and Trade (GATT), 96, 103
General equilibrium theory, 129, 143
Genetic engineering, 4
Georgescu-Roegen, N., 131
Geothermal power, 10
Gibbard, A., 144
Giddens, A., 64–65
Gladwell, M., 25
Global anti-realism, 81–83
Global capitalism, 67
Global catastrophe, 4
Global ecological collapse, 12, 13
Global economic chaos, 19, 101–111
Globalism, x, xi, xiv, xv, 25, 63, 101, 117, 135, 136, 147–151
Globalization, viii, x, xi, 25, 26, 63, 147–151
Global millennium meltdown, 19
Global supermarket, 136
Global super-organism, 102–103
Global warming, ix, 12, 46, 47–56, 60
Gödel, K., 123
Godwin, W., 35
Goeller, H. E., 10–11
Goldman, A. H., 92–93
Goldsmith, J., 116
Goudsblom, J., 70
Gowdy, J., 65
Grace Commission, 105
Graham-Smith, F. (Sir), 33, 35
Gray, J., 71, 96–97, 114–115, 142
Greeley, H., 113
Greens, 98
Gribbin, J,. 93
Guoxin, W., 6
Guzzo, L. R., x

Haines, M. R., 21, 22, 25
Hall, P. J., 87–88
Hamilton, A., 112
Harcourt, G., 121–122
Hardin, G., 15, 35, 123, 145, 147, 148–149, 150–151
Hardison, O. B., 19
Harré, R., 69, 75, 125

Harrison, P, 35–40
Hawkins, M., xvi
Heal, G. M., 120, 143
Health, 46–47
Heat-related mortality, 46–47
Heilig, G. K., 59
Hergenrother, C., xiii
Hern, W. M., 147
Herodotus, xii–xiii
Heyd, D., 59
Hiley, D. R., 73
Hill, R., 8
Hillis, W. D., 90
Hindley, B., 115
HIV, 22
Hobbes, T., 85
Hobson, J., 132
Hogben, L., 131
Hollywood fantasies, xii
Holocaust, 68, 82–83
Homo ecophagus, 148
Howard, J., 108
Howard, M. C., 121
Hoyle, F., 59, 90, 153
Hubbert, M. K., 15
Hughes, P. J., 55, 56
Humanism, 61–62
Humanistic economics, 132
Hydropower, 10

Iacuzio, D., 23
Ichiyo, M., 136
Ikkatai, S., 1–2
Immigration, xi, 2, 3, 7, 8, 12, 14, 47–56, 98–99
Impossibility of a Paretian liberal, 123
Independence of irrelevant alternatives principle, 123
Indeterminacy of translation, 80
India, 3, 30, 33
Indifference curve, 127
Indonesia, 3, 30, 116, 148
Induction, 75, 124
Industrialization, 46
Industrial society, 10
Infanticide, xi
Infectious disease crisis, 21
Infinity, 11, 14

Influenza, 22
Information technology, 18–20
Inscrutability of reference, 80
Intergovernmental Panel on Climatic Change (IPCC), 46
Internationalism, x, xi, xiv, 63, 99, 112, 147–151
Internationalization, vii, viii, x, xi, 108, 116, 147–151
International trade, 101–106
Interstellar migration, 34–35
Iran, 6
Iraq, 6
Isolationism, 25
Israel, 6

Jabri, M., 19
Japan, 1, 2, 110, 149
Japanese economic imperialism, 97
Jay, J., 112
Jews, 68, 86
Jones, E., 101, 142
Jordan, 6
Julien, P.-A., 137–138

Kagan, S., 145
Kahn, H., 16
Kaldor, N., 120
Kant, I., 73
Kaplan, R. D., 30, 153
Kapp, W., 131
Kapstein, E. B., 116–117
Kaufman, W., x, xi
Keating, P., 49, 107
Kekes, J., 98
Kemp, J, 126–127
Kennedy, P., 147–150
Kenya, 30
Keynes, J. M., 131
Khush, G., 4
Kiribati, 49, 50, 51
Knowledge, xv
Kohr, L., 137
Kosko, B., 89
Kritz, M. M., 51, 52, 53
Krugman, P., 116
Kuhn, A., 100
Kuru, 24

Lafrance, C., 137–138
Laissez-faire, 111
Lakatos, I., 83
Lampe, K., 2–3
Lancaster, K., 128
Lasch, C., 65
Latief, A., 116
Latin America, x, 5, 36, 46, 149
Laudan, L., 81
Law of action, 57
Law of information, 57
Law of prediction, 57
Lee, D. R., 101–102
Lehman, D., 68
Leibenstein, H., 125
Leucippus, 85
Levins, R., 17
Lewis, M. W., x, xi, 20, 26, 41
Liberalism, xi, xii, 13
Limitationism, ix, xi, xiv, xv, 1, 2, 9, 11, 12, 13, 25, 26, 32, 33, 57, 71–72, 130
Limits to growth, viii, ix, x, 1, 2, 13, 14, 33, 57, 71, 153
Lipsey, R. G., 128
List, F., 112–113, 143
Lloyd, W. F., 123
Lockwood, M., 92
Long range population projections, 31
Lorber, J,. 86–87
Lovelock, J, 103
Luce, R. D., 127
Luntley, M., 77
Lutz, M., 132
Lyons, G., 63
Lyotard, J.-F., 65–66

MacDonald, G. M., 115
Mad cow disease (bovine spongiform encephalopathy, BSE), 23–24
Madden, E. H., 75
Madison, J., 112
Major, J., 24
Malaria, 22
Malaysia, 49
Maley, B., x

Malignant epiecopathologic processes, 152
Malthus, T. R., 29, 35–36, 59, 132, 150
Malthusianism, 14, 35–36, 59, 150
Manes, C, 70
Mann, J., 24–25
Marginal preferences, 117
Marginal utility, 117–122
Markets, 13, 14
Markusen, J. R., 115
Mars, 34
Marshall Islands, 48–49, 51
Martinez-Alier, J,. 131
Marx, K., 35, 114
Marxism, 66
Materialism, xv, 63, 91
Mates, B., 73
Mathews, R,. 107
Maximization thesis, 124, 125
Maximum sustainable population, 44
Maxwell, N., 97–98
Mayur, R., 5
McCalla, A., 4
McCarthy, 73
McDonald, P., 22
McIntosh, D., 27
McKenzie, R. B., 101–102
McLaren, D. J., 35
McLaughlin, W. I., 19
McLean, I., 123
McNeill, W., 24
McNicoll, G., 31
Meadows, D. H., 9
Measurement problem, 93–94
Megill, A., 68–69
Mellor, D. H., 90
Metaphysical realism, 78, 90
Metaphysics, 67
Metaphysics of presence, 66
Mexico, 3, 30
Middle East, 6, 16
Migrants, 27
Migration, 47–56
Mill, J. S., 124, 132
Miller, D., 76
Mind-body problem, 84–91
Minerals, 9

Minimum viable population size, 44
Mirandola, P. D., 61
Mirowski, P., 131
Mishan, E. J., 122
Misplaced concreteness, fallacy of, 135
Modernism, 17, 86
Modernity, 1, 17
Modernization, 46
Modigliani, F., 144
Mogg, W. R., vii
Monetarism, 120–121, 144
Money, 16
Money-liquidity shortage, 103
Mooney, H., 5
Moore, E., 47, 60
Morgenstern, O., 124
Multiculturalism, viii, 55, 56, 72
Mumford, L., 131
Murphy's Law, 18
Murray-Darling Basin, 7
Murray-Darling River system, 8
Mutations, 21
Myers, N., 5

Nanotechnology, 20
National Aeronautics and Space Administration (NASA), 5, 7
Nationalism, 25, 102, 135
National systems economics, 114
Natural family planning (NFP), 34
Naturalism, 62–63
Natural selection, 21
Nature, 62–63
Nazis, 82, 86
Nazism, 82–83, 86
N-body problem, 128
Near Earth Objects (NEOs), xiii
Neoclassical economics, xi, xv, 13, 14, 16, 117–122
Neo-Darwinism, xii
Neoliberalism, 114
Neo-Malthusianism, 35
Neo-Ricardianism, 121
Net primary production (NPP), 45
Neurath, O., 131
Neurophysiology, 86–88
Neutral monism, 92

Newbery, D., 120
Newcomb's problem, 127
New dark ages, 26
New World Order (NWO), 136
New York, 8, 21, 29
New Zealand, 48, 49, 53, 54, 55, 56, 109–110
Ng, Y.-K,. 128
Nielsen, K., 73
Nietzsche, F., 63, 69
Nihilism, 70
Noble savage, xi
Nondictatorship principle, 123
Nonlinearity, xii, 45
Nonlocalism, 94
Nonrenewable resources, 10, 14, 38
North, R. D., x, xiv, 12, 17
North American Free Trade Agreement (NAFTA), 103, 106
Notestein, F., 31
Novick, R., 21
Nozick, R., 127

Objectivism, 74
Odden Feature, 60
Ohmae, K., 102
Open-border world, 25, 101–103
Optimal population size, 44, 59
Optimization, 118
Optimization theory, 123
Original sin, 33
Ormerod, P., 128
Ozone depletion, 47

Pacific-Asian Resource Center, 136
Pakistan, 3
Panspermism, 90
Papua New Guinea, 24, 48, 49, 50, 51, 54
Pareto optimality, 120, 128
Pareto principle, 123
Patriarchy, xi
Pattison, J., 24
Penrose, R., 93
Perelman, L., 10
Permissive cornucopia, viii
Pernetta, J. C., 55–56
Perry, T., xii
Perspectivism, 81

Pessimistic induction, 82
Pfaundler, L., 131
Philippines, 3
Philosophical pluralism, 90
Physicalism, 84–91
Pimentel, D., 44–45
Pimm, S., 5
Pinstrup-Anderson, P., 3, 6
Plagues, xiv
Plato, 73, 74
Podolinsky, S., 131
Political correctness, xi
Pontifical Academy of Sciences, 33–34
Poole, R., 69
Popper, K., 74, 76–77, 82
Popper-Lynkeus, J., 131
Population growth, ix, xiv, xv, 1, 2, 4, 8, 9, 13, 21, 29–60
Population impact, 41–43
Post, J., 85
Postmodernism, xv, 65–66, 69
Postmodernity, 65–66, 69
Prejudice, xi, 73
Preston, S. H., 41
Price, 13, 16
Price, D., 10, 141
Principle of transcendence, 81
Prions, 23–24
Prisoner's Dilemma, 123–124
Probability Agreement Theorem, 144
Productivity paradox, 18
Progress, 65
Protectionism, 112
Prusiner, S., 24
Putnam, H., 78–80, 86, 89, 94, 127
Pyrrhonism, 73

Q-infinity, 15
Quantum field theory, 94
Quantum logic, 93
Quantum mechanics, 92–96
Queensland, 53
Quesnay, F., 111
Quine, W., 80
Quinn, M., 109

Rabbit Calicivirus (RCD), 23
Racial coherence, 149
Racial conflict, viii, 48, 49, 56
Racism, xi
Rae, J., 113
Raiffa, H., 127
Rational Economic Man, xi, 125
Rationality, xv
Ray, D. L., x
Raymond, D., 113
Realism, 77–80
Reductionism, 85
Rees-Mogg, W. E., 111
Referential theory of language, 66
Refugees, 3
Refugees, ecological, 50
Reich, R., 102
Relativism, viii, 81–84
Renaissance, 62
Renewable energy, 10
Ricardo, D., 115
Robinson, J,. 121, 122
Romanticism, 63
Rorty, R., 73
Rothschild, G., 3
Routley, R., 123
Royal Society, 1
Rubin, C. T., x, xi
Ruskin, J., 132
Russell, B., 75, 92

Sachs, W., 136, 137
Sale, K., 137
Salinization, 37
Samoa, 48
Santamaria, B. A., 108
Santayana, G., 73
Sassone, R. L., 34
Sauer-Thompson, G,. 99
Savory, A., 9
Say, J. B., 112, 143
Scanning tunneling microscope, 20
Scerri, E. R., 95
Schmeidler, D., 144
Schonfeldt, K., 8
Schrödinger cat paradox, 94
Schumacher, E. F., 137
Schwartz, J. T., 89
Schwartz, T., 123

Science, xv, 11
Scientism, xi
Second best, theory of, 128–129
Second law of thermodynamics, 20, 131
Seers, D., 135
Self-reliance, xi, xv, 133, 135, 139, 140
Self-sufficiency, x, xv, 36, 133
Sen, A., 40, 123
Serageldin, I., 6
Sexism, xi
Sextus Empiricus, 74–75
Shackle, G.L.S., 124
Shelley, M., 19
Simon, H,. 125
Simon, J. L., x, xi, xiv, xv, 5, 9, 11–20, 22, 25, 26, 32–33, 35, 36, 40, 58
Sink constraints, ix, 9
Sismondi, J.C.L.S., 132
Skepticism, 73–77
Slote, M., 130
Smalls, I., 8
Smart, J.J.C., 85
Smil, V., 45
Smith, A., 111, 112, 113, 143
Smith, J. W., 63, 71–72, 97, 99, 115, 127
Snoddy, D., 110
Social chaos, vii, viii, 10
Soddy, F., 131
Soil degradation, 4
Soil erosion, 36
Solar power, 10
Solomon Islands, 49, 51, 54
Sonnenschein, H., 144
Sorites, 89
Source constraints, 9
South America, 36
South Australia, 7, 23
South Korea, 49
Space colonization, 34
Spahr, T., xiii
Spain, 148
Species, xii
Speciesism, 152
Species loss, 45
Spengler, O., xiii

Spiritual emptiness, viii
Spontaneous decoherence, 94
Sprigge, T. L., 91
Sraffa, P., 121
Steel, D., xiii
Stiglitz, J, 120
Stock, G,. 102
Stycos, J. M., 30
Sugeno, M., 89
Superbugs, drug resistant, 21–22
Superluminar communication, 94
Superposition problem, 94
Sustainability, 29
Swanson, G. J., 105
Sydney, 8
Syme, D., 113–114

Tainter, J. A., xiii
Tawney, R., 133
Technocratic society, 86
Technofeudalism, 10
Technological optimism, 17–26
Technological progress, 14, 15, 17, 32
Technology, vii, 10, 17, 41
Technophobia, 26
Thailand, 30
Third World, 32, 37, 40, 55, 148
Tokelau, 49
Tonga, 49
Toynbee, A. J., xiii
Tragedy of the commons, 123
Trainer, T., 9, 16, 141
Transformation curve, 129–130
Transnational corporations, 33
Tribal warfare, xi
Tuberculosis, 21, 22, 27
Turing machine, 89–90
Turkey, 6
Tuvalu, 49
Typhoid fever, 22

Übermensch, 63
Underdetermination of theory by data, 80
Underwood, R., 6–7
Union of Concerned Scientists, 1
United Nations, 29, 43, 45, 136

United Nations Conference on Environment and Development, (UNCED), 136–137
United Nations Food and Agricultural Organization (FAO), 4
United Nations Population Fund, xv, 29–30
United States of America, 4, 22, 27, 44, 48, 49, 54, 56, 102, 104–105, 106, 112, 148
Universalism, 63, 81, 96, 150
Universal reason, 62, 63, 97
U.S. Academy of Science, 1
U.S. Council on Foreign Relations, 116
Utilitarianism, xi, 117–129

Van Fraassen, B. C., 80
Venables, A. J., 116
Venus, 34
Vernon, C. A., 46
Vilks, A., 118, 119
Von Neumann, J., 127

War, 3, 6
Water resources, 5, 6, 7, 8, 36–37, 45
Water shortages, 5, 6, 7, 8, 36–37, 45
Wave function, 92–94
Wave-particle duality, 92–93

Weale, A., 123
Weintraub, E. R., 118
West Africa, x
White Australia policy, 142
Whitehead, A. N., 135
Whooping cough, 22
Wickramasinghe, C., 90
Wildavsky, A., x, xi, 5
Williams, M., 4
Wisdom, 97–98
Wood, C., 110
Woolley, R. G., 95
World Bank, 4, 6, 31, 45
World Commission on Environment and Development, ix
World Economic Forum, 117
World government, 116
World Health Organization, 22
World's Scientific Academies, 33, 35
World Trade Organization, 114
Wright, J., 79
Wrong, D. H., 69

Xenophobia, 116, 152

Yellow fever, 22
Young, J. O., 81–83
Yunker, J. A., 124

Zimbabwe, 30

About the Authors

JOSEPH WAYNE SMITH is Senior Research Fellow in Geography at the University of Adelaide in Australia. Dr. Smith is a widely published author on the subject of the future of the earth.

GRAHAM LYONS is a leading Adelaide businessman, cattle rancher, and environmentalist.

GARY SAUER-THOMPSON is a lecturer in the Department of Philosophy at The Flinders University of South Australia.

ISBN 0-275-95601-6

HARDCOVER BAR CODE